Understanding Multimedia Documents

Jean-François Rouet · Richard Lowe ·
Wolfgang Schnotz
Editors

Understanding Multimedia Documents

Foreword by Shaaron Ainsworth and Fons Maes

Springer

Editors
Jean-François Rouet
University of Poitiers
France
jean-francois.rouet@univ-poitiers.fr

Richard Lowe
Curtin University
Perth, WA, Australia
lower@educ.curtin.edu.au

Wolfgang Schnotz
University of Landau
Germany
schnotz@uni-landau.de

ISBN: 978-0-387-73336-4 e-ISBN: 978-0-387-73337-1
DOI: 10.1007/978-0-387-73337-1

Library of Congress Control Number: 2008920718

Printed on acid-free paper

springer.com

Foreword

The present volume, "*Understanding Multimedia Documents*" was prepared under the auspices of the European Association for Research on Learning and Instruction, Special Interest Group on "*Text and Graphics Comprehension*" (EARLI SIG 2).

The EARLI SIG 2 gathers together researchers and research students interested in comprehension processes as they apply to external representations of knowledge. Historically, the SIG has focused on text and picture comprehension. However, given the explosion of different representations that have become available with advances in information technology, the SIG now considers a broader range of representations including complex environments such as virtual reality, scientific visualization tools, haptics, multimedia, hypermedia, and simulations.

The SIG membership is multidisciplinary, including psychologists, educational scientists, linguists, computer scientists and specialists from other areas.

As part of its activities, the SIG organizes thematic meetings that alternate with the Biennial European Conference for Research on Learning and Instruction. Recent meetings have included "*Multimedia Comprehension*" (Poitiers, France, 2002), "*Comprehension of Text and Graphics: Basic and Applied Issues*" (Valencia, Spain, 2004) and "*Learning by interpreting and constructing educational representations*" (Nottingham, UK, 2006). At the time of printing, the 2008 SIG2 meeting was to take place in Tilburg, The Netherlands.

"*Understanding Multimedia Documents*" reflects the liveliness and productivity of our research field. It also shows the many connections of this field with areas of practice, such as instructional design, interface evaluation, and research methodologies. As the present coordinators of the EARLI SIG 2, we are proud and happy to introduce this new outcome of the SIG, and we hope that it will be of interest to a broad range of readers.

Shaaron Ainsworth and Fons Maes
EARLI SIG2 coordinators

Contents

Contributors

Shaaron Ainsworth
University of Nottingham, School of Psychology and Learning Sciences Research Institute, University Park, Nottingham, NG7 2RD, United Kingdom
shaaron.ainsworth@nottingham.ac.uk

Mireille Bétrancourt
Geneva University, Faculty of Psychology and Education, TECFA research center, 54 route des Acacias, CH-1227 Carouge, Switzerland,
mireille.betrancourt@tecfa.unige.ch

Raquel Cerdán
Department of Educational Psychology, University of Valencia, 21 avenue Blasco Ibanez, 46010 Valencia, Spain, Raquel.Cerdan@uv.es

Lionel Clavien
Geneva University, Faculty of Psychology and Education, TECFA research center, 54 route des Acacias, CH-1227 Carouge, Switzerland,
lionel.clavien@dolmen.ch

Pierre Dillenbourg
Ecole Polytechnique Fédérale de Lausanne, CRAFT research center, CH1015 Lausanne, Switzerland, Pierre.Dillenbourg@epfl.ch

Michel Fayol
Université Blaise Pascal, Laboratoire de Psychologie Sociale de la Cognition, Centre National de Recherche Scientifique, 34 avenue Carnot, 63 037 Clermont-Ferrand Cedex, France, michel.fayol@univ-bpclermont.fr

Laura Gil
Department of Educational Psychology, University of Valencia, 21 avenue Blasco Ibanez, 46010 Valencia, Spain, laugilpe@alumni.uv.es

Ramiro Gilabert
Department of Educational Psychology, University of Valencia, 21 avenue Blasco Ibanez, 46010 Valencia, Spain, Ramiro.Gilabert@uv.es

Cédric Hidrio
University of Rennes II, Laboratory of Experimental Psychology; Place du Recteur H. Le Moal, 35 043 Rennes Cedex, France, cedric.hidrio@uhb.fr

Éric Jamet
University of Rennes II, Laboratory of Experimental Psychology; Place du Recteur H. Le Moal, 35 043 Rennes Cedex, France, eric.jamet@uhb.fr

Chris Lankford
Department of Systems and Information Engineering, Eye Response Technologies, University of Virginia, P.O. Box 400747, 151 Engineer's Way, Charlottesville, VA 22904, Virginia, USA, chris@eyeresponse.com

Olivier Le Bohec
University of Rennes II, Laboratory of Experimental Psychology; Place du Recteur H. Le Moal, 35 043 Rennes Cedex, France, olivier.lebohec@uhb.fr

Richard Lowe
Faculty of Humanities, Curtin University of Technology, GPO Box U 1987, Perth Western Australia, 6845, lower@educ.curtin.edu.au

Lucia Lumbelli
Universitá Degli Studi di Trieste, Dipartimento Di Psicologia, Via S. Anastasio 12, 34134 Trieste, Italy, Lumbelli@univ.trieste.it

Rob L. Martens
Educational Technology Expertise Center, Open University of the Netherlands, Center for the Study of Education and Instruction, Leiden University, P.O. Box 2960, 6401 DL Heerlen, The Netherlands, rob.martens@ou.nl

Tomás Martínez
Department of Educational Psychology, University of Valencia, 21 avenue Blasco Ibanez, 46010 Valencia, Spain, Tomas.Martinez@uv.es

Fred Paas
Educational Technology Expertise Center, Open University of the Netherlands, P.O. Box 2960, 6401 DL Heerlen, The Netherlands, fred.paas@ou.nl

Francesca Pazzaglia
Universitá Degli Studi di Padova, Dipartimento di Psicologia Generale "Vittorio Benussi", Via Venezia 8, 35131 Padova, Italy, francesca.pazzaglia@unipd.it

Hervé Platteaux
University of Fribourg, Centre NTE, Faucigny 2, CH – 1700 Fribourg, Switzerland, herve.platteaux@unifr.ch

Mike Rinck
Behavioural Science Institute, Radboud University Nijmegen, PO Box 9104, 6500 HE Nijmegen, The Netherlands, m.rinck@psych.ru.nl

Jean-François Rouet
Center for Research on Cognition and Learning, University of Poitiers, MSHS, 99 avenue du Recteur Pineau, 86000 Poitiers, France, jean-francois.rouet@univ-poitiers.fr

Wolfgang Schnotz
Department of General and Educational Psychology, University of Landau, Im Fort 7, D-76829 Landau, Germany, schnotz@uni-landau.de

Huib K. Tabbers
Institute of Psychology, Erasmus University Rotterdam, Woudestein, T12-39, P.O. Box 1738, 3000 DR Rotterdam, The Netherlands, tabbers@fsw.eur.nl

Jeroen J. G. van Merriënboer
Educational Technology Expertise Center, Open University of the Netherlands, P.O. Box 2960, 6401 DL Heerlen, The Netherlands, jeroen.vanmerrienboer@ou.nl

Eduardo Vidal-Abarca
Department of Educational Psychology, University of Valencia, 21 avenue Blasco Ibanez, 46010 Valencia, Spain, Eduardo.Vidal-Abarca@uv.es

Chapter 1
Understanding Multimedia Documents: An Introduction

Jean-François Rouet, Richard Lowe, and Wolfgang Schnotz

Abstract This chapter introduces the domain and the issues dealt with in the volume. It provides a general characterization of comprehending multimedia documents as a process that is constrained by multiple interactions between learners' skills and knowledge, the structure and sequencing of information in the available multimedia documents, and contextual conditions such as time constraints, situational affordances, and so forth. The chapter provides an overview of the contributions presented within this book. It presents a general framework for the study of complex document comprehension, with memory processes in multimedia comprehension, and with contextual strategies in document-based learning. Finally the chapter addresses perspectives for further research on multimedia documents.

Keywords Comprehension · Context · Individual differences · Multimedia · Perspectives research methods

1.1 Introduction

The ability to read, understand and make use of documents is an essential skill in modern societies. Individuals must be able to access relevant information from text, pictures or other types of external representations, to decode and interpret the corresponding documents, and to integrate information from multiple sources. The cognitive processes involved in the reading, comprehension and use of multimedia documents have been the subject of increasing attention on the part not only of researchers, but also designers and educators. Sound theories of multimedia comprehension are essential to improve the quality of technical or instructional documents, and also to equip students with the skills and strategies required to use those documents effectively.

J.-F. Rouet
Center for Research on Cognition and Learning, University of Poitiers, MSHS, 99 avenue du Recteur Pineau, 86000 Poitiers, France
e-mail: jean-francois.rouet@univ-poitiers.fr

J.-F. Rouet et al. (eds.), *Understanding Multimedia Documents*,
DOI: 10.1007/978-0-387-73337-1_1, © Springer Science+Business Media, LLC 2008

Whether presented by print or electronically, multimedia documents are being used at a growing rate for a wide spectrum of purposes, ranging from technical information to distance education, personal development and the popularization of science. This increasing use of multimedia documents reflects a general belief that they facilitate people's understanding of technical, scientific or social phenomena. In addition, multimedia documents are widely credited with increasing students' motivation and their engagement in learning tasks. Such benefits, however, are yet to be conclusively demonstrated by empirical research evidence. In fact, despite growing interest on the part of the scientific community (e.g., psychologists, computer scientists, educationalists), the actual effects of multimedia documents on comprehension and learning remain in dispute.

The main purpose of this book is contributing to a better understanding of the information processing that underlie the comprehension of multimedia documents, particularly as it applies to learning. Users' perception and cognitive processing of multimedia information has been the subject of increased attention on the part of cognitive and instructional investigations in the past decade. Research has progressed from broad comparisons (e.g., written vs. spoken text) to fine-grained analyses that are more focused on individual behavior. This includes the use of sophisticated online technologies, e.g., eye tracking, automated data collection, that provide complementary multiple perspectives on the complex processes involved. The studies presented in this book cover a wide range of situations, tasks and domains that emphasize the role of comprehension processes in the use of multimedia information and learning systems. In its common sense, the concept of multimedia refers to the combination of verbal and pictorial information as, for example, in texts, realistic pictures, diagrams, and graphs, whereby the verbal information can be presented either in visual or the auditory modality. In some cases, we use the term *multimedia* also in a broader sense, when even complex text documents are considered to be multimedia because they generally include visual structuring devices such as content maps, frames, margins, typographical cues, and so forth.

Although the phrase "multimedia document" fits both printed and electronic information, the advent of personal computers has boosted the production of electronic multimedia documents to the extent that they are nowadays widely used across most developed societies. Electronic multimedia documents may include features that were not available via traditional, printed publishing. For example, computerized multimedia systems offer the possibility of interactive animations, that is, audio-visual documents in which the user may control the order, pace and position of the information being displayed. This book examines such possibilities by focusing on new ways of displaying and manipulating information through electronic displays.

In this introductory chapter, we provide an overview of the contributions presented throughout the volume that highlights their main themes, theoretical concerns, and perspectives on multimedia learning. We begin with a general framework that sets out some key cognitive dimensions of multimedia comprehension. This is followed by a review of the subsequent chapters that identifies the specific contribution of each chapter within that general framework.

1.2 A general Framework for the Study of Complex Document Comprehension

Comprehension is typically characterized in terms of the interaction of an individual (e.g., a learner), and a source of information (e.g., a text). The source is an external representation of the subject matter which may be read, understood and interpreted by the individual. To this external representation, the individual brings his or her cognitive resources, attention, motivation, and prior beliefs and knowledge to construct a mental representation of the "situation" described in the source. Although this view has prevailed both in research and in educational practice, it has also been criticized as being too narrow and limited. What is missing from this characterization is the awareness that contextual parameters strongly influence both the availability of text as an information source, and the individual's engagement and control of his or her activity (Snow, 2002; Rouet, 2006). Figure 1.1 illustrates the nature of comprehension as an interaction between reader, document and contextual parameters.

In Fig. 1.1, the individual (i.e., the learner) is defined as possessing general cognitive capabilities (e.g., working memory span), prior knowledge of the domain (e.g., meteorology) and purposes (e.g., to be entertained, to acquire new information, to pass a test). Other individual characteristics may of course come into play during multimedia comprehension. For instance, the reader may be more familiar or less familiar with the technology or tools being used to display the document, or with the learning task at hand; s/he may have specific beliefs about the nature of knowledge and information presented, and so forth. The point is that individual characteristics determine both how the learner will address the information source and how s/he will take account of contextual influences.

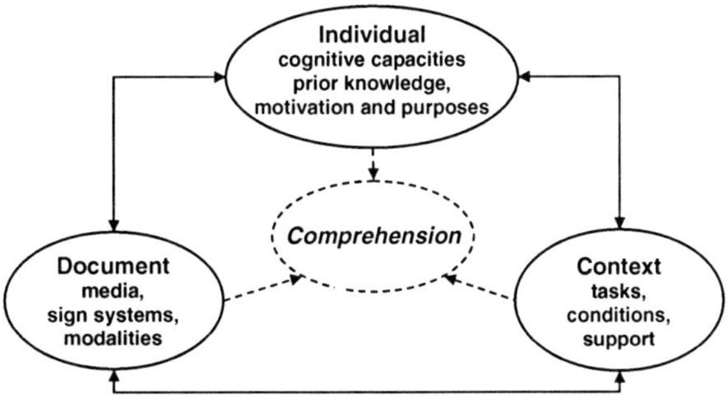

Fig. 1.1 Comprehension as a complex interaction between individual, context and document characteristics

Figure 1.1 also represents a document being presented via a particular "medium" or technology as involving one or more sign systems and as targeting one or more communication modalities (see also Schnotz, Chapter 2). The presentation medium or technology concerns the concrete means used to convey information: clay tablets, printed paper, radio and computer screens are examples of these information media and technologies. Sign systems concern the type of code used to communicate information: drawings, alphabets, road-signs and animated pictures are different sign systems (Schnotz, 2001). Sign systems also incorporate devices that signal the organization of the document. These include headings, bullets, indexes and hyperlinks. Finally, the communication modality concerns the fact that information may be conveyed via different sensory modalities (most typically visual and auditory). Although other modalities may sometimes be involved in multimedia comprehension (such as proprioception in simulation environments), they will not be considered here.

Finally, context includes the tasks, conditions, and support available during comprehension. Specific tasks are often assigned to comprehenders, for instance in school or work settings. Tasks come in various formats, including documents to be read and understood (see e.g., Cerdán et al., Chapter 7). The nature of such tasks is important in establishing standards for what aspects are relevant or important in the provided information set. Relevance and importance are in general not distributed evenly across the available information resources. In addition to task, the context is also defined by the set of conditions that prevails (such as available time or performance expectations) and by the support available. Other learners, coaches, and notetaking devices are examples of contextual support facilities. Our general claim in this volume is that the nature of multimedia comprehension can be properly understood only by articulating these three dimensions into a comprehensive theory. The purpose of the volume is to report the state of the art of research on the (long) road leading to such a theory.

We have organized the contributions into three main sections. Section 1 deals with the memory processes involved in multimedia comprehension; Section 2 addresses the issue of learn control during the comprehension of complex documents, and how it can be studied in real-time; Section 3 takes a broader perspective on multimedia comprehension, considering the evolution of media, technologies, research methods and theories in the short and longer terms. The chapters in Section 3 also include reflections on further research perspectives that may be drawn from the work gathered in the present volume.

1.3 Memory Processes in Multimedia Comprehension (Section 1)

The joint presentation of verbal and pictorial information is a hallmark of most documents within the broad informational genre. Newspapers, magazines as well as textbooks, popular science books and technical documents almost always use a combination of text, photographs, graphics and other types of pictorial information to convey meanings and present explanations. The pervasiveness of multimedia in editorial practice, across ages and cultures, is a de facto argument in favor of multimedia's effectiveness as a communicative approach. In recent years, however, research on learning and instruction has found that multimedia documents are not always as educationally effective as they were expected to be (Rouet, Levonen, & Biardeau, 2001). To make things worse, new types of multimedia documents offered by digital publishing tools, such as hyperlinks, interactive animations, and so forth, were often found to have little or no impact on comprehension (Bétrancourt & Tversky, 2000; Chen & Rada, 1996; Dillon & Gabbard, 1998).

As this field of research has progressed, theories have emerged that seek to explain the relative effectiveness of different multimedia document designs. Examples such as the Cognitive Load Theory by Sweller and his colleagues (Sweller, Chandler, Tierney, & Cooper, 1990; Sweller, van Merriënboer, & Paas, 1998; Van Merriënboer & Sweller, 2005) and cognitive theories of multimedia comprehension by Mayer (2001) and Schnotz (2005) rely on detailed accounts of perceptual and cognitive processes that occur when individuals use multimedia documents (Lowe, 2003). Within this framework, this section of the present volume provides theoretical and empirical analyses of working memory processes during the processing and comprehension of multimedia documents.

But, to start with, what is multimedia? In Chapter 2, Schnotz distinguishes three levels at which multimedia may be considered: The *technical level*, i.e. the concrete technical means used to communicate information; the *representational level*, i.e. the type of sign system used to convey meaning (e.g., words, pictures); and the *sensory level*, i.e. the perceptual modality used to receive information (e.g., auditory, visual). Design of multimedia systems, he claims, must take account of those three levels in order to be effective. Schnotz then reflects on the Cognitive Load Theory originally proposed by Sweller and his colleagues to provide a detailed analysis of the sources of cognitive load when learning from static vs. animated pictures. Next he establishes a distinction between facilitating and enabling functions of animations that leads him to predict interactions between sources of cognitive load, the learner's prior knowledge, and the demands of learning tasks. Findings from a series of experiments confirmed such predictions: For instance, studying animations instead of static pictures increased study time in high prior knowledge learners, but decreased study time in low prior knowledge learners. His chapter provides a very clear demonstration that a full theory of comprehension must take into account the characteristics of the learner, the learning materials and the task, as well as other dimensions of the learning context.

Pazzaglia (Chapter 3) examines the role of visuo-spatial working memory in the comprehension of illustrated text. She makes a well-argued case for the involvement of spatial processes both in one's perception and motion in real-life environments, and in the processing and representation of texts with spatial contents. The central question in her chapter is: under what conditions are pictures effective in supporting the comprehension of spatial text? In two experiments, she provides clear and informative answers. Participants listened to the description of a small town while either viewing an integrated picture, partial pictures of some landmarks, or no picture at all. Pictures were found to help when they represented spatial relations among objects (e.g. landmarks) within an integrated frame, as opposed to the mere location of particular objects. Pictures also helped when learners (or, in this case, listeners) could not spontaneously perform the processes needed to construct and internal representation of the spatial description. Thus, integrated pictures can help people with low spatial abilities to comprehend spatial relations that are explicit in the text. In addition, they can help listeners in general (irrespective of their spatial abilities) draw inferences about other, non-specified spatial relations.

Among the many types of documents that may be called "multimedia", computer animations have raised particular interest in recent years. Computer animations are often visually attractive, sometimes even spectacular, and they can convey a sense of empowerment when they let the learner control the presentation (moving forth and back, pausing, or opening pop-up explanations through hyperlinks, etc.). Unfortunately, and contrary to the intuitions of many instructional designers, animations are not always educationally effective or more motivating. Exceptions include cases where the contents to be taught are intrinsically dynamic. Calling upon the cognitive load theory, Bétrancourt, Dillenbourg, and Clavien (Chapter 4) hypothesized that the inclusion of static snapshots on the display, during the presentation of an animation may reduce the extraneous load and allow the learner to concentrate on the dynamic relations being displayed in the animation. They conducted an experiment in which college students learned about lightning through either static pictures or animations, either with or without static snapshots. The learners spent more time with the animated version but this did not result in superior performance on comprehension and transfer tasks. Further, the provision of a permanent snapshot added no value in the animation condition. Bétrancourt et al. consider different interpretations of these findings, including the fact that the particular snapshot used in their experiment may not have included the right type of information for their students. They suggest that verbal summaries may be more efficient in explicitly specifying relationships among steps in the process to be explained.

Le Bohec and Jamet (Chapter 5) offer a theoretical analysis of the concept of redundancy, (that is, repetition of information) in learning materials. Redundancy is widely used by communicators such as teachers or speakers who employ multimedia presentations. Research, however, has repeatedly found that redundancy may be detrimental to learning. Le Bohec and Jamet's literature review suggests that redundancy generally increases extrinsic cognitive load and may also have the effect of reducing learners' interest in the materials. One possible exception is when information is repeated across various formats (i.e., text and pictures) so that the presentation mode allows the student to encode the the different representations sequentially (see also Chapter 3). Le Bohec and Jamet make a case for *partial redundancy*, that is, the provision of visual summaries along with a spoken explanation. For example, the main points given in a lecture may be repeated on an overhead slide. However, in two experiments, these researchers found no learning benefit of partial redundancy compared to total redundancy (information repeated in print and speech) or no redundancy (speech only). Nevertheless, their data suggest that partial redundancy was "a good compromise", since it resulted in satisfactory learning outcomes and positive student evaluations. Their study confirms previous findings that the mere repetition of verbal information across perceptual modalities can interfere with learning.

In Chapter 6, Hidrio and Jamet discuss the processes involved in understanding spoken explanations of dynamic systems while studying either static pictures or animations. Based on Schnotz and Bannert's (2003) theoretical model, they point out that understanding a multimedia document poses a co-reference problem: as learners listen to speech, they must also locate the discourse referents in the visual display. Compared with static displays, animations may reduce the co-reference problem by providing timely updates in the visual display, something that is obviously impossible with a single static picture. They propose that series of visual pictures along with visual cues (in their case, arrows) may enhance comprehension, compared to single pictures with no cue. Their experiment only partially supported the latter expectation: Compared to a spoken explanation of the four-stroke engine with no illustration, an animation of the four-stroke cycle improved comprehension, recall and inferencing in novice students. The multiple picture with visual cues, however, failed to make any difference compared to the baseline condition. Hidrio and Jamet suggest that the type of information provided by their cues may be useful only to the extent that students have correctly identified the individual parts mentioned in the commentary, a requirement which was possibly too difficult in the static picture condition.

Although Chapters 4, 5, and 6 both confirm the value of a theory-based approach to multimedia design, they highlight the difficulty of turning theories into concrete design principles. More specifically, they clearly demonstrate that merely providing cues (such as snapshots or arrows) may not be enough to support multimedia learners. In order to be effective, the cues inserted in multimedia documents must be timely and match exactly the students' perceptual and cognitive needs. This can be challenging to implement in practice because these needs vary as a function of general cognitive capabilities (see Chapter 3) and according to learners' prior knowledge of the domain (see Chapter 2).

1.4 Contextual Strategies in Document-Based Learning (Section 2)

In naturalistic situations, people often deal with complex documents that include both multiple pieces of text and several types of pictorial information (pictures, diagrams, tables, graphs and to forth). In addition, complex documents may contain some information that is less relevant to the individual learner's purposes. Which passage or aspect of the document is most relevant depends on each individual learner's prior knowledge, as well as their expectations and purposes. Relevance of the information within a multimedia document also depends on contextual parameters, such as how much time is available and how accessible the particular piece of information is within the document. Finally, the relevance of a particular piece of information can be influenced by what is found in other parts of the documents. Cohesion, referential clarity, and congruence across documents or document parts strongly influence readers' comprehension processes.

In order to cope with the complexity of studying multimedia documents, readers must use sophisticated comprehension strategies (Rouet, 2006). Comprehension strategies involve both cognitive and metacognitive components (Lazonder & Rouet, 2008). They let the reader control the pace and distribution of attention over the document sections. The second section of this volume addresses the nature of study strategies as they apply to complex multimedia documents.

While studying a lengthy text, expert readers may skim or even skip some passages whereas for other passages they will slow down, read carefully, and possibly re-read the material several times. Cerdán, Martínez, Vidal-Abarca, Gilabert, Gil, and Rouet (Chapter 7) analyze the relationship between such context sensitive strategies and the level of comprehension reached by readers of instructional text. In two experiments, Cerdán et al. examined how college-level readers distributed reading time across the paragraphs of a science text as they searched the text in order to answer different types of questions. More specifically, they compared high level questions (requesting the integration of information across several paragraphs) with low level questions (that merely requested the localization of a piece of information within a paragraph). They found that high level questions needed to be revisited more often (to "refresh" one's understanding of the question, as they put it), and that these questions elicited broader text search patterns. Their data also indicate that comprehension performance (as assessed by students' ability to answer the questions accurately) was related to specific search patterns. Good comprehenders located relevant sections of the text faster and focused their efforts on those sections. Poor comprehenders, on the other hand, showed more "erratic" search patterns, spending more time on irrelevant portions of the materials. Chapter 7 illustrates the context-dependency of reading when it occurs in naturalistic, purposeful situations. Readers' understanding of the task demands guides the pace and depth of processing of text passages. Further, with efficient readers there may be huge difference in pace and depth of processing within a single text, depending on the relevance of text information for particular needs.

Self-regulation strategies are also important when learning from animations. Learners may need to adjust the pace at which a display presents information, to pause, to backtrack or to skip some sections of the materials. Lowe (Chapter 8) discusses the issue of learner control of animation and its potential effects on learning outcomes. He presents a multi-video technique designed to facilitate fine-grained investigation of learners' self-regulation activity when learning from controllable animations. The chapter makes an important theoretical point: learners need control but may not be able to use it wisely. Therefore, the type and level of control offered as part of electronic documents may be balanced against readers' expected level of skill and know how. Chapter 8 also makes a methodological contribution by demonstrating that when combined, multi-video and retrospective protocols offer a productive approach for studying multimedia learning.

In Chapter 9, Tabbers, Paas, Lankford, Martens and van Merriënboer illustrate the potential of another sophisticated technique, namely eye tracking, to study multimedia comprehension at a fine grain level. Their study raises a crucial question: to what extent can the learner make effective use of the available time when studying a complex multimedia document? The authors argue that the so-called modality principle (i.e., learners generally get more from materials that call upon the visual and auditory modality than from materials based on just one of those modalities. See also Chapter 6) must be reconsidered, taking into account contextual parameters such as how much time is available for study. When learners have enough time, they may be able to distribute their attention more "calmly" on different sections of a visual document, thus reducing the "split attention" effect often found to affect learning from visual multimedia documents. The analysis of learners' eye movements while they read a multimedia document under different timing conditions was found to be a most effective method to study this question. The data did not, however, provide a straightforward confirmation of Tabbers et al.'s prediction. Instead, the pattern of eye movement seemed to respond to a more complex combination of factors, some of them not identified in the study. Tabbers et al. acknowledged that the relation between presentation formats, time and cognitive load is rather complex, and that the use of a detailed cognitive model might help make more specific predictions.

Another important lesson from Chapter 9 is that, contrary to what many believe, eye tracking approaches may be poorly suited to exploratory investigations. Because eye trackers generate a huge quantity of data, and because eye movement patterns are highly variable, their use is likely to be better suited to experimental studies involving a tight and precise set of predictions to be tested. This is a precondition for the researcher to know exactly what to extract and what to compute from the flow of raw measures that come out of online behavioral technologies. In addition, studies based on a single item (i.e., a single text or document) with little control for the participants' prior knowledge run the risk of missing the kind of subtle interactions that occur between text, reader and contextual parameters (in this case, time pressure). The values and limits of various approaches in multimedia research are further discussed in Chapter 13.

Most current theories of multimedia comprehension assume that information acquired from texts and adjunct pictures must at some point be "integrated" to form a unique, coherent mental representation. But what are the conditions for such an integration to occur? In Chapter 10, Rinck draws upon Schnotz and Bannert's (2003) structure mapping hypothesis to claim that integration is reduced when information in a text and in a graph is not fully consistent. In two experiments, Rinck demonstrates that when quantitative phenomena (in his case, results from experiments) are reported in discrepant terms in a text and in an adjunct chart, study time increases, and subject's recall of the results is distorted. Using eye movement data, his second experiment further indicates that both the times spent on each of these media (text and graph) and the number of visual shifts across the media increase when information is discrepant. In other words, readers explore the materials more intensely when they notice a discrepancy, a further indication that they actively try to integrate the various sources into a single representation.

The data reported in Chapter 10 suggest, however, that the respective influence of text and graphs is not symmetrical. Text information has a larger impact on subjects' content recognition, interest ratings, and confidence in their recognition judgments. In other words, novice college students seem to rely much more on what was said in the text than on what is shown in the graph. As Rinck conjectures, however, it remains to be found if this pattern would apply to more experienced readers of scientific prose, or to other types of contents.

1.5 Multimedia Research in Perspective (Section 3)

This section of the volume takes a broader perspective on media, technologies and research into comprehension and learning processes. Whereas previous chapters of this volume have explored the features of multimedia documents at a fine grain level (e.g., assessing the effects of signals in computer animations), Section 3 reflects on multimedia as the continuation of a long term, on-going process of technological innovation in the making of texts and complex documents. The chapters in Section 3 also discuss the evolution of research issues and methodologies as advances in learning environments continue.

The concept of non-linearity has often been considered as a core difference between "old" printed documents and "new", hypermedia ones. Through a historical and semiological study, Platteaux (Chapter 11) demonstrates that non-linearity is in fact deeply rooted in the history of texts and books, through the progressive invention and improvement of content representation and selection tools. Platteaux reviews the history of those tools, in particular the table of contents, the index, and other text structuring techniques typical of the printed book. He shows the connection between text structuring devices and the social uses of text. Of particular interest is the parallel between the invention of sophisticated content representation devices and the diversification of reading strategies, with an ever growing need for fast and direct access to relevant content among a rapidly growing corpus of texts. Platteaux concludes that even though discourse is fundamentally linear, both modern printed texts and hypertext contain devices that let the reader depart from the linear course set forth by the author. Thus, nonlinearity and "reading tools" enable a diversity of cognitive strategies that mirror the diversity of reading purposes and functions. From this perspective, hypermedia documents may be considered to be consistent with the principles of written text that have been created over the centuries.

Current discussions of the promises and pitfalls of multimedia learning also mirror a more recent but classical discussion about so-called "media effects". In the course of the 20th Century, the popularization of movies and television raised both enthusiasm for the potential of these media and concern about their utility in practical educational contexts. As Lumbelli reminds us in Chapter 12, media theorists predicted either a facilitation or a decrease in learning from audio-visual materials, compared to more "traditional" instructional approaches. Many of the arguments in this debate are still present in current multimedia research – and some remain largely un-resolved. Of particular importance is the issue of learner motivation and investment of effort in the learning task (Guthrie & Wigfield, 2000). Learners' ability to comprehend complex information may vary as a function of how much mental effort they are willing to spend in a particular situation. Whether the student is interested or bored, active or passive, focused or un-focused, makes a lot of difference. Research into multimedia comprehension, however, has tended to overlook this basic dimension of learning. Instead, they try to measure aspects such as students' cognitive "load" as a function of situational variables, an approach whose predictive value is bound to remain limited.

Lumbelli also stresses the commonality of the mental processes at work during comprehension, regardless of the medium. In particular, she points out the production of inferences as a condition for deep comprehension. The influences of media or presentation conditions on comprehension may be interpreted in terms of inference production. In two experiments, Lumbelli showed that listening to text while watching pictures, either on television or on a computer screen, resulted in lower scores on comprehension questionnaires, compared to just reading a text which contained equivalent information. Lumbelli argues that images can have a "depressing" effect, i.e. they can decrease the production of inferences that normally characterize deeper text comprehension. Her experiments further confirm the dominance of textual over pictorial information in most comprehension situations (see also Chapters 5 and 10).

The section – and the book – end with two discussion notes about research methodologies and research issues in the area of multimedia learning.

In Chapter 13, Ainsworth analyses the evolution of research issues as well as the respective value and limits of various research approaches. She points out the progressive maturation of the field during the past two decades or so, with a progressive shift from the simple question of whether multimedia is effective, to a more analytic investigation of the complex interactions between environments, learners and learning processes. In particular, she argues that research needs to focus on the differential effects of a particular environment depending on learner characteristics and the broader learning context. Furthermore, researchers need to assess not just the outcomes of learning experiences (i.e., through post-tests and other measures) but also what happens during learning. Ainsworth makes the case for the use of a diversity of research approaches, whose relevance depends on the type of research question being investigated. She highlights the limits and potential misuses of standard factorial designs, and stresses the relevance of case-based, qualitative observations of learning processes especially when exploring complex learning processes.

Fayol and Rouet (Chapter 14) return to the theoretical analyses of the cognitive processes involved in text and multimedia comprehension. They point out the multiplicity of processes involved in comprehension, and the heavy demands these processes can impose on the individual's working memory. Their discussion stresses the importance of learners automatizing some processing components (like e.g., word decoding), and also building up effective processing strategies, in order to cope with the many general difficulties and specific challenges that may occur during the comprehension of a complex document. Fayol and Rouet conclude with the view that in the long run, comprehensive theories of comprehension will lead to more effective instructional approaches to helping students acquire knowledge from texts, pictures and complex documents in general.

1.6 Conclusions and Perspectives

Although the scientific study of multimedia comprehension is relatively recent, it has already proven to be a rich and multifaceted research area. The contributions gathered in the present volume provide a comprehensive overview of relevant issues and methods as well as lessons to be drawn so far. Meanwhile, more research questions and controversies are being raised and addressed within the multimedia research community. Let us briefly summarize a few of them.

An important issue at the theoretical level is to refine the concept of memory capacity. Most contributors to this volume adhere to the general view that cognitive processing occurs under a general working capacity limitation, or working memory span. There is, however, a debate over the dependence of working memory capacity on the learner's prior knowledge. In other words, to what extent is working capacity general and to what extent is it linked to the learner's experience in the particular domain being studied? Despite a large amount of evidence in favor of a general capacity limitation, recent works suggest that capacity maybe to some extent domain dependent (see e.g., Kalyuga, 2005). The relationship of memory capacity and prior knowledge is at the heart of current research efforts in the domain.

Most of the contributions in this volume have discussed the nature of the cognitive processes involved in multimedia comprehension. Other dimensions of learners' activity, such as engagement, effort, motivation, attitudes and so forth, have been investigated to a lesser extent. Yet those dimensions play a critical role in any learning situation. Integrating motivation and engagement into cognitive models of multimedia comprehension may help resolve some ambiguities, e.g. why rich information environments sometimes result in little cognitive processing, and why complex environments sometimes result in better learning even though they may pose more problems to learners.

At a more practical level, more research is needed in order to assess the scope of some findings regarding the effects of multimedia on comprehension and learning. The empirical studies reported in this volume have used samples drawn from various types of populations, whether children, teenagers, or young adults. The skills and capacities of those populations differ as a result of cognitive development, instruction, and academic selection. So far there is no general scale upon which the average ability level of a particular group could be mapped. Hence the need to be cautious about how well the findings may generalize to other populations.

In the context of rapidly evolving information technologies, multimedia comprehension remains a moving target for scientific research. Furthermore, the broader cognitive theories and research methods on which learning science relies are also constantly being updated. Nevertheless, we hope that the present volume provides a useful snapshot for those interested in this fascinating area of investigation. We extend our warm thanks to the contributors for their responsiveness and their patience, and to Christine Ros at the University of Poitiers for her assistance in the preparation of the manuscript.

References

Bétrancour, M., & Tversky, B. (2000). Effects of computer animation on users' performance: A review. *Le Travail Humain, 63*, 311–329.

Chen, C., & Rada, R. (1996). Interacting with hypertext: A meta-analysis of experimental studies. *Human-Computer Interaction, 11*, 125–156.

Dillon, A., & Gabbard, R. (1998). Hypermedia as an educational technology: A review of the quantitative research literature on learner comprehension, control and style. *Review of Educational Research, 68*(3), 322–349.

Guthrie, J. T., & Wigfield, A. (2000). Engagement and motivation in reading. In M. L. Kamil, P. B. Mosenthal, P. D. Pearson, & R. Barr (Eds.), *Reading research handbook* (Vol. III, pp. 403–424). Mahwah, NJ: Erlbaum.

Kalyuga, S. (2005). Prior knowledge principle. In R. Mayer (Ed.), *Cambridge handbook of multimedia learning* (pp. 325–337). New York: Cambridge University Press.

Lazonder, A. W., & Rouet, J. -F. (2008). Information problem solving instruction: some cognitive and metacognitive issues. *Computers in Human Behavior, 24*, 753–765.

Lowe, R. K. (2003). Animation and learning: Selective processing of information in dynamic graphics. *Learning and Instruction, 13*, 247–262.

Mayer, R. E. (2001). *Multimedia learning*. New York: Cambridge University Press.

Rouet, J. -F. (2006). *The skills of document use: from text comprehension to Web-based learning*. Mahwah, NJ: Erlbaum.

Rouet, J. -F., Levonen, J. J., & Biardeau, A. (2001, Eds.). *Multimedia learning: cognitive and instructional issues*. Oxford, UK: Elsevier Science.

Schnotz, W. (2001). Sign systems, technologies, and the acquisition of knowledge. In J. -F. Rouet, J. J. Levonen, & A. Biardeau (Eds.), *Multimedia learning: cognitive and instructional issues* (pp. 9–30). London: Elsevier Science.

Schnotz, W. (2005). An integrated model of text and picture comprehension. In R. E. Mayer (Ed.), *Cambridge handbook of multimedia learning* (pp. 49–69). Cambridge: Cambridge University Press.

Schnotz, W., & Bannert, M. (2003). Construction and interference in learning from multiple representation. *Learning and Instruction, 13*, 141–156.

Snow, C., & the RAND reading study group (2002). *Reading for understanding. Toward a R&D program for reading comprehension*. Santa Monica, CA : RAND Corporation.

Sweller, J., Chandler, P., Tierney, P., & Cooper, M. (1990). Cognitive load and selective attention as factors in the structuring of technical material . *Journal of Experimental Psychology: General, 119*, 176–192.

Sweller, J., van Merriënboer, J. G., & Paas, F. G. W. C. (1998). Cognitive architecture and instructional design. *Educational Psychological Review, 10*, 251–296.

Van Merriënboer, J., & Sweller, J. (2005). Cognitive load theory and complex learning: Recent developments and future directions. *Educational Psychology Review, 17*, 147–177.

Part I
Memory Processes in Multimedia Comprehension

Chapter 2
Why Multimedia Learning is not Always Helpful

Wolfgang Schnotz

Abstract The effectiveness of multimedia documents depends on a complex interaction between document design features, learners' characteristics and task demands. A series of experiments demonstrated that depending on learners' level of prior knowledge, animations may serve an enabling or a facilitating function. Those functions results in different patterns of learning processes and learning outcomes. The results are interpreted in terms of a general model linking document features, learner characteristics, task demands and learning outcomes. It is concluded that, in order for learning to occur, multimedia documents should not seek to facilitate any kind of cognitive processing. Instead, they should stimulate cognitive processes that are both learning effective and within the capabilities of the learners.

Keywords Animation · Cognitive load · Enabling · Facilitating · Prior knowledge

2.1 Introduction

Learning with multimedia is a research topic that has received increasing interest during the last years. The term 'multimedia' usually refers to a combination of multiple technical devices such as computers, information transfer networks, and electronic displays in order to present information through multiple presentation formats such as texts, pictures or graphs through multiple sensory modalities. A closer look reveals three levels of multimedia. First, there is the *technical level*, which refers to the technical devices used in multimedia; these technical devices can be considered as the *carriers* of signs (Cuban, 1986). Second, there is the *representational level*, which refers to the forms or representations used in multimedia, such as texts, static and animated pictures or graphs;

W. Schnotz
Department of General and Educational Psychology, University of Landau, Im Fort 7, D-76829 Landau, Germany
e-mail: schnotz@uni-landau.de

J.-F. Rouet et al. (eds.), *Understanding Multimedia Documents*,
DOI: 10.1007/978-0-387-73337-1_2, © Springer Science+Business Media, LLC 2008

these forms of representation can be considered as the *types* of signs (Schnotz, 1993, 2001). Third, there is the *sensory level*, which refers to the sensory modality used for the *reception* of signs used in multimedia (Mayer, 1997, 2001).

Discussions about multimedia learning often ignore the multi-level nature of the topic. Decision makers frequently assume that multimedia learning is primarily concerned with information technology and, therefore, is essentially a matter of information scientists and engineers. People who adopt this view are not aware that they only address one level. They ignore, that the other two levels are equally important and that these levels require expertise of cognitive science, psychology, and educational science. It is very easy to make huge false investments of time and money into multimedia, if only one level is taken into account. Effective multimedia learning requires that the learning content and the display of the learning content are adapted on the representational level and the sensory level to the functioning of the learner's cognitive system (Mayer, 2001; Sweller, 1999).

The present chapter will consider the interplay of different forms of representation and sensory modalities with the learner's cognitive system in multimedia learning. In a first step, the role of working memory in multimedia learning will be analysed. I will argue that multimedia learning can be associated with different kinds of cognitive load on working memory, depending on the learner's level of expertise. In a second step, a specific aspect of multimedia learning will be analysed more closely: learning from animation. I will show that different kinds of animations can put different kinds of cognitive load on the learner's working memory, depending on his/her level of expertise in the domain of learning. In a third step, the different effects of multimedia on cognitive load will considered more closely. It will be shown that simple thumb rules regarding the reduction of cognitive load are inadequate for the design of multimedia learning environments. I will argue that the different kinds of cognitive load are subject of multiple constraints, which have to be well balanced in media design to enhance effective multimedia learning.

2.2 Cognitive Load in Multimedia Learning

A basis assumption of recent theories on multimedia learning is that the human cognitive architecture includes different subsystems: various sensory registers, a working memory and a long term memory (cf. Atkinson & Shiffrin, 1971; Baddeley, 1986; Mayer, 2001, 2005; Schnotz, 2005; Schnotz & Bannert, 2003). According to these models, Information from the environment enters the cognitive system via sensory organs (e.g. the ear, the eye etc.) and is briefly stored in a sensory register (e.g. the auditory register, the visual register etc.). Information is then transmitted through different sensory channels from the sensory registers to working memory, where it is further processed together with information from long-term memory (i.e. prior knowledge) to construct different kinds of mental representations such as prepositional representations and mental models. The processes of constructing these mental representations in working memory are referred to as comprehension. When comprehension and other kinds of cognitive processing lead to changes in long-term memory, these changes are referred to as learning. The bottleneck of processing information from the environment is the human working memory due to its limited capacity of information storage and processing (Baddeley, 1986, 2000). All kind of information processing imposes, if the information originates from the outside world, a cognitive load on working memory. As working memory capacity is limited, this cognitive load has to be adapted to the available capacity (Chandler & Sweller, 1991; Sweller, 1999; Sweller & Chandler, 1994).

Multimedia can be considered as means to manipulate the cognitive load of learners. There are different possible effects that multimedia can have on cognitive load: an enabling effect, a facilitating effect, and an inhibiting effect. The enabling effect means that due to a reduction of cognitive load, processes become possible which otherwise had remained impossible. The facilitating effect means that due to a reduction of cognitive load processes that have been already possible, but still required high mental effort, become possible with less effort. Both the enabling effect (impossible processes become possible) of multimedia and the facilitating effect (possible difficult processes become easier) of multimedia result from a reduction of cognitive load. Of course, there is also the possibility of an unintended increase of cognitive load due to multimedia instruction. In this case, processes would become more difficult or even impossible, and multimedia would have an inhibiting effect on comprehension and learning.

2.2.1 Types of Cognitive Load

If multimedia has an enabling effect or a facilitating effect on comprehension and learning, one could argue that cognitive load should always be reduced as far as possible. Recent studies on cognitive load theory, however, have shown that such a general motto might be too simple, because one has to distinguish different kinds of cognitive load: intrinsic load, extraneous load, and germane load (Sweller, van Merriënboer & Paas, 1998).

The *intrinsic load* is determined by the intellectual complexity of the instructional content or the task to be performed, related to the degree of expertise of the learner. The complexity of the instructional content or task corresponds to the required element interactivity. Any interactions between elements to be held in working memory require working memory capacity. Intrinsic cognitive load therefore corresponds to the number of related elements to be held and coordinated simultaneously in working memory. With a specific learning task in a specific learning situation, the intrinsic load cannot be manipulated.

The *extraneous load*, on the contrary, is determined by the instructional format. More specifically, it is generated by an inappropriate instructional format; by the way the information is structured and presented to the learner. Extraneous load reflects the effort to process poorly designed instruction. When load can be reduced without changing the task, then the load is extrinsic. Accordingly, instructional design should aim to decrease extraneous cognitive load.

The *germane load* reflects the learner's effort of detecting regularities and of forming appropriate schemata during the process of learning. Individuals can and should be encouraged to engage in cognitive processing that triggers schema construction and increases the learners' level of expertise. Appropriate instructional design should therefore direct the learner's attention to processes that are relevant for learning by construction of schemata. In order to enhance learning, germane load should not be reduced, but rather increased provided that the total cognitive load stays within the limits of working memory capacity (Paas & van Merriënboer, 1994).

2.2.2 Differential Effects of Multimedia Presentations

How are the different kinds of cognitive load affected by multimedia and under which conditions are these effects beneficial for learning? The following considerations will demonstrate that this question can only be answered with regard to a specific expertise level of the learner: one and the same multimedia learning environment can be beneficial for one learner, whereas it can be harmful for another learner.

More than a hundred studies have demonstrated that in the vast majority of cases students learn better from words and pictures than from words alone (Levie & Lentz, 1982; Levin, Anglin & Carney, 1987). These kind of findings correspond to what Mayer (1997, 2001) has called the *multimedia effect*. This effect occurs under specific conditions. An external condition of the multimedia effect is that that the verbal and the pictorial information are simultaneously available in working memory, which requires that words and pictures have to be presented spatially close to each other on a paper or screen or that words are presented by an auditory narrative simultaneously with the picture. This presentation principle is called the spatial or the temporal *contiguity principle*. An internal condition of the multimedia effect is that learners have low prior knowledge but sufficient spatial ability (Mayer, 2001).

From the perspective of cognitive load theory, one can interpret these findings as effects of manipulating extraneous cognitive load. If the learner's task is to construct a mental representation of the subject matter in working memory, this task defines what is the unavoidable intrinsic cognitive load. Any kind of instruction that imposes a cognitive load higher than the required minimum for constructing a mental representation causes therefore an extraneous cognitive load on the learner's working memory. Under the conditions of low prior knowledge, constructing a mental representation from words and pictures is easier than constructing it from words alone. Presenting only words to the learner would therefore be an inappropriate instructional format, because it poses an additional and unnecessary cognitive load on the learners working memory, which is an extraneous load. In this case, adding a picture to the words would have an enabling effect on learning, because it takes away extraneous cognitive load from mental model construction (Mayer, 2001; Mayer & Moreno, 1998).

If learners have high prior knowledge, however, adding a picture to the words can have just the opposite effect. As Sweller and his colleagues have shown, multiple sources of information are frequently not needed. Instead, one source can be self contained, if it provides all the required information to construct a mental model of the subject matter (Chandler & Sweller, 1996; Sweller, van Merriënboer & Paas, 1998). In these cases, providing the same information in different formats through different sources generates an extraneous cognitive load, because the learner unnecessarily wanders between the different information sources, interrupts repeatedly ongoing processes of organisation and coherence formation, and looses time with unproductive search for unneeded information. This negative effect of attending to unnecessary (i.e. redundant) information, which require cognitive resources, that consequently are unavailable for learning, is called the *redundancy effect* by Sweller and his colleagues. Due to the redundancy effect, adding a picture to a text or a text to a picture can have an inhibiting effect on learning, because the additional source of information increases extraneous cognitive load.

In other words: A needed help for learners with low prior knowledge can become an unneeded help for high prior knowledge learners and thus lead to a so-called expertise reversal effect (Kalyuga, Chandler & Sweller, 2000; Kalyuga, Ayres, Chandler & Sweller, 2003). Accordingly, multimedia instruction which includes verbal and pictorial information is beneficial only under some well defined circumstances and can have negative consequences under other circumstances. It is therefore not possible to equate a specific kind of multimedia instruction with a decrease or increase of cognitive load. Instead, it depends on the learner and his/her learning prerequisites whether a specific change in the instructional format will result in an increase or decrease of cognitive load (see also Rouet, Lowe, & Schnotz, Chapter 1).

Multimedia designers often seem to assume that adding a picture to a text results in more elaborate cognitive processing, because the learner will not only read and understand the text, but also observe and understand the picture. The assumption that multimedia learning leads to additional cognitive processing is likely to be false. Instead, the learner has a choice: He/she can decide both for the text and for the picture how deep he/she will process the corresponding source of information. Accordingly, picture processing does not necessarily add up to the same amount of text processing that would occur without pictures. Instead, learners can use the picture partially instead of the text, because mental model construction based on pictorial information seems to be easier than mental model construction based on verbal information. Schnotz and Bannert (1999) found that learners with lower prior knowledge used a text to a considerably lower extent when there were also pictures presented than when no pictures were available. As a result, the text was processed less thoroughly and the mental model was less elaborated than if the participants had learned from a text without picture. In this case, multimedia instruction had a facilitating function. However, this facilitation had a negative effect on learning, because instead of the extraneous load the germane load was reduced. On the contrary, learners with higher prior knowledge were rather stimulated by the pictures to process the text more intensively. In this case, multimedia instruction stimulated deeper processing and, thus, increased germane load on the learners working memory.

2.3 Animation in Multimedia Learning

One of the frequently used features in computer-based multimedia learning environments is animation. Any element on a computer screen can be animated, but the most frequent use of animation concerns animated pictures. Animated pictures can be used to support 3D perception by showing an object from varying perspectives. They can be used to direct the observer's attention to important (and unimportant) aspects of a display, convey procedural knowledge (as e.g. in software training), demonstrate the dynamics of a subject matter, and allow exploratory learning through manipulating a displayed object. Furthermore, they can have a supplantation effect (Salomon, 1994), when they help learners to perform a cognitive process that the learners could not perform without this external support. Despite a widespread belief that animation is a powerful instructional device, however, it is still an open question under which conditions animated pictures really enhance comprehension and learning (Tversky, Morrison & Bétrancourt, 2002); see also Bétrancourt, Dillenbourg, & Clavien, Chapter 4).

Like other forms of multimedia instruction, animations can have different functions regarding cognitive load. If they reduce the cognitive load of tasks in order to allow cognitive processing that would otherwise be impossible, then animations have an *enabling function*. If they reduce the cognitive load of tasks that could otherwise be solved only with high mental effort, then animations have a *facilitating function* (cf. Mayer, 2001; Sweller & Chandler, 1994; Sweller, van Merriënboer, & Paas, 1998). For example, when students learn about time phenomena related to the earth's rotation, animated pictures like those in Figs. 2.1 and 2.2 can be useful. In these figures, the earth is depicted as a sphere viewed from the North Pole that rotates in a space where different locations are associated with different states of time.

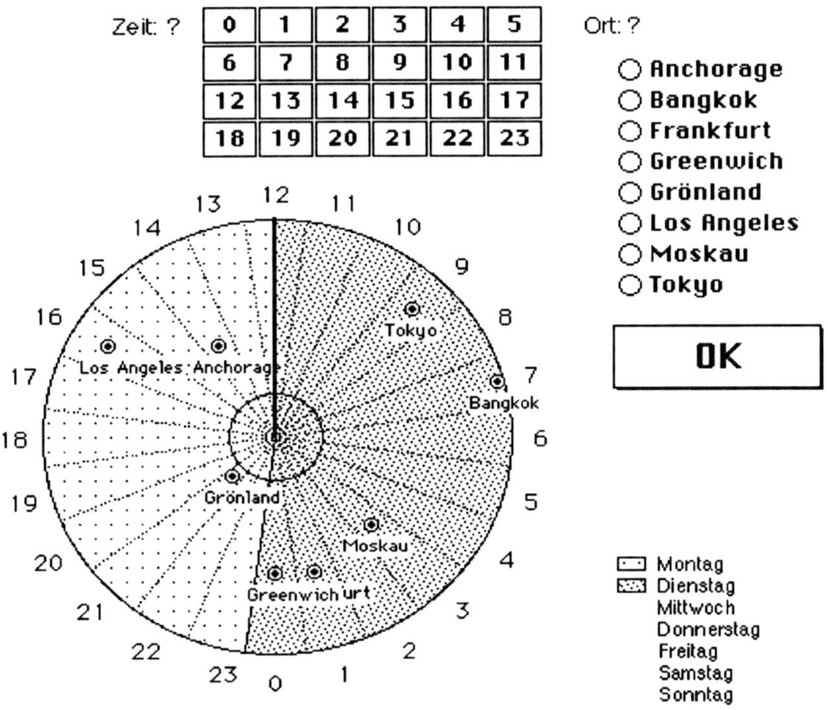

Fig. 2.1 Example of a manipulation picture that can be used to explore the depicted subject matter. The picture shows the earth with time zones seen from the North Pole. Learners can select different daytimes for different cities and turn the earth in the corresponding position

The picture shown in Fig. 2.1 can be manipulated by the learner who can define specific day-times for specific cities. After clicking on the OK-button, the earth moves into the corresponding time state. This type of picture will be called here a manipulation picture. Because a manipulation picture enables learners to investigate a high number of different time states, which would not be possible on the basis of a static picture, such a picture is assumed to have an enabling function.

The picture shown in Fig. 2.2 can be used to simulate the earth's rotation. The learner can choose different ways how a traveller can circumnavigate around the earth (symbolized by a black dot moving in Western or Eastern direction with different travelling speed depending on the learner's choice). After pressing the SIMULATION-button, the earth starts rotating and the traveler's dot starts moving on the rotating earth. This type of picture will be called here a simulation picture. It might be much easier for a student to observe the rotation of the earth and the movement of an object in a simulation picture than to perform the corresponding mental simulations on his/her own with only a static picture (Forbus, Nielsen & Faltings, 1991; Lowe, 1999, 2003; Sims & Hegarty, 1997). Thus, such a picture is assumed to have a facilitation function.

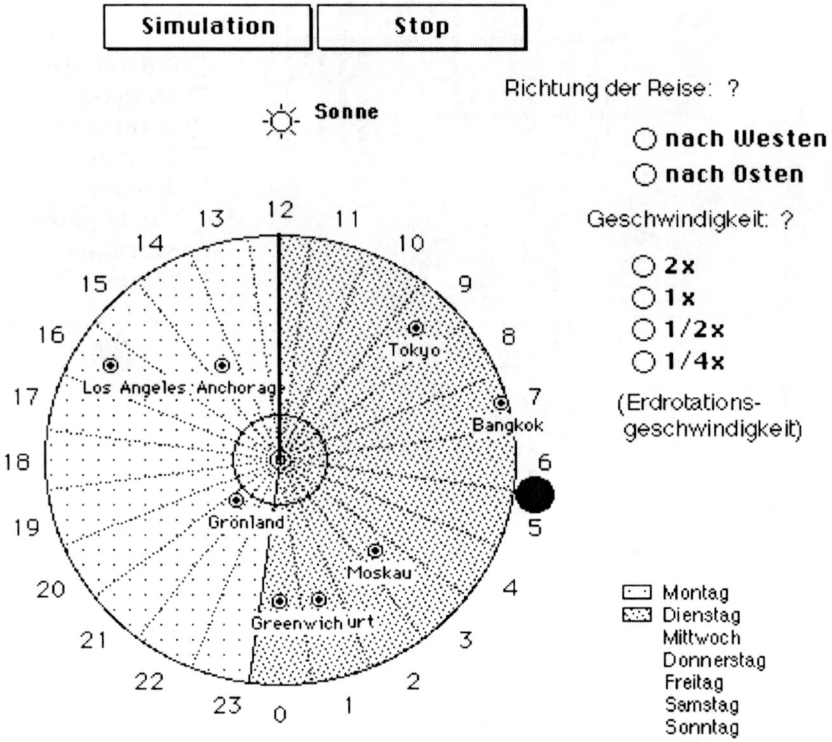

Fig. 2.2 Example of a simulation picture that can be used as external support for mental simulations. The picture shows the earth with time zones seen from the North Pole. Learners can select among different kinds of circumnavigations of a traveler (symbolised by a *black dot*) around the world and observe the Earth's rotation plus the circumnavigation

2.3.1 Differential Effects in Learning from Static and Animated Pictures

In a study on learning from animation from a cognitive perspective, Schnotz and Rasch (2005) compared learning from animated (manipulation and simulation) pictures and learning from static pictures. The rationale of this study was the following. If animated pictures *enable* the learner to perform additional cognitive processing, the learner's total amount of processing should increase. As additional processing needs additional time, the enabling function of animations should lead to an increase of learning time compared to the corresponding static pictures. The enabling function is expected to be more pronounced when individuals have high learning prerequisites (high cognitive ability and high prior knowledge) because these learners will be able to use the possibilities of animations more extensively than individuals with low learning prerequisites. If animated pictures *facilitate* cognitive processing, the learner needs less effort with animated pictures than with static ones, because the animation reduces cognitive load to a degree that is easier to cope with. Thus, if the facilitating function of animations applies, learners will invest less learning time into animated pictures than into corresponding static pictures. The facilitating function is expected to be more pronounced when learners have low prerequisites because these individuals need more external support than learners with high prerequisites.

If animated pictures enable individuals with high learning prerequisites to do additional cognitive processing, these learners will spend more time observing animated pictures than static pictures. If animated pictures facilitate processing for individuals with low learning prerequisites, these learners will spend less time observing animated pictures than static pictures. Following this line of reasoning, one can assume an interaction between learning prerequisites (high/low) and type of pictures (animated/static) on learning time.

Forty university students participated in the study and were tested for their prior knowledge about the topic and for their intelligence. Both variables were combined into a joint variable of learning prerequisites. Then, the students received a hypertext about time and date differences on the earth either with static pictures or with animated pictures. After the learning phase, the participants received a comprehension test, which consisted of items referring to time differences between different places on the earth (e.g., *What is the time in Anchorage, if it is Thursday 9 o'clock p.m. in Tokyo?*) or which referred to time phenomena related to circumnavigations of the world (e.g., *Why did Magellan's companions think, upon their arrival after sailing around the world, that it was Wednesday when it was actually already Thursday?*).

The results of this study are presented in Figs. 2.3, 2.4 and 2.5: Figure 2.3 shows the picture observation times for learners with low and learners with high prerequisites when learning from static or from animated pictures. The figure displays a significant interaction *Picture Type x Learning Prerequisites* ($F(1,36) = 3.171$, $p = 0.042$). When students had high learning prerequisites, they spent more time for animated pictures than for static pictures. When students had low

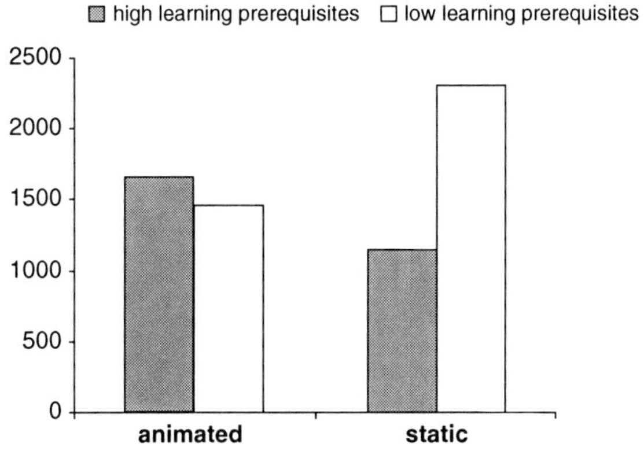

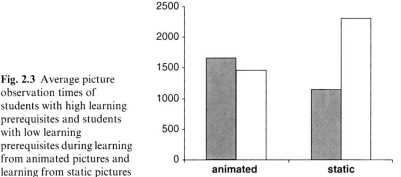

Fig. 2.3 Average picture observation times of students with high learning prerequisites and students with low learning prerequisites during learning from animated pictures and learning from static pictures

Fig. 2.4 Average performance of students with high learning prerequisites and students with low learning prerequisites in answering time difference items after learning from animated pictures and after learning from static pictures

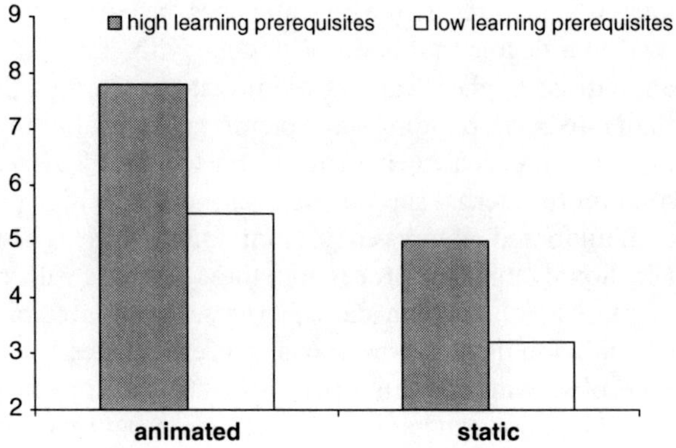

learning prerequisites, they spent less time for animated pictures than for static pictures. Thus, the results supported the assumption that the enabling function of animations applies to students with higher learning prerequisites, whereas the facilitating function applies to students with lower learning prerequisites.

Figure 2.4 shows how well the participants answered the time-difference items. There was a highly significant effect of picture type ($F(1, 36) = 8.553$, $p = 0.003$), but no interaction effect. Students with animated pictures outperformed students with static pictures in answering time difference questions.

Figure 2.5 shows the students' performance with the circumnavigation items. This pattern of results was totally different from the previous pattern. There was neither a significant main effect nor a significant interaction effect. However, students with low learning prerequisites answered circumnavigation questions significantly better after learning with static pictures than after animated ones ($t(13.5) = 2.380$, $p = 0.033$). Animated pictures did not have positive effects on answering these questions, but were harmful when students had lower learning prerequisites.

To summarize: For individuals with high prerequisites animations seemed to have an enabling rather than a facilitating function, increasing the time needed for

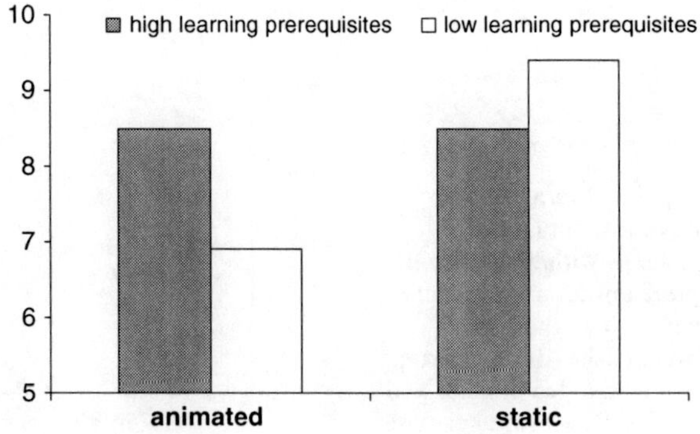

Fig. 2.5 Average performance of students with high learning prerequisites and students with low learning prerequisites in answering circumnavigation items after learning from animated pictures and after learning from static pictures

them to study. For individuals with low learning prerequisites, animations seem to have a facilitating rather than an enabling function. The findings concerning answering time-difference questions supported the assumption that animations result in better learning due to their enabling or facilitating function. The findings concerning answering circumnavigation questions, however, did not give any evidence for this assumption: Learners with high learning prerequisites did not profit from the animations, and learners with low learning prerequisites surprisingly performed even better with static pictures than with animated ones.

In order to understand this unexpected divergence between time-difference and circumnavigation scores, it might be helpful to analyse the cognitive processes required by the corresponding test items more closely. Answering time difference items requires knowledge about time coordinates of various cities in the world and the time differences between them. Manipulation pictures such as shown in Fig. 2.1 can be used to display a high number of different time states, which should be a good basis to extract information about time differences. Thus, the high performance of the animation group in answering time difference questions might correspond to the enabling function of such animations.

Answering circumnavigation items requires mental simulations. Simulation pictures such as displayed in Fig. 2.2 provide external support for such simulations. Possibly, this function is under specific conditions beneficial for learning, namely if the individual has too low abilities to perform a mental simulation on his/her own (Salomon, 1994; Sweller & Chandler, 1994). This study, however, indicates that facilitation can also have a negative effect on learning. If individuals are capable of performing such mental simulations by themselves, external support can make processing unnecessarily easy. Accordingly, students invest less cognitive effort in learning from animation than when learning from static pictures. From the perspective of cognitive load theory, animation can unnecessarily reduce cognitive load associated with deeper meaningful cognitive processing. Most students had obviously sufficient skills for mental simulations without external support, but students with lower cognitive prerequisites were apt to accept unneeded external support.

Animations can obviously have different effects on different tasks. As the manipulation pictures seem to allow deeper analysis of time differences, their enabling function results in better performance with time difference questions. Simulation pictures, on the contrary, seem to make mental simulations easier, but this facilitating function can obviously be harmful for learning. In this case, animation has an inhibiting effect on learning due to an inadequate reduction of cognitive load.

2.3.2 Learning from Different Kinds of Animations

In a second study, Schnotz and Rasch (2005) analysed the effects of different kinds of animations. Based on the previous experiment, it was assumed that manipulation pictures have primarily an enabling function, which is especially important for time-difference questions, whereas simulation pictures have primarily a facilitating function, which is especially important for circumnavigation questions. 26 university students participated in the study. The learning material was the same as in the previous study except that one group received a text including only manipulation pictures, whereas the other group received a text including only simulation pictures. The further procedure was the same as in the previous study.

The results of the study are presented in Figs. 2.6 and 2.7. Figure 2.6 shows how well the participants answered the time-difference items. There was a marginally significant effect of the animation type ($F(1, 22) = 1.743, p = 0.10$) and a significant interaction between animation type and learning prerequisites ($F(1, 22) = 4.511, p = 0.023$). Students with manipulation pictures outperformed students with simulation pictures. When learners had high learning prerequisites, they had significantly higher scores after learning from manipulation pictures than after learning from simulation pictures ($t(12) = 2.287$, $p = 0.021$), whereas learners with low learning prerequisites had lower scores with manipulation pictures than with simulation pictures. Accordingly, manipulation pictures seem to have an enabling function that is helpful for answering time difference questions, but only if learners have sufficiently high learning prerequisites.

Figure 2.7 shows how well the participants answered the circumnavigation items. There was a significant effect of animation type ($F(1, 22) = 5.020, p = 0.018$), but no significant interaction effect. Especially students with low learning prerequisites had lower performance in answering circumnavigation questions after learning from simulation pictures than after learning from manipulation pictures ($t(10) = 2.928$, $p = 0.008$). Simulation pictures seem to have a facilitating function especially for students with low learning prerequisites, and this affects the answering of circumnavigation questions. However, this function

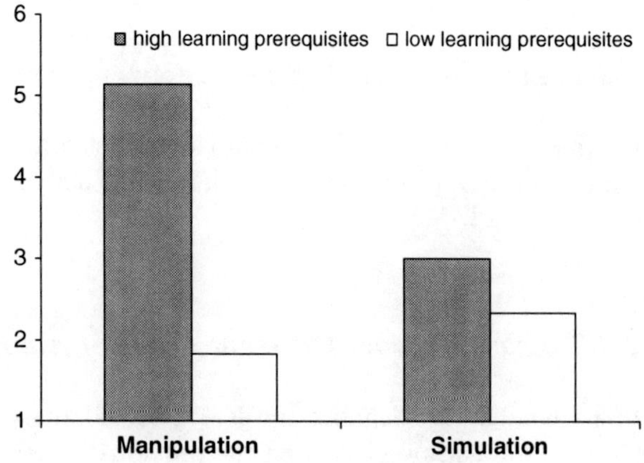

Fig. 2.6 Average performance of students with high learning prerequisites and students with low learning prerequisites in answering time difference items after learning from manipulation pictures and after learning from simulation pictures

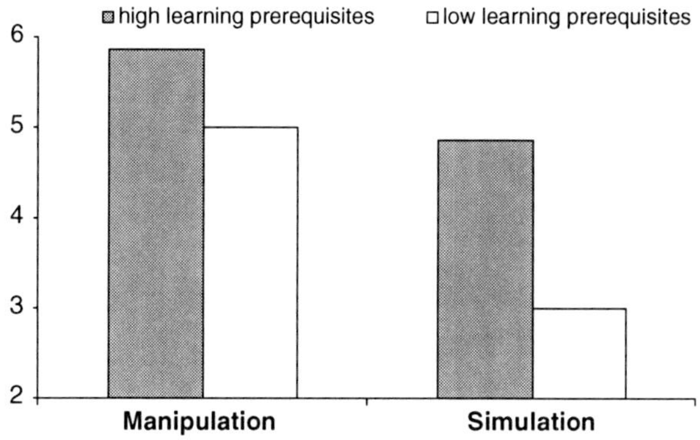

Fig. 2.7 Average performance of students with high learning prerequisites and students with low learning prerequisites in answering circumnavigation items after learning from manipulation pictures and after learning from simulation pictures

turned out again to be harmful for these learners, because the external support had made processing unnecessarily easy.

The results indicate that the different kinds of animations have indeed different functions in the process of learning. Whereas the manipulation pictures seem to have primarily an enabling function, the simulation pictures seem to have primarily a facilitating function. Manipulation pictures seem to be primarily beneficial for answering time-difference questions. Learners can use such pictures to generate various time states of the earth in order to extract information about time differences, which was obviously helpful for answering time-difference questions. This function seems to be especially pronounced when students have higher learning prerequisites, because these learners have sufficient resources available to use these possibilities. Simulation pictures seem to affect primarily the answering of circumnavigation questions. They have a facilitating function insofar as they allow following an external simulation process that makes the corresponding mental simulation much less demanding. This function might be beneficial for learners who would not be able to perform this mental simulation at all without external support (cf. Mayer, 1997, 2001; Salomon, 1994; Schnotz, Böckheler, & Grzondziel, 1999). However, if learners are able to perform the mental simulation on their own, the external support prevents students from performing learning-relevant cognitive processes. In this case, the facilitating function is beneficial for processing, but not for learning.

Did the simulation pictures unintentionally increase extraneous load? At the first sight, one could suspect that they did. Learners were able to perform the mental simulations on their own. Thus, the simulation pictures provided process information, which was in fact no longer required by the learner and which was therefore redundant. Providing redundant information is generally considered as an increase of extraneous cognitive load, because learners have to process additional unneeded information. Such redundancy can result in an expertise reversal effect, when individuals with higher learning prerequisites perform better without, rather than with, additional information (Kalyuga,

Chandler, & Sweller, 2000). However, this pattern does not fit to the results of the experiments presented above, because the negative effects of animation were found primarily when students had low learning prerequisites rather than high learning prerequisites. Therefore it seems that the negative facilitating effect is something different from the expertise reversal effect.

2.4 A Closer Look on the Enabling and Facilitating Function of Multimedia

I have argued before that multimedia learning environments can reduce the cognitive load for the learner and the reduction of cognitive load can have either an enabling function or a facilitating function. The enabling effect means that due to a reduction of cognitive load, processes become possible which otherwise had remained impossible. The facilitating effect means that due to a reduction of cognitive load processes that are already possible, but which still require high mental effort, become possible with less effort. The following considerations will aim at a closer analysis of the enabling effect and the facilitating effect. For the sake of simplicity, the analysis will assume that there is no extraneous load.

2.4.1 The Zone of Proximal Development from a Cognitive Load Perspective

As has been mentioned already, intrinsic load is determined by the intellectual complexity of the task to be performed, related to the degree of expertise of the learner. Figure 2.8 shows an assumed relation between different levels of learners' expertise, learners' performance on a specific hypothetical task X and the intrinsic load imposed by this task on working memory.

The upper part of Fig. 2.8 shows how the learner's expertise (represented on the abscissa of the figure) determines the likelihood of the learner's successful performance (represented on the ordinate of the figure) on a task X. Within the area of low expertise on the left hand, the likelihood of successful performance remains at 0% up to the expertise level L1. Between the expertise level L1 and the expertise level L2, the likelihood of successful performance increases from 0% to100%. Beyond the expertise level L2, the likelihood of successful performance remains at 100%. In other words: If the learner's expertise level is below L1, then the task is too difficult for the learner. If the learner's expertise level becomes higher than L1, then the task becomes more and more easy for the learner. At the expertise level L2 and beyond, the task is so easy that performance is likely to be perfect.

The lower part of Fig. 2.8 shows how the intrinsic cognitive load associated with task X varies with the learner's level of expertise. Up to L1, the cognitive

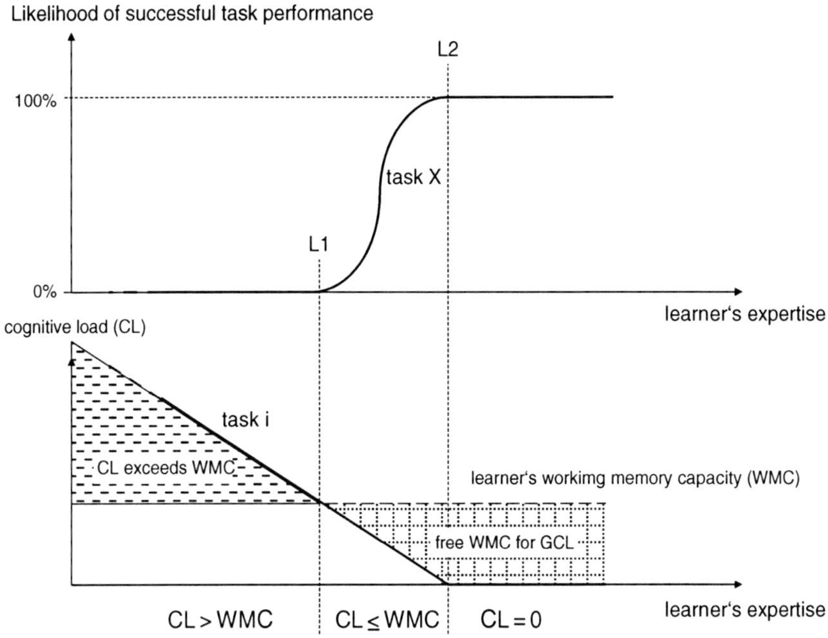

Fig. 2.8 Task performance (*top*) and cognitive load (*bottom*) of a hypothetical task X for learners with different levels of expertise

load (CL) of task X exceeds the learner's working memory capacity (WMC). The learner is therefore unable to perform the task successfully. Between L1 and L2, the cognitive load of the task is lower than the learner's working memory capacity: The learner is able to perform the task, and there is free capacity of working memory left that can be used for germane cognitive load activities (GCL). At L2, the cognitive load of task X drops down to zero, because task performance becomes automated and does not need working memory capacity any more. The available working memory capacity can therefore in principle be used for other activities.

Whereas Fig. 2.8 has shown the learner's performance on one hypothetical task X and the cognitive load in relation to the learner's expertise, Fig. 2.9 shows the same dependencies for different hypothetical tasks A, B, and C, which are ordered according to their difficulty from the most easy task A to the most difficult task C. Any task can be performed without additional help or with additional help. If a task has to be performed without help, this is indicated in Fig. 2.9 by the symbol '–'. If help is available during task performance, this is indicated by the symbol ' + '.

For a student who has reached learning state L3, task A is very easy. Its likelihood of successful performance is 100%, even if no help is provided (A–). The cognitive load of doing task A is zero for the student, because task

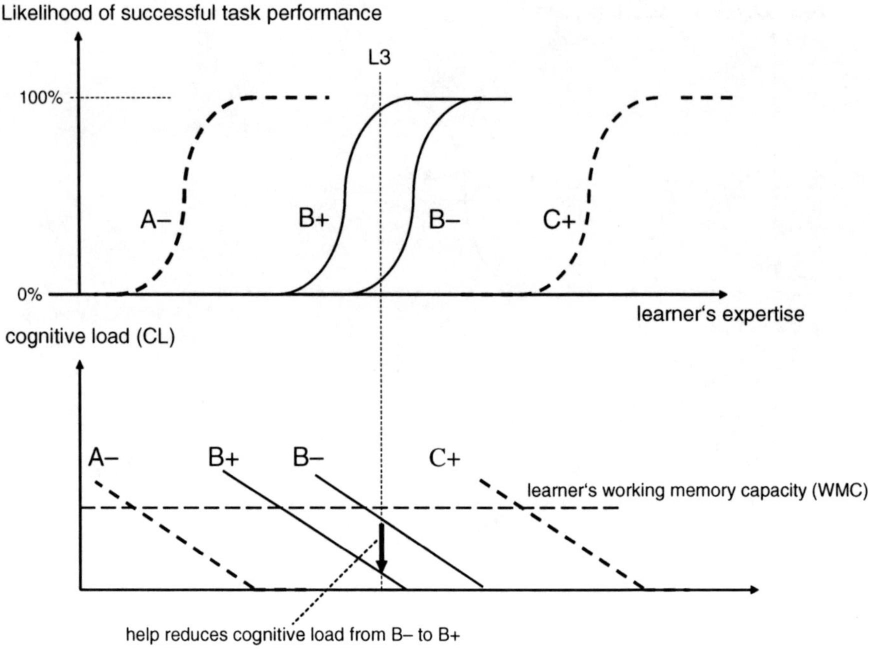

Fig. 2.9 Task performance (*top*) and cognitive load (*bottom*) of an easy task A, a medium task B and a difficult task C with help (+) or without help (–) for learners with different levels of expertise

performance is already automated and no working memory capacity is required any more. For the same student, task B has a high difficulty, because the likelihood of successful performance is very low as long as no help is provided. This is indicated in Fig. 2.9 by the function 'B–'. In the case of no help, the cognitive load of task B is very high, as the task requires most of the learner's working memory capacity.

If help is available, however, the same student performs considerably better. If the learner has the best possible help available for the task at hand, he/she performs successfully with a very high likelihood, which is indicated in Fig. 2.9 by the function 'B + '. The cognitive load of doing the task with this kind of help is very low, because the help reduces the required working memory capacity from the function 'B–' down to the function 'B + '. Finally, task C is so difficult for a student at learning state L3, that he/she is unable to perform this task successfully even if additional help is provided. The cognitive load of doing task C exceeds the learner's working memory capacity and the likelihood of successful performance is 0% even with help (C +).

The increase of performance as a result of instructional help is the core of the zone of proximal development (ZPD). The zone of proximal development has been defined by Vygotski (1963) as the range between a lower limit and an upper

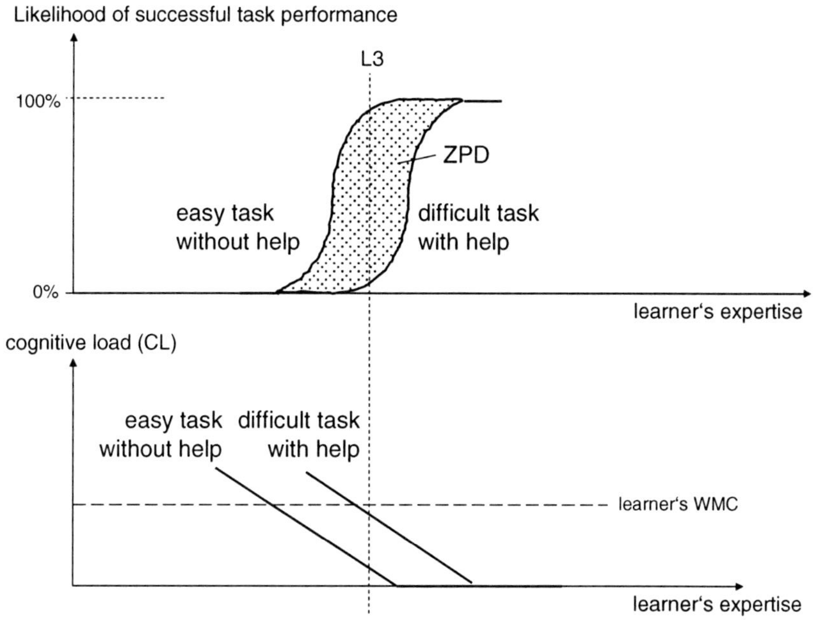

Fig. 2.10 Task performance (*top*) and cognitive load (*bottom*) of an easy task which can be solved by a learner at expertise level L3 without help as well as task performance (*top*) and cognitive load (*bottom*) of a difficult task which can be solved by learner at expertise level L3 only with help. The range of difficulty between the two tasks is known as the zone of proximal development (ZPD)

limit of task difficulty. The lower limit of the ZPD is defined as the most difficult task the learner can perform successfully without help. The upper limit of the ZPD is defined as the most difficult task that the learner can perform successfully with optimal help. The lower limit task is of course easier than the upper limit task. In Fig. 2.10, the ZPD is represented by the shaded area between these two tasks, the easier performed without help and the more difficult one performed with help. The left-hand curve shows the performance characteristics of the easier task, which is the most difficult task a learner at state L3 can perform successfully without help. The right hand curve shows the performance characteristics of the most difficult task that the learner can perform successfully only with optimal help.

Any instruction that aims at promoting learning should include learning tasks within the limits of the ZPD. If the task difficulty would be higher than the ZPD, the learner's cognitive capacity would be overwhelmed, because the cognitive load would exceed the learner's working memory capacity. If the task difficulty would be lower than the ZPD, the learner would be subchallenged and a great deal of the available cognitive capacities would remain unused for the learning process.

2.4.2 *Cognitive Load Effects of Manipulation and Simulation Pictures*

Based on the previous analysis, the effects of animation on learners' working memory can be described now more precisely. In the studies mentioned above, manipulation pictures provided learners the possibility to explore a high number of different time states on the earth. The assumed effects of manipulation pictures compared to static pictures in terms of cognitive load theory are visualized in Fig. 2.11. Accordingly, generating a high number of different time states only on the basis of a static picture is too difficult for learners at the expertise level L3, the average expertise level of participants in these studies. Under this condition, only very few time states can be generated (if any) beyond the states shown explicitly in the static pictures. Most learners in the studies described above were probably unable to generate a higher number of time states in their mind according to their limited processing capacity.

The use of manipulation pictures changed the situation dramatically. Learners were now able to click on a few buttons in order to generate a high number of time states and explore them systematically, which was beyond the learners' possibilities on the basis of static pictures. In other words: The manipulation

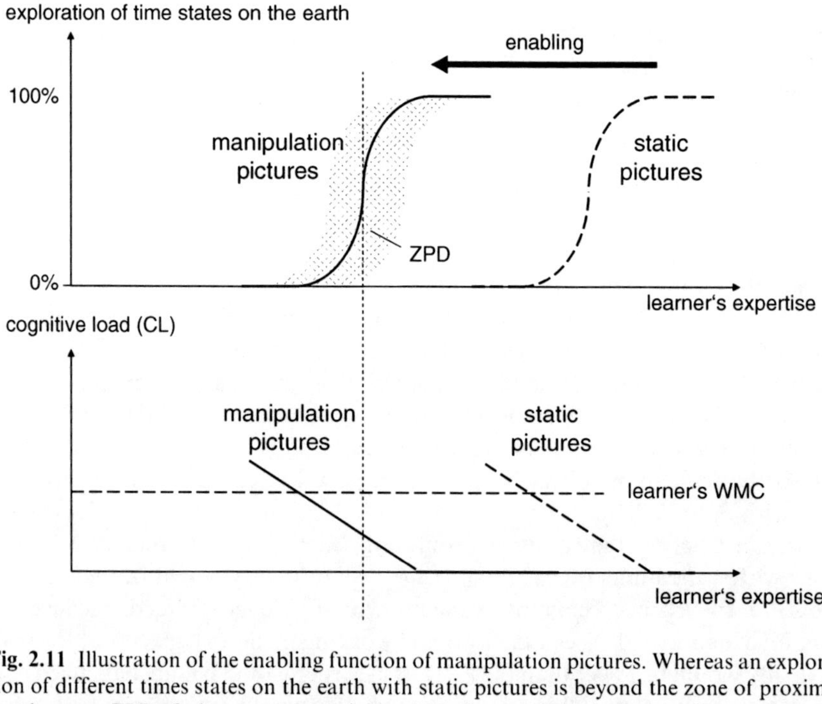

Fig. 2.11 Illustration of the enabling function of manipulation pictures. Whereas an exploration of different times states on the earth with static pictures is beyond the zone of proximal development ZPD of a learner at expertise level L3, the use of manipulation pictures shifts the task difficulty into the learner's ZPD

pictures shifted the task of generating multiple time states from a too high level of difficulty down to a lower level of difficulty within the students' zone of proximal development. The students were enabled in this way to perform a task that they could not perform on the basis of static pictures. Accordingly, the manipulation pictures had an enabling function for the learners.

The function of simulation pictures used in the studies described above was different from those of the manipulation pictures. The simulation pictures demonstrated the earth's rotation around its axis and, thus, facilitated the corresponding mental simulations compared to static pictures. The assumed effect of simulation pictures compared to static pictures in terms of cognitive load theory is visualized in Fig. 2.12. Accordingly, learners at the expertise level L3 (which is again the assumed average expertise level in the studies) were able to perform a mental simulation of the earth rotation even on the basis of a static picture. In other words: The mental simulation on the basis of a static picture was within the learners' zone of the proximal development.

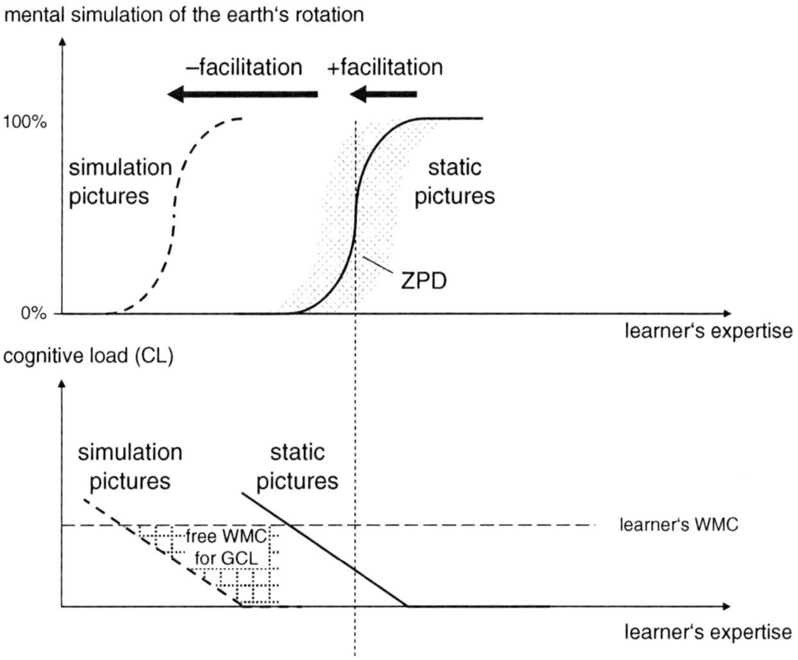

Fig. 2.12 Illustration of facilitating functions of simulation pictures. For a learner at expertise level L3, performing a mental simulation of the earth's rotation on the basis of static pictures is within his/her zone of proximal development (ZPD). A minor facilitation through a better graphical design, for example, could still have a beneficial effect on performing this mental simulation (+ facilitation). However, simulation pictures make the process of mental simulation too easy, because the learner can watch the simulation and follow it in a relatively passive mode. In this case, the use of simulation pictures shifts the task difficulty out of the learner's ZPD (-facilitation)

The use of simulation pictures reduced the difficulty of the mental simulation dramatically. Learners are now able to click on a few buttons in order to see a picture of the earth rotating around its axis. Thus, they did not have to infer the movement of the earth any more without external support. Instead, they could perform the mental simulation just by watching the animated picture, by passively following the perceived rotation of the earth. Accordingly, one can assume that the simulation pictures used in the studies had a facilitating function for the learners, because the mental simulation became much easier. However, this facilitation turned out to have a negative effect on learning. As Fig. 2.12 illustrates, the simulation pictures shifted the task of mental simulation, which was inside the learners' zone of proximal development with static pictures, down to the area of too low task difficulty outside the students' zone of proximal development. In other words: The simulation pictures had a facilitating function, but they made the mental simulation too easy by providing unneeded support for the learners.

Of course, this is not to say that a facilitating function has always negative effects of learning. If a task is very difficult and if the facilitation remains within the zone of proximal development, the facilitating function may well be beneficial for learning. This possibility is indicated in Fig. 2.12 as a positive facilitating effect. However, if the facilitation shifts the task difficulty out of the learner's zone of proximal development, this facilitation is likely to have negative effects on learning.

2.4.3 Constraints on Germane Cognitive Load

Whereas the considerations described in 4.1 and 4.2 focused on the constraints of intrinsic load, the following analysis will focus on the constraints of germane load. Remember that we have hypothesized in the previous paragraphs for the sake of simplicity that there is no extraneous load. Accordingly, we have assumed that the learner's working memory capacity is available only for intrinsic load and for germane load. Germane load has been described above as the load of cognitive processes, which aim at detecting regularities, forming appropriate schemata and, thus, to increase the individual's expertise during the process of learning. Whereas intrinsic load is a performance oriented concept, germane load is a learning oriented concept. Although performance and learning are closely related, they are different kinds of processes.

Germane load requires an extra amount of working memory capacity beyond the intrinsic load (or any extraneous load), and this extra capacity is used for learning. The fact, that there are cognitive activities, which aim at learning and which require working memory capacity, does not imply, however, that all kinds of learning require germane load. Learning can also occur as a by-product of performance without any conscious extra reflection about the conditions of performance and, thus, without any extra processing in working memory.

Germane load should therefore *not* be considered as a prerequisite for all kinds of learning. It should be considered only as the load of some specific cognitive processing (such as conscious monitoring of one's own performance, for example) which requires working memory capacity and which is directed at learning.

Germane load seems to be constrained in different ways. The first constraint is that germane load, as any other kind of cognitive load, is constrained by the available working memory capacity. If the intrinsic load of a task is very high and uses most of the learner's working memory capacity, there is not much capacity left for any germane load. If the intrinsic load of a task would require all of the learner's working memory capacity, the germane load would even drop down to zero. However, this would not imply that there is no learning, because germane load should not be considered as a prerequisite of all kinds of learning.

A second constraint of germane load seems to be the nature of the learning task. If we consider the simulation pictures in the studies above as an example, we have to notice that a mental simulation with the help of a simulation picture puts only a low intrinsic cognitive load (if any) on working memory, because the learner has only to follow the displayed process on a perceptual basis. Insofar, a high amount of working memory capacity should be available for germane load (see Fig. 2.12). In fact, however, there was less learning from simulation pictures than from static pictures, although the static pictures were more demanding than the simulation pictures. Obviously, a higher proportion of free working memory capacity is not always beneficial for learning, because the free capacity cannot always be used for germane cognitive load. If a task becomes too easy, there is not much to learn, even when there is much working memory capacity available. One can speculate that the amount of working memory capacity available for germane load is also limited by the task difficulty, that is, by the intrinsic load of the task.

A third constraint of germane load is the learners motivation to use his/her available mental resources in a strategic manner for cognitive processing that deliberately aims to increase his/her own expertise. Learners do not automatically invest all their available cognitive capacity which is not used for intrinsic load or extraneous load into learning. Instead, they decide whether they do engage or do not engage into specific learning activities and how much amount of cognitive resources they invest into it. Germane cognitive load depends not only on the available working memory capacity. It also depends on general learning orientations, on affective and on motivational aspects of learning. For example, learners who follow a deep approach in their learning will more likely adopt a higher germane load than learners who follow a surface approach in their learning (Entwistle & Ramsden, 1983; Marton & Säljö, 1984). Similarly, learners with high interest in the learning content or are for other reasons highly motivated in learning will more likely adopt a higher germane load than learners who are not interested (Renninger, Hidi & Krapp, 1992). In other words: Germane load is an aspect of the learner's self-regulation (Winne & Hadwin, 1998).

Although germane load is subject of the individual's willingness to engage in additional learning-oriented cognitive processing, learning environments can encourage individuals to engage into this kind of processing. In other words: It is not sufficient that learners have cognitive resources available for learning. It is necessary to take care as far as possible that they really invest their available working memory resources into learning.

2.5 Conclusions

We have considered multimedia as a means to manipulate cognitive load of learners, which again raised the question of how cognitive load *should* be manipulated. One possible answer is given by a widespread thumb rule in the field of instructional design, which is simple and clear. Accordingly, cognitive load should be reduced as far as possible. Unfortunately, this advice is wrong, because things are not as simple like that. As the previous analysis has shown, cognitive load should not generally be reduced as far as possible. Instead, the relevant question is, when cognitive load should be reduced and when it should not be reduced. More specifically, we should ask which kind of cognitive load should be manipulated in which way under which conditions.

The standard answer given by cognitive load theory to this question is the following. Intrinsic load is given by the task and, thus, cannot be manipulated. Extraneous load results from an inappropriate instructional design, that is, from an inappropriate presentation of information to the learner. Extraneous load should therefore be reduced as far as possible. Whereas intrinsic load cannot be manipulated and extraneous load should be reduced as far as possible, the germane load should be adapted to the specific conditions at hand. As germane load is assumed to enhance learning, it should not be reduced, but rather increased within the limits of available working memory capacity. This is a much more differentiated view than the simple thumb rule 'reduce cognitive load whenever you can'. However, our previous considerations suggest that even this view is still too simplistic.

Learning tasks presented in the instructional process should be adapted to the learner's zone of proximal development, which depends on his/her level of expertise based on prior knowledge and cognitive abilities. If learning tasks are too difficult, the learner is unable to perform these tasks successfully, because the requirements exceed the learner's working memory capacity. In this case, successful performance is impossible, and there is no learning. If learning tasks are too easy, they do not challenge the learner's capabilities, because task performance is automated to a large extent and therefore requires very few working memory capacity (if any). In this case, performance is successful, but there is also little learning besides further automation. If learning task difficulty is adapted to the learner's zone of proximal development, then intrinsic load is adapted to the learner's working memory capacity, as the intrinsic load should neither exceed nor subchallenge the available working memory capacity.

We have seen that a reduction of intrinsic or extraneous load through multimedia can have either an enabling function or a facilitating function. The reduction of cognitive load has an enabling function, if a previously impossible task performance becomes possible due to its decreased difficulty. An example of the enabling function of animation was given by the manipulation pictures in the two studies described above. The pictures allowed the learner to generate a large number of different time states, which could not have been generated on the basis of a static picture. The reduction of cognitive load has facilitating function, if a task performance that required so far high mental effort becomes possible with less effort due to its decreased difficulty. An example of the facilitating function of animation was given by the simulation pictures in the two studies. The pictures provided external support for the corresponding mental simulations and, thus, made these mental processes easier.

The facilitating function can be helpful for learners under specific conditions (cf. Wallen, Plass & Brünken, 2005). However, the studies mentioned above showed that the facilitating function can also be harmful for learning. The negative effects of facilitation obviously occur, when learners who would be able to perform cognitive processes on their own make nevertheless use of external support, which they do not really need. The unneeded external support can keep a learner away from doing learning-relevant cognitive processes by him/herself due to an inappropriate facilitation of the task. Although the facilitation makes performance easier, it does not necessarily make learning easier. The essential point here is that learning is different from performance. Accordingly, performance aids are not necessarily also learning aids.

As we did not deal with the role of extraneous cognitive load here, we can simply adopt the standard view of cognitive load theory in this respect, which suggests that extraneous load should be reduced as far as possible. With regard to germane load, however, our analysis leads to a suggestion that differs somewhat from the standard view of cognitive load theory. Accordingly, germane load is not only constrained by the available working memory capacity, that is, it's full capacity minus intrinsic minus extraneous load. Germane load is also constrained by the difficulty of the task, that is, by its intrinsic load. In the previous example, the simulation pictures made the mental simulation considerably easier, as the intrinsic load was much lower and, accordingly, more working memory capacity was left for germane load. Nevertheless, the simulation pictures resulted in lower learning than the static pictures despite the high amount of available working memory capacity. It seems that if a task is too easy, there is not much to learn about it. Although much working memory capacity is available in this case, there is not much to be invested into learning. In other words: The amount of germane load seems to be constrained also be the intrinsic load. Accordingly, germane cognitive load cannot be increased to any degree whatever within the limits of available working memory capacity. Instead, germane load should be balanced against the required intrinsic load of the task. Finally, germane load is also constrained by the individual's willingness to invest his/her energy into cognitive processes that promote learning.

Accordingly, successful teaching and learning with multimedia is not only a matter of instructional design. It is also a matter of the learner's strategies and his/her own initiative to apply these strategies. A central question is what possibilities exist to make learners more engaged into this kind of processing.

The present chapter has made obvious that multimedia does not guarantee effective learning. Rich multimedia environments that offer high amounts of information do not necessarily result in elaborated knowledge structures. Instead, as the human cognitive resources are limited, less can be more. It has also become obvious, that simple didactic thumb-rules do not provide appropriate guidelines for the design of powerful learning environments. Instead of applying simple thumb-rules, we need a better understanding of how people learn from multimedia. We need to know under which conditions multimedia learning is effective, and why it is effective under these conditions. In other words: We need further theory driven empirical research on learning from multimedia.

References

Atkinson, C., & Shiffrin, R. M. (1971). The control of short-term memory. *Scientific American, 225*, 82–90.

Baddeley, A. (2000). The episodic buffer: a new component of working memory? *Trends in Cognitive Science, 4*, 417–423.

Baddeley, A. (1986). *Working memory*. Oxford, U.K.: Oxford University Press.

Chandler, P., & Sweller, J. (1991). Cognitive load theory and the format of instruction. *Cognition and Instruction, 8*, 293–332.

Chandler, P., & Sweller, J. (1996). Cognitive load while learning to use a computer program. *Applied Cognitive Psychology, 10*, 151–170.

Cuban, L. (1986). *Teachers and machines. The classroom use of technology since 1920*. New York: Teachers College Press.

Entwistle, N. J., & RamsdenRamsden, P. (1983). *Understanding student learning*. London: Croom Helm.

Forbus, K. D., NielsenNielsen, P., & FaltingsFaltings, B. (1991). Qualitative spatial seasoning: the Clock project. *Artificial Intelligence, 51*, 417–471.

Kalyuga, S., Chandler, P., & Sweller, J. (2000). Incorporating learner experience into the design of multimedia instruction. *Journal of Educational Psychology, 92*, 126–136.

Kalyuga, S., Ayres, P., Chandler, P., & Sweller, J. (2003). Expertise reversal effect. *Educational Psychologist, 38*, 23–31.

Levie, H. W., & LentzLentz, R. (1982). Effects of text illustration: A review of research. *Educational Communication and Technology Journal, 30*, 195–232.

Levin, J. R., Anglin, G. J., & Carney, R. N. (1987). On empirically validating functions of pictures in prose. In D. M. WillowsWillows & H. A. HoughtonHoughton, (Eds.), *The psychology of illustration*, (Vol. 1, pp. 51–86). New York: Springer.

Lowe, R. K. (1999). Extracting information from an animation during complex visual learning. *European Journal of Psychology of Education, 14*, 225–244.

Lowe, R. K. (2003). Animation and learning: Selective processing of information in dynamic graphics. *Learning and Instruction, 13*, 157–176.

Marton, F., & Säljö, R. (1984). Approaches to learning. In F. Marton, D. J. Hounsell, & N. J. EntwistleEntwistle (Eds.), *The experience of learning* (pp. 36–55). Edinburgh: Scottisch Academic Press.

Mayer, R. E. (1997). Multimedia Learning: Are we asking the right questions? *Educational Psychologist, 32*, 1–19.

Mayer, R. E. (2001). *Multimedia learning*. New York: Cambridge University Press.

Mayer, R. E. (Ed.) (2005). *Cambridge Handbook of Multimedia Learning*. Cambridge: Cambridge University Press.

Mayer, R. E., & Moreno, R. (1998). A split-attention effect in multimedia learning: Evidence for dual processing systems in working memory. *Journal of Educational Psychology, 90*, 312–320.

Paas, F., & van Merriënboer, J. G. (1994). Instructional control of cognitive load in the treining of complex cognitive tasks. *Educational Psychology Review, 6*, 357–371.

Renninger, A., Hidi, S., & Krapp, A. (Eds.) (1992). The role of interest in learning and development. Mahwah, NJ: Erlbaum.

Salomon, G. (1994). *Interaction of media, cognition, and learning*. Hillsdale, NJ: Erlbaum.

Schnotz, W. (1993). On the relation of dual coding and mental models in graphics comprehension. *Learning and Instruction, 20*, 247–249.

Schnotz, W. (2001). Sign sytems, technologies, and the acquisition of knowledge. In J. F. RouetRouet, J. LevonenLevonen & A. BiardeauBiardeau (Eds.), *Multimedia Learning – Cognitive and Instructional Issues* (pp. 9–29). Amsterdam: Elsevier.

Schnotz, W. (2005). An Integrated Model of Text and Picture Comprehension. In R. E. Mayer (Ed.), *Cambridge Handbook of Multimedia Learning* (pp. 49–69). Cambridge: Cambridge University Press.

Schnotz, W., & Bannert, M. (1999). Einflüsse der Visualisierungsform auf die Konstruktion mentaler Modelle beim Bild- und Textverstehen. *Zeitschrift für experimentelle Psychologie, 46*, 216–235.

Schnotz, W., & Bannert, M. (2003). Construction and interference in learning from multiple representations. *Learning and Instruction, 13*, 141–156.

Schnotz, W., & Rasch, T. (2005). Enabling, facilitating, and inhibiting effects of animations in multimedia learning: Why reduction of cognitive load can have negative results on learning. *Educational Technology Research and Development, 53*, 47–58.

Schnotz, W., Böckheler, J., & Grzondziel, H. (1999). Individual and co-operative learning with interactive animated pictures. *European Journal of Psychology of Education, 14*, 245–265.

Sims, V. K., & Hegarty, M. (1997). Mental animation in the visuospatial sketchpad: Evidence from dual-tasks studies. *Memory & Cognition, 25*, 321–332.

Sweller, J. (1999). *Instructional design in technical areas*. Camberwell, Australia: ACER Press.

Sweller, J., & Chandler (1994). Why some material is difficult to learn. *Cognition and Instruction, 12*, 185–223.

Sweller, J., van Merriënboer, J. G. & Paas, F. G. W. C. (1998). Cognitive architecture and instructional design. *Educational Psychological Review, 10*, 251–296.

Tversky, B., Morrison, J. B., & Bétrancourt, M. (2002). Animation: Does it facilitate? *International Journal of Human-Computer Studies, 57*, 247–262.

Wallen, E., Plass, J. L., & Brünken, R. (2005). The function of annotations in the comprehension of scientific texts: cognitive load effects and the impact of verbal ability. *Educational Technology Research and Development. 53*, 59–72.

Winne, P. H., & Hadwin, A. F. (1998). Studying as self-regulated learning. In D. J. Hacker, J. Dunlosky, & A. C. Graesser (Eds.), *Metacognition in educational theory and practice* (pp. 277–304). Mahwah, NJ: Lawrence Erlbaum Associates.

Vygotski, L. S. (1963). Learning and mental development at school age (J. SimonSimon, Trans.). In B. Simon & J. Simon (Eds.), *Educational psychology in the U.S.S.R.* (pp. 21–34). London: Routledge & Kegan Paul.

Chapter 3
Text and Picture Integration in Comprehending and Memorizing Spatial Descriptions

Francesca Pazzaglia

Abstract Spatial processes are involved both in subjects' perception and motion in real-life environments, and in the comprehension of texts with spatial contents. Two experiments examined the effectiveness of pictures in supporting the comprehension of spatial text. Undergraduate students listened to the description of a town while either viewing an integrated picture, partial pictures of some landmarks, or no picture at all. Integrated pictures resulted in better comprehension especially in participants with a lower spatial working memory capacity. It is concluded that integrated pictures help low spatial ability individuals comprehend spatial relations that are explicit in the text. Integrated pictures also help any listener draw inferences about other, non specified spatial relations.

Keywords Integrated pictures · Spatial text · Working memory

3.1 Introduction

Spatial language is very common in every-day life. People often describe the shape and the position of certain objects, different spatial configurations and both indoor and outdoor environments. Particularly frequent is the task in which a person describes a particular environment thus allowing others to create a mental model, which can help them to move successfully therein. These spatial descriptions can be given from different perspectives, for example in relation to the cognitive style of the descriptor or the spatial features of the environment. Several studies (as reviewed by Devlin, 2001) have demonstrated that, in describing their environment, women generally prefer to adopt a route perspective based on egocentric terms of reference, and particularly centered on the description of salient landmarks. By contrast, men prefer to adopt a survey

F. Pazzaglia
Universitá Degli Studi di Padova, Dipartimento di Psicologia Generale "Vittorio Benussi", Via Venezia 8, 35131 Padova, Italy
e-mail: francesca.pazzaglia@unipd.it

J.-F. Rouet et al. (eds.), *Understanding Multimedia Documents*,
DOI: 10.1007/978-0-387-73337-1_3,

perspective, based on exocentric terms of reference, such as compass directions. It has also been demonstrated that description-perspectives can change according to environmental complexity. Modern cities, with straight roads intersecting at 90° angles, are more frequently described from a survey perspective than are historic centers of European cities characterised by very narrow, non-linear routes (Pazzaglia, 2000). These results demonstrate that the use of spatial language is quite complex, requiring the speaker to choose among several possibilities as regards to perspective (Taylor & Tversky, 1992; Tversky, 2003), linearisation (Levelt, 1989) and use of landmarks for their description (Daniel & Denis, 1998; Tversky & Lee, 1999a,b). Despite this complexity, people can quite efficiently describe their environment, so as to allow others, unfamiliar with it, to successfully navigate through it following verbal instructions alone. Guidebooks with verbal descriptions of places to see are a typical example. Pictures and maps often accompany and integrate verbal information. Substantial research has also addressed the interesting question regarding which sort of mental representations derive from processing spatial descriptions. In an attempt to answer this question, many studies, in the last twenty years, have focused on the concept of "spatial mental models" (as reviewed by Tversky, 1991).

3.2 Theoretical Framework

3.2.1 Spatial Mental Models and the Role of Imagery in the Comprehension of Spatial Texts

In Johnson-Laird's (1983) theory, the final mental representation emerging from the processing of a text is a mental model representing the situation described therein. In the case of spatial texts, mental models are supposed to have spatial properties isomorphic to those of the environments represented (Mani & Johnson-Laird, 1982). In their analysis of how spatial texts are understood and comprehended, Perrig and Kintsch (1985) drew a distinction between a text-based representation, which maintains the verbal characteristics of the message, and a situation model, spatial in nature. The nature and the features of mental models derived from spatial descriptions have been intensively studied during the last two decades (Tversky, 2003). Amongst the numerous questions addressed by these empirical studies, some remain particularly relevant and continue to be debated: e.g. the nature, verbal or spatial, of the mental model (de Vega, Cocude, Denis, Rodrigo, & Zimmer, 2001); its dependency on the perspective assumed in the description (Bosco, Filomena, Sardone, Scalisi, & Longoni, 1996; Pazzaglia, Cornoldi, & Longoni, 1994; Perrig & Kintsch, 1985; Taylor & Tversky, 1992); the dimension accessibility in mental frameworks (Franklin & Tversky, 1990; Franklin, Tversky, & Coon, 1992; Maki & Marek, 1997; de Vega et al., 2001).

The studies on the comprehension of spatial descriptions assume that the mental models derived from spatial descriptions are themselves spatial in nature.

Supposedly, they tend to maintain the characteristics of the original spatial configuration: people build mental models to represent significant aspects of their physical world and manipulate them when thinking and planning (Bower & Morrow, 1990). Further support to this is provided by Morrow, Bower and Greenspan (1989).

Indeed, they showed that, when people memorise a building layout and then read narratives that describe a protagonist moving around in the building, they focus on information that is relevant to the protagonist. Evidence to that supplied by the fact that objects from the room where the character was located were most accessible (Morrow, Greenspan, & Bower, 1987).

Bryant (1997) claims that people possess a spatial representation system that constructs spatial mental models on the basis of perceptual and linguistic information. This issue has been discussed also by de Vega et al. (2001) and Baguley and Payne (2000). Nieding and Ohler (1999) have demonstrated that six year-old children can construct spatial situation models from narratives and that these models differ from a text-based representation (van Dijk & Kintsch, 1983).

Literature on spatial descriptions shows that the description of an environment can assume two different main route and survey perspectives (Tversky, 1991). The route descriptions assume the point of view of a person who is moving along the environment. They are characterized by the use of an intrinsic frame of reference and egocentric terms, such as right, left, front and back, and have a linear organisation, given by the order in which landmarks appear along the route itself. The survey descriptions provide an overview of the spatial layout, sometimes with a strong hierarchical organization (Taylor and Tversky, 1992). An extrinsic frame of reference and canonical terms such as north, south, east and west are used. The question of whether the mental model derived from spatial descriptions is perspective dependent was investigated by some studies with different results (Bosco et al., 1996; Pazzaglia et al., 1994; Perrig & Kintsch, 1985; Taylor & Tversky, 1992). Bosco et al. (1996) found that representations of repeatedly experienced descriptions were shown to be perspective independent. Lee and Tversky (2005), even if demonstrated that switching perspective plays a significant role in comprehension of spatial texts, found that the relevance of this role, in turn, diminishes with repeated retrieval.

Studies on mental models have also considered what kind of temporary memory functions are involved in their construction. However less attention has been devoted to studying which cognitive functions are involved in the construction of spatial mental models. For example the involvement of visuo-spatial working memory has only recently been studied.

3.2.2 *Visuo-Spatial Working Memory in Comprehending Spatial Descriptions*

Working memory is generally defined as the dynamic control and co-ordination of processing and storage that takes place during the performance of complex cognitive tasks, such as language processing and visuo-spatial thinking (Miyake & Shah, 1999). In Baddeley's model (Baddeley, 1986; Baddeley & Hitch, 1974; Cornoldi & Vecchi, 2003; Logie, 1995) working memory is thought of as a temporary storage and processing system with a central executive and two slave sub-components: verbal working memory (VWM) and visuo-spatial working memory (VSWM).

Visuo-spatial working memory maintains and processes spatial and visual information, thus ensuring the formation and manipulation of mental images. Several studies (see below) have recently demonstrated that VSWM has a role in processing spatial texts.

Indirect evidence of the involvement of VSWM in the comprehension of spatial descriptions has emerged from data on individual differences in spatial abilities, where visuo-spatial working memory ability is related to the comprehension of spatial texts (Conte, Cornoldi, Pazzaglia, & Sanavio, 1995; de Vega, 1994; Pazzaglia & Cornoldi, 1999). Pazzaglia and Cornoldi (1999, Exp. 1) selected two groups of participants presenting no differences as regards performance on the digit span test (which measures verbal abilities) and, respectively, high and low performances on Corsi' s block task (which measures visuo-spatial abilities). Group participants were asked to listen to the description of a city and subsequently recall the spatial text. As expected, the high visuo-spatial ability group performed the memory task significantly better than the other group.

Having controlled for differences in verbal abilities, they demonstrated that the comparatively poorer performance of the low visuo-spatial ability group in the comprehension of the spatial description was effectively due to differences in spatial ability.

This experiment contributes to support the idea that the differentiation of intelligence into different components, among which spatial and verbal, allows to explain individual diversity in many every-day cognitive tasks, critical dissociations, differences between groups (Cornoldi & Vecchi, 2003). Further support in this direction is provided by the fact that even popular tests aimed at measuring intelligence are often based on the distinction between verbal and spatial (performance) intelligence. Examples are the Primary Mental Abilities (PMA) test (Thurstone & Thurstone, 1947) and Wechsler scale (Wechsler, 1981).

Other studies have shown more direct evidence of the involvement of VSWM in spatial texts processing by using a dual-task paradigm. In the dual task methodology participants have to perform a primary and a secondary task concurrently. The rationale is that performance on the primary task should be less efficient when a secondary task is presented concurrently than in the single task condition, because in the former condition the two tasks compete for the same limited resources of working memory. Many studies have explored the effects of various secondary tasks on performance during diverse cognitive activities, and it is now generally agreed that visuo-spatial tasks such as spatial tapping (continuous tapping of a series of keys or buttons) compete for maintenance of spatial information in VSWM (Farmer, Berman, & Fletcher, 1986).

Vandierendonck and De Vooght (1997) studied the comprehension of temporal and spatial relations in four-term series problems. Participants had to perform, concurrently to the problem-solving activity, an articulatory suppression task, a tapping task and a random interval repetition task. Results showed that all three secondary tasks interfered with reasoning accuracy, but that the tapping task was particularly interfering when it was performed concurrently with processing the premises of the spatial problems. This result supports the idea that VSWM is involved in constructing a mental representation of the initial data of the given spatial problem.

Pazzaglia and Cornoldi (1999, Exp. 2) investigated the involvement of verbal and visuo-spatial WM during memorisation of short abstract and spatial texts. The spatial texts consisted of instructions that required the filling-in of cells in an imagined 4 x 4 matrix, in order to follow a route within it (Brooks, 1967). Participants had to listen to the instructions while concurrently performing either a verbal or a spatial task. Results showed an interference effect of the concurrent spatial task on the spatial sentences: Average recall of spatial sentences under the concurrent spatial condition was lower than under the concurrent verbal condition.

More recently, De Beni, Pazzaglia, Gyselinck, and Meneghetti (2005), and Pazzaglia, De Beni, and Meneghetti (2006), studied the involvement of the verbal and visuo-spatial components of working memory in the memorisation and retrieval of spatial descriptions from a route perspective. In several experiments recall and recognition of spatial and non-spatial texts were compared under different conditions of concurrent spatial and verbal tasks. In accordance with their hypothesis, both memorisation and retrieval of the spatial texts was impaired by the concurrent spatial task. By contrast, the performance in the non-spatial texts was mainly affected by the concurrent verbal task.

Studies on the involvement of VSWM in the construction of spatial mental models are relevant because, on one hand, they support the models' spatial nature, and on the other because in these studies the focus has shifted from the models' characteristics to the cognitive functions and abilities required for their construction. As a consequence, they offer the theoretical basis for developing tools and training methodologies to improve comprehension and memorisation of spatial texts. Given that spatial representations are isomorphic to spatial configurations, and that they require VSWM, we can assume that pictures, being a sort of external representation of the mental model, can help the comprehension of spatial texts. However, it remains to be established if certain kinds of pictures are more effective in supporting the implementation of the spatial model than others.

3.2.3 Discourse-Picture Integration in Spatial Descriptions: An Empirical Study

Although it has been well documented that pictures improve comprehension and memorisation of texts (Levie & Lentz, 1982; Glenberg & Langston, 1992;

Hannus & Hyona, 1999), the cognitive mechanisms of this phenomenon are not entirely known. Some authors (see for example Gyselinck & Tardieu, 1999) have suggested that the "power" of pictures consists in enhancing the construction of mental models of the texts. For this reason they affirm that only certain types of pictures are effective i.e. those which help the reader obtain relevant information so as to organise and represent it mentally. Scientific texts accompanied by graphics and illustrations are generally used as materials in research on text/picture integration, rather less attention has been devoted to the role of pictures in improving comprehension and memorisation of spatial texts, such as environments' description from either survey or route perspectives. However, the hypothesis that effective pictures are faithful external representations of an internal model can be advanced also for illustrated spatial texts. More specifically we would expect the most effective pictures to be those, which not only represent all the landmarks described in the text, but also clearly mark their reciprocal spatial relations.

To date, only a few studies have analysed the role of pictures in spatial text comprehension (e.g. Ferguson & Hegarty, 1994; Tversky & Lee, 1999a), intending spatial text as description of routes and environments. The present study intends to be an empirical investigation of this topic. More specifically, we address three questions: 1. whether pictures really improve comprehension of spatial texts; 2. which kind of pictures is particularly effective (for example by comparing pictures representing the position of single landmarks with others also representing the spatial relation between landmarks); and finally 3. whether pictures in spatial texts differently affect individuals having respectively high versus low VSWM.

In the following two experiments these questions were addressed by presenting spatial texts, either with or without pictures, to different samples of undergraduate students. The aim of the first experiment was to investigate the role of pictures in spatial text comprehension, by comparing a 'no-picture' condition with two other picture conditions: (a) the single-picture condition, in which each sentence was accompanied by a picture representing the exact location of the landmark described within and (b) the map-picture condition, in which the same pictures were inserted in the perimeter of the described environment as framework.

The second experiment used the same materials and procedure, but introduced the theme of individual differences by creating two participant groups with a high versus low spatial abilities score as measured by the Mental Rotations Test (MRT; Vanderberg & Kuse, 1978).

The hypotheses made as regards to questions 1 and 2 were that pictures would be effective in improving comprehension, but only when the relative position of the landmarks were made explicit, thereby aiding the construction of a spatial mental model. Thus, we expected the best comprehension to occur in the map-picture condition when compared to the single-picture and no-picture conditions.

As for the third question, we tested the following hypotheses: given that VSWM is involved in the construction of spatial mental models, individuals with high spatial abilities were expected to perform better than the low spatial abilities group in the no-picture condition because of their superior ability in spontaneously constructing a good spatial mental model and using the VSWM to do so. However, in the picture condition we expected a smaller difference between groups, since the low spatial abilities group was expected to use the pictures as aids more than the high spatial abilities group and hence show greater improvement.

3.3 Experiment 1

3.3.1 Method

3.3.1.1 Participants

A total of 28 (7 male and 21 female) undergraduate students from the Faculty of Psychology of the University of Padua (Italy), participated in the experiment.

3.3.1.2 Materials

- Texts

Three spatial descriptions (from Taylor & Tversky, 1992; Pazzaglia, Cornoldi, & Longoni, 1994), which adopt a survey perspective and describe three fictitious environments: a zoo, a park and a farm were used. The descriptions were all ten sentences long, consisted of 120 words and had the same number of landmarks (7). Part of the description entitled "The zoo" is shown in Table 3.1.

- Verification test

Sixteen assertions, half true and half false, were formulated for each text. Half the assertions were paraphrased, half inferential (examples of assertions are reported in Table 3.2).

Table 3.1 The first five sentences of the spatial text "The zoo". The entire text is composed by ten sentences

The Zoo
The zoo extends over a large rectangular area.
It has only one entrance in the middle of the south side of the whole frame.
In front of the entrance there is a bar.
The bar is exactly in the centre of the zoo.
In the south-west corner of the zoo there is the amusement park.
...

Table 3.2 Examples of paraphrased (P) and inferential (I) assertions referred to the texts "The zoo"

The zoo (assertions)
1. (P) In the middle of the south side of the whole fence there is the only zoo entrance.
2. (P) Right in the middle of the zoo there is the service bar.
3. (P) The zoo extends on a large square area.
4. (I) The amusement park is to the south-east of the bar.
5. (I) The elephants are to the north-west of the penguins.

- Pictures

Two different types of pictures were created for each descriptive sentence. The first type, the "single-picture", depicted the local spatial information contained in each sentence, i.e. one landmark and its position. The second type of pictures, i.e. the "map-pictures" was identical to the single-pictures, but assembled so as to form a map of the environment described in the text (example of single- and map-pictures, and of the sentences they referred to, are shown in Fig. 3.1).

3.3.1.3 Procedure

Each participant was tested individually for approximately 40 minutes. They were informed that the experiment required them to listen to and memorise three descriptions in order to answer a questionnaire and that two of these were accompanied by some pictures, one for each sentence. Descriptions were tape-recorded. Each participant listened to three descriptions, each in a different condition: 1. listening, 2. single-picture, 3. map-picture. The order of text and picture type presentation was counterbalanced across participants. During the single-picture and the map-picture conditions, each picture was presented on an A4-format paper, for the duration of each sentence description. Limited to the single-picture, the participants could inspect in any time all the old pictures. Immediately after having listened to each description, participants were asked to respond to the true/false assertions presented on a computer screen in random order.

3.3.2 Results and Discussion

A 3 X 2 Analysis of Variance (ANOVA) with presentation condition (listening, single-picture, map-picture) and assertion type (paraphrased vs. inferential) as factors was performed on the total correct responses given. The analysis revealed the expected best performance in the map-picture condition (M = 6.86, SE = 0.19), compared to single-picture (M = 6.14, SE = 0.20) and listening (M = 6.05, SE = 0.24), $F(2, 54) = 6.49$, MSE = 1.67, $p < 0.005$. Paraphrased

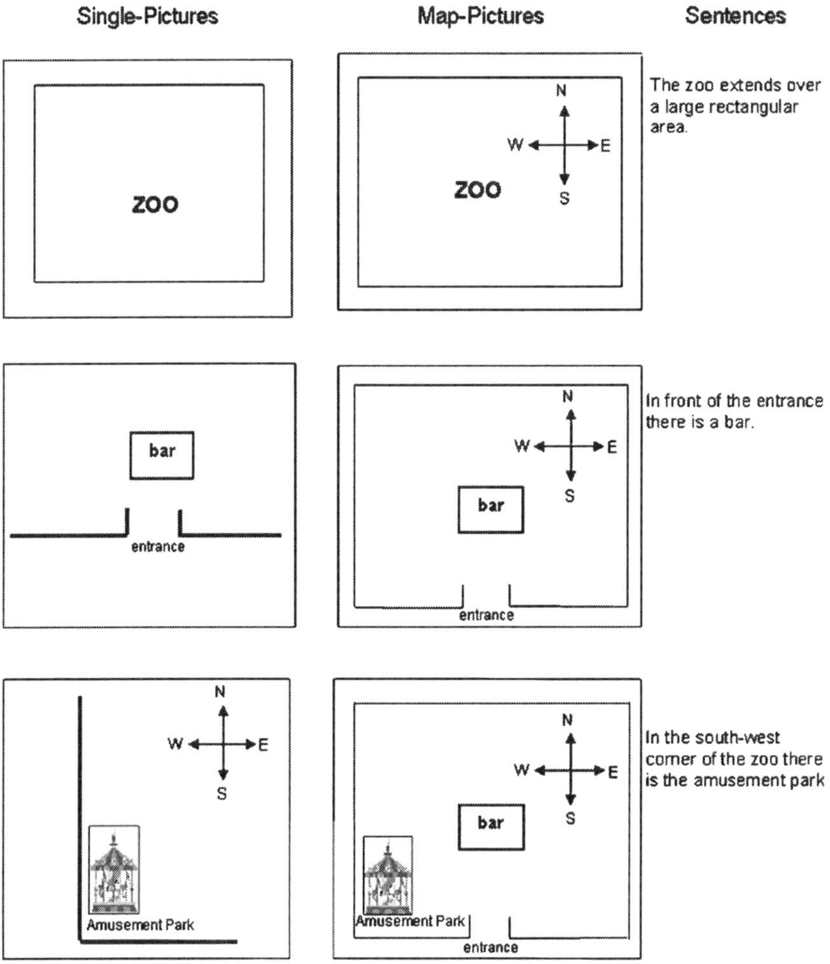

Fig. 3.1 Example of single-pictures and map-pictures used in the text "The zoo" and relative sentences

assertions were simpler than inferential ones (respectively: M = 6.85, SE = 0.17; M = 5.84, SE = 0.18), $F(1, 27) = 50$, MSE = 0.84, $p < 0.001$.

As expected, the results of Experiment 1 demonstrate that pictures presented concurrently with spatial texts improve text comprehension. Pictures are effective not only in helping the memorisation of single pieces of information, but also in aiding the formation of a spatial mental model of the text. In fact both responses to paraphrased and inferential assertions improved with picture presentation. However, this positive effect was restricted to the map-pictures condition. Only the presentation of a map-picture together with the spatial text was effective in enhancing comprehension of the spatial description. This is in accordance with our hypotheses that the map-picture condition would aid the construction of a mental model of the text by making the relation between elements of the description explicit.

This experiment contributes to demonstrate that comprehension of spatial texts is enhanced by the presence of accompanying pictures. The paradigm adopted in the experiment, i.e. comparing two different kinds of pictures, contributes also to explain the cognitive mechanisms underlining this phenomenon and results so far suggest that this is not entirely due to a dual-code effect (Paivio, 1978), but to the construction of mental models of the text.

3.4 Experiment 2

3.4.1 Objectives

Experiment 2 aimed to investigate the involvement of spatial abilities in processing spatial texts and to verify whether participants with high and low spatial abilities were differently influenced by illustrations. Existing research on spatial abilities provides evidence that they are not as a single component but that they are articulated to varying extent (Cornoldi & Vecchi, 2003; Devlin, 2001). Linn and Petersen (1985), conducting a meta-analysis of 172 studies, argued for the existence of three spatial factors: spatial perception, determining spatial relations with respect to one's own body; mental rotation, a gestalt-like analogue process; spatial visualisation, multistep manipulation of spatially presented information. Spatial abilities have been examined either through pencil-and-paper psychometric tests, such as mental rotation tests, or more real-world tasks, such as distance judgments, way-finding, pointing in the direction of unseen locations, map learning (Kirasic, 2000).

In our study, individual differences in spatial abilities were measured using the Mental Rotations Test (Vanderberg & Kuse, 1978). This choice was due to the fact that the MRT can be solved only using a global spatial ability, it is correlated with survey spatial representation (Pazzaglia & De Beni, 2001) and derives from studies on imagery. All these factors were important in our experimental procedure, where a description from a survey perspective was used and where imagery abilities could be considered important.

We expected to replicate the results found in the previous experiment on the different efficacy of single and map pictures in improving text comprehension. Regarding individual differences, we hypothesized that participants with high spatial abilities would perform better than those with low spatial abilities, in considering the spatial features of the texts. However, we expected that this effect, dramatic in the no-picture condition, would be reduced in the map-picture condition because, for individuals in the low spatial ability group, the presentation of pictures would constitute an external spatial representation i.e. a useful aid in integrating their poor internal representation.

3.4.2 Method

3.4.2.1 Participants

Participants were 36 undergraduate students (7 males, 29 females) divided in two groups with high and low spatial abilities, each comprising 18 participants. They were selected from a sample of 174 students by administering the Mental Rotations Test (MRT) (Vanderberg & Kuse, 1978). Participants with scores in the MRT lower than, or equal to the 25th percentile of the entire sample were considered as having low spatial abilities and participants with scores higher than or equal to the 75th were considered as having high spatial abilities. Two sub-groups, composed of 12 low – and 9 high-spatial individuals respectively were administered with a standardised comprehension test (Cornoldi, Rizzo, & Pra Baldi, 1991) in order to verify that they did not differ in comprehension ability. The mean scores were 7.75 and 8.11 respectively for low and high spatial ability groups, and difference was not significant, $t(19) = -0.46$, $p = 0.65$.

3.4.2.2 Materials and Procedure

The Materials and Procedure were the same as in Experiment 1, except that there were 24 assertions instead of 16.

3.4.3 Results and Discussion

A 3 X 2 X 2 ANOVA with presentation condition (listening, single-picture, map-picture), assertion types (paraphrased, inferential) and group (high and low in spatial abilities) as factors, was performed on the percentage of correct answers to the true/false assertions. As expected the analysis revealed best performance in the map condition (M = 84.81, SE = 2.22), compared to picture (M = 77.17, SE = 2.44) and listening (M = 73.26, SE = 2.63), $F(2, 68) = 9.99$, MSE = 248, $p < 0.001$. Paraphrased assertions resulted simpler than inferential ones (respectively: M = 83.10, SE = 1.90; M = 73.72, SE = 2.16), $F(1, 34) = 39.21$, MSE = 121, $p < 0.001$.

High-spatial (M = 84.12, SE = 2.69), performed better than low-spatial group (M = 72.68, SE = 2.69), $F(1, 34) = 8.02$, MSE = 785, $p < 0.01$.

There was a significant interaction effect between presentation condition, assertion type and group, $F(2, 68) = 4.55$, MSE = 126, $p < 0.05$. A post-hoc Newman-Keul analysis (c.d. = 9.35) revealed, as shown in Fig. 3.2, different patterns of results for high and low spatial individuals in relation to pictures and assertions.

In answering paraphrased assertions high spatial abilities individuals had the same performance for both listening and pictures conditions. This is due to their very high performance (more than 85%) in all conditions. By contrast, the low spatial abilities group had a significantly poorer performance in the listening

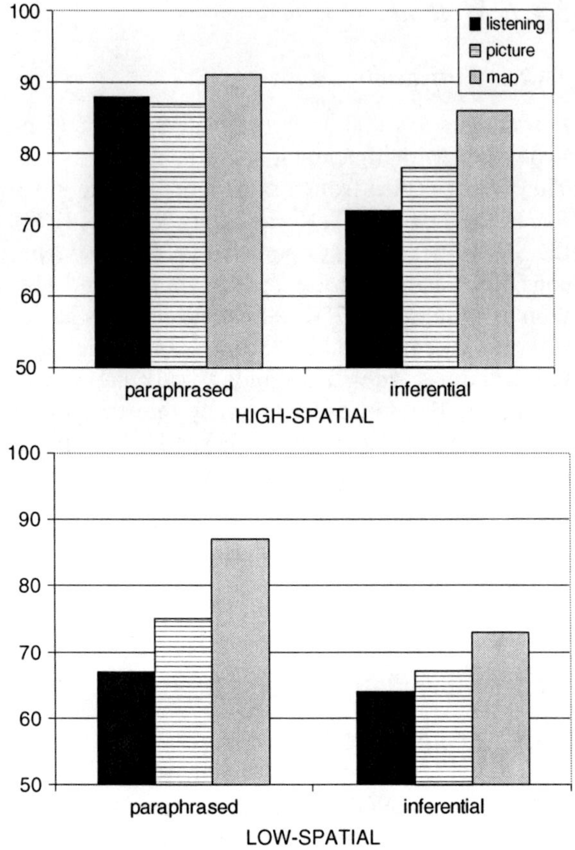

Fig. 3.2 Percentage of questions correctly responded in Experiment 2: Interaction group (high and low spatial abilities) by picture (no picture, single-picture, map-picture) by assertions (paraphrased and inferential)

and single-picture condition (with no significant difference between them), as compared to the map-picture condition. Compared to the high spatial abilities individuals, they performed worse both in the listening and single-picture conditions, but performance of the two groups was equal in the map-picture condition. Taken together, these results support the hypothesis that pictures are effective because they help the construction of an internal spatial mental model. In fact, as observed in the first experiment, only map-pictures, which make explicit the spatial relations between landmarks, are effective in improving memory performance.

It is also interesting to note that this beneficial effect is limited to individuals with low spatial abilities. A possible interpretation is that participants in the high spatial abilities group can spontaneously activate an internal spatial model, using their superior abilities in maintaining and processing visuo-spatial materials. The external representation is in this case superfluous, because their internal representation is good enough to answer the paraphrased assertions presented (see also Schnotz, Chapter 2). By contrast, low spatial individuals do not have sufficient cognitive resources to construct a good mental model. However, given the external aid, i.e. the map-picture, their performance improves sufficiently to equal that of the high spatial abilities group.

A reverse pattern of results was found for inferential assertions. In this case the low spatial abilities group showed the same, low, performance in all three conditions, although it should be noted that the difference between the listening and the map-picture conditions was close to significance. The high spatial abilities group, however, performed significantly better in the map-picture than in the listening condition. Furthermore, the two groups did not differ in the listening condition, but did differ in the predicted direction in both single- and map-picture conditions. This is consistent with our hypotheses in that when questions require a more complex and stable spatial representation individuals with good spatial abilities take advantage from inspecting the map-picture during text presentation.

Results of Experiment 2 confirm that illustrations enhance text comprehension when they make explicit the relationship between units of information contained in texts and that spatial abilities are indeed involved in processing verbal information when the content of the text is spatial.

3.5 Conclusions

Describing spatial configurations and comprehending spatial texts are tasks that involve both spatial and verbal cognitive systems. They require a conversion from an internal spatial representation to a linguistic expression, or the creation of a mental spatial representation from a verbal description. In the latter case, the presence of pictures can enhance the construction of the correspondent spatial mental model. The results of the present study suggest that of the two types of pictures used (single-picture versus map-picture), the most effective in helping to memorize a spatial text are those which describe the relation amongst landmarks present in the text. This is thought to be because this type of picture presentation aids individuals in the creation of an internal mental map, matching that of the text. Furthermore both people with high and low spatial abilities can take advantage, even if at different levels, of the use of pictures accompanying spatial texts.

Given the results above, the role of pictures is now clear: they constitute external representations that facilitate the creation and maintenance of an internal mental model. A possible objection is that the superiority of "listening plus picture" condition was due to the fact that pictures were available for review and participants could inspect them whenever they want. Conversely, they could not listen again to the descriptions in the "listening" condition. However, the goal of these experiments was not to demonstrate that listening plus picture was better than listening twice or more (dual-code vs. single-code), but to compare two very common and ecological conditions: listening the spatial description of an environment and listening the same description accompanied by pictures. Further, the main focus was on the comparison between the two picture conditions, identical in the procedure. In these comparisons the map-picture turned out to be superior not only respect to listening but to the single-picture condition too.

Some questions still remain unanswered. An important question is the property of the test used to assess comprehension. In our experiments we used a verification task of paraphrased and inferred information. This task allowed us to assess more directly the construction of a mental model. Free-recall is a different index commonly used to assess comprehension and memorisation of the whole content of a text, but it has the limit to be less sensitive in distinguishing between literal and inferential processes. A further index, which should be useful to our goals, is response times in the verification task. In fact, if a reader has built a mental model properly, with a lot of inferences, then these inferences should be readily and quickly available. This should result in faster verification times. It would be interesting to verify if pictures affect response times and to compare response times of participants with high and low spatial abilities.

In our experiments picture-presentation was concurrent to text-presentation, hence each picture added only the units of information contained in each sentence. Thus, the increment of knowledge offered by each picture corresponded to that given by each sentence and the construction of the mental model followed the sequential procedure typical of text processing. It would be interesting to verify the effect of pictures containing all the information of the text given either at the beginning, at the end or during the presentation.

Furthermore in the present study we compared "listening" to "listening plus picture", finding a superiority of the latter condition, thus we can claim that pictures help the comprehension of spatial texts. Yet the question remains whether the reverse is also true, i.e. if the presence of text can help the comprehension of pictures (on this issue see also Rinck, Chapter 10). In order to answer this question it could be useful to compare a "picture" to a "listening" and to a "listening plus picture" condition. If it is true that "a picture is worth a thousand words" we would expect the "picture" condition to be more efficient than the "listening" condition but perhaps equal to the "listening plus picture" combination. We hope to answer these and other questions in future research.

Acknowledgments The author wishes to thank Sabina Scattola and Francesca Zanardi for collecting data of the two experiments.

References

Baddeley, A. D. (1986). *Working Memory*. Oxford: Oxford University Press.

Baddeley, A. D., & Hitch, G. (1974). Working memory. In G. A. Bower (Ed.), *Recent advances in learning and motivation* (Vol. 8). New York: Academic Press.

Baguley, T., & Payne, S. (2000). Long-term memory for spatial and temporal mental models includes construction processes and model structure. *Quarterly Journal of Experimental Psychology: Human Experimental Psychology, 53A*, 479–512.

Bosco, A., Filomena, S., Sardone, L., Scalisi, T. G., & Longoni, A. M. (1996). Spatial models derived from verbal descriptions of fictitious environments: The influence of study time and the individual differences in visuospatial ability. *Psychologische-Beitrage, 38*, 451–464.

Bower, G. H., & Morrow, D. G. (1990). Mental models in narrative comprehension. *Science, 247*, 44–48.

Brooks, L. R. (1967). The suppression of visualization by reading. *Quarterly Journal of Experimental Psychology, 19*, 289–299.

Bryant, D. J. (1997). Representing space in language and perception. *Mind and Language, 12*, 239–264.

Conte, A., Cornoldi, C., Pazzaglia, F., & Sanavio, S. (1995). Lo sviluppo della memoria di lavoro visuospaziale e il suo ruolo nella memoria spaziale./The development of the visuo-spatial working memory and its role in spatial memory. *Ricerche di Psicologia, 19*, 95–114.

Cornoldi, C., Rizzo, A., & Pra Baldi, A. (1991). *Prove avanzate di comprensione della lettura./Reading comprehension advanced tests.* Firenze: Organizzazioni Speciali.

Cornoldi, C., & Vecchi, T. (2003). *Visuo-spatial working memory and individual differences.* Philadelphia, PA: Psychology Press.

Daniel, M. P., & Denis, M. (1998). Spatial descriptions as navigational aids: A cognitive analysis of route directions. *Kognitionswisssenchaft, 7*, 45–52.

De Beni, R., Pazzaglia, F., Gyselinck, V., & Meneghetti, C. (2005). Visuo-spatial working memory and mental representation of spatial descriptions. *European Journal of Cognitive Psychology, 17*, 77–95.

Devlin, A. N. (2001). *Mind and maze: Spatial cognition and environmental behavior*. Westport, CT: Praeger Publishers/Greenwood Publishing Group, Inc.

van Dijk, T. A., & Kintsch, W. (1983). *Strategies of discourse comprehension.* New York: Academic Press.

Farmer, E. W., Berman, J. V. F., & Fletcher, Y. L. (1986). Evidence for a visuo-spatial scratchpad in working memory. *The Quarterly Journal of Experimental Psychology, 38A*, 675–688.

Ferguson, E. L., & Hegarty, M. (1994). Properties of cognitive maps constructed from texts. *Memory and Cognition, 22*, 455–473.

Franklin, N., & Tversky, B. (1990). Searching imagined environments. *Journal of Experimental Psychology: General, 119*, 63–76.

Franklin, N., Tversky, B., & Coon, V. (1992). Switching points of view in spatial mental models. *Memory and Cognition, 20*, 507–518.

Glenberg, A. M., & Langston, W. E. (1992). Comprehension of illustrated texts: Picture help to build models. *Journal of Memory and Language, 31*, 129–151.

Gyselinck, V., & Tardieu, H. (1999). The role of illustration in text comprehension: what, when, for whom and why? In H. van Oostendorp & S. Goldman (Eds.), *The construction of mental representations during reading* (pp. 195–218). Mahvah, NJ: Lawrence Erlbaum Associates.

Hannus, M., & Hyona, J. (1999). Utilization of illustrations during learning of science textbook passages among low and high-ability children. *Contemporary Educational Psychology, 24*, 95–113.

Johnson-Laird, P. (1983). *Mental models.* Cambridge, MA: The MIT Press.

Kirasic, K. C. (2000). Age differences in adults' spatial abilities, learning environmental layout, and wayfinding behavior. *Spatial Cognition and Computation, 2*, 117–134.

Lee, P. U., & Tversky, B. (2005). Interplay Between Visual and Spatial: The Effect of Landmark Descriptions on Comprehension of Route/Survey Spatial Descriptions. *Spatial Cognition and Computation, 5*, 163–185.

Levelt, W. J. M. (1989). *Speaking: From intention to articulation.* Cambridge, MA: The MIT Press.

Levie, W. H., & Lentz, R. (1982). Effects of text illustration: A review of research. *Educational Communication of Technology Journal, 30*, 195–232.
Linn, M. C., & Petersen, A. C. (1985). "Emergence and characterization of sex differences in spatial ability: A meta-analysis" *Child Development, 56*, 1479–1498.
Logie, R. H. (1995). *Visual-spatial working memory*. Hillsdale, NJ: Lawrence Erlbaum Associates.
Maki, R. H., & Marek, M. N. (1997). Egocentric spatial framework effects from single and multiple points of view. *Memory and Cognition, 25*, 677–690.
Mani, K., & Johnson-Laird, P. (1982). The mental representation of spatial descriptions. *Memory and Cognition, 10*, 181–187.
Miyake, A., & Shah, P. (1999). Emerging general consensus, unresolved theoretical issues, and future research directions. In A. Miyake & P. Shah (Eds.). *Models of working memory: Mechanisms of active maintenance and executive control*. New York, NY, US: Cambridge University Press (pp. 1–27).
Morrow, D. G., Bower, G. H., & Greenspan, S. L. (1989). Updating situation models during narrative comprehension. *Journal of Memory and Language, 28*, 292–312.
Morrow, D. G., Greenspan, S. L., & Bower, G. H. (1987). Accessibility and situation models in narrative comprehension. *Journal of Memory and Language, 26*, 165–187.
Nieding, G., & Ohler, P.(1999). Der Einfluss von Protagonisten Zielstrukturen auf raeumliche mentale Modelle beim narrativen Textverstehen von Kindern./The effect of protagonists' movements on spatial mental models in narrative text comprehension by children. *Sprache and Kognition, 18*, 146–158
Paivio, A. (1978). Comparisons of mental clocks. *Journal of Experimental Psychology: Human Perception and Performance, 4*, 61–71.
Pazzaglia, F. (2000). Tipologie di descrizione di ambienti in funzione delle caratteristiche ambientali, individuali, e di familiarità con i luoghi. (Typology of environmental descriptions in function of environmental, individual, and familiarity characteristics of place). *Giornale Italiano di Psicologia, 27*, 133–159.
Pazzaglia, F., & Cornoldi, C. (1999). The role of distinct components of visuo-spatial working memory in the processing of texts. *Memory, 7*, 19–41.
Pazzaglia, F., Cornoldi, C., & Longoni, A. (1994). Limiti di memoria e specificità di rappresentazione nel ricordo di descrizioni spaziali "dall'alto" o "entro il percorso". (Limits of memory and the specificity of representations in the memory of survey and route descriptions). *Giornale Italiano di Psicologia, 21*, 267–286.
Pazzaglia, F., & De Beni, R. (2001). Strategies of processing spatial information in survey and landmark-centred individuals. *European Journal of Cognitive Psychology, 13*, 493–508.
Pazzaglia, F., De Beni , R., & Meneghetti, C. (2006). The effects of verbal and spatial interference in the encoding and retrieval of spatial and nonspatial texts, *Psychological* Research, Feb 16; [Epub ahead of print; DOI: 10.1007/s00426-006-0045-7].
Perrig, W., & Kintsch, W. (1985). Prepositional and situational representations of text. *Journal of Memory and Language, 24*, 503–518.
Taylor, H. A., & Tversky, B. (1992). Spatial mental models derived from survey and route descriptions. *Journal of Memory and Language, 31*, 261–292.
Thurstone, L. L., & Thurstone, T. G. (1947). *Primary mental abilities*. New York: Psychological Corporation.
Tversky, B. (1991). Spatial mental models. In. G. H. Bower (Ed.), *The psychology of learning and motivation: Advances in research and theory* (pp. 109–145). San Diego, CA: Academic Press.
Tversky, B. (2003). Structures of mental spaces: How people think about space. *Environment and Behavior, 35*, 66–80.
Tversky, B., & Lee, P. U. (1999a). Pictorial and verbal tools for conveying routes. In C. Freksa & D. M. Mark (Eds.), *Spatial Information Theory. Cognitive and computational foundations of geographic information science: International Conference COSIT'99* (pp. 51–64). Heidelberg: Springer-Verlag.

Tversky, B. & Lee, P. U. (1999b). Why do speakers mix perspectives? *Spatial Cognition and Computation, 1*, 399–412.

Vanderberg, S. G., & Kuse, A. R. (1978). Mental rotations: A group test of three-dimensional spatial visualization. *Perceptual and Motor Skills, 47*, 599–604.

Vandierendonck, A., & De Vooght, G. (1997). Working memory constraints on linear reasoning with spatial and temporal contents. *The Quarterly Journal of Experimental Psychology, 50A*, 803–820.

de Vega, M. (1994). Characters and their perspectives in narratives describing spatial environments. *Psychological-Research/Psychologische-Forschung,* 56, 116–126.

de Vega, M., Cocude, M., Denis, M., Rodrigo, M. J., & Zimmer, H. D. (2001). The interface between language and visuo-spatial representation. In M. Denis, R. H. Logie, C. Cornoldi, M. de Vega, & J. Engelkamp (Eds.), *Imagery, Language and Visuo-Spatial Thinking* (pp. 109–136). Hove, East Sussex: Psychology Press Ltd.

Wechsler, D. (1981). *Wechsler Adult Intelligence Scale-Revised.* New York: Psychological Corporation.

Chapter 4
Display of Key Pictures from Animation: Effects on Learning

Mireille Bétrancourt, Pierre Dillenbourg, and Lionel Clavien

Abstract Research carried out so far has failed to establish systematic learning benefits of animated graphics over static ones, even in the case of dynamic systems. We hypothesize that animation promotes the understanding of dynamic systems if delivery features decrease the perceptual and cognitive load of processing the animation. We therefore report an experimental study investigating the effects of two delivery features: the continuity of the information flow (animation vs. series of static graphics) and the permanence of critical snapshots from the animation. The animation group outperformed the static group for retention and transfer performance. However, the presence of snapshots of critical steps had no significant effect. The results are discussed in terms of cognitive load and metacognitive processing engaged by learners while processing the multimedia instruction.

Keywords Cognitive load · Computer animation · Continuity · Mental model

4.1 Introduction

In the last decade, with rapid advances in computing capacities and the progress of graphic design technologies, multimedia learning environments have evolved from the mere presentation of a series of static text and picture frames to increasingly sophisticated visualizations. However, the design of dynamic and interactive visualizations remains most often driven by esthetics or visual appeal rather than by pedagogical or cognitive considerations. In the present chapter we review some key research advances into the use of animations for explaining dynamic systems. Then we present an experiment that investigated the use of snapshots as means to reduce cognitive load during multimedia learning.

M. Bétrancourt
Geneva University, Faculty of Psychology and Education, TECFA research center,
54 route des Acacias, CH-1227 Carouge, Switzerland
e-mail: mireille.betrancourt@tecfa.unige.ch

J.-F. Rouet et al. (eds.), *Understanding Multimedia Documents*,
DOI: 10.1007/978-0-387-73337-1_4,

4.2 Multimedia Instruction for Understanding Dynamic Systems

Multimedia learning refers to situations in which one of the main learning resources is multimedia instruction that can be defined as "[...] a presentation involving words and pictures that is intended to foster learning." (Mayer, 2001, p. 3). According to this definition, multimedia instruction can range from illustrated textbooks to dynamic and interactive simulations. However, the term multimedia is predominantly used for computer-based instruction that can include some navigation devices and verbal or illustrative auditory information. In this chapter multimedia instruction refers to a presentation including graphic and symbolic information (e.g., natural language, formulas, conventional notations) presented by means of a computer. We will focus here on the format of the multimedia instruction and its effects on cognitive processes, and will not consider other dimensions of the learning situation that can affect learning outcomes.

4.2.1 Multimedia Animations as Instructional Devices

As graphics are proliferating in instructional material and particularly in computer-based documents, it is legitimate to ask whether they increase learners' motivation and performance compared to pure symbolic information. In the eighties, a large body of research supported the idea that graphics are beneficial to learning. In most studies, graphics improved recollection of the illustrated information and comprehension of the situation described in the text (Levie & Lentz, 1982; Levin, Anglin, & Carney, 1987). One of the most generally accepted explanations for that effect is provided by mental model theories. According to this framework, understanding a text requires the reader to build a *mental model*, which is structurally analogical to the concept represented. A mental model is a cognitive representation elaborated from the reader's previous knowledge along with new information provided in the text. The mental model allows the reader to infer new information, fill-in absent information and resolve contradictions (Johnson-Laird, 1983). Providing an analogical visualization through the use of graphics would facilitate the construction of the mental model (Mayer, 1989). Schnotz and Bannert (2003) provided an elaborated model of how verbal-symbolic information and depictive information are conjointly and interactively processed in order to form a mental model, which eventually may affect conceptual organization (see also Schnotz, Chapter 2). More pragmatically, graphics also offer an external representation supporting an internal representation, thus offloading working memory and increasing processing capacities.

According to Schnotz and Lowe (2003), the concept of animation can be characterized using three different levels of analysis: technical, psychological and semiotic. The technical level refers to the format of animation: real movies with all details in each picture versus simplified or abstract computer-generated movies. TIF or static pictures, the degree of abstraction has an effect on cognitive processing (Dwyer, 1982/1983) and can be manipulated for pedagogical purposes. The psychological level refers to the perceptual and cognitive processes involved when animations are displayed to learners. This issue will be further discussed in section 2. Finally, the semiotic level refers to the type of signs used in the multimedia instruction, namely the kind of dynamics that are conveyed in the representation. Lowe (2004) identified three types of dynamics that are relevant for understanding dynamic systems:

- *Transformation* involves form changes in graphical features such as size, shape, color, and texture, such as when illustrating the change in a boiling liquid.
- *Translation* refers entities moving from one location to another, either with respect to the border of the animation or relative to other elements within the animation. One example is the trajectory of the planets around the sun.
- *Transition* involves the appearance or disappearance of entities (either fully or partly) by zooming in, out or changing the view point, as for instance in shifting from an earth to a galactic point of view.

In order to pictorially represent changes in dynamic systems, instructional designers can use either animation or a series of static graphics. Besides practical considerations, the choice between the two possibilities pertaining to perceptual and cognitive processes will be discussed later on. Regarding the semiotic level, identifying the dynamic information conveyed in an animation, usually a combination of at least two types of change, is one of the promising steps toward categorizing animations. Discussions about the design of animation often focus on technical or surface characteristics. From a learning perspective, these characteristics have to be taken into consideration insofar as they may change the way the content to be learned is perceived and apprehended by learners.

4.2.2 Does Animation Improve Learning?

It is generally expected that computer animations facilitate the comprehension of dynamic systems such as weather patterns, circuit diagrams, the body circulatory system or the mechanics of a bicycle pump. Computer animation is a powerful medium for displaying how dynamic systems function in a space and time scale accessible to human perception. However, research failed to find systematic benefits of using animation over static graphics (Lowe, 1999; Morrison & Tversky, 2001); Pane, Corbett, & John, 1996; Rieber, 1989 or over text instructions (Palmiter & Elkerton, 1993). Further studies showed that the structure and the content of the instructional material had more effect on learning outcomes than presentation modalities (Narayanan & Hegarty, 2002).

Another common belief is that learners find animations more motivating than text and static pictures and would therefore be inclined to process the material more deeply. However, the processing of animation requires heavy perceptual and cognitive processing. Novice learners tend to pay more attention to perceptually salient features than to conceptually relevant changes in the animation (Lowe, 1999, 2003). If it is not obvious to learners how they can benefit from an animation, they may just not use it at all (Pane, Corbett, & John, 1996).

In a few cases, animations did result in better comprehension than static graphics. It turns out, however, that in these studies the animation actually provided additional information compared to the static graphics. The transitions between steps were explicit in the animation whereas they had to be inferred in the static display. Research by Thompson and Riding (1990) supported the hypothesis that animation facilitates learning when it presents the 'microsteps' of a process that static graphics do not present. They used a standard lesson explaining the Pythagorean Theorem to junior high school students. Two sets of graphical aids were designed. The animated set was a sequence of 10 diagrams using shears and rotations to depict the equivalence of area of three different figures. The static set consisted of two diagrams. After a 15-minutes lesson on the Pythagorean Theorem, one group viewed the animation, a second group viewed the static diagrams, and a third group did not see any computerized instruction (control group). The group viewing the continuous animation outperformed the other two groups on comprehension questions. The animation depicted all the microsteps, while that information had to be inferred from both of the other graphics.

In order to illustrate a text explaining the functioning of sorting algorithms, Catrambone & Fleming Seay (2002) used two graphical aids: a continuous animation or the succession of static frames taken from the animation. They found that the animation group performed slightly better than the static group for far transfer but not for close transfer problems. Both graphical aids groups performed better than the control group, which only used the standard text. However, the benefits from graphical aids disappeared when the instructional text was designed using a task analysis method. Our claim is that the critical gain of animations over static graphics comes from the visualization of the microsteps in a dynamic process that are difficult to mentally infer for novices (Tversky, Bauer-Morrison, & Bétrancourt, 2002).

The literature review above shows that computer animation is potentially beneficial to learning. However, research often failed to find this advantage, even when the instructional animation was carefully designed. The most common explanation is based on the idea that learning from animation may be cognitively too demanding for novices of a domain. An experimental study carried out by Schnotz, Böckheler, and Grzondziel (1999) provided evidence that animation can impair learning in some circumstances. The study compared static and animated displays for understanding time zones. In individual settings, learners who received an animated and interactive display performed better on transfer tests than learners who received the static display. However, this advantage of animated displays disappeared when learners were in pairs. The authors interpreted the results in terms of cognitive load: the animation imposed a heavy cognitive load for processing the information in addition to the load of interacting with a peer and with the device. The construction of a mental model is impaired by a cognitive overload. The cognitive load assumption is described in detail in section 3.

According to Bétrancourt & Tversky (2000), processing a changing visual situation introduces high demands on perception, conception and working memory.

- *Perception* as learners must be attentive to simultaneous changes in the display;
- *Conception* as learners build a "runnable mental model" (Mayer, 1989) while they are watching the animation;
- *Working memory* as they have to keep in memory the previous states and trajectory of each element of the system.

Examples in which the human system is not effective in processing visually changing information are numerous. Kaiser, Proffitt, Whelan, and Hecht (1992) found that students enrolled in a physics curriculum were unable to draw the correct trajectory of a point on a bicycle tire from an animation of the rolling tire. Using a weather forecast task, Lowe (2003, 2004) found that the processing of animation by novices was driven by the perceptual salience of the dynamics of the elements rather than by their thematic relevance. Another drawback of animations is that they can induce a surface processing strategy, memorizing visual changes rather than trying to understand them. For instance, when learning to use a software program, participants who studied with animations outperformed participants using text only conditions immediately after the training. However, performance of the participants in the animation condition declined dramatically one week later whereas performance of participants in the text condition remained stable (Palmiter & Elkerton, 1993). For the authors, the decrease of performance with time revealed that participants in the animation condition just mimicked the instruction and did not elaborate a complete understanding of the procedure. In this case, animation had an *inhibiting* effect, inducing a shallow processing of the subject matter instead of a deeper and more demanding processing. In such situations, animation did not produce benefit because of what Lowe (2004) called the "underwhelming effect" (Lowe, 2004): not enough cognitive resources are allocated to the processing of the graphical information. In summary, these results suggest that learners need guidance to process animations, otherwise they may be overwhelmed with the continuous flow of information, or the processing may remain at the surface.

4.2.3 Cognitive Load and the Design of Multimedia Instruction

In this paper, we deal with multimedia instructional material aiming at the acquisition of new conceptual knowledge, and particularly how dynamic systems function. Conceptual learning, also considered 'deep learning' is characterized by the transformation of learners' cognitive structures in a way that the acquired knowledge, procedures or schemata could be used in other situations or domains (De Corte , 2003). Deep learning is measured through transfer problems, i.e. problems requiring learners to infer new information from the learning material and from their previous knowledge. On the contrary, surface learning or rote memorization, enables the learner to apply the learned schema only to similar situations. In contrast to surface learning, deep learning is demanding with respect to cognitive resources.

A framework commonly used in the study of multimedia instruction is the cognitive load theory (see for example, Paas, Renkl, & Sweller, 2004; see also Schnotz, Chapter 2; Le Bohec & Jamet, chapter 5). Tenets of the cognitive load theory claim that if the instructional material imposes a heavy processing load which restraints the cognitive resources available for the acquisition of new knowledge. This claim is based on the view that the capacity of working memory is limited, as described in Baddeley's model (Baddeley, 1997, 2000). Nevertheless, recent findings showed that the processing capacity of working memory can expand tremendously when dealing with well-known materials or situations (Ericsson & Kintsch, 1995); Sweller, 2003). Consequently, an important purpose of instructional design research consists in finding ways to reduce the cognitive burden required for students to process multimedia materials.

Current developments of the cognitive load theory consider three sources of load when learners have to process instructional material in order to achieve the learning task (Paas, Renkl, & Sweller, 2004):

- *Intrinsic load* refers to the load required to process the instructional task and is related to the complexity of the content itself, and particularly the number of elements that must be held in working memory simultaneously (what is called level of interactivity in the material).
- *Germane load* is the quantity of resources involved in the construction of new knowledge in long term memory, which is the goal of deep learning.
- *Extraneous load* refers to the additional load that is affected by the format of instruction (material presentation or structure of the learning task) and that does not contribute to learning.

According to the cognitive load theory, deep learning occurs only if cognitive resources are sufficient to cover the processing requirements. Cognitive overload is a plausible explanation of why learning situations sometimes fail to induce deep learning. Extraneous load should thus be reduced to its minimal by adequate presentation format and learning tasks. For example, Sweller and Chandler (1994) demonstrated that multimedia instructional materials in which mutually referring verbal and graphic information are displayed separately on the page are detrimental to learning compared to material in which graphic and verbal information are spatially integrated. According to the authors, the separated display forced learners to repeatedly shift their attention from one source to the other and thus increased the cognitive resources that should be dedicated to mentally integrate the two sources of information. The cognitive overload induced by the 'split-attention effect' would explain the learning impairment.

As shown in the literature review, processing the animated information while elaborating a mental model of the topic to be understood imposes a heavy cognitive demand. In the last decade, research has started to investigate the effects of instructional manipulation of animations using the cognitive load framework as a predictive and explanatory framework. For example, Mayer and his colleagues investigated various presentation factors on the means used for the commentary (aural vs. written), or the synchronization of the commentary and the animation (Mayer & Moreno, 2002). Practical guidelines for designing animations that foster the understanding of dynamic phenomena were drawn from this line of research (Mayer, 2003; Narayanan & Hegarty, 2002). One factor that has been investigated is the learner's control over the pace of the animation. In two experiments, Mayer and Chandler (2001) investigated the effects of simple user control on learning. The users controlled the pace of the presentation in a minimal way: The animation was segmented into meaningful 8 second-sequences, and after each sequence, learners had to click on a button to run the next sequence. The results of the two experiments showed that learners performed better on transfer tests when they controlled the pace of the presentation. Moreover, students who received the presentation with control followed by the presentation without control performed better than students who received the two presentations in the reverse order. The control enabled learners to process all information of a frame before proceeding to the next. In other words, interactivity decreases cognitive load and enables the formation of local mental models that can then be integrated when the whole presentation is displayed. These results are consistent with the two-stage mental model construction hypothesis (Hegarty, 1992; Hegarty & Sims, 1994), which states that learners first build local mental models, and then incorporate these local models into an integrated representation.

Another drawback of animation is that information is not only continuously changing but is also transient, which implies that learners must keep previous states of the animation in working memory. Series of static frames are often used in order to represent systems involving complex motion, such as operating a machine or assembling an object. Each step is portrayed in a separate frame and the frames are ordered by the sequence of steps. In addition to complying with the way dynamic systems are conceived (Hegarty, 1992), series of frames have an additional advantage: they facilitate the detailed comparison and reinspection of the actions.

4.2.4 Research Hypotheses

In the second part of this chapter, we report here an experimental study that was designed to investigate if adding static snapshots of the critical steps of an animation had an effect on understanding a dynamic phenomenon (i.e. the formation of lightning). We compared two types of presentations: a series of animated frames and a series of static graphics depicting the steps. Our hypotheses were the following.

According to our first hypothesis, animations would facilitate novices' understanding of the way a dynamic system works compared to a series of static graphics depicting the same thing, since an animation displays all the transitions between steps that otherwise have to be inferred from static graphics. We used a series of static graphics and a series of animations, ensuring a certain amount of informational equivalence and a correspondence between the verbal commentary and the graphic source (animated or static). We assumed that novice learners studying static graphics and text would be unable to infer the transitions between steps and consequently, animation would facilitate the elaboration of a dynamic mental model.

According to our second hypothesis, providing snapshots of critical steps to accompany the animation would facilitate the elaboration of a functional mental model from which inferences can be generated. Snapshots provide a permanent representation of the previous steps and would reduce the need for learners to memorize these steps, thus hypothetically saving cognitive resources for learning. An alternative assumption is that the presence of snapshots while the animation runs could cause a split-attention effect and impair learning (Mayer, Heiser, & Lonn, 2001). However, since learners have control over the pace of the animation, they should be able to process both visual sources of information (Tabbers, Martens, & van Merriënboer, 2004).

4.3 Experiment

4.3.1 Method

4.3.1.1 Participants and Design

The participants were 72 French-speaking students from the University of Geneva, 45 of which were women (mean age = 28). They participated voluntarily and without remuneration. We used a factorial 2 X 2 between-subjects design. The first factor was continuity (animation vs. static graphics), and the second factor, permanence with two modalities (with permanence vs. no permanence) according to whether snapshots of the presentation remained on the screen or not. There were 18 subjects in each condition. All participants reported low knowledge in meteorology in a self-evaluation scale.

4.3.1.2 Material and Apparatus

All the instruction and test materials were computer-based. The instructional material was designed after the "How lightning works" multimedia instruction kindly provided by Richard Mayer (University of Santa Barbara, USA) using *Macromedia Flash* and *Authorware* software. The material (visual animation and audio narration) aimed at explaining the formation of lightning. This material was used in previous experiments (e.g., Mayer, Heiser, & Lonn, 2001; Mayer & Chandler, 2001) with novices (undergraduate students with little knowledge in meteorology). The narration (accompanying text in auditory mode) was a strict translation of the original commentary. The original material included sixteen frames that were reduced to eight according to the model of lightning formation: : 1) air rises, 2) water condenses, 3) water and crystals fall, 4) wind is dragged downward, 5) negative charges fall to the bottom of the cloud, 6) the leaders meet, 7) negative charges rush down, and 8) positive charges rush up. After each segment, the animation stopped and the execution was controlled by the learner, as recommended from Mayer and Chandler's (2001) results.

Four versions of the material were designed. In the animated presentation without permanence, the animation ran in the centre of the screen. In the animated presentation with permanence, the animation ran in the centre of the screen and when a new sequence began, the last frame of the previous sequence was placed at the top of the screen (see Fig. 4.1).

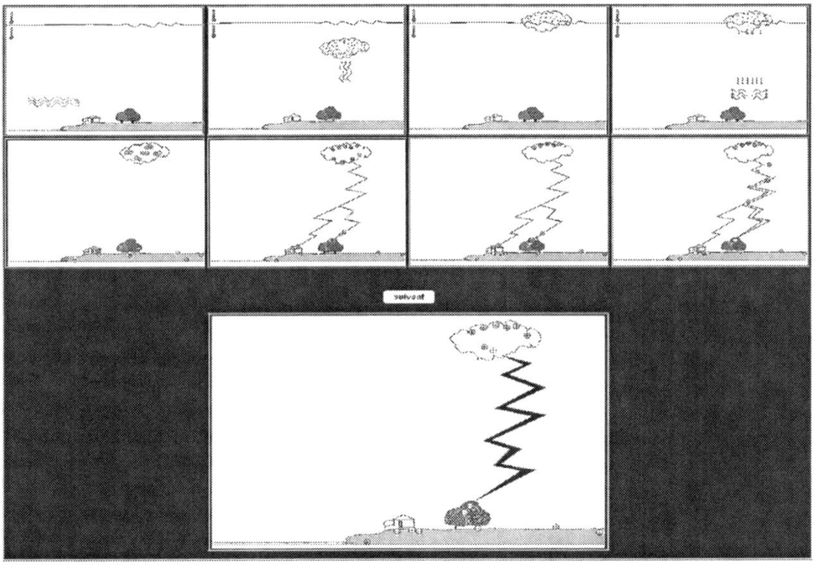

Fig. 4.1 Screen display in the last step of the presentation in the conditions with permanence. In the conditions without permanence, the upper part of the screen remained empty

The testing procedure followed the conventional paradigm for studying construction of mental models (Schnotz, 2001). The retention test consisted of 10 multiple choice questions measuring surface level understanding through paraphrases of statements explicitly included in the instructional material. Then a transfer test followed with 4 questions requiring to infer information from the text. Examples of transfer questions are: "Suppose you see clouds in the sky and no lightning, why not?" and "What could you do to decrease the intensity of lightning?". These questions were proposed as multiple-choice questions, with all propositions being plausible from a surface point of view.

4.3.1.3 Procedure

Participants were randomly assigned to one of the four conditions. They first evaluated their knowledge in the domain on a 4 point-scale (from very little knowledge to very good knowledge). Then they studied the animation twice, at their own pace. Immediately after, they had to perform a retention test and a transfer test. Finally, participants evaluated their perceived difficulty and interest in the material on two five-point scales.

4.3.2 Results and Discussion

4.3.2.1 Study Time

Participants had the control over the pace of the presentation and studied the animation twice. The total time the participants took to study the material was recorded. Figure 4.2 displays the mean study times and standard deviations for each condition. We conducted a two-way analysis of variance (ANOVA), with continuity as the first factor and permanence as the second factor.

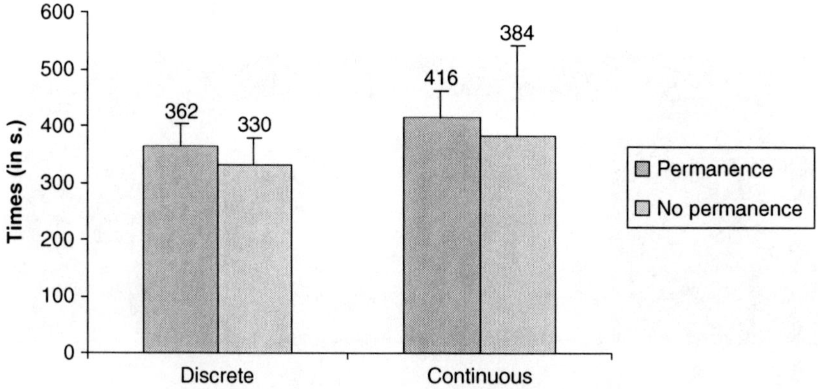

Fig. 4.2 Study times (means and standard deviations) for each condition

Participants in the animation conditions spent significantly more time studying the presentation than did participants in the static graphics conditions ($F(1,68) = 49.45$, $MSE = 52056.89$, $p < 0.0001$). There was also a significant main effect with permanence ($F(1,68) = 18.06$, $MSE = 19012.5$, $p < 0.0001$). Participants in the conditions with permanence spent more time studying the presentation than did participants in the conditions without permanence. There was no significant interaction between continuity and permanence ($F(1,68) < 1$).

4.3.2.2 Time Spent in the Retention and Transfer Tests

Table 4.1 presents the mean response times and standard deviations for each condition.

The two-way analysis of variance on the time spent answering the test questions did not reveal any significant difference between the four conditions (continuity: $F(1,68) = 0.56$; permanence: $F(1,68) = 2.12$).

4.3.2.3 Score for Retention and Transfer Tests

A first MANOVA with continuity and permanence as between-subjects factors and type of question as the within-subject factor revealed a significant difference between retention and transfer scores ($F(1,68) = 816.5, p < 0.0001$). Therefore retention and transfer performance were analyzed separately. As study times were significantly different across conditions, they were included in the variance analysis as a covariate. Figures 4.3 and 4.4 present the mean scores and standard deviations to the retention and transfer tests for each condition.

In the retention test, participants in the animation conditions did significantly better than participants in the static conditions ($F(1,67) = 5.98$, $MSE = 15.6$, $p < 0.05$). The effect size, using Cohen's d (Cohen, 1988), was 1.47. The effect of permanence was not statistically significant ($F(1,67) = 2.10$). However, the interaction between permanence and continuity was significant ($F(1,67) = 4.9$, $MSE = 12.84, p < 0.05$). As shown in Fig. 4.3, permanence had no effect on retention scores when the presentation was animated, whereas permanence decreased retention scores when the presentation was a series of static frames.

In the transfer test, participants in the animation conditions significantly outperformed participants in the static graphics conditions ($F(1,67) = 13.53$,

Table 4.1 Time (in seconds) spent on the retention and transfer tests for each condition. Permanence refers to the inclusion of snapshots

	Permanence	No permanence
Static graphics M (SD)	639 (205)	554 (224)
Animation M (SD)	592 (316)	519 (142)

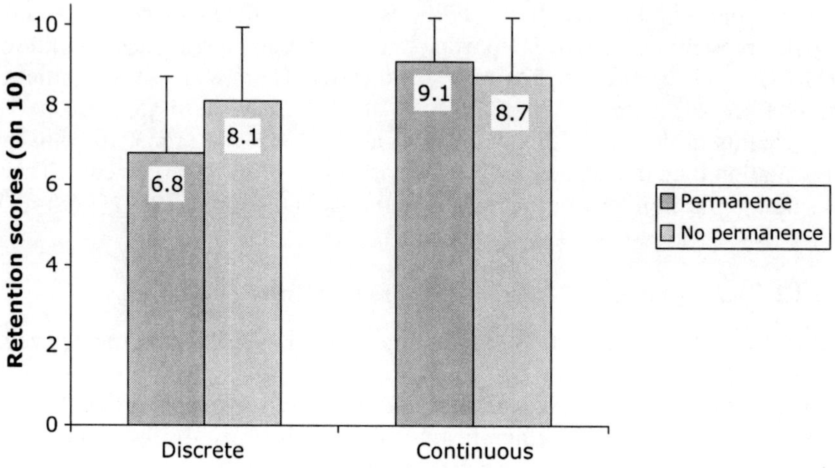

Fig. 4.3 Scores to the retention test (means and standard deviations) for each condition

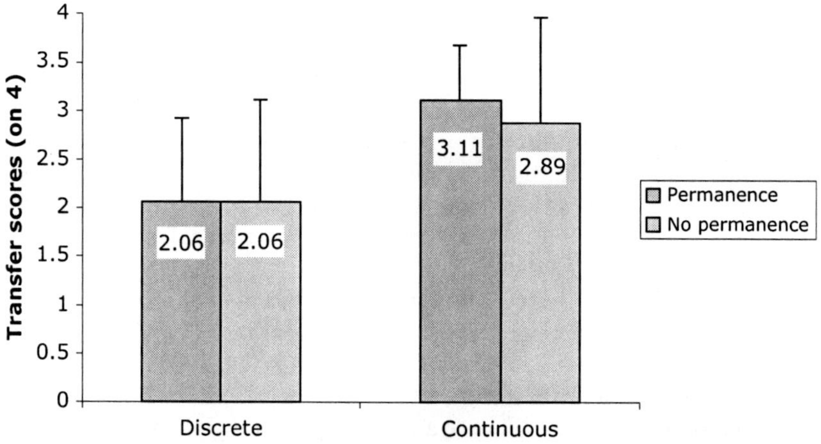

Fig. 4.4 Scores to the transfer test (means and standard deviations) for each condition

$MSE = 11.57$, $p < 0.05$), yielding an effect size of 1.38. The effect of permanence was not significant ($F(1,67) = 0.41$), nor was the interaction between permanence and continuity ($F(1,67) = 0.25$).

4.3.2.4 Subjective Evaluation

The participants evaluated the difficulty and their interest in the material on two five-point scales (see Fig. 4.5).

The perceived difficulty was considered as an indicator of the cognitive load that participants felt they engaged while studying the material. A

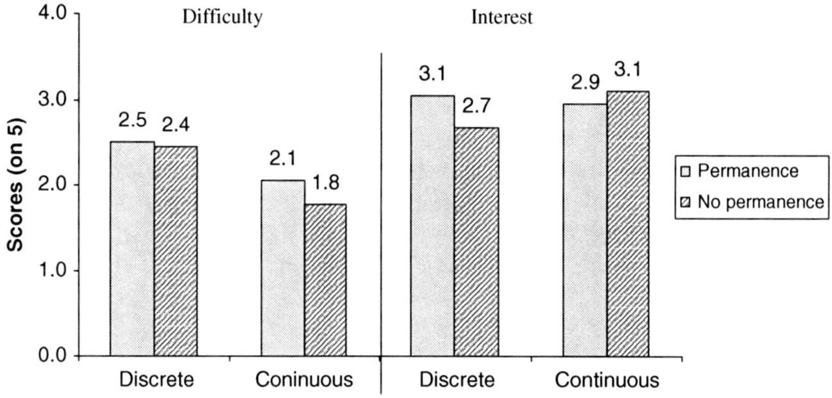

Fig. 4.5 Mean ranking of the perceived difficulty and interest for each condition

Mann-Whithney U test showed that participants in the static graphics conditions reported a significantly higher difficulty than participants in the animation conditions (U = 388.5, z = –3.218, $p < 0.01$). The effect of permanence was not significant (U = 585.0, z = –0.781).

For the question whether they found the material interesting, participants gave similar judgments across conditions (continuity effect: U = 578.0, z = –0.853; permanence effect: U = 588.0, z = –0.731).

4.3.3 Discussion

This chapter addressed two main questions: First, does animation help learners understand the functioning of dynamic systems? Second, does the permanent display of critical snapshots from the presentation reduce cognitive load and facilitate construction of the mental model?

From the literature review we concluded that animations may be made more effective by reducing the level of extraneous cognitive load induced by remembering the various steps and their relations. We hypothesized that snapshots would be helpful with that respect. The experiment showed that animation facilitates learners' understanding of dynamic systems compared to the presentation of successive static graphics of the main steps. The participants in the animation conditions had better performance to transfer questions than the participants in the static graphics conditions, which suggests that learners in the animation conditions elaborated a 'runnable' mental model of the dynamic systems in Mayer's (1989) sense. Moreover, they got higher retention scores, which means that even the surface structure was better memorized with the animation than with the static snapshots. This result is consistent with Tversky, Bauer-Morrison, and Bétrancourt's (2002) claim that animation is beneficial if it depicts the micro-steps of the system that otherwise would be inferred from static diagrams. In the static graphics conditions, participants had to infer the transitions between steps from the verbal commentary while trying to construct the mental model, which induced a cognitive overload. Indeed, the participants in the static graphics conditions reported significantly higher difficulties in studying the material than participants in the animation conditions.

It should be noted, however, that participants in the animation condition took longer to study the material than participants in the static graphics conditions. Several non exclusive hypotheses can explain this longer time. First, the continuous presentation involves more pieces of information that take time to mentally integrate, as suggested in Mayer & Chandler (2001). Second, the formation of a dynamic mental model could call for longer mental elaboration than surface representation of the explicit content. Finally, learners in continuous conditions could be more eager to study the instruction. No data in this study can either support or infirm any of the three explanations. But we found that although they took longer times, the students in the animation condition did experience lower difficulty than the students in the static graphics conditions. It has to be noted that learners had control over the pace of the presentation. As in Mayer & Chandler (2001), the learners could choose when to start the next sequence, both in the animation and static graphics conditions. Thus they could control the cognitive demand of viewing the material and mentally integrating the information.

The second question deals with the delivery features of animation. How should the interface be designed in order to facilitate cognitive processing of animation? This research investigated the effect of sequentially displaying snapshots of the main steps of a process while the presentation runs. We called this feature "permanence" as the previous steps are permanently displayed on the screen, instead as being replaced by the succeeding steps. The results did not show any effect of permanence on transfer performance. However, permanence significantly increased study times compared to the conditions without permanence both in the animated and static graphics conditions. Moreover, there was a significant interaction between continuity and permanence in the retention test: While permanence had no effect for the animation condition, it decreased retention performance in the static graphics condition. The results can be explained in terms of split-attention effect (Sweller & Chandler, 1994). In the static condition with permanence, the snapshots were identical to the graphics displayed. Under those circumstances of redundancy, learners had to split their attention between the main presentation and the snapshots, which decreased the cognitive resources allocated to learning, even at the rote level. However, this explanation was not confirmed by data from the subjective evaluation since learners in the permanent condition did not report higher difficulty. An alternative explanation lies at the meta-cognitive level. Since learners were not used to the permanence device, it may be that they simply did not know what to do with the snapshots. They might have considered them as additional information whereas the snapshots were meant to be used as "just in case" optional aids, as memory support. A follow-up study was done to investigate that particular issue by providing the snapshots in pop-up windows that learners could activate at will (Rebetez, Sangin,

Bétrancourt, & Dillenbourg. 2004). Time devoted to the snapshots, as well as the particular moments learners activated them were recorded. The results showed that the students barely used the snapshots, even though they were explained how to use them in the instructions. However, the permanence significantly increased the time students took reflecting on the sequences during the pauses, though it has no significant effect on performance or difficulty rating. Finally, a more practical explanation is that, as learners were novices, the permanence did not help because the snapshots displayed only the graphical elements and not the verbal commentary. Further studies should investigate whether in such situation, the verbal summary of the steps, alone or with the accompanying graphics, would be a better cognitive aid than pure graphic information.

From a methodological point of view, our study failed to provide enough data on students' cognitive load. Assessing the difficulty of the materials on a simple scale, as participants did, is far from evaluating the subjective cognitive load involved in processing the material. Further studies may benefit from finer instruments, like the standardized questionnaires *Nasa TLX* (Hart & Staveland, 1988) or *Workload Profile* (Tsang & Velazquez, 1996), or ad hoc questionnaires adapted to multimedia learning situations (Gerjets, Scheiter, & Catrambone, 2004). Another method to evaluate cognitive load is the dual task paradigm; measuring how a secondary simple task is hindered by the primary task. The dual-task method is worth considering since it provides less indirect measures than learning outcomes or subjective evaluation, and is easier to handle in a learning situation than physiological measures (heart rate, neuro-imaging or eye-tracking techniques). Though Brünken, Steinbacher, Plass, and Leutner (2002) claimed that the dual-task method would bring interesting insights in multimedia learning, it seems more suitable for laboratory experiments focusing on a particular aspect of the cognitive processing (for example auditory vs. visual processing like in Gyselink, Ehrlich, Cornoldi, de Beni, & Dubois, 2000) rather than for drawing general recommendations for the design of multimedia instructions. To date, the issue of measuring cognitive load, particularly extraneous cognitive load, remains a tough one (Dillenbourg & Betrancourt, 2006).

The results of the study reported here show that contrary to our expectation, the permanence of previous steps of an animated presentation failed to offload working memory, though no data can depart between the split-attention effect and the lack of cognitive relevance assumptions. Further investigation is needed combining fine observation techniques, like eye-tracking or post-task verbalization methods and more valid instruments to measure cognitive load.

4.4 Conclusion

The study reported in this paper provided both theoretical knowledge and practical guidelines for the use of animation in multimedia instruction. From a theoretical point of view, this research reinforces the hypothesis that a continuous animation helps learners to elaborate the mental model of a dynamic system. It depicts the transitions between steps that are difficult to infer from static schemas and verbal commentaries alone. It is important to note that we observed that benefits from animations showing mainly translational and transitional changes according to Lowe's (2004) distinction.

According to the experiment reported here, animations can be more effective than static graphics but not more efficient if we take into account the time needed to study the presentation. From an instructional design point of view, the time needed is less an issue than the learning outcomes. Furthermore, animation is likely to be beneficial only if learners do not have the knowledge or skills necessary to infer the transitions between steps by themselves. Further studies should be carried out investigating the effects of animation during the course of learning for beginning students as opposed to complete novices in a domain.

From an interface design point of view, the research showed that displaying static snapshots depicting the previous steps along with the animation did not act as an effective cognitive aid. Future research will have to investigate whether verbal information could be more useful as a memory aid than snapshots displaying only graphical elements.

In summary, this research provides evidence for the high potential of animation in future educational settings. This point is particularly important now that a growing number of universities and colleges propose distance training. Animation can be a powerful explanative device, provided it is used with respect to learners' cognitive processes.

Acknowledgments The research reported here was part of the third author's master thesis. We are grateful to Cyril Rebetez and the two anonymous reviewers for their helpful comments on earlier draft of this chapter. We thank Monica Axelrad for proofreading the final version.

References

Baddeley, A. (1997). *Human memory: Theory and practice*. London: Lawrence Erlbaum.

Baddeley, A. (2000). The Episodic Buffer: A New Component of Working Memory?" *Trends in Cognitive Sciences, 4*, 417–423.

Bétrancourt, M., & Tversky, B. (2000). Effects of computer animation on users' performance: A review. *Le Travail Humain, 63*, 311–329.

Brünken, R., Steinbacher, S., Plass, J. L. & Leutner, D. (2002) Assessment of cognitive load in multimedia learning using dual-task methodology. *Experimental Psychology, 49*, 1–12

Catrambone, R., & Fleming Seay, A. (2002). Using animation to help students learn computer algorithms. *Human Factors, 44*, 495–511.

Cohen, J. (1988). *Statistical power analysis for the behavioral sciences* (2nd ed.). Hillsdale, NJ: Lawrence Earlbaum Associates.

De Corte, E. (2003). Designing learning environment that foster the productive use of acquired knowledge and skills. In E. De Corte, L. Verschaffel, N. Entwistle & J. van Merrienböer (Eds.) *Unravelling basic components and dimensions of powerful learning environments*. (pp. 21–33). Pergamon: Elsevier Science Ltd.

Dillenbourg, P., & Betrancourt, M. (2006). Collaboration load. In J. Elen & R. E. Clark (Eds.), *Dealing with complexity in learning environments* (pp. 141–165) Advances in Learning and Instruction Series, Pergamon.

Dwyer, F. M. (1982/1983). The program of systematic evaluation: A brief review. *International Journal of Instructional Media, 10*, 23–38.

Ericsson, K. A., & Kintsch, W. (1995). Long-term working memory. *Psychological Review, 102*, 211–245.

Gerjets, P., Scheiter, K., & Catrambone, R. (2004). Designing instructional examples to reduce intrinsic cognitive load: Molar versus modular presentation of solution procedures. *Instructional Science, 32*, 33–58

Gyselink, V., Ehrlich, M. -F., Cornoldi, C., de Beni R., & Dubois, V. (2000). Visuospatial working memory in learning from multimedia systems. *Journal of Computer Assisted Learning, 16*, 166–176.

Hart, S. G., & Staveland, L. E. (1988). Development of NASA-TLX (Task Load Index): Results of experimental and theoretical research. In P. A. Hancock & N. Meshkati (Eds.), *Human mental workload* (pp. 39–183). Amsterdam: North Holland.

Hegarty, M. (1992). Mental animation: Inferring motion from static displays of mechanical systems. *Journal of experimental psychology: Learning, Memory and Cognition, 18*, 1084–1102.

Hegarty, M., & Sims, V. K. (1994). Individual differences in mental animation during mechanical reasoning. *Memory & Cognition, 22*, 411–430.

Johnson-Laird, P. N. (1983). *Mental models: Toward a cognitive science of language, inference and consciousness*. Cambridge: Cambridge University Press.

Kaiser, M. K., Proffitt, D. R., Whelan, S. M., & Hecht, H. (1992). Influence of animation on dynamical judgements. Journal of experimental Psychology: *Human Perception and performance, 18*, 669–690.

Levie, W. H., & Lentz, R. (1982). Effects of text illustration: A review of research. *Educational Communication and Technology Journal, 30*, 195–232.

Levin, J. R., Anglin G. J., & Carney, R. N. (1987). On empirically validating functions of pictures in prose, in D. M. Willows & H. A. Houghton (Eds.), *The psychology of illustration: I. basic research* (pp. 116–135). New York: Springer.

Lowe, R. (1999). Extracting information from an animation during complex visual processing. *European Journal of the Psychology of Education, 14*, 225–244.

Lowe, R. (2003). Animation and learning: selective processing of information in dynamic graphics. *Learning and Instruction, 13*, 157–176.

Lowe, R. K. (2004). Interrogation of a dynamic visualization during learning. *Learning and Instruction, 14*, 257–274.

Mayer, R. E. (1989). Models for understanding. *Review of Educational Research, 59* (1), 43–64.

Mayer, R. E. (2001). *Multimedia learning*. Cambridge: University Press.

Mayer, R. E. (2003). The promise of multimedia learning: using the same instructional design methods across different media. *Learning and Instruction, 13*, 125–139.

Mayer, R. E., & Chandler, P. (2001). When learning is just a click away: Does simple interaction foster deeper understanding of multimedia messages? *Journal of Educational Psychology, 93*(2), 390–397.

Mayer, R. E., Heiser, J., & Lonn, S. (2001). Cognitive constraints on Multimedia learning: When presenting more material results in less understanding. *Journal of Educational Psychology, 93*(1), 187–198.

Mayer, R. E., & Moreno, R. (2002). Aids to computer-based multimedia learning. *Learning and Instruction, 12*, 107–119.

Morrison, J., & Tversky, B. (2001). The (in)effectiveness of animation in instruction. In J. Jacko & A. Sears (Eds.), *Extended abstracts of the ACM conference on human factors in computing systems* (pp. 377–378). Seattle: ACM.

Narayanan, N. H., & Hegarty, M. (2002). Multimedia design for communication of dynamic information. *International Journal of Human-Computer Studies, 57*, 279–315.

Paas, F., Renkl, A., & Sweller, J. (Eds.). (2004). Advances in cognitive load theory: Methodology and instructional design [Special issue]. *Instructional Science, 32*, 1–189.

Palmiter, S., & Elkerton, J. (1993). Animated demonstrations for learning procedural computer-based tasks. *Human-Computer Interaction, 8*, 193–216.

Pane, J. F., Corbett, A. T., & John, B. E. (1996). Assessing dynamics in computer-based instruction. In M. J. Tauber (Ed.), *Proceedings of the ACM conference on human factors in computing systems* (pp. 797–804). Vancouver: ACM.

Rebetez, C., Sangin, M., Bétrancourt, M., & Dillenbourg, P. (2004). Effects of collaboration in the context of learning from animations, In *Proceedings of the EARLI SIG meeting on comprehension of texts and graphics: basic and applied issues* (pp. 187–192). September 2004, Valencia (Spain).

Rieber, L. P. (1989). The effects of computer animated elaboration strategies and practice on factual and application learning in an elementary science lesson. *Journal of Educational Computing Research, 5*, 431–444.

Schnotz, W. (2001). Sign sytems, technologies, and the acquisition of knowledge. In J. F. Rouet, J. Levonen, & A. Biardeau (Eds.), *Multimedia learning: Cognitive and instructional issues* (pp. 9–29). Amsterdam: Elsevier.

Schnotz, W., & Bannert, M. (2003). Construction and interference in learning from multiple representation. *Learning and Instruction, 13*, 141–156.

Schnotz, W., Böckheler, J., & Grzondziel, H. (1999). Individual and co-operative learning with interactive animated pictures. *European Journal of Psychology of Education, 14*, 245–265.

Schnotz, W., & Lowe, R. K. (2003). External and internal representations in multimedia learning. *Learning and Instruction, 13*, 117–123.

Sweller, J., & Chandler, P. (1994). Why some material is difficult to learn. *Cognition and Instruction, 12*, 185–233.

Sweller, J. (2003). Evolution of human cognitive architecture. In B. H. Ross (Ed.), *The psychology of learning and motivation* (Vol. 43, pp. 215–266). New-York: Academic Press.

Tabbers, H. K., Martens, R. L., & van Merriënboer, J. J. G. (2004). Multimedia instructions and cognitive load theory: effect of modality and cueing. *British Journal of Educational Psychology, 74*, 71–81.

Thompson, S. V., & Riding, R. J. (1990). The effect of animated diagrams on the understanding of a mathematical demonstration in l- to 14-year-old pupils. *British Journal of Educational Psychology, 60*, 93–98.

Tsang, P. S., & Velazquez, V. L. (1996). Diagnosticity and multidimensional subjective workload ratings. *Ergonomics, 39*, 358–381.

Tversky, B., Bauer-Morrison, J., & Bétrancourt, M. (2002). Animation: Can it facilitate? *International Journal of Human-Computer Studies, 57*, 247–262.

Chapter 5
Levels of Verbal Redundancy, Note-Taking and Multimedia Learning

Olivier Le Bohec and Eric Jamet

Abstract We examine the influence of redundancy in multimedia comprehension, within the framework of cognitive load theory. In two experiments, we examined whether totally or partially repeating a spoken comment in print could improve undergraduate students' comprehension of an introductory course on accountancy rules. In Experiment 1, the participants studied a multimedia document made of a series of graphs with a spoken explanation. The explanation was either totally, partially or not repeated in print. We found that the totally redundant format (diagram plus spoken and written text) was evaluated positively, but affects negatively comprehension processes. In Experiment 2, students were allowed to take notes while studying the multimedia course. The three conditions resulted in similar comprehension outcomes and subjective evaluations. The results suggest that redundancy must be used with caution in multimedia design, because it may increase the cognitive load of learning without facilitating the deep comprehension of the materials.

Keywords Cognitive load · Diagrams · Note taking · Recall · Redundancy · Subjective estimates

5.1 Introduction

Documents that call upon two sensory modalities (i.e., visual and auditory) are generally thought to be more effective than those using a single modality. Indeed, multimedia designers often duplicate spoken messages through the use of visual materials, with the underlying intention to improve users' understanding. Similarly, speakers sometimes use IT-based slide presentations to repeat the content of their spoken presentation. Other speakers, however, prefer to present mere summaries. What are the implications of these presentation strategies on

O. Le Bohec
University of Rennes II, Laboratory of Experimental Psychology; Place du Recteur H. Le Moal, 35 043 Rennes Cedex, France
e-mail: olivier.lebohec@uhb.fr

J.-F. Rouet et al. (eds.), *Understanding Multimedia Documents*,
DOI: 10.1007/978-0-387-73337-1_5,

students' comprehension and learning? In other words, what are the effects of various levels of redundancy on the cognitive and connotative processes involved in the comprehension of instructional discourse? These are the questions we address in the present study. In the theoretical section, we briefly present the cognitive load theory and the generative theory of multimedia learning, which both provide explanatory mechanisms to explain redundancy effects. Then we examine various types of redundancy effects in document comprehension, from a theoretical standpoint. In the second part of the chapter, we present two experiments in which we examined the effects of various levels on redundancy on students' comprehension of course contents. In these experiments, we examined the effects of redundancy both on measures of comprehension and transfer, and on students' satisfaction with the learning experience.

5.2 Theoretical Background

5.2.1 The Cognitive Load Theory

Cognitive Load theory (CLT, see e.g., Sweller, 1999; Sweller, Chandler, Tierney, & Cooper, 1990) provides a well-known and established literature for improving the training of complex cognitive skills and their transfer to new situations (Bannert, 2002; see also Schnotz, Chapter 2). According to the cognitive load theory, domain experts possess mental schemata defined as "a mental construct permitting problem solvers to categorize problems according to solution modes" (Sweller, Chandler, Tierney, & Cooper, 1990, p. 176). Mental schemata allow experts to solve problems faster and better, and to achieve deeper levels of comprehension of technical materials. CLT also assumes that studying documents or solving problems generate a certain amount of "cognitive load", which can be decomposed into three major sources: intrinsic (due to the number of components to be learned, and to their interactions); extrinsic (due to the way the materials are structured and presented); and germane (due to the amount of mental effort invested in the task). Finally, CLT describes two strategies that are supposed to facilitate the acquisition of expertise in a given content area:

1. Reduce extraneous cognitive load, or the amount of unnecessary cognitive processing, which is linked to the inadequate presentation and/or structuring of learning materials.
2. Increase germane cognitive load, that is, the load generated by cognitive processes directly relevant for learning (van Merriënboer, Schuurman, de Croock, & Paas, 2002).

These purposes may be achieved by avoiding split attention, setting up specific learning goals, or avoiding unneeded redundancy, as we further discuss below.

5.2.2 The Generative Theory of Multimedia Learning

The generative theory of multimedia learning proposed by Mayer and his colleagues draws on: 1 – a modal view of information processing that is "most consistent with Paivio's distinction between verbal and nonverbal systems" (Mayer, 2001); 2 – A sensory modality view of Working Memory that is "most consistent with Baddeley's distinction between the visuo-spatial sketch-pad and the phonological loop" (Mayer, 2001); and 3 – the generative-learning theory which states that meaningful learning involves selecting relevant verbal and non-verbal information, organizing it into coherent representations, and making connections between representations and with prior knowledge.

Some aspects of Mayer's theory help explain what may happen in situations where contents are presented in various formats, as it is the case in multimedia documents. More specifically, we shall consider three types of materials or formats: spoken words (e.g. narration), written words (e.g. on-screen text), and pictures (e.g. diagram, plan, animation and video). Let us first consider the issue of presenting pictures with written vs. spoken words. When verbal and pictorial materials are both presented visually, readers must split their attention among the two sources. This may overload the visual channel in working memory. This problem can be bypassed by the use of spoken rather than written texts. In this way, the load is distributed across the two channels. There is evidence that students learn better from pictures presented with spoken comments, than from pictures presented with written comments (e.g., Mousavi, Low, & Sweller, 1995).

The strict application of the modality principle is not always possible. Indeed, many multimedia scenarios include the presentation of visual materials such as animations, video or graphics with simultaneous redundant verbal information, that is, narration with identical on-screen text. In this case, written words and illustrations compete for attention and time as both must also be processed in the visual/pictorial channel. Moreover, the processing of the two verbal sources must be synchronized to be understood. Mayer (2001) uses the term "redundancy effect" to refer to the situation when learning is hindered by the superfluous duplication of verbal contents.

Thus, the cognitive load theory and the generative theory of multimedia learning both indicate that redundancy may be detrimental to document-based learning. It is important, however, to further analyze the concept of redundancy, as different kinds of redundancy may have different effects on learning.

5.2.3 Redundancy in Document Comprehension

The concept of redundancy is used in research areas of psychology, ergonomics, educational sciences, human/machine interactions and even marketing studies. In this paper, we are primarily interested in the way redundancy affects the comprehension of spoken instructional discourse (see Jamet & Le Bohec, 2007). According to the cognitive load theory by Sweller and colleagues (see Sweller, 1999 for a review) and the generative theory of multimedia learning by Mayer (see Mayer, 2001 for a review), three types of redundancy may be distinguished.

5.2.3.1 Redundancy Defined as Superfluous Information

Most instructional documents tend to elaborate on key notions by providing additional materials, such as examples, illustrations, or the mere repetition of information at various locations. Mayer (2001, p. 113) pointed out that adding unnecessary information does not always help, a problem that he identified as the "coherence effect", defined as follows: "students learn better when useless material is excluded than when it is included." In this case, information that is not directly relevant for learning tends to decrease the document coherence, which generates an increased cognitive load. This, in turn, might impair students' performance. For example, Mayer and his colleagues examined information intended to make multimedia documents more interesting, amusing or motivating, but which was useless in terms of learning, regardless of whether this information took the form of text, images or sound (e.g., Harp & Mayer, 1998; Moreno & Mayer, 2000). They provided direct evidence that learning is facilitated when superfluous information is removed from the documents.

5.2.3.2 Redundancy and Learners' Prior Knowledge

Applying the coherence principle is less easy as it may seem, because it is sometimes difficult to tell whether a piece of information is useful or not. In fact, the necessary or superfluous nature of information depends on other factors, e.g. the level of expertise of the readers of the document, their motivation, the task type, etc. Thus, a source of information might be essential for a beginner but redundant – and thus useless or even harmful – for someone who possesses more specific domain knowledge. As Kalyuga, Ayres, Chandler, and Sweller (2003) suggest, there may be a threshold beyond which a highly condensed document may be too concise to be properly understood by beginners, since it requires too many inferences to be made. Thus, one should consider learner's prior knowledge level when designing effective learning materials (McNamara, Kintsch, Songer, & Kintsch, 1996; but see also Gilabert, Martinez, & Vidal-Abarca, 2005).

Several studies found empirical evidence for the detrimental effect of adjunct information that does not match students' needs; For example, Yeung, Jin, and Sweller (1997) found that word definitions inserted in a foreign language text helped readers with a low level of language proficiency, while they were disruptive for more experienced ones. Jamet and Le Bohec (2000) replicated this effect, controlling the participants' age and prior knowledge and distinguishing. In addition, they controlled whether the defined words were known by a majority of the participants or not. The results indicated that the definition of already known words generated a redundancy effect on the comprehension of the text passages that contained the words. Another study by Kalyuga, Chandler, and Sweller (1998) demonstrated that explanations inserted in an electrical wiring plan are clearly beneficial to beginners in electricity but not to individuals who are more familiar with electrical circuits. The latter operate more effectively if given only the wiring plans: in this case, the explanations are clearly redundant with their knowledge. Kalyuga, Chandler, and Sweller (2000) replicated this pattern of results using spoken explanations concerning the operation of industrial machines. Only the beginners benefited from these explanations, with individuals who were more familiar with the equipment performing better when using only the machine diagrams. This effect was called the "expertise reversal effect".

5.2.3.3 Redundancy Associated with Multiple Presentation Formats

The third type of redundancy effect corresponds to the presentation of a given piece of information in several different formats. Or, to put it in Tricot's (1998) words, "when the same information is present a number of times in different forms (for example, in text form and in pictorial form), it results in a heightened cognitive load (and thus poorer performance) than when the same material is presented without redundancy". Contrary to the widespread idea that presenting the same information in different formats facilitates learning, a large number of experiments tend to indicate that this form of redundancy may have a deleterious effect. Chandler and Sweller (1991, Exp. 3, 4 & 5) showed detrimental effects of redundant information, using multimedia documents which presented an electrical wiring plan and blood circulation with the make-believe help of a text reproducing items from the illustrations. In this case, illustrations were understandable on their own.

Mayer (2001, p. 153) defined the redundancy effect in a narrow sense "to refer to any multimedia situation in which learning from animation (or illustrations) and narration is superior to learning from the same materials along with printed text that matches the narration". Kalyuga, Chandler and Sweller (1999, Exp. 1) worked with beginners whose aim was to learn a diagram relating to the fusion of materials. They compared the effectiveness of three presentation formats: (1) a diagram together with a text to be read; (2) a diagram together with the same text which, in this case, was read to the participants; (3) a diagram together with the text presented both in speech and writing. The performance indicators used consisted of a multiple choice questionnaire to evaluate memory retention (recall task) and an error detection task designed to evaluate the participants' ability to transfer the knowledge to new situations (transfer task). A subjective indicator of the load level (Paas & van Merrienboër, 1993) based on a seven-point, Likert-type scale was also used. Two types of results were observed: First, the format "diagram plus spoken text" was more effective than the format "diagram plus written text"; second, better performances were obtained for the format "diagram plus spoken text" than the format "diagram plus spoken and written text". Here, the duplication of the text clearly generates an extraneous cognitive load, which hampers learning. Studies by Mayer, Heiser, and Lonn (2001; Exp. 1 & 2), Moreno and Mayer (2002; Exp. 2), and Craig, Gholson, and Discroll (2002) have since replicated this type of redundancy effect using one and the same document intended to explain storm formation while modifying certain parameters such as the presence of virtual pedagogical agents.

It should be noted that these studies used static illustrations, and not sequential presentations in which pieces of information are presented one after the other. Moreno and Mayer (2002) included this simultaneous aspect of the presentation in their definition of the redundancy principle. Indeed, when an animation was introduced before the redundant verbal information, which was presented both in speech and writing, no redundancy effect was obtained since readers did not have to split their attention between two sources of visual information (verbal and pictorial). In fact, "when students were able to hold the graphic information before attending to the textual information in visual working memory, redundant verbal explanations enhanced learning" (Moreno & Mayer, 2002, p. 162).

Moreno and Mayer (2002) defined "verbal redundancy" as "the simultaneous presentation of text and narration using exactly the same words. Consequently, verbal redundancy constitutes a subclass of redundant information in general which includes cases in which verbal and non-verbal material is used to represent the same information via different modes." In the first experiment conducted as part of their study, Moreno and Mayer (2002) obtained a positive effect of verbal redundancy on learning in two distinct situations: on the one hand, when no animation was provided in parallel and, on the other hand, when animation was introduced before the redundant verbal message. According to Moreno and Mayer (2002), such results are compatible with ergonomic studies designed to investigate the simultaneous processing of bimodal information (see, for instance, Lewandowski & Kobus, 1993; Le Bohec & Jamet, 2001).

5.2.4 Study Objectives

In this study, we focus on the redundancy associated with the duplication of information. To sum up the literature so far, the negative effect of redundant verbal information during the learning of an illustrated document appears to be clearly established (e.g., Kalyuga, Chandler, & Sweller, 1999). However, Moreno and Mayer (2002, Exp. 2) succeeded in showing that the interfering nature of redundancy emerges only in situations of simultaneous presentation, which yields working memory overloads due to the division of attention between the sources of visual information. The aim of a recent study (Jamet & Le Bohec, 2007) was to examine this hypothesis, i.e. that the visual channel is overloaded by a redundant presentation as the cognitive theory of multimedia learning suggests.

Documents consisting of diagrams and spoken information on the development of memory models were presented to three groups of students. In the first group, no written text was presented. In the second group, written sentences redundant with the spoken information were progressively presented on the screen (sequential presentation) while in the third group, these written sentences were all presented together (static presentation). The study found that whatever the presentation (sequential or static), the duplication of information in the written mode led to a substantial impairment in subsequent retention and transfer tests as well as in a task in which the memorization of diagrams was evaluated. The latter result supports the assumption that the visual channel is overloaded as proposed by the underlying theory of multimedia learning (Mayer, 2001, 2005) given that the learning performance that is most affected by the redundancy is associated with the information source that directly competes with the written text in terms of visual processing (i.e. the diagram).

More studies need to be conducted in order to clearly identify conditions under which the redundancy effect is more likely to appear. For example, the study led by Moreno and Mayer (2002) suggests that we should be cautious with regard to the transferable nature of the classical redundancy principle (Mayer, 2001). We can assume that many various contextual factors are able to influence the redundancy effect and the personal impressions concerning the characteristics of the document or the quality of learning.

In the experiments cited above (Craig, Gholson, & Discoll, 2002; Jamet & Le Bohec, in press; Kalyuga, Chandler, & Sweller, 1999; Mayer, Heiser, & Lonn, 2001; Moreno & Mayer, 2002), multimedia documents were presented in such a way that learners could not control pacing of presentation. This situation is probably sufficient to explain a part of the observed cognitive overload by the absence of possible compensations in terms of time. This assumption was the purpose of a recent study (Le Bohec, 2006). Documents consisting of diagrams/tables and spoken information presenting the fundamentals of French accountancy rules were presented to four groups of students. Presence of written redundant text (bulleted text) and pacing were manipulated. Results indicated than in a classic condition where learners had no control, better transfer performances were obtained in the condition without redundant verbal explanation than in a redundant condition. This redundancy effect was coherent with the classical literature presented above. On the other hand, negative effect of redundancy was not yet observed when learner processed instructions at their own pace. Here, the students did not have to split their attention between the different information sources with a limited time-on-task. In this condition, learners had more time flexibility to sequentially integrate narration, redundant bulleted text and diagrams/tables.

In the first experiment, we manipulated the level of verbal redundancy by using the same multimedia slide show with three conditions: full-text and totally redundant audio delivery, partial-text (bulleted) with full-audio delivery, or no-text (graphics only) with full-audio delivery. We assume that the partial text in bulleted units can guide students' attention, by passing the redundancy effect (Mautone & Mayer, 2001).

In the second experiment, we used the same materials and task, but the participants were allowed to take notes. The main purpose was to evaluate how note taking impacts the redundancy effect.

5.3 Experiment 1

The redundancy effects have been analyzed virtually only within the framework of "all or nothing" paradigms. If the strict duplication of the information in the spoken and written modes generates a cognitive overload, then one may wonder if reducing the quantity of written information by presenting it in summarized form will be sufficient to eliminate this redundancy effect. This is the major question we asked in Experiment 1.

Barron and Atkins (1994) may have provided a unique case of partial redundancy in an experimental study. They examined the implications of audio and textual redundancy into a computer-based training program. Three experimental groups completed the program with materials presented in one of the three following conditions:

An audio-based version with total textual redundancy – the audio is word-for-word the same as the instructional text on the screen.

An audio-based version in which the audio and graphics are the same as version # 1, but the visual text of # 1 is reduced to bulleted items, rather than full text.

An audio-based version in which the audio and graphics are the same as version # 1 and # 2, but there is no visual text.

Barron and Atkins (1994) found no significant difference in learning outcomes across groups. However, several specific features of this experiment preclude any final conclusion regarding the possible benefits of partial redundancy. There was no time limit to complete the lesson; the students could "replay the audio segments and back up to review previous instructional screens" (p. 304); and last, "Ninety-seven percent of the students responded the audio was easy to understand" (p. 303). These characteristics made the task easy enough to prevent any cognitive overload. In fact, the authors concluded that "future research may investigate whether or not more difficult content, evaluated at higher cognitive levels, would differentiate among students' achievements levels" (p. 304). This suggestion will constitute the basis of our experiment.

The main goals of this experiment were as follows. First, we aimed at verifying if duplicating a spoken presentation in writing impairs comprehension of multimedia documents, by comparing two formats comparable to those employed by Kalyuga, Chandler, and Sweller (1999).

Second, we examined whether an intermediate redundancy format with visual bulleted items (as in Barron & Atkins, 1994) can bypass the negative redundancy effects. We predict that the intermediate format can facilitate the active cognitive process of selecting relevant pieces of information making the learning process easier. In terms of cognitive load, this format, by signaling main concepts, may reduce extraneous processes of selecting relevant information and, at the same time, may increase germane cognitive load by redirect learners' attention toward the construction and abstraction of schemas. Third, we wanted to assess, in an exploratory way, some participant's impressions relating to the characteristics of the multimedia lesson and the effectiveness of learning as a function of the level of redundancy.

5.3.1 Method

5.3.1.1 Subjects

The experiment took place as part of the initial presentation of a number of accounting concepts within a 3-month training program intended for students enrolled in their first year of Business Studies or Business and Public Authority Administration. Three experimental groups of 41 students enrolled in either of these two relatively similar courses were formed. The participants (70 males and 53 females) were arbitrarily assigned to the three experimental conditions in order to build three equal groups. The mean age was approximately 20 years. All the students from each experimental group were present at the same time in the classroom. The business studies teacher and one researcher introduced the course and the specific features of the experimental session. The participation in the experiment was voluntary but encouraged as a way to receive a first introduction to the course contents.

5.3.1.2 Materials

For this experiment, we constructed three different half-hour versions of one and the same document presenting the fundamentals of French accountancy rules. In the "no redundancy" version, there was no duplication of the spoken message in writing; in the "total redundancy" version, there was a strict duplication of the spoken and written explanations; finally, the "partial redundancy" included a written summary presented as bulleted text (Barron & Atkins, 1994). The written summary was constructed using an extremely schematic syntax. For example, a sentence presenting the equivalence of two accounting terms A and B was summarized as "A = B". Accountancy teachers in accordance with the importance of the different idea units made the selection of the partially redundant information.

In the three conditions, the time and the pacing of the instruction were based on the duration of the narration. Thus, exposure time was identical in the three groups.

The document, which was created using "flash 5 Macromedia®" software, was presented using a video projector on a white screen and the recorded text was played loud enough for all the students to hear it comfortably.

1) Initial funding phase.

- At this stage, it is important to make a terminological remark.
- In everyday life, the words ĒŹbank ŹČand ĒŹcapital are ŹČare often confounded and they do not mean the same as in the present context.
- However, for an accountant, the capital is the amount of money brought by the associates, whereas the word bank means the total amount on the bank account.
- These are two distinct notions, as can be seen on the Table.

Table 2 b
Balance sheet as of February 1, 2001

ASSETS		DEBIT	
		CAPITAL	250
BANK	300	LOAN	50
Total	300	Total	300

Fig. 5.1 Example of the format with "total redundancy"

It is also important to note that the graphs and balance sheets – which were updated as a function of the explanations – were always presented on the right-hand side of the screen in all the experimental conditions. When the speech was transcribed into writing, it was presented on the left-hand side of the screen as can be seen in Figs. 5.1, 5.2 and 5.3 below:

1) Initial funding phase.

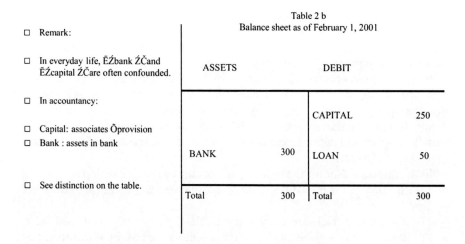

- Remark:
- In everyday life, ĒŹbank ŹČand ĒŹcapital ŹČare often confounded.
- In accountancy:
- Capital: associates Õprovision
- Bank : assets in bank
- See distinction on the table.

Table 2 b
Balance sheet as of February 1, 2001

ASSETS		DEBIT	
		CAPITAL	250
BANK	300	LOAN	50
Total	300	Total	300

Fig. 5.2 Example of the format with "partial redundancy"

Fig. 5.3 Example of the format without any redundancy

1) Initial funding phase.

Table 2 b
Balance sheet as of February 1, 2001

ASSETS		DEBIT	
		CAPITAL	250
BANK	300	LOAN	50
Total	300	Total	300

5.3.1.3 Dependent Measures

We developed a pre-test questionnaire consisting of a set of 12 sentences with blanks for completion in order to evaluate the students' prior knowledge of accountancy, with the list of possible words being provided (e.g., "In an accountancy context, we found in the liabilities: ________"). We also measured participant's impressions on eight criteria relating to the characteristics of the document and the effectiveness of learning as a function of the format of presentation. Appendix presents the scales that we selected in the order in which they where presented to the students (i.e., difficulty, pleasantness, speediness, interest, memorization, comprehension, feelings about competences).

In view of the dependent variables used to measure the quality of learning, we decided to distinguish between two types of questionnaires that are frequently used in the literature on presentation formats, namely a recall questionnaire and a transfer questionnaire.

The first questionnaire assessed the recall of information explicitly provided in the explanations. This involves the construction of the microstructure and macrostructure to use Kintsch's (1998) terminology. The test took the form of 11 sentences that had to be completed using suitable terms without any list of possible words being provided (e.g., "The production period permits to build: _______").

The transfer questionnaire, which consisted of 15 items and was scored out of a possible 15 points, measured the ability to transfer the processed information to another context of use (Mayer, 2001). Here, we asked the students to solve problems corresponding to new financial situations in fictitious businesses by employing inferential processes. (e.g., question 3: A firm reimburses a loan, what happens with regards to the liabilities?). This task requires the production of inferences, i.e. an integration of both the information presented in the document and knowledge present in long-term memory. The transfer of knowledge to new situations which are significantly different from the presented situations would be a much better indicator of the depth of processing since it tests the final step, namely the quality of the mental representation (Mayer, 2001).

We scored the prior knowledge test, the recall test and the transfer test by basically adding together the correct answers.

5.3.1.4 Procedure

First of all, we asked all the students, irrespective of the experimental condition they were assigned to, to complete the pretest questionnaire. We also asked the students whether, during their course, they had had the chance to attend accounting classes and, if so, for how long. We retained only the students who were not repeating the accountancy program. The participants were told that they would be assessed on the basis of what they had learned following the presentation of the document. Once the document had been projected, the students were handed the recall questionnaire. The questionnaires were only collected when the students were finished and there was no time pressure associated with its completion. Once the recall questionnaire had been completed, we distributed the transfer questionnaire and then, when this had been filled in, we handed out the impression questionnaire, which made use of eight 4-point Lickert-type scales.

5.3.2 Results

5.3.2.1 Performance

- Pretest questionnaire
  Once we had checked the homogeneity of the variances in the pre-presentation questionnaire ($F(2, 120)$ 1.09; NS), we tested the equivalence of prior knowledge of the three groups. The analysis of variance showed no significant difference ($F(2, 120)$ 0.60; NS). Thus, the three groups were equivalent in terms of their prior knowledge. The average performance, for the three groups was 5.78 (SD 2.20). To sum up, almost half of the questions were correctly answered. The students were not entirely novices in accountancy.
- Memory and transfer performance
  Figure 5.4 presents the scores on the memory and transfer post-test as a function of presentation condition.

The analysis of variance indicated that the three experimental groups had equivalent performance on the recall questionnaire ($F(2, 120) = 0.17$; NS). As

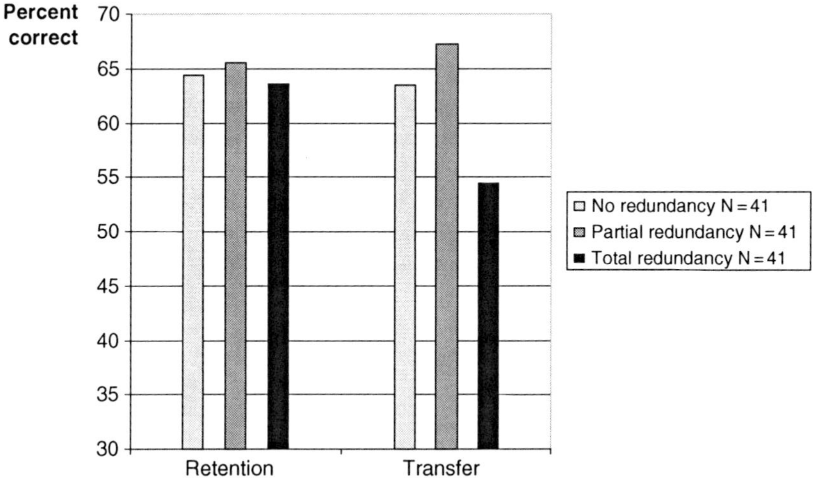

Fig. 5.4 Experiment 1: Percentage of correct answers for each type of test

far as the transfer questionnaire is concerned, the analysis of variance indicated a simple effect of redundancy level ($F(2, 120) = 4.50$; $p = 0.01$; $\eta 2 = 0.07$). The pairwise comparison (Least Significant Difference) indicated that performance on the format "total redundancy" was worse than that obtained with the format "partial redundancy" (Difference between means = 1.92; $p = 0.004$) or with the format "no redundancy" (Difference between means = 1.36; $p = 0.04$).

5.3.2.2 Subjective Evaluation

Subjects' impressions were analyzed as a function of presentation condition using chi2 test (see Table 5.1). Table 5.1 present the median evaluation scores on each of the questionnaire items, as a function of presentation condition.

Table 5.1 Median evaluation score for each of the eight assertions, as a function of presentation condition

	Level of redundancy				
Item	None	Partial	Total	χ^2 (df)	p value
Difficulty of the document	3	3	3	(4) = 3.33	NS
Pleasantness of the document	2	2	3	(6) = 18.38	005
Speed of the document	4	3	3	(6) = 14.98	0.02
Interest of the document	3	3	3	(6) = 10.93	NS
Understanding of the document	3	3	3	(6) = 6,56	NS
Suitability of speed	2	2	2	(6) = 19.22	0.004
Memorization of the document	3	3	3	(6) = 9.95	NS
Transfer abilities	3	3	2	(6) = 15.73	0.015

The manipulation of redundancy had an effect on three dimensions. When using total redundancy, document was evaluated as more pleasant than with no redundancy and partial redundancy. The feeling to be able to re-use knowledge for another countable assessment (capacity of transfer) was less important than with the two other formats. The document speed was perceived as unsuited in the no redundancy group, probably because of the absence of written information to read. In other words, the "total redundancy" format was perceived more positively (pleasantness and speed) than the "no redundancy" format although, as indicated by the transfer test, its pedagogical effectiveness was lesser.

5.3.3 Discussion

According to the cognitive load theory (Chandler & Sweller, 1991); Sweller, 1999), the duplication of verbal information generates an additional cognitive load which impairs learning performance. Mayer (2001) explains the redundancy effect as follows:

"When pictures, printed words, and spoken words are all presented, the system can become overloaded in two ways. First, pictures and printed words compete for limited cognitive resources in the visual channel because both enter the information processing through their eyes. Second, when verbal information is presented both visually and auditorily, learners may be tempted to attend to both in an attempt to reconcile the two information streams; this extraneous activity requires cognitive resources that consequently are not available for processing the animation [illustration] and mentally linking it with the narration, an integration process that is essential for meaningful learning." (p. 153)

In this experiment, redundancy only seemed to have an impact on the transfer questionnaire, which is not fully consistent with previous studies (e.g. Kalyuga, Chandler, & Sweller, 1999). Our results suggest that redundancy affects the high-level integrative processes rather than the surface processing of explicitly provided information. Consistent with our result, Mayer, Heiser, and Lonn (as presented in Mayer, 2001) have observed lesser redundancy effects on recall performances (effect size: 0.77; Percent gain: 28) than on transfer performances (effect size: 1.24; Percent gain: 79). In fact, the transfer questionnaire investigates the mobilization of inferential processes, which are known as extremely costly in terms of cognitive resources.

Partial redundancy (with only main verbal information in a visual form) reduces the superfluous division of attention between the visual information sources and help students in focusing their attention toward germane idea units. The partial redundancy format represented a good compromise since it equaled the performances obtained with the "no redundancy" format but without being perceived negatively. Indeed, as Mautone and Mayer (2000; p. 378) pointed out "one function of signaling is to guide the search for specific information and to simplify decisions the reader may have to make about which information is relevant." We can also assume that partial redundant information serves as an external memory aid and, therefore, facilitates activities like rereading and mental revision.

The students in the "no redundancy" group tended to judge the document as very unpleasant and very slow. They also considered the document presentation speed to be very unsuitable. Based on informal observations in the classroom, we found that students were annoyed by the blanks between two succeeding slides. In the partial and total redundancy conditions, rereading activity was possible during the inter-slide interval: this may have made the presentation pace seem more normal to students in those groups. Thus, the learning benefit of the no redundancy condition was acquired at the expense of students' global impression of the document. What do the results tell us regarding the psychological processes at work during the study activity? First of all, redundancy requires additional processing time, as evidenced in students' evaluation of presentation speed. The analysis of the participants' evaluations reveals another interesting result. After the evaluation, many of the students in the "total redundancy" group thought they would not be able to write the same type of balance sheet for a different example. This opinion concerning the ability to transfer the acquired knowledge to analogous situations was observed even in the absence of objective feedback concerning their performance (cf. problem correction sheet). We did not observe this phenomenon in the other two groups. This corroborates the results obtained for performances on the transfer questionnaire and supports our hypothesis concerning the increased load weighing on the high-level integrative processes.

The partial redundancy format yielded the same data pattern as was observed for the format without redundancy. Furthermore, the students in the partial redundancy group had more positive opinions about the documents. Thus, overall, the experiment confirmed that partial redundancy can be beneficial both in terms of learning outcomes and students' enjoyment of the learning task.

5.4 Experiment 2

5.4.1 Objectives

In Experiment 1, we used a condition in which the students were not allowed to take notes in order to make our experiment comparable with those reported in the literature. This procedure was consistent with most of the studies reported in the introduction, were the participants are simply asked to understand the content and memorize as much information as possible. The main objective of Experiment 2 was to replicate the effects of partial redundancy in an ecological situation requiring participants to perform a supplementary parallel task. During the presentation of the redundant slide show, students must continuously and simultaneously listen, read and keep an eye on graphics or tables. Moreover, they must "select important ideas, hold and manipulate ideas, interpret the information, decide what to transcribe, and record notes. Some resources are additionally spent on the mechanical aspects of note-taking such as spelling, grammar, and notational style."(Kiewra & Dubois, 1991, p. 241).

Note-taking, or NT, is practiced almost systematically both in higher education, where the use of IT-based slide presentations is rapidly increasing, and in professional conferences such as scientific symposia. According to Piolat (2001), NT requires the following to be activated in parallel "1 – listening in order to understand what is said by the speaker or speakers; 2 – writing in order to transcribe what needs to be retained on paper depending on the aim of the work; 3 – reading in order to check that what is being written is valid with regard to what is being said and the objectives in terms of information storage." NT depends on the students' level of familiarity with the materials. According to Piolat (2001), "the less well known the subject matter is, the more difficult it is for note-takers to distinguish between what is and what is not essential." In other words, beginners may find it more difficult to construct a global representation of the meaning of the text (or macrostructure, according to Kintsch's (1998) theory) due to the lack of the specific knowledge that would facilitate the activities of generalization and the suppression of useless information.

The review conducted by Kiewra (1985) indicates the presence of contrasting results concerning NT, with 35 studies revealing positive effects on performance, 23 obtaining no effect and 3 pointing to better performance in the absence of note-taking. The evidence to support a positive effect of note-taking is, thus, somewhat inconsistent. There are, indeed, many factors that influence the effectiveness of NT such as, for example, the presence of structural cues in the passages or the individual differences in the manner of processing information. For example, Rickards, Fajen, Sullivan, and Gillespie (1997) found a complex interaction between signaling, note-taking and cognitive style. The first experiment involved having students take or not take notes while listening to two passages with or without structural cues. Regression analyses suggested that note-taking in the presence of structural cues increased recall of field-dependent but not field-independent learners. On the basis of the second experiment's results, "field-independent learners seemed to spontaneously use a tacit structure strategy when left to their own devices and field-independent learners appeared to immediately display powerful structuring skills when induced to do so via notetaking."(p. 508). In our view, this result illustrates that NT is a complex activity which comprises various aspects and which derives from a diversity of personal objectives and strategies (Piolat, 2001). Other important factors that need to be considered are students' prior knowledge (Piolat, 2001) or the length of the presentation (Scerbo, Warm, Dember, & Grasha, 1992).

We recognize the possibility that "different techniques for note-taking might produce differential encoding or external storage effects" (Kiewra & Dubois,

1991). Several effects of note-taking can be expected: taking notes can provoke a cognitive overload and, on the other hand, repeated exposures to text or lecture information classically results in greater learning (e.g., Kiewra, Mayer, Christensen, Kim, & Risch, 1991).

5.4.2 *Method*

Like Experiment 1, Experiment 2 was conducted with students enrolled in their first year of Business Studies or Business and Public Authority Administration. The results of students with a good knowledge of accountancy (e.g., students repeating a year.) were excluded from the analysis. Eighty-four participants (44 males and 40 females) were randomly assigned to the different experimental conditions. More precisely, three groups of 28 individuals each were thus formed for this condition in which note-taking was permitted.

We re-used the same material as in the first experiment which corresponded to the three formats: "total/partial or no redundancy". The procedure was also similar, with one exception: the instructions advised participants to take their own notes, as they would do in a regular class.

5.4.3 *Results*

5.4.3.1 Learning Outcomes

Once we had checked the homogeneity of the variances in the pre-presentation questionnaire ($F(2, 81) = 2.22$; NS), we tested the equivalence of the prior knowledge of the three groups. The average performance, for the three groups was 5.80 (SD = 2.02). There was no effect of the Group factor ($F(2, 81) = 0.38$; NS). Since the variables are homogeneous (recall questionnaire: $F(2, 81) = 1.33$; NS; transfer questionnaire: $F(2, 81) = 1.58$; NS), we analyzed these two indicators of learning separately by analyzing the variances (ANOVA). Figure 5.5 presents the results on the recall and transfer post-test as a function of presentation condition.

The performances of the three experimental groups were equivalent on the recall questionnaire. We did not obtain any simple effect of redundancy ($F(2, 81) = 0.58$; NS). Moreover, the analysis of variance did not, unlike what we had observed in the preceding experiment, reveal any simple effect of redundancy on the transfer questionnaire ($F(2, 81) = 0.61$; NS).

5.4.3.2 Analyses of Students' Impressions

Table 5.2 presents the median ratings on the subjective impression questionnaire.

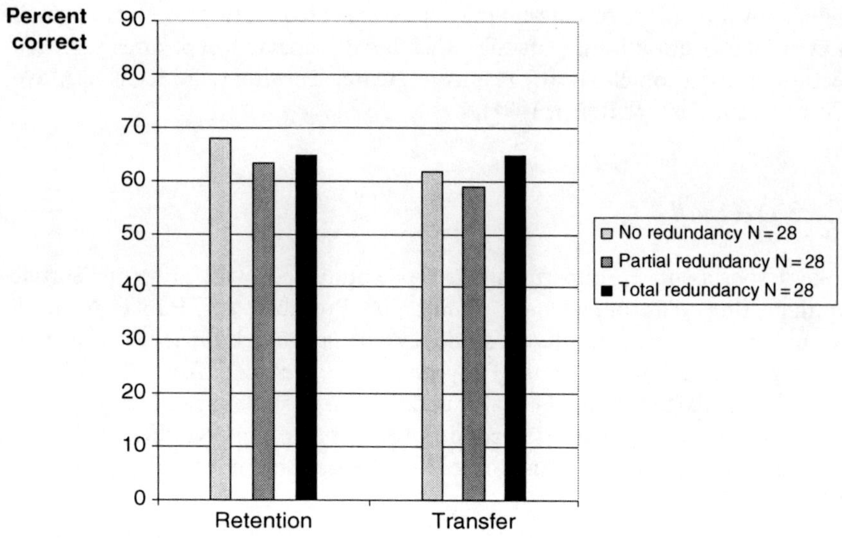

Fig. 5.5 Percentage of correct answers for each type of test

Table 5.2 Median evaluation score for each of the eight assertions, as a function of presentation condition

Item	No redundancy	Partial redundancy	Total redundancy	χ^2(df)	p value
Difficulty of the document	3	3	3	(4) = 4.05	NS
Pleasantness of the document	3	2,5	3	(4) = 6.09	NS
Speed of the document	3	3	3	(6) = 6.37	NS
Interest of the document	3	3	3	(6) = 7.86	NS
Understanding of the document	3	3	3	(6) = 5.03	NS
Suitability of speed	3	3	3	(4) = 7.84	NS
Memorization of the document	3	3	3	(6) = 1.02	NS
Transfer abilities	3	3	2	(6) = 4.45	NS

The level of redundancy did not affect the scores on any of the scales.

5.4.4 Discussion

We did not observe any effect of redundancy level on performances on the recall questionnaire: indeed, the three groups were equivalent from this point of view, just as in the first experiment. Contrary to Experiment 1, all the groups were equivalent on the transfer questionnaire. As a tentative explanation, we suggest that NT distracts the students' visual attention away from the redundant text and towards their notepads. With NT, the various experimental conditions lead to more similar psychological processes, i.e. an attentional focus (Cowan, 1988) which concentrates more on the tables, the spoken explanations and the notepad. This more uniform focus then may result in analogous performances in the different experimental conditions.

The analysis of students' evaluations showed no significant difference across conditions.

5.5 Discussion and General Conclusion

In this study, we have focused on the influence of levels of redundancy on learning and on participants' impressions as a function of whether or not a parallel note-taking (NT) activity is performed.

In the first experiment, the significant difference observed between the "no redundancy" and "total redundancy" groups at the level of the second questionnaire, seems to confirm our first hypothesis. The results we obtained are compatible with those reported in Kalyuga, Chandler, and Sweller's study (1999). In addition, our results indicate that redundancy affects the high-level integrative processes rather than the surface processing of explicitly supplied information as has also been observed in the researches conducted by Mayer and co-workers (for a review, see Mayer, 2001).

According to Kintsch's (1998) comprehension theory, once the text base has been constructed, the representation in working memory is thought to contain "redundant, irrelevant or even mutually contradictory information" (Seigneuric, 1998). The integration process which takes place at the end of each processing cycle in working memory makes it possible to construct a coherent, integrated representation of the text, or "situation model", thanks to the reinforcement of important information and the suppression of irrelevant or peripheral information. We tentatively suggest that the integration stage is more susceptible to failure when the material for processing is redundant. In such a case, the elimination of the useless information requires additional mechanisms (see, for example, Gernsbacher & Faust, 1991). Experiments have demonstrated that these inhibitory processes are very costly in terms of attentional resources (e.g. Engle, Conway, Tuholsky, & Shisler, 1995). This would explain why redundancy particularly affected performance on the transfer questionnaire.

Here, the intermediate format seems to represent a good compromise since it equals the performances obtained with the "no redundancy" format but without being perceived negatively. We assume that the written text, which is presented in summarized form, conveys only the key information which is then retained in working memory in order to establish the coherence of the text.

The absence of differences between the no-redundancy condition and the partially redundant condition is somewhat problematic. The data do not allow us to conclude that the partially redundant condition is more learning effective. This may be because the information that was retained in the partially redundant condition was not the most important or useful. Future studies should use a more explicit procedure in selecting the partially redundant information (terms importance, quantity of information, etc.).

The main difference between the first and second experiment relates to the "total redundancy" format, which in the latter experiment led to performances equivalent to those obtained with the other formats. A possible explanation is that students focused on spoken explanations when taking notes, and spent little time processing the written verbal information (which was totally or partially redundant). The time that is left over is probably devoted to examining the tables. This would explain the equivalence of our three groups here: since the redundancy receives little or no processing, it is largely non-disruptive.

Generally speaking, our results suggest that we should be cautious with regard to the transferable nature of the experimental results taken from studies of presentation formats. Activities, like note-taking, could, like expertise, lead to differentiated effects of the presentation formats on performance and consequently require further investigation. A precise analysis of the various contextual parameters – number of sources of information, sequential or simultaneous presentation, mode and modality of information presentation, element interactivity – will make it possible to understand results which seem contradictory. For example, Moreno and Mayer (2002) defined the redundancy effect by specifying the simultaneous nature of the presentation of the information, thus reducing the generality of this effect. Moreno and Mayer (2002, Exp. 1) have also demonstrated the importance of the sharing of visual attention in order to observe the redundancy effect: in effect, in their study, verbal redundancy is positive when visual attention is not shared between a written text and an animation. At the same time, the work conducted by Kalyuga, Ayres, Chandler, and Sweller (2003) found a close link between expertise and the redundancy of information. For their part, Craig, Gholson, and Driscoll (2002) have examined whether they could replicate the redundancy effect associated with the duplication of information by incorporating virtual pedagogical agents in their document. In fact, this additional factor does not seem to modify the effect.

Our study represents a continuation of this type of research and, we believe, provides new information by adopting a broader perspective on redundancy effects, by operationalizing redundancy in a non-dichotomic way and by using an activity, here the NT task, in parallel to the learning task.

Many more studies need to be conducted in order to identify clearly and precisely the general scope of the redundancy effect – or, rather, the redundancy effects – if we are to provide reliable recommendation schemas to the designers of pedagogical, multimedia documents and the education professionals who make use of these new technologies...

5.6 Appendix

First scale: You found the document: 1 – very difficult; 2 – difficult; 3 – easy; 4 – very easy.
Second scale: You found the document: 1 – very unpleasant; 2 – unpleasant; 3 – pleasant; 4 – very pleasant.
Third scale: You found the document: 1 – very fast; 2 – fast; 3 – slow; 4 – very slow.
Fourth scale: You found the document: 1 – very uninteresting; 2 – uninteresting; 3 – interesting; 4 – very interesting.
Fifth scale: You rate your understanding of the document as: 1 – very bad; 2 – bad; 3 – good; 4 – very good.
Sixth scale: You rate the speed of presentation of the document as: 1 – very unsuitable; 2 – unsuitable; 3 – suitable; 4 – very suitable.
Seventh scale: You rate your memory of the document as: 1 – very bad; 2 – bad; 3 – good; 4 – very good.
Eighth scale: Do you now feel capable of writing the same type of balance sheet but using a different example? 1 – Absolutely not; 2 – with difficulty; 3 – quite easily; 4 – easily.

References

Bannert, M. (2002). Managing cognitive load-recent trends in cognitive load theory. *Learning and instruction, 12,* 139–146.

Barron, A. E., & Atkins, D. (1994). Audio instruction in multimedia education: Is textual redundancy important? *Journal of Educational Multimedia and Hypermedia, 3,* 295–306.

Chandler, P., & Sweller, J. (1991). Cognitive load theory and the format of instruction. *Cognition and Instruction, 8,* 293–332.

Cowan, N. (1988). Evolving conceptions of memory storage, selective attention and their mutual constraints within the human information-processing system. *Psychological Bulletin, 104* (2), 136–191.

Craig, S. D., Gholson, B., & Discoll, D. M. (2002). Animated pedagogical agents in multimedia educational environments: effects of agent properties, picture features, and redundancy. *Journal of Educational Psychology, 94* (2), 428–434.

Engle, R. W., Conway, A. R. A., Tuholski, S. W., & Shisler, R. J. (1995). A resource account of inhibition. *Psychological Science, 6,* 122–125

Gernsbacher, M. N., & Faust, M. E. (1991). The mechanism of suppression: A component of general comprehension skill. *Journal of Experimental Psychology: Learning Memory and Cognition, 17,* 245–262.

Gilabert, R., Martinez, G., & Vidal-Abarca, E. (2005). Some good texts are always better: Text revision to foster inferences of readers with high and low prior background knowledge. *Learning and Instruction, 15,* 45–68.

Harp, S. F., & Mayer, R. E. (1998). How seductive details do their damage: A theory of cognitive interest in science learning. *Journal of Educational Psychology, 90,* 414–434.

Jamet E., & Le Bohec O. (2000, July 19–21). Does the position of words' explanations play a role during text comprehension?*Paper presented at the tenth annual meeting of the society for Text and Discourse.* Lyon, France.

Jamet, E., & Le Bohec, O. (2007). The effect of redundant text in multimedia learning. *Contemporary Educational Psychology, 32,* 588–598.

Kalyuga, S., Ayres, P., Chandler, P., & Sweller, J. (2003). The expertise reversal effect. *Educational Psychologist, 38,* 23–31.

Kalyuga S., Chandler P., & Sweller J. (1998). Levels of expertise and instructional design. *Human Factors, 40,* 1–17.

Kalyuga S., Chandler P., & Sweller J. (1999). Managing split, attention and redundancy in multimedia instruction. *Applied Cognitive Psychology, 13,* 351–372.

Kalyuga S., Chandler P., & Sweller J. (2000). Incorporating learner experience into the design of multimedia instruction. *Journal of Educational Psychology, 92,* 126–136.

Kiewra, K. A. (1985). Investigating notetaking and review: A depth of processing alternative. *Educational Psychologist, 20,* 23–32.

Kiewra, K. A., & Dubois, N. F. (1991). Note-Taking Functions and Techniques. *Journal of Educational Psychology, 83,* 240–245.

Kiewra, K. A., Mayer, R. E., Christensen, M., Kim, S., & Risch, N. (1991). Effects of repetition on recall and note-taking: Strategies for learning from lectures. *Journal of Educational Psychology, 83,* 120–123.

Kintsch, W. (1998). *Comprehension: A paradigm for cognition.* New York: Cambridge University Press.

Le Bohec, O. (2006). Présentation multimodale et apprentissage en ligne. [Multimodal redundant courses and e-learning] In A. PiolatPiolat (Ed.), *Lire, écrire, communiquer et apprendre avec Internet* (pp. 529–555). Marseille : Editions Solal.

Le Bohec, O., & Jamet, E. (2001, 29–30 Oct). Effet de redondance et effet de modalité. Communication présentée aux *Journées d'Études en Psychologie Ergonomiques (EPIQUE).* Nantes, France.

Lewandowski, L. J., & Kobus, D. A. (1993). The effects of redundancy in bimodal word processing. *Human Performance, 6,* 229–239.

Mautone, P. D., & Mayer, R. E. (2001). Signaling as a cognitive guide in multimedia learning. *Journal of Educational Psychology, 93,* 377–389.

Mayer, R. E. (2001). *Multimedia learning.* Cambridge: Cambridge University Press.

Mayer, R. E. (2005). *The Cambridge handbook of multimedia learning.* Cambridge: Cambridge University Press.

Mayer, R. E., Heiser, J., & Lonn, S. (2001). Cognitive constraints on multimedia learning: When presenting more material results in less understanding. *Journal of Educational Psychology, 93,* 187–198.

McNamara, D. S., Kintsch, E., Songer, N. B., & Kintsch, W. (1996). Are good texts always better? Interactions of text coherence, background knowledge, and levels of understanding in learning from text. *Cognition and Instruction, 14*(1), 1–43.

Moreno, R., & Mayer, R. E. (2000). A coherence effect in multimedia learning: The case for minimizing irrelevant sounds in the design of multimedia messages. *Journal of Educational Psychology, 92,* 117–125.

Moreno, R., & Mayer, R. E. (2002). Verbal redundancy in multimedia learning: When reading helps listening. *Journal of Educational Psychology, 92,* 724–733.

Mousavi, S.Y., Low, R., & Sweller, J. (1995). Reducing cognitive load by mixing auditory and visual presentation modes. *Journal of Educational Psychology, 87,* 319–334.

Paas, F. G. W. C., & Van Merrienboer, J. J. G (1993). The efficiency of instructional conditions: An approach to combine mental-effort and performance measure. *Human Factors, 35,* 737–743.

Piolat, A. (2001). *La prise de notes.* Paris : Presse Universitaire de France.

Rickards, J. P., Fajen, B. R., Sullivan, J. F., & Gillespie, G. (1997). Signaling, Notetaking, and FieldField Independence-Dependence in Text Comprehension and Recall. *Journal of Educational Psychology, 89,* 508–517.

Scerbo, M. W., Warm, J. S., Dember, W. N., & Grasha, A. F. (1992). The role of time on cueing in college lecture. *Contemporary Educationnal Psychology, 17,* 312–328.

Seigneuric, A. (1998). *Mémoire de travail et compréhension de l'écrit chez l'enfant*. Doctorat. Université René Descartes, Paris.

Sweller, J. (1999). *Instructional design in technical areas*. Camberwell, Australia: ACER Press.

Sweller, J., Chandler, P., Tierney, P., & Cooper, M. (1990). Cognitive load and selective attention as factors in the structuring of technical material. *Journal of Experimental Psychology: General, 119*, 176–192.

Tricot, A. (1998). Charge cognitive et apprentissage. Une présentation des travaux de John Sweller. *Revue de Psychologie de l'Éducation, 1*, 37–64.

Van Merriënboer, J. J. G., Schuurman, J. G., de Croock, M. B. M., & Paas, F. G. W. C. (2002). Redirecting learners' attention during training: Effects on cognitive load, transfer test performance and training efficiency. *Learning and Instruction, 12*, 11–37.

Yeung, A. S., Jin, P., & Sweller, J. (1997). Cognitive load and learner expertise: Split-Attention and redundancy effects in reading with explanatory notes. *Contemporary Educational Psychology, 23*, 1–21.

Chapter 6
Learning from a Multimedia Explanation: A Comparison of Static Pictures and Animation

Cédric Hidrio and Éric Jamet

Abstract When comprehending multimedia documents, readers face the problem of establishing co-reference between texts and pictures. We hypothesized that cues inserted in animations may reduce the co-reference problem by providing timely updates in the visual display. Students were asked to study an explanation of the four-stroke engine in three different formats. Compared to a spoken explanation alone, an explanation of the four-stroke cycle improved comprehension, recall and inferencing in novice students. A multiple picture version with visual cues, however, failed to make any difference compared to the baseline condition. We suggest that cues may be useful only to the extent that students already possess a visual representation of the verbal referents.

Keywords Animation · Cues · Mapping · Mechanical systems · Pictures · Spoken text · Working memory

6.1 Introduction

The association of texts and pictures in educational resources can be an effective way to facilitate the learning of new subject matter (Anglin, Towers, & Levie, 1996; Carney & Levin, 2002; Levie & Lentz, 1982). For example, the inclusion of illustrations (i.e., analogue representations of the contents to be learned) can improve the understanding and the recall of associated texts (Mayer, 2001). According to multimedia comprehension theorists, the information gained from illustrations supports the construction of mental models (Mayer, 2001); Schnotz, 2001; Gyselinck & Tardieu, 1999). It is not clear, however, whether static and dynamic illustrations have specific effects when presented along with a verbal explanation. The purpose of this study was to assess the effectiveness of

C. Hidrio
University of Rennes II, Laboratory of Experimental Psychology; Place du Recteur H. Le Moal, 35 043 Rennes Cedex, France
e-mail: cedric.hidrio@uhb.fr

J.-F. Rouet et al. (eds.), *Understanding Multimedia Documents*,
DOI: 10.1007/978-0-387-73337-1_6,

static *vs.* animated illustrations as means to support the comprehension of dynamic systems, in this case a mechanical device (see also Bétrancourt et al., Chapter 4). We review current issues concerning the role of pictorial information in the construction of mental models. Then we present an experiment in which we manipulated the amount of pictorial information presented as part of an instructional document.

6.2 Constructing Mental Models from Multimedia Documents

6.2.1 Constructing Mental Models from Texts and Pictures

Several theories have been developed to account for the construction of mental models on the basis of verbal and pictorial information (e.g. Mayer, 2001; Narayan & Hegarty, 1998; Schnotz, 2001). Mayer (2001) suggested that verbal and pictorial information are handled by different processing systems that result in the construction of two mental models – one verbal, the other pictorial – which are finally integrated within a single mental model on the basis of prior knowledge. However, as Schnotz, Böckheler, and Grzondziel (1999) pointed out, there is no specific empirical support for this parallelism between verbal and pictorial processing. Moreover, the process responsible for integrating the representations resulting from the two sources of information is not stated and seems problematic, since it would have to operate between representations that are different in nature (i.e., symbolic *vs.* analogue). The model proposed by Narayanan and Hegarty (1998) accounts for the construction of mental models on the basis of texts and illustrations in the specific case of the description of mechanical systems. One of the interests of this model lies in the fact that it distinguishes the construction of a static model of the system that is thought to precede the construction of a dynamic model (i.e., that relates to the functioning of the system). But here again, it is necessary to address the question of the cooperation between representations involving signs that are fundamentally different in nature.

In their general model of text and picture comprehension, Schnotz and his colleagues (Schnotz, 2001; Schnotz, 2002; Schnotz, Böckheler, & Grzondziel, 1999; Schnotz & Bannert, 2003) make a distinction between the different systems of representations involved in the processing of pictures and the processing of language. According to Schnotz (2001), language constitutes a system of symbolic representation (which is called descriptive) in the sense that words are arbitrarily related to what they represent. In contrast, a picture shares properties and dimensions of reality with the referent. Pictures thus constitute a system of analogue representations (which Schnotz calls depictive). These two systems of representation, descriptive and depictive, are thought to complement one another in contributing to the construction of the mental model.

As far as text information is concerned, linguistic processes ensure the construction of a propositional textbase that represents the ideas in the text in the form of a hierarchical series of semantic propositions (cf. van Dijk & Kintsch, 1983). Following the textbase construction, semantic processes operate in order to achieve a deeper level of representation, which integrates text information with the reader's prior knowledge (or mental model of the text). This construction phase implies the transition from a symbolic representation (descriptive) to an analogue representation (depictive). Once the mental model has been established, model inspection processes make it possible to read off new information that is not explicitly expressed by the text. This new information can then be formulated in propositional form before being integrated in the propositional representation.

Illustrations, for their part, constitute a system of analogue representations. Pictures convey meaning directly without using an arbitrary symbolic code (e.g., language). The semantic information to be extracted is here directly dependent on the environment, i.e. on its actual perception. Faced with an illustration, the initial stages of processing consist in creating a perceptual representation of the graphic information. First, visual information is selected through the top-down activation of schemata and then visually organised via automated visual routines. The application of schemata further allows the mapping of the perceptual representation onto the model that is being built. The graphical entities are mapped to the entities of the mental model, and the spatial relations that structure the picture are mapped to the semantic relations. The mapping process can help both to build a mental model from a picture and to evaluate the quality of an already constructed mental model in the light of a presented picture. Finally, a mental model constructed on the basis of illustrations can generate a propositional representation via model inspection processes.

Schnotz (2002) also states that picture perception and imagery both point to the same cognitive processes. In other words, the construction of a mental model based a perceived picture or a mentally generated picture operates in the same way. Denis and de Vega (1993) have suggested a similar idea, considering "mental images" to be a means of instantiating a mental model.

In summary, the construction of a mental model in a learning context based on illustrated text documents depends both on (i) the construction process that operates on the basis of a propositional representation and (ii) the analogue mapping to visually perceived information. As a result, actual perception (direct or in imaged form) of the analogue information appears to be a key factor in the establishment of mental models.

6.2.2 Processing Static and Dynamic Illustrations

In the design of electronic learning resources, a central question is whether to choose static or animated visuals to complement an explanatory text. Despite the widespread assumption that animated visuals are more effective than static ones, the research literature reveals no clear advantage of one format over the other (Betrancourt & Tversky, 2000; see also Bétrancourt et al., Chapter 4). It seems that a variety of factors have to be taken into account in order to make valid comparisons of static and animated pictures. These factors include the subject matter of the document, learner characteristics, the type of task, and the modality of the accompanying text presentation.

When comparing static and dynamic illustrations, it is necessary to consider how these two depictive informational sources differ and how these differences may affect the construction of mental models. One representational advantage of animations over static pictures is their capacity to represent dynamic changes directly (Lowe, 1999). This direct depiction can convey different levels of analogue information about the referent situation. Animations may contribute three levels of additional information, depending on the subject matter of the depicted situation:

(1) The animation does not contribute any additional analogue information. The order of the pictures is not informative (random order) and the sequential character of the animation is used either simply to present a variety of static images or to direct attention to certain parts of a static illustration. The former case covers, for example, the presentation of various software screen shots in order to depict the program's user interface (e.g. in the form of an animated GIF). In the latter case, a dynamic guidance code is applied to the static illustration in order to attract the subject's attention to certain specific parts of the visual (e.g. by highlighting them). This type of presentation using highlighted images would primarily be of use for the synchronised presentation of verbal auditory material: the highlighting would ensure that the verbal information and the corresponding images are simultaneously present in WM, thus constituting an optimised presentation format to permit their co-referencing (see, e.g., the. *temporal contiguity effect,* Mayer & Anderson, 1991, 1992; *or the split-attention effect*, Jeung, Chandler, & Sweller, 1997; Sweller, 1999). An example of this type of dynamic presentation that provides no additional information would be the sequential highlight-based presentation of a system in its static state.

(2) The animation contributes analogue information relating to a single dimension of the situation to be explained. The animation is used for the sequential presentation of information relating to a situation in a precise order. In most cases, this order of presentation reflects the temporal progression of the situation (e.g. the stages in a cycle). To a lesser extent, the sequence of images may also reflect non-temporal dimensions, such as spatial dimension (the order may correspond, for example, to spatial distances, e.g. an animation presenting the planets of the solar system one after the other as a function of their increasing distance from the sun), or even dimensions that are not directly perceptible such as a hierarchical or thematic organization etc. However, in the case of such dimensions, there is little point using a sequence for representational purposes since they can be represented more appropriately via the spatial medium (i.e. use of static illustrations).

(3) The animation contributes analogue information relating to the visuospatial events characteristic of a situation. The sequence of images is used in order to create an illusion of movement intended as a continuous representation of the transformations of the situation's spatio-temporal dimension. In other words, the animation enables the analogue representation of the visual and spatial characteristics of a given situation. For example, this type of animation makes it possible to represent the operation of moving systems (e.g. pump systems etc.).

Thus, a dynamic presentation of visual information can communicate different levels of analogue information concerning the reference situation. It appears that sequences of pictures are particularly efficient when they represent movements, directions, and spatial relations. When presented with a static illustration representing such information, subjects must engage in active processes in order to extract the corresponding analogue information. The effective extraction of this information would depend firstly on the perception of the visual information that is to be manipulated (Hegarty & Just, 1989), and then on the application of a spatial visualization process (Sims & Hegarty, 1997). These inferences from static materials can be particularly costly in terms of cognitive resources (Narayanan & Hegarty, 1998), since they are dependent, in particular, on the complexity of the material to be manipulated (e.g. Hegarty & Kozhevnikov, 1999), the subjects' visuospatial skills (Hegarty & Just, 1989, 1993) and prior knowledge (cf. Mayer, 2001). The use of a code to guide these spatial visualization processes is therefore thought to benefit the processing of static illustrations (Weidenmann, 1994).

Thus, as far as situations involving visuospatial events are concerned, static illustrations must be the object of supplementary processes in order to extract certain items of analogue information that are necessary in order to establish the mental model. The animations directly supply this information in perceptual form. Nevertheless, despite this apparent benefit, animation can result in specific processing difficulties:

(1) The fleetingness of animation imposes information extraction difficulties (Schnotz, 2001). The speed at which events are displayed and the number of animated elements that have to be taken into account appears to be a main source of processing difficulty (Lightner, 2001). Lowe (2003) refers to this as the imposition on learners of excessive information processing demands ("overwhelming").
(2) The presence of animated illustrations may exempt learners from mentally animating the iconic information, i.e. they fail to process the pictorial material deeply ("learners as viewers", Schnotz, 2001). This results in a reduction in the extent to which learners engage in valuable processing activities ("underwhelming", Lowe, 2003). Static illustrations may therefore be more effective than animations for the construction of the mental models (Schnotz, Böckheler, & Grzondziel, 1999). When confronted with static illustrations, subjects would therefore necessarily be active given the required spatial visualization operations.

(3) Animations also seem to impose specific difficulties on learners who are novices in the depicted domain because they select non relevant visuospatial information (Lowe, 1999).

The first point seems to be particularly important since the complexity of the visual material may have negative consequences on the subject's involvement in the activity of comprehension. The excessive information density of certain animations may discourage subjects from actively processing the document. Given these considerations, the use of animations may be beneficial (i) when the information density is sufficiently low to be apprehended by the learner's cognitive system (ii) when the learner adopts the strategy of actively processing the information.

However, these processing difficulties have been observed in situations in which animations were displayed with on-screen texts or no text at all. One way to overcome difficulties caused by on-screen texts or lack of verbal support would be to use the auditory modality to present explanatory text.

6.2.3 Auditory Presentation of Verbal Information

The use of spoken texts allows the verbal and corresponding pictorial information, to be processed simultaneously in working memory. Beneficial effects of animation on learning audio texts are observed when the audio commentary is presented at the same time as the animation, but not when it follows or precedes the animation (Mayer & Anderson, 1991, 1992). The effective co-referencing of the verbal and pictorial information is a central process since (i) the effective construction of a mental model requires the presence of depictive elements corresponding to the descriptive elements and (ii) the effective generation of propositions on the basis of the mental model requires the existence of descriptive elements corresponding to the depictive elements.

The role of the auditory information is not limited to presenting content information. Auditory information can also assist the visuospatial processing of animations by directing learner attention to relevant parts of the display. The synchronisation of the two presentations allows verbal information to guide processing of the pieces of pictorial material by sequentially signaling the pictorial information that has to be extracted. Synchronicity could also promote the active processing of the animation. In effect, the simultaneously provided verbal information could act as a series of instructions resulting in the active processing of certain parts of the animation. As a result, the subjects would be less inclined to behave as viewers since they are asked to perform the indicated visuospatial processing. Thus, the use of audio text seems particularly well suited for the processing of animations because of the synchronicity it allows.

One may question whether static pictures with audio text can be as efficient as an animation. Static illustrations can indeed be presented with a simultaneous accompanying audio text. However specific processing difficulties should arise from (i) the need to locate the relevant parts of the picture (corresponding to the audio material) and (ii) the mental manipulations required to re-create the dynamics of the phenomenon to be understood (e.g. the mental rotation of an object). Indeed, the beneficial effects of illustrations appear when the co-referencing between verbal and pictorial information is performed (e.g. Mayer & Anderson, 1991, 1992). When a spoken comment is used in addition to the static illustration and the described situation involves visuospatial events, co-referencing between what is verbally described and the corresponding analogue information can occur only if a perceptual simulation of the events is simultaneously performed on the basis of the illustration. This simulation cannot start until the subject has identified the point on the illustration to which the spatial visualization processes are to be applied.

6.3 Experiment

6.3.1 Rationale

The continuous presentation of auditory verbal information means that co-referencing operations have to be performed within a very brief period of time. As a consequence, we can expect static illustrations to be less effective than animations when simultaneously presented with an audio text. To address this issue, we examined the effectiveness of different kinds of illustrations (static and dynamic) on the learning of a spoken text describing the functioning of a mechanical system. To this end, we designed illustrations that differed in the way the analogue spatiotemporal information was represented (Single static illustration *vs.* Multiple static pictures with arrows *vs.* Animation). As we manipulated the ease of analogue information extraction in the illustrations, we manipulated the possibility of (i) mapping this information onto mental models and (ii) connecting this information with the corresponding verbal information. We predicted that the easier the extraction of analogue information relating to a situation (i.e. provision at the perceptual level of this information or the resources that permits it to be extracted), the better the mental model. In other words, compared to an audio-only baseline situation, a single static picture should lead to no or little beneficial effect because of the difficulty of coreferencing. Supplementary static illustrations successively representing the main steps of the situation with arrows simulating visuospatial events (e.g., translation) should minimise these difficulties and help learners to instantiate higher quality mental models. Finally, the animated format should be more effective than both static formats by providing directly the analogue information required for the construction of mental models, and facilitating coreference with the spoken text.

6.3.2 Method

6.3.2.1 Participants

The participants were 97 French student volunteers from the psychology department at the University of Rennes 2, France. One hundred and thirty-nine subjects originally took part in the experiment. Eleven subjects were dropped because of their high prior knowledge of the functioning of 4-stroke engines (as assessed in a pre-test, see below). The remaining 128 subjects were randomly assigned to one of the four conditions (32 subjects per group). At the end of the experiment, the results of 19 subjects proved to be unusable because of a computer-related problem. The results of 12 further subjects were excluded from the analyses because these subjects did not reply to any of the questions on the questionnaire. These subjects had decided to give up the experiment following the presentation of the documents. As a consequence, there were 17 subjects in the audio only group, 22 in the single illustration group, 27 in the multiple illustrations with arrows group and 31 in the audio plus animation group. Only 4 males participated in the experiment (1 per group). This was due to the low proportion of males enrolled for psychology courses and our requirement for novice participants. Males appeared to have more knowledge about car mechanics than females (of the 11 subjects removed because of their prior knowledge of car mechanics, 10 were males).

6.3.2.2 Materials

Four versions of an instructional document explaining the functioning of the four-stroke engine were constructed using *Macromedia*® *Flash*™ 5.0 software (2000), based on a web site that aims to explain the functioning of different systems (www.howstuffworks.com). The same verbal material was used for all 4 experimental conditions and consisted of two texts narrated by a male voice at constant speed.

1. *Introduction (Text 1)*. The Introduction text (145 words lasting 50 s) explained the underlying operation of an engine by analogy with the operation of a canon. It also provided general information about engines (e.g. engines typically have four cylinders). The function of this part was to introduce the second text. Two versions of this introduction were built: one presented only the verbal material (spoken text alone) and the other presented the spoken text with static pictures. The spoken text alone version was designed for the audio only condition and the picture version for the three illustrated conditions.
2. *Function description (Text 2)*. The Function description text described the four-stroke combustion cycle (i.e. intake, compression, ignition, exhaust) by which an engine converts gasoline into motion. This part of the document contained 180 words and lasted about 80 s. Below is the portion of the text describing the first stroke:

"During stroke 1, intake: (i)The piston moves down into the cylinder; (ii) The intake valve opens due to the operation of the camshaft; (iii) Air and gas enter the cylinder (iv) When the piston has fully descended, the outlet valve closes due to the operation of the camshaft."(translated from French).
Four versions of this description, each using an identical narration, were designed as a function of the quantity of iconic information provided simultaneously with the verbal description:

- No pictorial information

  The spoken text was presented with no other information.

- Single illustration

  A single static picture was presented simultaneously with the spoken text. The illustration consisted of a cross-section of an engine (see Fig. 6.1).

- Multiple illustrations with arrows

  Four different illustrations appeared successively and succeeded each other on the screen as the narration progressed. Each illustration depicted a cross-section of an engine identical to the one provided in the single illustration

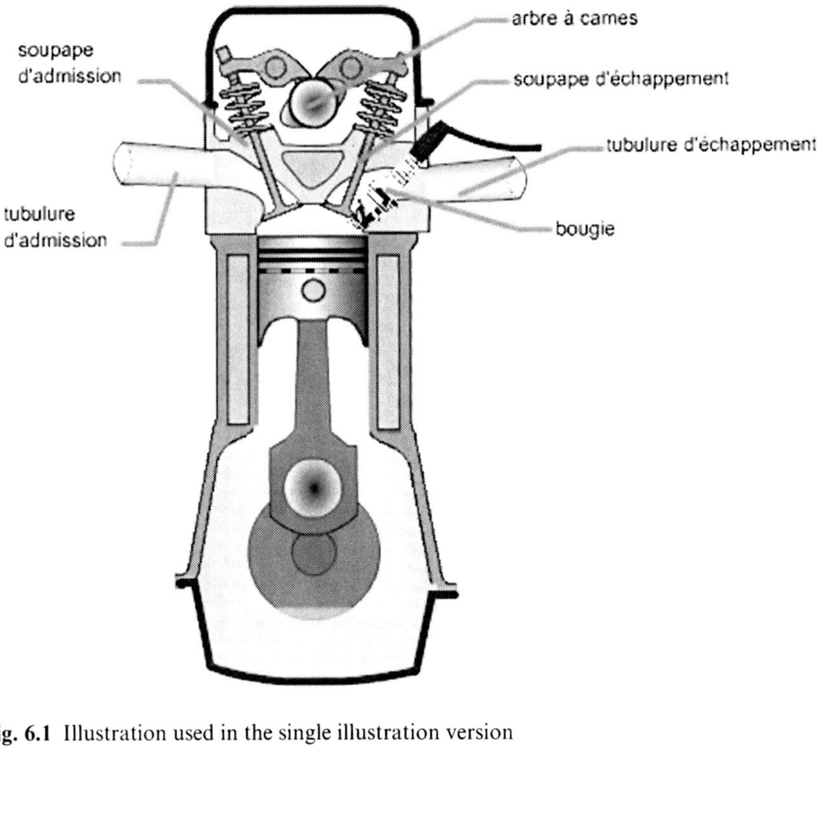

Fig. 6.1 Illustration used in the single illustration version

version of the document, except that the relevant elements (i.e. piston, valves and camshaft) were displayed in the specific positions corresponding to the stroke that was being described (i.e. the middle of the stroke). Arrows were also added to simulate element movements (for the piston, crankshaft and camshaft). Valves were depicted as either opened or closed. Arrows were also provided to indicate the current state of the air-gasoline mixture (e.g. incoming arrows for the intake stroke). Figure 6.2 shows the sequence of these frames.

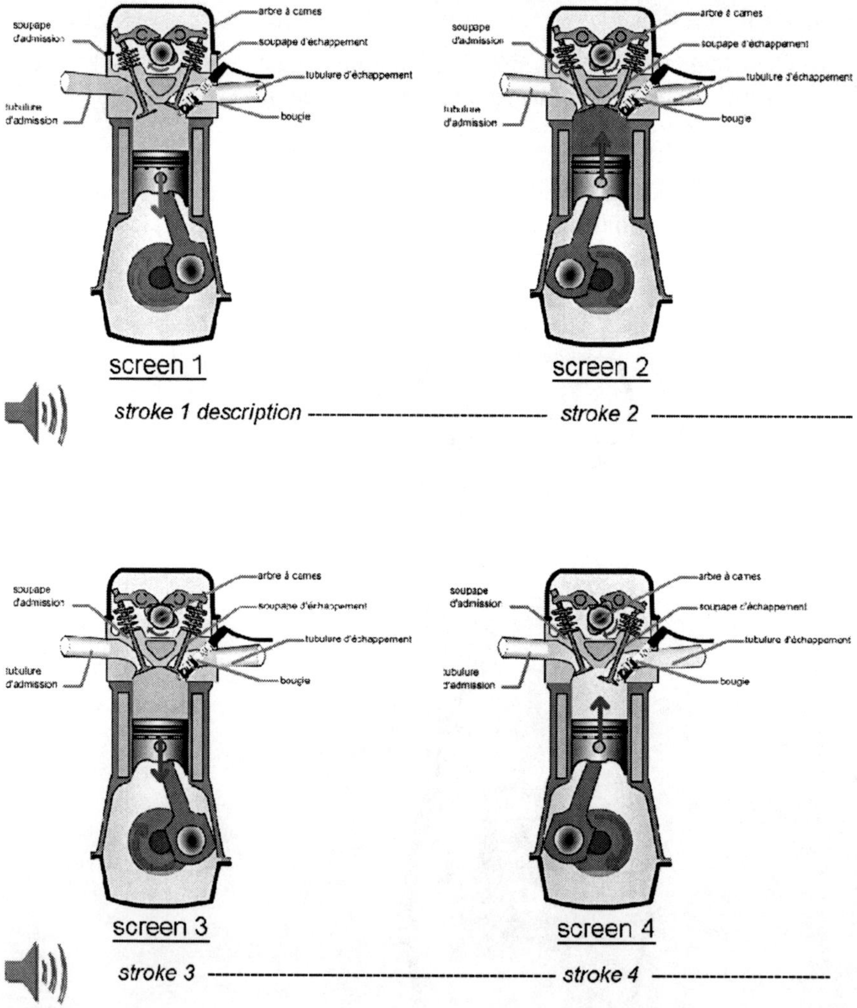

Fig. 6.2 Succession of illustrations provided in the "multiple illustrations with arrows" condition

- Animation

The verbal description was synchronised with an animated version of the cross-section illustration used in the other illustrated documents. The visuospatial events described in the commentary were simultaneously illustrated on screen and therefore did not have to be inferred.

The three picture conditions shared some additional features:

- Smooth transitions were inserted between the descriptions of two successive strokes in order to avoid any movement effect due to the succession of the static pictures in the multiple static illustration condition.
- Labels were displayed for the most important parts (see Figs. 6.1 and 6.2) (identical for all picture conditions).
- Pictures were available only when the verbal material was playing. At the end of the spoken description, the pictures disappeared.
- In all four conditions, the document (i.e., text 1 + text 2) was presented 3 times in succession, with the subjects clicking on a button to start each new presentation.

A pre-test and the two post-tests were presented on separate 21 × 29.7 cm sheets of paper. The pre-test consisted of three questions (only one answer was accepted for each question): "how many pistons does a 6 cylinder engine have?"; "what is a two-liter engine?" and "what is the function of the crankshaft in an engine?". This pre-test was designed to select people with no background knowledge of the functioning of 4-stroke engines. The post-tests included a recall questionnaire and an inference questionnaire. The recall questionnaire asked subjects to recall the functioning of each stroke (four open-ended questions, e.g. question 1 "What happens during the first stroke? "). This post-test simply asked subjects to recall semantic information explicitly stated in the auditory description of the system (the subjects were not asked for literal recall). The purpose of this test was to determine the quality of the subjects' propositional representation of the document.

The inference test consisted of ten inferential questions concerning the functioning of four-stroke engines. The answers were not explicitly stated in the document, but had to be inferred from the newly acquired knowledge. One example of these questions is "What stroke is really active? Justify". This type of question required the production of elaborative inferences and was intended to draw upon subjects' mental model of the situation.

6.3.2.3 Procedure

The participants started by answering the pre-test. Only the subjects who did not answer any of the questions in this test were invited to continue the experiment. The subjects were then randomly allocated to one of the four groups and seated individually in front of a computer. The experimenter informed them that they were about to listen (and to watch, depending on the processing mode assigned to the group) to an explanation of how a car's engine works. The experimenter told them to understand and memorise as much information as possible in order to answer questions in the testing phase. The subjects were informed that the document would be presented three times and that they only had to click on the buttons that were displayed one after the other on the screen throughout the experiment. To begin the experiment, they put on headphones and launched the document themselves by clicking the Start button on the screen. After the subjects had finished the learning phase (which lasted about six minutes), they were asked to answer the two post-tests. No time limit was imposed for this testing phase. The entire experiment lasted about forty minutes.

6.3.3 Results

A scorer who was not aware of the experimental conditions assessed the answers given in the two post-tests. The recall questionnaire was scored on the basis of the number of correctly recalled "idea units". Fifteen idea units corresponding to the fifteen steps described in the narration were extracted from the text and one point was given for each correctly recalled idea unit. Half a point was given for answers that were correct but incomplete (e.g., recalling that in the first stroke "the valve opens" instead of "the intake valve opens"). The maximum score for this post-test was fifteen.

Each correctly answered question in the inference test scored one point. Half a point was given if the answer was correct but incomplete. For instance, consider the question:

"Some four-cylinder car engines have sixteen valves instead of eight. What is this increase in the number of valves intended to do? "

A *correct answer* (one point) may be formulated as follows "It speeds up the first and the last stroke" (i.e., the correct answer must contain the two ideas that (i) incoming air and gas enters the cylinder more rapidly and (ii) are ejected more rapidly".

An *incomplete answer* would contain only a part of the requested answer (e.g. "it speeds up the last stroke" or "it speeds up the first stroke").

6.3.3.1 Data analysis

The results obtained on the two questionnaires, expressed as a percentage of the maximum possible score, are presented in Fig. 6.3. An analysis of variance was performed taking account of both between (learning conditions) and within-group factors (type of question). The dependent variable used in these analyses was the percentage of correct responses provided in the two post-tests.

The percentage of correct responses given to the inference questions (M = 39.84, SD = 19.65) was lower than the text information recall percentage (M = 50.36, SD = 25.28; $F(1, 93) = 21.88$, $p < 0.05$). We observed a main effect

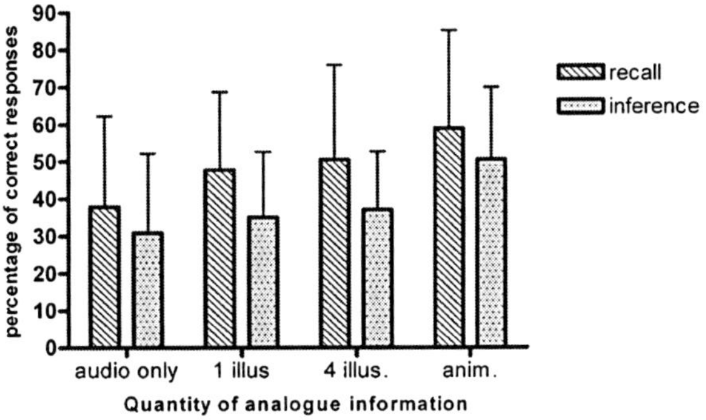

Fig. 6.3 Proportion correct on recall and inference tests for the four groups

of the presentation condition: $F(3, 93) = 4.88, p < 0.05$. There was no Question type x Quantity of analogue information interaction: $F(3, 93) = 0.52, p < 0.05$.

A multivariate analysis of variance applied to recall and inferences and taking Quantity of analogue information as sole factor, revealed a significant effect of this factor on the two learning indicators (recall: $F(3, 93) = 2.83$, $p < 0.05$, inferences: $F(3, 93) = 5.64, p < 0.05$).

As far as recall is concerned, multiple comparisons (Dunn-Bonferroni adjustment) indicated a significant difference between two of the groups: on average, the Animation group (M = 58.98, SD = 26.21) recalled more core ideas than the Audio only group (M = 37.81, $p = 24.45$), MD = 21.17, $p < 0.05$. No other comparison was significant.

As far as the production of elaborative inferences is concerned, the multiple comparisons indicate that, on average, the Animation version allowed subjects to respond more accurately (M = 50.64, SD = 19.26) than in the Audio only (M = 30.88, SD = 21.30), MD = 19.76, $p < 0.05$, the Single illustration (M = 35, SD = 17.66), MD = 15.64, $p < 0.05$, and the Multiple illustrations (M = 37.03, SD = 15.70), MD = 13.61, $p < 0.05$ conditions. There was no significant difference between the Audio, Single illustration and Multiple illustrations groups.

6.4 Discussion and Conclusions

The purpose of our study was to examine the specific properties of dynamic illustrations, as means to foster the comprehension of an explanation presented as spoke text. Based on a theoretical model of multimedia comprehension, we assumed that animated illustrations would improve the comprehension of a spoken explanation of a dynamic system, compared to static illustrations or no illustration at all, because they would facilitate coreference across sources of information.

Animations did improve the quality of students' mental model, as evidenced by their production of more accurate elaborative inferences. This beneficial effect of the animation on comprehension can also be seen in the greater level of recall of verbal information. We interpret this phenomenon as the consequence of the construction of a more effective mental model: the model inspection processes (Schnotz, 2001) make it possible to generate verbal information relating to the situation irrespectively of whether or not this information refers to the explicit context of the text.

The addition of a single static illustration or multiple static illustrations with arrows did not result in the construction of a better mental model compared to the control condition. It may be that these static illustrations were not as attractive as the animations, and that the subjects were frustrated at not seeing the events on screen while they were being verbally described. This might have resulted in a fall-off in motivation and a reduced commitment to the task. However, we observed no difference between the single illustration and multiple illustrations with arrows controls. If this were due to a motivation-related effect, we would have expected to observe better results in the multiple illustrations with arrows condition because this was visually more attractive, with new pictorial information being displayed on screen every 3 or 4 sentences.

An alternative explanation could be formulated in terms of the processing difficulties imposed by the static conditions. In order to ensure the co-referencing of the verbal and analogue information while listening to the explanations, the subjects in both static conditions had to (i) locate the referents in the illustration and (ii) simulate the described visuospatial events. In the animation condition, the synchronisation between the spoken text and the animation permitted the co-presence in working memory of the visuospatial events and the corresponding verbal labels. This facilitated the localisation process and there was no need to simulate the visuospatial events. These additional processes involved in the processing of static illustrations may have been too complex to undertake during the simultaneous processing of the verbal information (excessive cognitive load). Since the subjects were unable to locate the information and perform the required mental simulations in the time available, they could not access the analogue information required for the instantiation of an effective mental model (cf. Schnotz, 2001).

If this explanatory hypothesis is correct, any cue that facilitates the localisation and simulation of visuospatial events within static illustrations should result in the construction of higher quality mental models. However, the addition of static illustrations and arrows did not have the expected effect on performance. Instead, this additional information may have improved the simulation of the visuospatial events, not the localisation of the elements. Since these visuospatial simulations are subordinate to the actual localisation of the elements, the subjects were apparently unable to exploit the additional information provided in the multiple illustrations with arrows condition.

More experiments are needed in order to verify this explanatory hypothesis. Such experiments could, for example, assess the effects of pauses in the spoken commentary while the static illustration continues to be displayed on screen. The pauses should provide the time necessary to identify the locations of the elements and perform the pictorial simulations necessary for co-referencing.

Similarly, during the processing of the spoken commentary, highlighting the visual elements that are to be processed mentally should make it easier to locate them. Jeung, Chandler, and Sweller (1997) have shown that the use of highlighting helps ensure better co-referencing of the auditory and visual information sources. Another way of facilitating the localisation of the elements might be to provide information concerning their location prior to the processing of the illustrations. Mayer, Matthias, and Wetzell (2002) have demonstrated the positive effect of a pre-training consisting of the presentation of the elements of a system. This pre-training preceded the learning of a commented animation describing the functioning of the system in question. In the case of static visual information, prior knowledge of the location of the elements on the illustration should allow subjects to allocate all their resources to the mental simulation of the described events. This might make it possible to observe the benefits associated with the joint presentation of auditory and static visual information.

References

Anglin, G. J., Towers, R. L., & Levie, W. H. (1996). Visual message design and learning: The role of static and dynamic illustrations. In D. H. Jonassen (Ed.), *Handbook of research for educational communications and technology* (pp. 755–794). New York: MacMillan.

Bétrancourt, M., & Tversky, B. (2000). Effects of computer animation on users' performance: A review. *Le Travail Humain, 63,* 311–329.

Carney, R. N., & Levin, J. R. (2002). Pictorial illustrations still improves students' learning from text. *Educational Psychology Review, 14,* 5–26.

Denis, M., & De Vega, M. (1993). Modèles mentaux et imagerie mentale. In M. F. Ehrlich, H. Tardieu, & M. Cavazza (Eds.), *Les modèles mentaux : Approche cognitive des représentations.* Paris: Masson.

Gyselinck, V., & Tardieu, H. (1999). The role of illustrations in text comprehension: What, when, for whom and why? In S. R. Goldman & H. van Oostendorp (Eds.), *The construction of mental representations during reading* (pp. 195–218). N.J.: Lawrence Erlbaum Associates.

Hegarty, M., & Just, M. A. (1989). Understanding machines from text and diagrams. In H. Mandl & J. Levin (Eds.), *Knowledge acquisition from text and pictures.* Amsterdam: North Holland (Elsevier Science Publishers).

Hegarty, M., & Just, M. A. (1993). Constructing mental models of machines from text and diagrams. *Journal of Memory and Language, 32,* 717–742.

Hegarty, M., & Kozhevnikov, M. (1999). Spatial reasoning abilities, working memory, and mechanical reasoning. In J. S. Gero & B. Tversky (Eds.), *Visual and Spatial Reasoning in Design* (pp. 1–19). Sydney: Key Center of Design Computing and Cognition.

Jeung, H. J., Chandler, P., & Sweller, J. (1997). The role of visual indicators in dual sensory mode instruction. *Educational Psychology, 17,* 329–343.

Levie, W. H., & Lentz, R. (1982). Effects of texts illustrations: A review of research. *Education Communication and Technology Journal, 30,* 195–232.

Lightner, N. (2001). Model testing of users' comprehension in graphical animation: The effects of speed and focus areas. *International Journal of Human-Computer Interaction, 13*(1), 53–73.

Lowe, R. K. (1999). Extracting information from an animation during complex visual learning. *European Journal of Psychology of Education, 14,* 225–244.

Lowe, R. K. (2003). Animation and learning: selective processing of information in dynamic graphics. *Learning and Instruction, 13,* 157–176.

Macromedia. (2000). *Flash 5.0* [Computer program]. San Francisco: Author.

Mayer, R. E. (2001). *Multimedia learning*. Cambridge University Press.

Mayer R. E., & Anderson R. B. (1991). Animations need narration: An experimental test of dual coding hypothesis. *Journal of Educational Psychology, 83,* 484–490.

Mayer R. E., & Anderson R. B. (1992). The instructive animation: Helping students build connections between words and pictures in multimedia learning. *Journal of Educational Psychology, 84,* 444–452.

Mayer, R. E., Matthias, A., & Wetzell, K. (2002). Fostering understatnding of multimedia messages through pre-training: Evidence for a two-stage theory of mental model construction. *Journal of Experimental Psychology: Applied,* 8, 147–154.

Narayanan, N. H., & Hegarty, M. (1998). On designing comprehensible interactive hypermedia manuals. *International Journal of Human-Computer Studies, 48,* 267–301.

Schnotz, W. (2001). Sign systems, technologies, and the acquisition of knowledge. In J. -F. Rouet, J. J. Levonen, & A. Biardeau (Eds.), *Multimedia learning: Cognitive and instructional issues* (pp. 9–30). London: Elsevier Science.

Schnotz, W. (2002). Towards an integrated view of learning from text and visual displays. *Educational Psychology Review,* 14, 101–120.

Schnotz, W., & Bannert, M. (2003). Construction and interference in learning from multiple representation. *Learning and Instruction, 13,* 141–156.

Schnotz, W., Böckheler J., & Grzondziel, H. (1999). Individual and cooperative learning with interactive and animated pictures. *European Journal of Psychology of Education, 2,* 245–265.

Sims, V. K., & Hegarty, M. (1997). Mental animation in the visual-spatial sketchpad: Evidence from dual-task studies, *Memory and Cognition, 25,* 321–332.

Sweller, J. (1999). *Instructional design in technical areas*. Camberwell, Australia: Acer Press.

Van Dijk, T. A., & Kintsch, W. (1983). *Strategies for discourse comprehension*. New-York: Academic Press.

Weidenmann, B. (1994). Codes of instructional pictures. In W. Schnotz & R. Kulhavy (Eds.), *Comprehension of graphics* (pp. 29–42). Amsterdam: North Holland.

Part II
Contextual Strategies in Document-Based Learning

Chapter 7
Search and Comprehension Processes in Learning from Text

Raquel Cerdán, Tomás Martínez, Eduardo Vidal-Abarca, Ramiro Gilabert, Laura Gil, and Jean-François Rouet

Abstract We analyzed the relationships between comprehension skill and search strategies in instructional text. In two experiments, college-level readers were asked to search a computer-presented science text in order to answer different types of questions. High level questions required the integration of information across paragraphs, whereas low level questions requested the localization of information within a single paragraph. High level questions were re-read more often and they resulted in broader text search patterns. Furthermore, students who were diagnosed as good comprehenders located relevant sections of the text faster and spent more time on those sections. Poor comprehenders, on the other hand, showed more "erratic" search patterns, spending more time on irrelevant portions of the materials. The results support the view that skilled comprehension involves the ability to allocate various levels of attention to different portions of the text, depending on contextual constraints.

Keywords Comprehension skill · Individual differences · Monitoring · On-line measures · Questions · Search

7.1 Introduction

This chapter investigates the cognitive processes at work when readers search texts in order to answer questions. More specifically, our purpose is to elicit the strategic aspects of text-based question answering, and the relationship between search strategies and comprehension outcomes.

Text comprehension is a complex ability in which simultaneous processes need to be carried out by the reader. According to Kintsch and van Dijk model (Kintsch, 1998; Kintsch & van Dijk, 1978; van Dijk & Kintsch, 1983) these processes are mainly a series of processing cycles. During each cycle, the reader acquires a small amount of information, roughly corresponding to one sentence.

R. Cerdán
Department of Educational Psychology, University of Valencia, 21 avenue Blasco Ibanez, 46010 Valencia, Spain
e-mail: Raquel.Cerdan@uv.es

J.-F. Rouet et al. (eds.), *Understanding Multimedia Documents*,
DOI: 10.1007/978-0-387-73337-1_7, © Springer Science+Business Media, LLC 2008

This involves constructing semantic propositions that underlie the meaning of the sentence, connecting the propositions through various types of links (e.g., coreference, causal and temporal relationships), and maintaining a small subset of propositions in working memory, in order to connect them to the next processing cycle. This process goes on during each subsequent cycle, allowing the reader to construct progressively an interconnected network of semantic propositions, or *textbase* in Kintsch and van Dijk's (1978) terminology.

Text comprehension also involves the retrieval of knowledge from the reader's long term memory. Retrieval from long term memory is cued by the concepts and propositions encountered in the current cycle. Knowledge retrieved from LTM is integrated with text information and becomes part from the reader's representation in long term memory, or *situation model* (van Dijk & Kintsch, 1983). The amount of knowledge available prior to reading a text determines the elaborateness of a reader's situation model.

These processes involved in text comprehension are, on the one hand, highly resource demanding and, on the other hand, not always carried out by all the readers, who many times fail to construct a well integrated representation of the text which both captures the ideas present in the text itself and connects them to the reader's background knowledge.

The requirements may increase when students are asked not only to comprehend the ideas in the text, but also to use them in order to perform a specific task, such as answering questions or solving problems. Despite the potential overload in resources, giving the students questions to answer after or before reading a text has been traditionally used to foster comprehension and learning from text. In fact, there is a vast literature on the use of different types of questions to improve and facilitate the above mentioned processes involved in text comprehension. (e.g., Andre, 1979; Hamilton, 1985; Hartley & Davies, 1976; Rickards, 1979; Wixson, 1983; Vidal-Abarca, Mengual, Sanjose, & Rouet 1996; Vidal-Abarca, Gilabert, & Rouet, 1998). But the extent to which answering questions contributes to building a mental representation from text will depend on which comprehension processes they are specifically inducing, either higher level processes such as integration of distant information via inferences or low-level processes such as location of one or two pieces of information. Broadly speaking, high-level questions, those that precisely require connecting distant information via inferences, have been found to help readers reach a better comprehension of the text, in comparison to low-level questions (Andre, 1979; Rouet & Vidal-Abarca, 2002; Vidal-Abarca et al., 1996).

7.2 Theoretical Background

7.2.1 Cognitive Processes in Searching for Information in Documents to Answer Questions

Answering questions after or before reading a text is, therefore, an activity which can be used to increase text comprehension. Nevertheless, answering questions requires additional strategic processes, presumably different from those needed when students are merely requested to read. Generally, when students are asked to answer questions, they have to use question-answering strategies and to engage in a search for the information, either in memory or in the text.

Graesser and Franklin (1990) proposed a cognitive model of question answering from memory. According to the QUEST model, question answering involves a categorization mechanism, that identifies the *type* of question (e.g., why-, how- type of question), its *focus* (e.g., "water is heated" in "How is water heated?"), and relevant information *sources*, that is, the episodic or general knowledge structures which may be tapped for answers to the question. Simple questions focus on a single concept or a semantic proposition. However, more complex questions focus on broader conceptual structures. The actual process of answering a question starts with the activation of a knowledge node, either directly if the node matches a term in the question, or indirectly through the contextual activation of relevant knowledge structures (see also Whilite, 1985). Search continues through a radiation mechanism called *arc-search procedure*. Arc-search allows the propagation of activation through a knowledge network, based on constraints specific to each type of question. For instance, how-questions call for the search of causal antecedents or subordinate goals. Arc-search reduces the search space by identifying those knowledge nodes that may be chosen for an answer. The search space is further reduced by constraints propagation and pragmatic rules.

When answering questions from text, the processes of categorization and focusing also apply, as well as the initial activation of knowledge nodes. However the actual search process includes text inspection in addition to memory arc-search. Goldman and Durán (1988) presented a conceptual model of question-answering that takes into account both memory search and text inspection. It describes four major processing events and goals associated with each. The first processing event is question encoding, in which goals are to determine the type of answer required by the question and the starting point for searching for an answer. As Goldman and Durán pointed out, the search space can be reasonably well defined when the question uses words that match those used in the text. Nevertheless, these matching words can also be misleading, when the question is requiring more than locating specific segments of the text (i.e., the application of knowledge presented in the text). After question encoding, search for an answer then proceeds in either memory or in an external source such a text book. According to the model, in a memory-based search a threshold is established, against which candidate answers are tested. An answer exceeding the threshold would be given as a response, whereas inability to find an answer exceeding this threshold would lead to an external search. One of the goals of an external search is to delimit the search space by using the results of question encoding and memory search and a second goal is finding relevant information relevant to the question, which should be meaningfully processed so as to fulfill the task demands. It should be noted that the evaluation process in extracting relevant information might fail, thus leading to unsuccessful text searches (i.e., accepting as relevant a piece of information that is actually irrelevant). Finally, the model includes an evaluation-monitoring component that might be used in any of the question-answering processing events, for regulating the degree to which the search is in agreement with the demands of the search task.

Rouet and Tricot (1998) proposed a general framework for search processes that focuses mainly on external searches and includes three phases that unfold in a cyclical and partly interactive way. In the evaluation phase (E), the searcher builds a representation of the search objective as well as a search strategy. At this point, the searcher may decide whether to answer based on memory processes or if a text inspection is needed. Evaluating the need for an external search will imply a selection phase (S), in which the searcher selects units of information from the external source. Finally, there is a processing phase (P), when the searcher extracts relevant information from the selected text passage and integrates it within the goal representation under construction. The ESP framework assumes that complex search tasks are handled through numerous iterations of the ESP cycle, each iteration ending with an evaluation of whether the search is satisfactory.

These two models (i.e., Goldman & Durán, Rouet & Tricot) present a similar conceptualization to describe search processes. Mainly, they both include three main processing events in any search task: (a) Evaluating the task demands; (b) Finding relevant sources of information; (c) Extracting and processing this information from the relevant sources. They also include a monitoring component to regulate iterations in search cycles until goals are satisfied. We will use the Rouet and Tricot ESP model for the description of search tasks in our next studies, as it is more focused on external searches, similar to those included in our experimental designs.

7.2.2 Differential Processes Involved in Answering Questions

Even though both answering high or low level questions require search processes, either in memory or in an external source, the specific processes involved in answering high vs. low-level questions from text differ in several aspects. High-level questions are those that require integrating distant information via inferences, whereas low-level questions only make the reader locate specific pieces of information. Thus, answering high-level questions, in comparison to answering low-level questions, promotes the processing of more textual units as well as the activation of a greater number of knowledge nodes. Additionally, high-level questions require that the reader establishes more connections between textual and knowledge-based information. Therefore, the role of high-level questions is similar to that of self-explanations (Chi, de Leeuw, Chiu, & LaVancher, 1994). On the contrary, low-level questions involve few textual units to be answered and require few or no inferences. In any case, text-based inferences to connect close sentences in the text.

These above mentioned differences in answering different types of questions are apparent in the pattern of information search that they trigger. Vidal-Abarca et al. (1998) conducted two experiments in which high-school (experiment 1) and University students (experiment 2) read a 2500-word physics text presented paragraph-by-paragraph on a computer screen. Then, half of the students in each experiment answered text-based explicit questions whereas the other half answered global and inference questions. In both conditions, the students were allowed to search information in the text to answer the questions. Answering both types of questions required that students focused on the same textual information. Students who answered explicit questions searched fewer numbers of paragraphs per question than those answering global and inference questions. Moreover, students who answered global and inference questions significantly spent less time searching information than students who answered text-based explicit questions. Using a similar procedure, Rouet, Vidal-Abarca, Bert-Erboul, and Millogo (2001) asked undergraduate students to search a 35-paragraph text in order to answer high level or low level questions. They observed that each type of questions promoted specific review patterns. Whereas high-level questions promoted a review and integrate search pattern, low-level questions triggered a locate and memorize search pattern.

The distinction between high vs. low-level questions regarding the kinds of processing they induce is not unique. In fact, there is ample literature on the use of different types of questions in text comprehension and learning (Hartley & Davies, 1976; Andre, 1979; Rickards, 1979; Wixson, 1983; Hamilton, 1985; Langer, 1985; Goldman & Durán, 1988; Trabasso, van den Broek, & Lui, 1988; Graesser & Franklin, 1990; Graesser, Lang, & Roberts, 1991). Specifically, Goldman and Durán (1988) identified five types of questions depending on the relationship between the question and the text and the demands made on the knowledge base. These questions varied in terms of their relation to the text and the types of processing required to answer them. In type 1 questions there was a verbatim relationship between the question and the text, that is to say, the answer was explicitly given in the text and there was a direct match between the question wording and the text wording. In type 2 questions, the answer was also explicitly stated in the text, but differently to type 1 questions, the learner should made some vocabulary conversions. Thus, there was a paraphrase relationship between the question and the text. Type 3 questions also usually had a direct match between the question wording and the text but they required not only locating but comparing the information found to other information (i.e., concepts, quantities). The fourth type of question required integration of information across several paragraphs of the text. Hence, information must have been coordinated and analyzed to construct a correct answer. Finally, Goldman & Durán (1988) described a fifth type of question, in which the learner should use textual information to apply it to a new situation. Thus, type 5 questions required that the learner reasoned beyond the boundaries of the text. In summary, type 1, 2 and 3 questions had in common their verbatim relationship to the text, type 4 questions required integration across segments and, finally, type 5 questions required reasoning beyond the text.

In the present study, we will stick to the general distinction high vs. low- level questions. With high-level questions we will refer to questions in which the answer is not explicitly stated in the text but requires integration across several and distant paragraphs. They would be equivalent to Goldman and Durán type 4 questions. On the other hand, we will consider low-level questions those in which the answer can be located in specific segments of the text and can be extracted either by copying or by making minimal inferences across close sentences. Therefore, there is always going to be a verbatim relationship between the question and the text, such as in Goldman and Durán's type 1, 2 and 3 questions. This way, the biggest distinction between high and low-level question will be the location of the answer (concentrated vs. dispersed) and the need or not of integration across segments (e.g., by summarizing, comparing, and contrasting).

7.2.3 The Role of Strategic Monitoring and Comprehension in Answering Questions from Text

Learners have to behave strategically when answering questions from a text. In fact, when answering questions, strategies used to regulate the question-answering process seem to be crucial to the final success or failure in the answer. Thus, answering questions, either from memory or inspecting the text, may be seen as a constructive problem- solving activity (e.g., Brandsford & Johnson, 1973; Collins, Brown, & Larkin, 1980; Goldman, 1985), in which the learner first has to establish the demands of the task and then undertake some actions to reach an optimal end. In question-answering situations, one of the main actions to be taken is finding relevant sources of information to match to the question demands. This obviously requires having analyzed in detail which strategies and search inspection patterns are most useful and actually implementing them. More specifically, the ability to discriminate the pertinent sources of information has been proved to have a determinant role when answering questions from text. Raphael, Winograd, and Pearson (1980) found that the ability to recognize appropriate information sources appeared to be related to the quality of answers students gave to questions. They also found that the more successful students tended to show a flexible question answering behavior in the use of information sources for providing an answer. Their flexibility was apparent in that they tended: (a) to use explicitly stated information when a low level literal question was asked, (b) to integrate information when the question required it, and (c) to use information from prior knowledge when the external source did not provide the answer. In contrast, the less successful students were apparently unaware of the variations in the task demands and they tended to use a similar question answering strategy, regardless of the question variation.

The importance of self-monitoring one's question answering behavior according to the question demands was also apparent in Wonnacott and Raphael (1982). They examined the relationships between third and sixth grade students' knowledge of the question-answering process and their performance on three types of comprehension questions. Results indicated that metacognitive insight, as measured by students' ability to verbalize their understanding of the process of question answering, was a strong positive correlate of performance on comprehension questions.

Goldman and Durán (1988) analyzed the interaction between learner's characteristics and solution strategy patterns apparent in a question-answering task. Students read two selections from an Oceanography text and answered questions. Verbal protocols were collected and analyzed. Generally, they found that the more successful learners engaged in more cognitive monitoring than the less successful learners. Additionally, good learners also engaged more in question analysis and reasoning processes. In contrast, poor learners showed relatively short searches, with a tendency to answer quickly and lacking of metacognitive behavior.

Therefore, there is evidence that metacognitive behavior in regulating the question-answering process directed to the relevant sources of information is the key to succeeding in these kinds of tasks. Especially, flexibility in adapting specific search and answering strategies depending on the type of cognitive processes questions are asking for. Nevertheless, an important issue arises as regards to the role of text comprehension in the efficiency of the search task. Is successful strategic behavior in locating relevant sources of information and answering questions linked to good comprehension? Or, in other words, are good comprehenders good searchers and bad comprehenders inefficient ones? Kirsch and Guthrie (1984) and Guthrie and Kirsch (1987) concluded that comprehension and searching skills were not related. Nevertheless, as Cataldo and Oakhill (2000) argue, this conclusion was dependent on the type of search task used by the authors. When the search task is simple and does not require text integration, such as locating data in nonprose material or schematics, the ability to locate specific pieces of information may not depend so much on text comprehension ability. On the other hand, when searching requires one to locate and integrate several pieces of information from a continuous text, text comprehension may have a determinant role in the efficiency of the search (MacLatchy-Gaudet & Symons, 1999; Symons & Specht, 1994, Cataldo & Oakhill, 2000). Comprehension determines one's ability to discriminate the relevant sources of information and one's use of successful strategies depending on the type of question. In fact, Cataldo and Oakhill (2000) found that good comprehenders performed a better search directed to relevant sources of information. In contrast, poor comprehenders showed an undirected search that was additionally time consuming.

In the present study, one of our main claims is that search processes in complex documents to perform learning tasks (i.e., answering questions) are dependent on good understanding. The rationale for that claim is that the ability to discriminate the pertinent sources of information and to perform effective search cycles until a final answer is given needs comprehension of: (a) the question demands, (b) the relevant text paragraphs and (c) the implementation of inferencing and connection across paragraphs when the type of task requires it. Consequently, the search patterns of good and bad performers in answering high and low level questions will be inspected in the following studies.

7.3 Empirical Studies of Text Search

In the rest of this chapter, we report two experiments that were conducted with the following objectives in mind:

- Objective 1

The first objective was to study the differences between information search processes to answer either high or low-level questions, and their relation with comprehension processes. We took into account prior results found by Vidal-Abarca, Rouet et al. (Vidal-Abarca et al., 1996, 1998, Rouet et al., 2001), in which low-level questions promoted different information search patterns to the ones promoted by high-level questions. Generally, we expect to find locate and memorize search patterns associated to low-level questions and review and integrate search patterns associated to high-level questions (Rouet et al., 2001). On the other hand, we will use Rouet and Tricot search framework (1998) to study information search processes in complex documents.

- Objective 2

The second objective was to study the relation between search processes and the performance level (good vs. poor) reached when answering high and low-level questions. Several questions arise: are information search processes that conclude in a good performance level different from those that conclude in a poor performance level? Which relation have search processes with comprehension processes? With search processes we refer to the cognitive processes unfolded to inspect a text with a specific purpose and for which we assume the information search model proposed by Rouet and Tricot (1998). Broadly speaking, participants reaching higher scorings in learning questions should show a more effective search pattern than participants reaching lower scorings. We expected that the most marked differences would appear in the selection and processing phase (Rouet & Tricot, 1998), so that better performers should have consulted and read a higher percentage of relevant information for the question than worse performers. As the type of search undertaken could interact with the type of question, both variables will be considered simultaneously.

We designed two experiments in which university students read a scientific text of 1900 words approximately and they answered either high or low-level questions. Both text and questions were presented on a computer screen. Whereas in experiment 1 students read the text and then answered the questions, in experiment 2 students were firstly presented with the questions and then searched for information in the text to answer them. Thus, students in the second experiment could not form an initial representation of the text prior to reading the questions. Therefore, search processes could be studied without the influence of the prior representation of the text. Putting together the results from the two experiments, the relationship between search and comprehension processes could be analyzed in greater detail.

7.3.1 Experiment 1: Reading a Text and Answering Questions

We conducted the first experiment in order to assess search and comprehension processes in learning from text. Participants read a long scientific expository text and then they answered either high or low-level questions on a computer screen, using a software tool that allowed us to record the pattern of text search for each question.

7.3.1.1 Method

- Participants

Twenty-two university students took part in the experiment. They were randomly assigned to two experimental conditions. In the first one twelve students had to answer high-level questions, that required the reader to integrate and revise information from different paragraphs of the text and to make many inferences. In the second condition, ten students answered low-level questions. For those questions the answer was explicitly stated in one or two consecutive paragraphs and required few or no inferences.

It was verified that both groups were equivalent in a set of measures that could contaminate subsequent results. Thus, participants were firstly tested on prior knowledge about the text they would be reading in the experimental session, with no significant differences between the high ($M = 5.50$, $SD = 1.62$) and low-level question groups ($M = 4.70$, $SD = 1.49$). Additionally, participants were assessed on lexical access. They read aloud a word and another non-word list, each of them consisting of 40 items. We measured the number of errors made when reading both lists. As for errors reading the word list, no differences appeared between the high ($M = 0.16$, $SD = 0.57$) and low-level question group ($M = 0.10$, $SD = 0.31$). Neither did they appear significant differences between the high-level ($M = 0.66$, $SD = 0.88$) and low-level group ($M = 1.90$, $SD = 2.68$) when reading non-words.

Finally, we measured participants' keyboard typing speed. Participants were asked to copy a 146 word text on the computer, within a two minutes time period. The high-level question group (M = 60.08, SD = 17.95) and low-level question group (M = 70.90, SD = 32.56) did not differ in the number of words written during the established period of time.

- Materials

Text. The text used in the experiment dealt with the evolution from the atomic models from the initial proposal by Dalton to the Rutherford Model. We used the simpler version of a text used in a previous experiment (Vidal-Abarca et al., 1996). It had 1768 words, divided into 59 paragraphs and distributed in 9 pages, including a table of contents. The text was transformed to a format compatible with the application *Read&Answer*, so that it could be presented on a computer screen. All sections in the text were explicit in a table of contents which precedes the text.

Prior Background Knowledge. In order to asses the subject's level of prior knowledge on atomic models a nine item questionnaire was used (Vidal-Abarca et al., 1996). It consisted of five questions on static electricity, a content necessary to understand the text, and four more questions specifically related to atomic models.

Treatment questions. Participants had to answer either high or low-level questions, whose purpose was to help the reader understand and learn the text better. High-level questions were those that required revising distant segments of the text and making inferences to integrate the information. In contrast, information to answer low-level questions was explicitly stated in one or two consecutive segments and required making few or no inferences. It should be noted that text information to answer both types of questions was the same. Participants belonging to the high-level questions group answered five questions, whereas participants belonging to the low-level group answered nineteen questions, both covering the same textual information. We included more low-level than high-level questions so as to equate the total amount of text needed to answer the questions across conditions.

Let us take an example of a high-level question covering several distant pieces of information in the text: *Can the Dalton Model explain radioactivity by emission of alpha particles?* Textual information necessary to answer correctly was located in eight different paragraphs along two pages. The answer to the question was not explicitly stated in any of those paragraphs, but required the student to construct a new answer using the textual information presented in the two pages. Therefore, the student had to generate inferences and then construct an integrated answer.

Students answering low-level questions were also presented with questions covering the same textual information as required to answer the above high-level question. However, given that each of the low-level questions only covered a specific piece of information, more questions were needed to cover the total amount of textual information involved in the high-level question. As an example, this is one of the low-level questions that covered part of the information needed for the high-level question presented above: *How would be the atoms that Dalton imagined in 1803?* Differently to the high-level question, it focused on a specific piece of information located in one paragraph and only required that the student found it in the text.

Software. The text was presented on a computer screen using the application *Read&Answer* developed at the University of Valencia. Like previously developed experimental text presentation tools (e.g., *Select-the-text*, Goldman & Saul, 1990b), *Read&Answer* presents readers with a full screen of text. All text except the segment (i.e., a sentence or a paragraph) currently selected by the reader is masked, and the white spaces denote sentence boundaries. Readers unmask a segment by clicking on it; when they unmask another segment, the first segment is remasked. Thus, only one segment at a time is visible, but the graphic features of the text (e.g., paragraph indentation, length of the paragraphs, position of the segment in the text) are visible to the reader. Readers can reread the segments in any order they choose (see Fig. 7.1).

Read&Answer includes other possibilities which are especially useful for recording the reader's behavior when she or he is involved in question-answering tasks from a long text. *Read&Answer* presents the text on different screens corresponding to the different pages. A simple interface allows the user to navigate among them. In addition, visual information (e.g., diagrams,

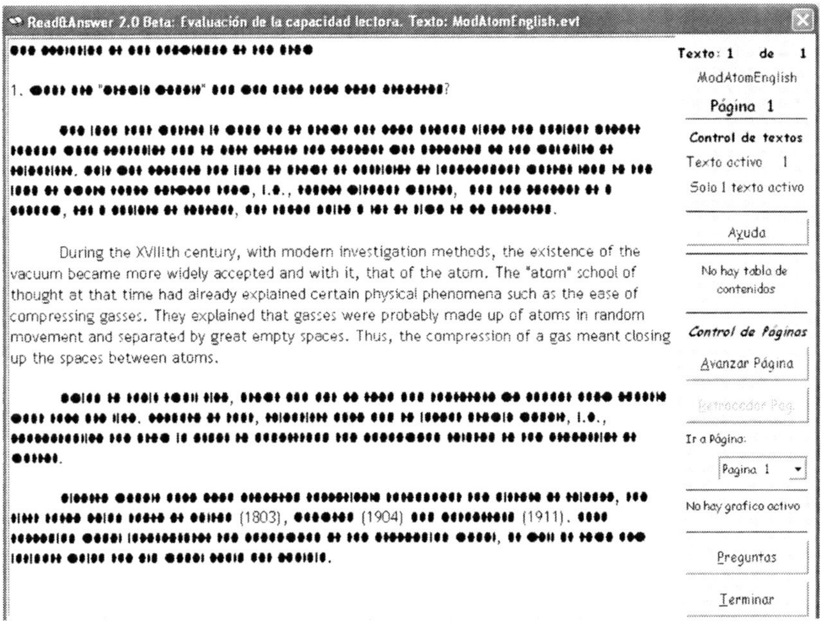

Fig. 7.1 *Read&Answer*: Text Screen

figures, pictures, etc) can be inserted into the text as a segment. *Read&Answer* also presents the reader with a question screen, which is divided into two parts, the upper part for the question and the lower part for the answer. The user clicks on each part to either read the question (see Fig. 7.2) or write in the answer box (see Fig. 7.3). A simple interface allows the reader to move from one question to another and from the question screen to the text screen, and vice versa.

Read&Answer automatically generates three outputs. The first is a list of all the segments active at any given moment, and the length of time each was active. A piece of the text (e.g., a paragraph), a specific question, and the answer to every question are all segments. Thus, every action the reader undertakes, whether it be reading a text segment, reading a question, rereading a text segment, or writing an answer, is recorded and included in the list. The second output is a summary of the reader's behavior when he or she reads the text and answers the questions. *Read&Answer* provides a different summary of the two types of study behavior, reading the text and answering the questions. The summary includes: (1) the number of words in the text segment, (2) the total amount of time for which the segment was exposed, (3) the rate per word, and (4) the process time per word. The third output is the record of the reader's answers to each question.

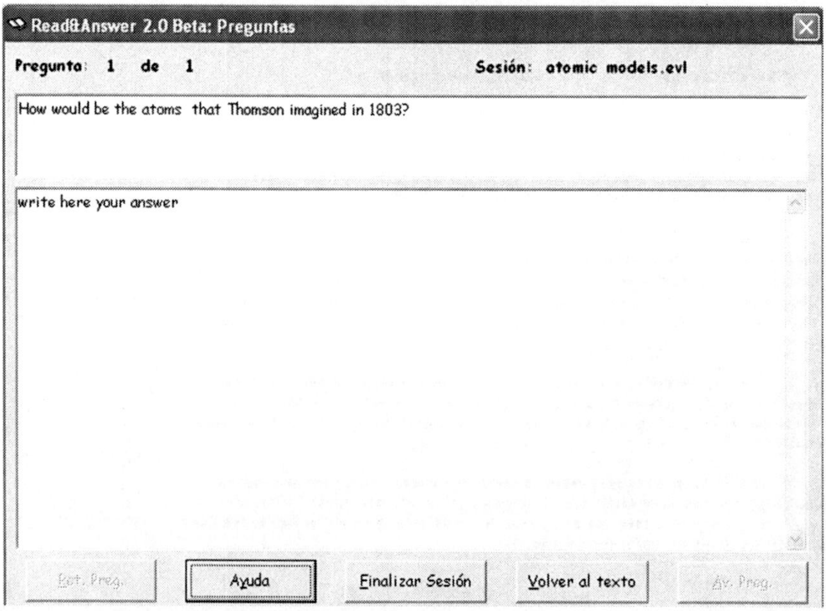

Fig. 7.2 *Read&Answer*: Reading question on question screen

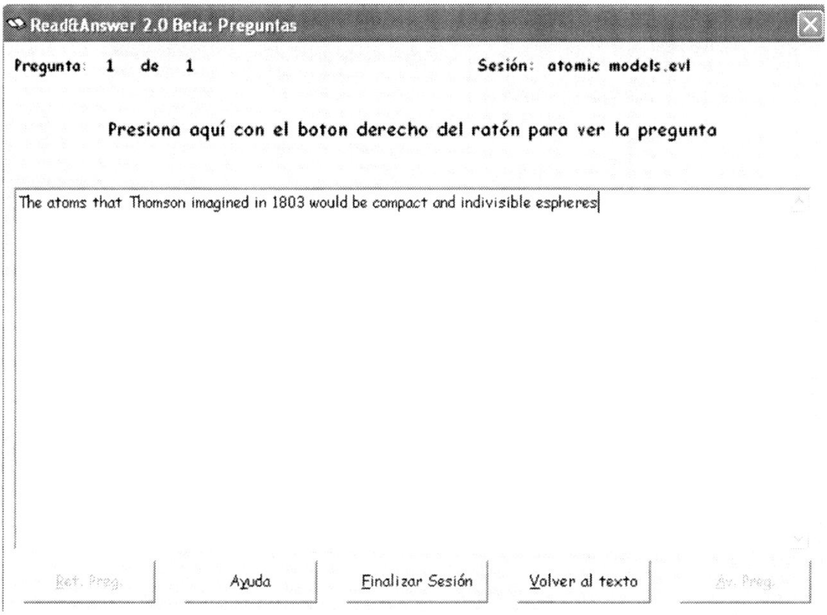

Fig. 7.3 *Read&Answer*: Answering question on question screen

- Procedure

Experimental sessions were carried out individually and during a unique session, similarly for all the participants. Each subject was firstly measured on previous background knowledge and then randomly assigned to one experimental condition, i.e., high-level questions group vs. low-level questions group. After that they were tested on writing speed on the keyboard.

Participants then started a training phase with the software *Read&Answer*, so that they got used not only with the task they were expected to undertake, but also with the presentation format and the different menus available. They read a 333 word text, consisting of 13 paragraphs, and then answered 4 questions. They were allowed to go back to the text as many times as they wished, to look for the information needed to answer the questions, in a similar way as they would have to do in the experimental phase.

Following the training phase, participants began the experimental phase. They all had to read the text carefully and then answer either five high-level or nineteen low-level questions, depending on the condition they were in. It was strictly indicated to follow this reading-answering sequence. Nonetheless, once in the answering module, participants could move from the questions screens to the text screens at will. Finally, the experimental session ended with the reading skills assessment. Participants were given two lists, one with words and other containing pseudowords, being both read aloud. Both speed and errors while reading were recorded. No time limit was indicated for the experimental phase. The total duration of the procedure was about one hour and a half.

- Dependent measures

On-line Measures. Based on the Rouet and Tricot (1998) proposal, a set of on-line measures was obtained, corresponding to the Evaluation, Selection and Processing phases of the search process. For the Evaluation phase (E) two dependent variables were considered: the number of visits to the question and the total time spent reading the question. For the Selection phase (S) three measures were considered, namely, total number of paragraphs visited, number of relevant paragraphs visited, and percentage of relevant paragraphs visited over the total number of paragraphs visited. For the Processing phase (P) only one dependent variable was considered, i.e., the percentage of time reading relevant segments over the total time devoted to reading within the question. Finally, we measured the executive control processes with the number of QTW cycles, i.e., reading the question (Q), reading the text (T) and writing an answer (W), these cycles are closely related to the iterations of ESP in the framework by Rouet and Tricot (1998).

7.3.1.2 Results

- Experimental design

We conducted 2x2 ANOVAs, with two between-subjects independent variables, i.e., performance level in the questions (poor vs. good) and type of question (low-level vs. high-level). The performance level for each subject was established by considering the percentage of success in all the questions each subject had to answer, either high level or low level. Those equal or above 50% in percentage of success were considered good performers, and those below 50% were considered poor performers.

Table 7.1 presents the average value of online search measures, as a function of question type of comprehension level.

- Evaluation Phase (E)

There was a significant effect of question type on the number of times the participants read the questions while searching ($F(1, 18) = 11.342$, $p < 0.05$). High-level questions were read more times (M = 8.28, SD = 4.24) than low-level questions (M = 3.29, SD = 1.18). Poor comprehenders also tended to re-read the question more often than good comprehenders, but the difference was not significant. Neither was the interaction between the two factors.

Concerning the time reading the question (Table 7.1), the type of question was again significant ($F(1, 18) = 19.74$, $p < 0.05$). Participants spent more time reading (and rereading) high-level questions (M = 258.93 seconds, SD = 108.40) than low-level questions (M = 89.06 seconds, SD = 26.07). There was a nonsignificant trend for good performers to spend less time reading the

Table 7.1 Means of on-line dependant measures for Experiment 1 (standard deviation in parenthesis)

		High-level questions		Low-level questions	
		Good	Poor	Good	Poor
Evaluation	Times reading question	7.76 (1.94)	8.65 (8.49)	3.57 (1.28)	2.88 (1.02)
	Time reading question	250.69 (67.91)	264.81 (135.55)	83.34 (25.35)	97.64 (28.37)
Selection	Total paragraphs	21.06 (12.92)	27.57 (17.44)	9.48 (4.63)	9.67 (0.31)
	Relevant paragraphs	7.64 (2.88)	7.57 (3.50)	2.24 (1.06)	2.10 (0.45)
	% of relevant paragraphs	43.02 (12.77)	21.61 (4.66)	29.21 (9.89)	22.04 (13.42)
Processing	% of time reading relevant paragraphs	61.81 (13.82)	40.69 (6.98)	39.40 (11.36)	28.30 (13.82)
Control	QTW cycles	2.58 (0.92)	2.45 (1.19)	1.98 (1.16)	1.72 (0.71)

questions (M = 159.41, SD = 99.01) than poor performers (M = 204.02, SD = 135.57). Again, there was no significant interaction.

In short, the participants visited high-level questions more frequently and for longer than low-level questions. The data suggest that, as search processes were more complex, students had to "refresh" the question's content during the answering process. There was no significant effect of comprehension performance on the Evaluation measures, but the trends were in the expected direction, i.e. good performers tended to read questions fewer times and faster, possibly because their representation of the search goal was established sooner and more firmly than that of poorer performers.

- Selection Phase (S).

The *total number of paragraphs* visited varied as a function of question type (Table 7.1; $F(1, 18) = 7.93$, $p < 0.05$). Participants answering high-level questions visited a larger number of text paragraphs (M = 24.86, SD = 15.42) than those answering low-level questions (M = 9.56, SD = 3.46). Poor performers also tended to visit more text segments than good performers, but results failed to reach significance.

The pattern of effects was similar for the *number of relevant paragraphs visited* (Table 7.1). More relevant paragraphs were visited for high level questions (M = 7.6, SD = 3.12) than for low-level questions (M = 2.18, SD = 0.83; $F(1,18) = 24.61$, $p < 0.05$). This result, however, was over-determined since more of the text's paragraphs were relevant high than for low level questions. Good and poor performers visited a similar amount of relevant information (Table 7.1), which indicates that merely locating the relevant segments was not enough for providing relevant answers to the questions.

Comprehension performance had a significant effect on the *percentage of relevant paragraphs visited* (Table 7.1). Good performers visited a higher percentage of relevant paragraphs (M = 35.48, SD = 12.89) than poor performers level (M = 21.76, SD = 8.19; $F(1,18) = 24.61$, $p < 0.05$). Answering the questions correctly was associated with a selective search pattern, concentrating on those segments that contained the information relevant to answer the question. Poor performers showed a more "chaotic" search, searching among a larger set of text segments, fewer of which were relevant to the question.

To sum up, high-level questions were visited more often and they implied revising a higher number of text segments. This result can be explained by the complexity of the search processes necessary to answer this type of questions which involve revising and integrating many pieces of distant text information. Good comprehenders were more selective, visiting a higher proportion of passages relevant to their questions. It should be noted that both good and poor performers visited relevant passages. However, good performers were able to find which information matched the question, whereas this did not occur in poor performers. This result illustrates the interplay of comprehension processes and search tasks in complex documents.

- Processing Phase (P)

Both the type of question and the performance level had a significant effect on the percentage of time spent reading relevant segments ($F(1,18) = 12.60$, $p < 0.05$ and $F(1,18) = 10.80$, $p < 0.05$, respectively). Participants answering high level questions spent a greater percentage of time reading relevant segments (M = 49.49, SD = 14.64) than those answering low-level questions (M = 34.96, SD = 12.97). The effect of question type is little surprising since the probability of opening irrelevant segments was higher for low level than for high-level questions, due to the difference in the number of segments relevant per question.

On the other hand, good performers spent a significantly larger amount of time reading relevant segments (M = 35.48, SD = 12.89) than poor performers (M = 21.76, SD = 8.19). This suggests, once again that comprehension played a role in focusing students' attention to the information that was actually useful for constructing one's answer to the questions.

- Executive control processes

Finally, we measured the executive control processes with the number of QTW cycles, i.e., reading-the-question (Q), reading the text (T) and writing an answer (W), (Table 7.1). These cycles are closely related to the iterations of ESP in the framework by Rouet and Tricot (1998). Results of the analysis showed no significant differences in any of the independent variables. Despite that, we found a tendency in high-level questions having a higher number of QTW cycles (M = 2.50, SD = 1.04) than low-level questions (M = 1.87, SD = 0.96), which is in agreement with previous results, as high-level questions imply more processing iterations due to the higher number of inferences they require.

7.3.1.3 Discussion

- Processes of searching information to answer high and low-level questions

One of the aims of this experiment was to examine differences for high and low-level questions in the processes of searching for information. For this first research objective, we depart from the results found by Vidal-Abarca et al. (1998) in which high-level questions were associated with revising more text sources than low-level questions. In the same vein, Rouet et al. (2001) also described different search patterns for high and low-level questions. Whereas high-level questions promoted the revision and integration from different text sources, low-level questions implied a locate and memorize information search pattern.

Our experiment confirmed the results reported above. High level questions were read longer and more times, in comparison to low-level questions. They were also associated with visiting more text segments, both relevant and non-relevant for answering the question and they tended to require more QTW cycles. This set of results indicates that high-level questions required, in fact, the revision and integration of many textual units dispersed in the text. On the contrary, in low-level questions, the total amount of text segments visited was lower, as well as the time devoted to reading the questions. They promoted a more specific search pattern with fewer QTW cycles, in comparison to high-level questions.

In addition, answering high-level questions implied opening and reading more relevant segments than answering low-level questions, a result due to the inherent characteristics of each type of question. In high-level questions the students had to integrate several text units, whereas in low-level questions only one or two segments were needed. Therefore, the probability of coming across relevant segments was much higher in high-level questions.

This set of results is consistent with the findings of Halpain, Glover, and Harvey (1985), who concluded that answering high-level questions after reading a text was more resource consuming than answering low-level questions using a secondary task method. Students answering high-level questions had to integrate a high number of dispersed text units and make many inferences. These cognitive operations are complex and imply an overload in working-memory, resulting in more complex search patterns, i.e., reading questions more times, opening more text segments and using more QTW cycles. On the contrary, students answering low-level questions only had to find some specific pieces of information and make few or no inferences. After having understood the question demands, students had to locate and understand the relevant pieces of information for the question. Thus, search processes to answer low-level questions were simpler.

- Relation between search processes and the performance level (good vs. poor) reached when answering high and low-level questions

It seems that reaching a good performance level after reading a text depends on complex cognitive and metacognitive search and comprehension strategies.

When answering at a good level, unlike answering at a poor level, students tended to read the questions fewer times, opened a lower number of paragraphs, though the percentage of relevant paragraphs over the total number of paragraphs opened was higher as well as the percentage of time devoted to reading relevant information. It seems that answering questions at a good level involved forming a good representation of the search objective very quickly when reading the question, selecting the right information also quickly, and understanding the text deeply either when it was read firstly or when it was reread during the processing phase. Thus, answering at a good performance level involved displaying a strategic question-answering behavior directed to the relevant information. In contrast, when answering questions at a poor level, questions were read more times and a higher number of paragraphs were opened, though the percentage of relevant paragraphs opened over the total selected was smaller. It means that many non-relevant segments were visited when answering poorly, as opposed to answering at a good level, where a more selective search pattern was apparent. Therefore, when answering at a poor performance level, the search pattern to answer the questions was more chaotic, in comparison to the good performance level. This erratic pattern suggests that students got lost in the search task due to their lack of understanding of contents, i.e., the same reason that prevented them from giving a correct answer.

These conclusions should be considered with caution considering that students were given the opportunity to read the text prior to answering questions. Thus, the role of text comprehension on search may have been overemphasized. For this reason, we conducted a second experiment in which students searched for information to answer questions, without having previously read the text.

7.3.2 Experiment 2: Searching for Information to Answer Questions

In this experiment participants searched for information to answer high and low-level text questions but they did not have a prior representation of the text before reading the questions, given that there was not a previous initial reading of the text. Therefore, information search processes to answer the questions could be studied more precisely, without the influence of the prior comprehension of the text. Thus, differences between information search processes and processes of comprehension should turn out to be clearer.

Our main research objectives were the same as in experiment 1. Briefly, our purpose was first to study different search patterns when answering high and low-level questions and its relation with comprehension processes. Secondly, we wanted to examine the relation between search processes and the performance level (good vs. poor) reached with high and low-level questions.

7.3.2.1 Method

- Participants

Sixteen university students took part in this second experiment, with similar characteristics to the participants in experiment 1. Half of the students were randomly assigned to the high-level questions group and the other half to the low-level questions group.

We verified that both groups did not differ in a set of measures that could contaminate subsequent results. Using the same tasks as in experiment 1, we found no difference between the high level and the low level question groups in measures of prior knowledge (M = 4.50, SD = 2.37 and M = 4.12, SD = 1.88, respectively); lexical access (M = 0.38, SD = 0.52 and M = 0.13, SD = 0.35) non-word reading (M = 1.13, SD = 1.55 and M = 1.75, SD = 1.58) or typing speed (M = 65.50, SD = 25.22 and M = 59.50, SD = 16.73).

- Materials, measures and procedure

Materials and dependent measures were identical to the ones used in experiment 1. Regarding the general procedure used in this second experiment, there was a key difference with experiment 1, as we have already mentioned. Students did not read the text before answering the questions but first read the questions and then searched for information in the text to answer them. As we did in the experiment 1 students had an exhaustive table of contents at the beginning of the text to facilitate the process of searching information to answer the questions. Differently to the first experiment, in this one students used the table of contents to search the text information to answer the questions, which sounds logical as in this experiment students had not read the text before receiving the questions.

As in experiment 1, the training and the experimental parts of the study took place on the same day. Both of them were carried out on a computer screen, using the *Read&Answer* software. Participants could invest all the time they needed to carry out the experimental session, spending, as in experiment 1, an hour and a half on average.

7.3.2.2 Results

- Experimental design

Similarly to experiment 1, we conducted 2x2 ANOVAs with performance level (poor vs. good) and type of question (low vs. high-level) as independent variables, as we did in experiment 1. The same dependent variables used in experiment 1 were taken here, i.e., a number of on-line measures representative of the three search phases mentioned by Rouet and Tricot, i.e. Evaluation, Selection and Processing, and of the executive control processes. To classify the performance level (good vs. poor), we also considered the students reaching a global percentage of success in the questions equal or above 50% (i.e., good performance level) and the students reaching a percentage of success in all the questions below 50% (i.e., poor performance level).

Table 7.2 Means of on-line dependent measures for Experiment 2 (standard deviation in parenthesis)

		High-level		Low-level	
		Good	Poor	Good	Poor
Evaluation	Times reading question	9.00	8.20	2.95	2.33
		(6.66)	(1.84)	(0.72)	(0.62)
	Time reading question	47.58	50.44	15.73	16.86
		(5.13)	(28.32)	(6.06)	(5.55)
Selection	Total paragraphs	25.75	34.00	11.29	10.71
		(6.71)	(6.09)	(1.84)	(2.63)
	Relevant paragraphs	8.45	13.75	2.70	2.31
		(2.25)	(3.34)	(0.46)	(0.57)
	% of relevant paragraphs	67.29	28.25	61.49	34.82
		(7.70)	(8.20)	(15.02)	(2.03)
Processing	% of time reading relevant paragraphs	35.90	35.98	52.55	42.97
		(3.82)	(0.66)	(6.11)	(6.91)
Control	QTW cycles	4.15	7.75	3.23	2.64
		(0.70)	(2.48)	(0.54)	(0.23)

Table 7.2 shows the online measures of Evaluation, Selection and processing as a function of question type and comprehension level.

- Evaluation Phase (E)

High-level questions were read more times (M = 8.6, SD = 4.5) than low-level questions (M = 2.72, SD = 0.71; $F(1,12) = 11.25$, $p < 0.05$). Thus, the lack of an initial reading of the text did not affect the number of times the students read the question, as means were very similar in experiments 1 and 2. High-level questions were also read longer (M = 49.01 seconds, SD = 18.91) than low-level questions (M = 16.15, SD = 5.49, $F(1,12) = 18.44$, $p < 0.05$). Unexpectedly, the questions were read much faster than in experiment 1. Good performers also tended to spend less time studying the questions than poor performers (M = 29.89, SD = 17.60 and M = 36.05, SD = 27.08, respectively), but the difference was not significant.

In summary, high-level questions were read more times and longer than low-level questions. Questions were also read faster than in experiment 1. We interpret this unexpected result in terms of availability of a prior representation of the text which permitted the students to connect the information acquired during the initial reading with the information and demands presented in each question. In other words, in experiment 1 students were able to reflect more on the question as they were reading it, because they already had a representation of the text in memory.

- Selection Phase (S)

The same three measures considered in experiment 1 were taken here, i.e., number of total paragraphs , number of relevant paragraphs visited and percentage of relevant paragraphs visited over the total number of paragraphs visited. In relation to the number of total paragraphs visited to answer the questions (Table 7.2), only the type of question was significant. Thus, a higher number of total paragraphs was visited in high-level questions (M = 29.87, SD = 7.39) than in low-level questions (M = 11.07, SD = 2.00), $F(1,12) = 60.32$, $p < 0.05$. Similarly to experiment 1, this result can be explained by the higher number of text segments that were necessary to revise to answer high-level questions. Good comprehenders tended to visit fewer paragraphs (M = 17.71, SD = 8.75) than poor comprehenders (M = 24.02, SD = 13.25), but the difference failed to reach significance. Finally, the interaction between the two main variables was nearly significant ($F(1,12) = 3.29$, $p = 0.94$). The difference between good and poor comprehenders was larger for high level questions.

Regarding the number of relevant paragraphs visited to answer the questions (Table 7.2), significant differences were apparent for the two main effects and their interaction, differently to experiment 1. Firstly, more paragraphs were visited for high level questions (M = 11.10, SD = 3.87) than for low level questions (M = 2.55, SD = 0.51, $F(1,12) = 68.21$, $p<0.05$). Secondly, good comprehenders visited fewer relevant paragraphs (M = 5.25, SD = 3.34) than poor comprehenders (M = 8.84, SD = 6.56), $F(1,12) = 5.57$, $p<0.05$. Finally, there was a significant interaction between question type and comprehension level ($F(1,12) = 7.48$, $p < 0.05$). The difference between good and poor comprehenders was larger for high level than for low level questions.

Finally, good performers were selective in their search, visiting a higher percentage of relevant paragraphs (M = 64.07, SD = 12.02) than poor performers (M = 31.07, SD = 6.88). No other comparison was significant.

- Processing Phase (P)

The participants spent a larger proportion of time reading relevant information for low level than for high level questions (M = 48.96, SD = 7.71 and M = 35.94, SD = 2.54, $F(1,12) = 22.35$, $p < 0.05$). This pattern of effect was the reverse of that observed in experiment 1. It suggests that without a prior representation of the texts, participants spent less time on irrelevant passages when processing low level, but not high level questions.

- Executive control processes

Both the type of question and the performance level had significant effects on the number of QTW cycles (Table 7.2). High-level questions implied more QTW cycles (M = 5.95, SD = 2.56) than low-level questions (M = 3.01, SD = 0.52, $F(1,12) = 19.78$, $p < 0.05$). Additionally, good comprehenders searched for fewer cycles (M = 3.63, SD = 0.75) than poor comprehenders (M = 5.56, SD = 3.24, $F(1,12) = 4.97$, $p < 0.05$). Finally, there was a significant question type x comprehension level interaction ($F(1,12) = 9.54$, $p < 0.05$). The effect of comprehension level on the number of cycles as larger in the high level than in the low level condition. Therefore, students who answered poorly showed a more chaotic search pattern, using more search cycles and visiting more irrelevant segments for the question. And this happened especially in high-level questions, those that required not only locating but also comprehending and integrating distant information via inferences. It should be noted that these effects did not appear in experiment 1. This suggests that the role of self-monitoring strategies (i.e., apparent in the number of QTW cycles) is stronger when students have a search task to solve, without having read the text at first.

7.3.2.3 Discussion

- Processes of searching information to answer high and low-level questions

Through a set of on-line measures corresponding to the search phases proposed by Rouet and Tricot (1998) we wanted to confirm if search processes when answering high-level questions were different to search processes when answering low-level questions, as we already did in experiment 1. Our results for experiment 2 also showed a similar search pattern depending on the type of question in each of the three search phases (i.e., Evaluation, Selection & Processing) described by Rouet and Tricot (1998). Therefore, high-level questions implied a higher number of times and a longer time reading the questions. Additionally, the number of paragraphs visited was greater than in low-level questions, as they required revising and integrating a higher number of distant text segments. Finally, high-level questions implied using more QTW answering cycles than low-level questions. The opposite tendency appeared for low-level questions, in which questions were read fewer times, fewer text segments were visited and less QWT were used. Surprisingly, the percentage of relevant segments visited was higher for low level than for high level questions. When readers do not have the opportunity to form a mental representation of the text prior to searching, they tend to focus on relevant segments especially for specific, low level questions. Good comprehenders achieve this selection process better than poor comprehenders, as assessed by their higher percentage of relevant nodes for both types of questions.

Consistent with experiment 1, as well as with prior studies (Rouet et al., 2001; Vidal-Abarca et al., 1998), high-level questions promoted a review and integrate search pattern, whereas low-level questions were associated with a locate and memorise search pattern. Contrary to findings by Halpain, Glover, and Harvey (1985), high-level questions even took more resources (i.e., being read more times and for longer, visiting more text segments, using more QTW cycles) than low-level questions, even though students did not read the text at first. Therefore, the need to connect and integrate ideas is likely to be already present in the question itself. Students reading higher level questions realize that a higher amount of cognitive resources are required to face those kinds of questions, hence the more complex search patterns.

- Relation between search processes and the performance level (good vs. poor) reached when answering high and low-level questions

As we already concluded for experiment 1, it seems that reaching a good performance level depends on complex search and comprehension monitoring strategies. In this second experiment, it could be appreciated how students answering at a good performance level tended to read the questions more quickly, they knew which information was relevant for the question and went directly in search for it, even though there had not been an initial reading of the text. They were even more selective, having higher percentages of visits to relevant segments than those found in experiment 1, which they evidently needed, as they had no previous knowledge of the text. An exhaustive table of contents helped them look for the relevant information to comply with the demands of the questions. On the contrary, students answering at a poor performance level visited a greater number of text segments, most of them irrelevant for the question. Thus, they were lost in their search task and had not probably completely understood neither the question demands nor the relevant segments they encountered while inspecting the text, as opposed to students answering at a good level. Therefore, those students understanding what they were asked for as well as the relevant information sources to comply with the question demands were the ones who displayed a better and more effective search pattern. This clearly demonstrates the link between search and comprehension processes. Good understanding leads to an effective search, and effective search is hardly possible without a good level of understanding of the contents. On the other hand, differences between a good and a poor performance level were stronger and clearer in this second experiment, especially in search control measures, such as cycles. Generally, good performers did as well as in experiment 1. Thus, they invested more cognitive resources when the task was more demanding (i.e., answering high-level questions). In contrast, students answering poorly in experiment 2 did much worse than poor performers in experiment 1, especially when answering high-level questions, those that precisely required more cognitive resources.

In the absence of an initial representation of the text (experiment 2), poor performers were even more lost in their search task than when they had the opportunity to read the text first. In experiment 1 the differences between good and poor performers in the search task were softened by the initial representation of the text, which served as a guide to look for information in the text. In experiment 2, nevertheless, students had no initial representation of the text. Nevertheless, good performers did it as well as in experiment 1, which suggests that they had sufficient strategies to look for information using the table of contents, that they understood the questions demands and stopped their search when they found the relevant information for the question. In contrast, poor performers seemed to get lost, showing the opposite search pattern (i.e., reading questions more times, searching for information in irrelevant segments) when the task was more demanding.

To sum up, students answering at a good performance level displayed a search pattern directed to relevant information and dependent on the type of question. That clearly indicates strategic self-monitoring, which was lacking for students answering at a poor level. Results were consistent in experiment 1 and 2, but the gap between good and poor performers was even bigger when the task was more demanding (i.e., without an initial reading of the text and when answering high-level questions).

7.4 General Discussion and Conclusions

Our main research objective for this chapter was to explain the role of search and comprehension processes when answering high and low-level questions, in two different experimental situations (i.e., answering questions after reading a text and looking for information to answer questions in a text). More specifically, we wanted to study the differences between information search processes to answer both high or low-level questions, and its relation with comprehension processes. Another purpose was to study the relation between search processes and the performance level (good vs. poor) reached with high and low level questions.

In the main, answering questions and searching for information in complex documents are processes highly dependent on understanding and on strategic performance. Search processes to answer questions require that the reader first constructs a representation of the search objective that will permit selecting the relevant information for the question, as well as monitoring this process in a way that fits not only the type of question to be answered, but also the kind of search and answering strategies to be displayed to answer correctly. Indeed, as we had hypothesized, the main difference between good and poor performers appeared when selecting and processing the relevant units of information for the questions. Therefore, in agreement with previous studies (Raphael, Winograd, & Pearson, 1980; Wonnacott & Raphael, 1982; Goldman & Durán, 1988) metacognitive behavior in regulating the question-answering process is strongly associated with success in these kinds of learning tasks (Lazonder & Rouet, 2008). And this metacognitive behavior was even more apparent in good performers in experiment 2, where the search task was more pure and without the aid of an initial representation of the text. On the other hand, both in experiment 1 and 2 we found a clear connection between search processes to answer questions and comprehension processes. Our claim, based on previous research (MacLatchy-Gaudet & Symons, 1999; Symons & Specht, 1994; Cataldo & Oakhill, 2000) that comprehension and search processes are highly linked, was supported by our empirical findings. It may be concluded that comprehension is a prerequisite for building up effective search strategies used to answer the questions. In both experiments, good performers formed a good representation of the search objective when reading the question and then went direct in search for the textual information that matched the question demands. That process implied comprehending both the question and the information they were selecting, and realizing what was the key information for giving a correct answer. Thus, students answering at a good performance level read questions fewer times, selected more relevant segments and used fewer QTW cycles to give a correct answer. In other words, a good comprehension of both the question and the textual information made them display an effective search pattern, whereas the opposite was observed for students answering at a poor performance level.

Comprehension is not only a prerequisite for displaying effective search patterns, but also guarantees the use of specific answering strategies depending on the type of question. We found that good performers were able to differentiate between high vs. low-level questions. Thus, when answering high-level questions they would review the majority of the textual segments involved in the question and they would connect and integrate that information in a way that would fit the question demands. Conversely, when answering low-level questions they would try to find the right information located in one or two paragraphs that matched the question demands, without needing to construct a whole new answer. These processes were apparent in the pattern of results that students answering at a good performance level showed (i.e., when reading the question, when selecting information and in the number of cycles used to answer either high or low level questions), especially in experiment 2. On the contrary, students answering at a poor performance level seemed not to distinguish between specific strategies to answer high vs. low-level questions. Therefore, they showed a rather chaotic answering pattern for the two types of questions.

Finally, both experiments showed clear search patterns associated to the good and poor performance levels. Nevertheless, there were some differences in the pattern of results for the good vs. poor performance level, especially when the complexity of the search task increased (i.e., with high-level questions). Generally, students answering at a good performance level did it as well as in experiment 1, showing effective search patterns directed to the relevant information and fitting the kind of question. Nevertheless, students answering at a poor level did worse in experiment 2, especially with high-level questions. We already argued that differences between the good and poor performance level were possibly softened by the initial reading in experiment 1, whereas in experiment 2 those differences turned out to be clearer and stronger. Two main factors could explain these differences for experiment 2: firstly, the task was more difficult (i.e., searching for information in a complex expository text) and secondly, differences between the good and poor answering level were more apparent in high-level questions, as the level of difficulty increased by the new question demands (i.e., not only locating but reviewing and integrating a high number of text segments).

In conclusion, searching for information to answer questions in complex documents is highly dependent on understanding and on strategic performance.

Strategic behavior when reading both narrative and expository texts has been widely studied (e.g., Goldman & Saul, 1990b; Trabasso, Suh, Payton, & Jain, 1995; Trabasso & Magliano, 1996b; Cote, Goldman, & Saul, 1998), but the use of different types of strategies when searching for information in expository texts for different purposes has been subject to little research so far. As students are more and more exposed to complex multimedia materials, effective handling of search assignments is becoming a critical skill. The contextual and individual factors that influence the acquisition of this skill are a new research avenue that should deserve further attention in the future.

References

Andre, T. (1979). Does answering higher level questions while reading facilitate productive reading? *Review of Educational Research, 49*, 280–318.

Brandsford, J. D., & Johnson, M. K. (1973). Considerations of some problems of comprehension. In W. G. Chase (Ed.), *Visual information processing* (pp. 383–438). New York: Academic.

Cataldo, M. G., & Oakhill, J. (2000). Why are poor comprehenders inefficient searchers? An investigation into the effects of text representation and spatial memory on the ability to locate information in text. *Journal of Educational Psychology, 92*, 791–799.

Chi, M. T. H., de Leeuw, N., Chiu, M. -H., & LaVancher, Ch. (1994). Eliciting self-explanations improves understanding. *Cognitive Science, 18*, 439–477.

Collins, A., Brown, J. S., & Larkin, K. M. (1980). Inference in text understanding. In R. J. Sprio, B. C. Bruce, & W. F. Brewer (Eds.), *Theoretical issues in reading comprehension* (pp. 385–407). Hillsdale, NJ: Erlbaum.

Cote, N., Goldman, S. R., & Saul, E. U. (1998). Students making sense of informational text: Relations between processing and representation. *Discourse Processes, 25*, 1–53.

Goldman, S. R. (1985). Inferential reasoning in and about narrative texts. In A. Graesser & J. Black (Eds.), *The psychology of questions* (pp. 247–276).Hillsdale, NJ: Erlbaum.

Goldman, S. R., & Durán, R. P. (1988). Answering questions from Oceanography Texts: Learner, Task and Text Characteristics. *Discourse Processes, 11*, 373–412.

Goldman, S. R., & Saul, E. U. (1990b). Flexibility in text processing: A strategy competition model. *Learning and Individual Differences, 2*, 181–219.

Graesser, A. C., & Franklin, S. P. (1990). QUEST: A model of question answering. *Discourse Processes, 13*, 279–303.

Graesser, A. C., Lang, K. L., & Roberts, R. M. (1991). Question answering in the context of stories. *Journal of Experimental Psychology, 120* (3), 254–277.

Guthrie, J. T., & Kirsch, I. (1987). Distinctions between reading comprehension and locating information in text. *Journal of Educational Psychology, 79*, 220–227.

Halpain, D. R., Glover, J. A., & Harvey, A. L. (1985). Differential effects of higher and lower order questions: Attention hypotheses. *Journal of Educational Psychology, 77*, 703–715.

Hamilton, R. J. (1985). A framework for the evaluation of the effectiveness of adjunct questions and objectives. *Review of Educational Research, 55*, 47–85.

Hartley, J., & Davies, I. K. (1976). Preinstructional strategies: The role of pretests, behavioral objectives, overviews and advance organizers. *Review of Educational Research, 46*, 239–265.

Kintsch, W., & van Dijk, T. A. (1978). Toward a model of text comprehension and production. *Psychological Review, 85*, 363–394.

Kintsch, W. (1998). *Comprehension: a paradigm for cognition.* Cambridge, MA: Cambridge University Press,.

Kirsch, I., & Guthrie, J. T. (1984). Adult reading practices for work and leisure. *Adult Education Quarterly, 34*, 213–232.

Langer, J. A. (1985). Levels of questioning: An alternative view. *Reading Research Quarterly, 20*, 586–602.

Lazonder, A. W., & Rouet, J. -F. (2008). Information problem solving instruction: some cognitive and metacognitive issues. *Computers in Human Behavior, 24*, 753–765.

MacLatchy-Gaudet, H., & Symons, S. (1999). *The role of reading comprehension in text search*. Unpublished manuscript.

Raphael,T. E., Winograd, P., & Pearson, P. D. (1980). Strategies children use when answering questions. In M. L. Kamil & A. J. Moe (Eds.), *Perspectives on reading research and instruction*. Washington, D.C: National Reading Conference.

Rickards, J. P. (1979). Adjunct postquestions in text: A critical review of methods and processes. *Review of Educational Research, 49*, 181–196.

Rouet, J. -F., Vidal-Abarca, E., Bert-Erboul, A., & Millogo, V. (2001). Effects of information search tasks on the comprehension of instructional text. *Discourse Processes, 31*(2), 163–186.

Rouet, J -F., & Vidal-Abarca, E. (2002). "Mining for meaning": a cognitive examination of inserted questions in learning from scientific text. In J. Otero, J. A. León, & A. C. Graesser (Eds.), *The Psychology of science text comprehension* (pp. 417–436). Mahwah, NJ: Lawrence Erlbaum Associates.

Rouet, J. -F., & Tricot, A. (1998). Chercher de l'information dans un hypertext: vers un modèle des processus cognitifs. In A. Tricot & J. -F. Rouet (Dir.) *Les hypermedias: approches cognitives et ergonomiques* (pp. 57–74). Paris: Hermès.

Symons, S., & Specht, J. A. (1994). Including both time and accuracy in defining text search efficiency. *Journal of Reading Behavior, 26*, 267–276.

Trabasso, T., van den Broek, P., & Lui, L. (1988). A model for generating questions that assess and promote comprehension. *Questioning Exchange, 2*, 25–38.

Trabasso, T., Suh, S., Payton, P., & Jain, R. (1995). Explanatory inferences and other strategies during comprehension: Encoding effects on recall. In R. Lorch & E. Brien (Eds.), *Sources of coherence in text comprehension* (pp. 219–239). Hillsdale, NJ: Lawrence Erlbaum Associates, Inc.

Trabasso, T., & Magliano, J. (1996b). How do children understand what they read and what can we do to help them ? In M. Craves, P. Van den Broek, Van den Broek & B. M. Taylor (Eds.), *The first R: Every child's right to read* (pp. 158–181). New York: Teachers College Press.

van Dijk, T. A., & Kintsch, W. (1983). *Strategies of Discourse Comprehension*. Hillsdale, NJ: Lawrence Erlbaum Associates.

Vidal-Abarca, E., Gilabert, R., & Rouet, J. -F. (1998). El papel del tipo de preguntas en el aprendizaje de textos cientificos [The role of question type on learning from scientific text.] *Seminario "Comprension y produccion de textos cientificos" [Meeting on Comprehension and production of scientific texts]*. Aveiro (Portugal), July 8–10, 1998.

Vidal-Abarca, E., Mengual, V., Sanjose, V., & Rouet, J. -F. (1996). Levels of comprehension of scientific prose: The role of text and task variables. Paper presented at the *International Seminar on Using Complex Information Systems*. Poitiers, France, September 4–6.

Whilite, S. C. (1985). Differential effects of high-level and low-level postpassage questions. *American Journal of Psychology, 98*, 41–58.

Wixson, K. K. (1983). Postreading question-answer interactions and children's learning from text. *Journal of Educational Psychology, 75*(3), 413– 423.

Wonnacott, C. A., & Raphael, T. E. (1982). Comprehension monitoring: An investigation of children's question-answering strategies. Paper presented at the *National Reading Conference*, Clearwater, Florida.

Chapter 8
Searching User-Controllable Animations During Learning

Richard Lowe

Abstract Complex animated information poses challenges for learners with respect to spatial and temporal search. Although user control of animations is widely regarded as a way to ameliorate these challenges, its potential often remains unfulfilled for learners who are novices in the depicted domain. Efforts to improve the effectiveness of user controllable animations should be based on a sound understanding of why such learners fail to extract crucial task relevant information. This chapter gives an account of an approach of fine-grained investigation of how learners interrogate animations. Three complementary sets of synchronized video recordings providing tight integration of different perspectives on a learner's activity are employed. These records permit detailed analysis of task performance on the basis of closely coordinated quantitative and qualitative data sets. Learners' concurrent verbalizations are supplemented by timely stimulated retrospective accounts. Results obtained suggest that domain novices rely on perceptually based interrogation strategies and set task-inappropriate goals.

Keywords Animation · Integrated methodology · Interrogation · Perceptually-based strategies · Self regulation · User control

8.1 Introduction

This chapter reports an approach for collecting fine-grained data about how individuals interact with user-controllable animations while engaging in learning tasks. The technique described permits data that give multiple perspectives on learner activity to be recorded and combined in a synchronized manner. For example, video recordings of learners' search of a user-controllable animation can be integrated with corresponding records of associated learning activities.

R. Lowe
Faculty of Humanities, Curtin University of Technology, GPO Box U 1987, Perth Western Australia, 6845
e-mail: lower@educ.curtin.edu.au

J.-F. Rouet et al. (eds.), *Understanding Multimedia Documents*,
DOI: 10.1007/978-0-387-73337-1_8, © Springer Science+Business Media, LLC 2008

Such combined records are then available for immediate replay to each learner for the purpose of eliciting stimulated recall of approaches employed while using the animation to carry out the learning task.

Animation is a potentially powerful way of presenting information to learners. It appears well suited to the challenge of communicating dynamic subject matter to learners in an effective manner (Narayanan & Hegarty, 2002). Until comparatively recently, the production of animations was a highly labour-intensive activity. Production costs generally ruled animation out of consideration by developers of educational resources. Distribution of educational animations also posed considerable challenges in past years. However, progress in information and communications technology has completely changed the situation. Because today's hardware and software greatly facilitate the production and distribution of animations, they have proliferated in computer-based learning environments. There has also been increasing attention to animation from researchers who investigate the efficacy of these learning environments (e.g. Mayer & Anderson, 1992; Mayer & Moreno, 2002; Palmer & Elkerton, 1993). The growing popularity of animations in multimedia learning resources suggests that many educational designers consider these dynamic explanations to be intrinsically superior to static alternatives. A preference for animated over static depictions often appears founded in animation's capacity to depict dynamic aspects of the content in an *explicit* fashion. Static depictions lack this capacity for direct representation of dynamics and so can provide *implicit* information only about how subject matter changes over time. They rely on the addition of indirect indications (dynamic symbols such as arrows, dotted lines, etc.) to designate temporal change and therefore learners are required to infer the actual situational dynamics. Carrying out this inferential activity with static depictions imposes an additional processing burden on learners that is not present with animations. In the absence of explicit dynamic information, learners are required to perform 'mental animation' (Hegarty, 1992; Hegarty & Sims, 1994), a process that can be both difficult to perform and uncertain in terms of its outcomes. Using static depictions to portray dynamic subject matter carries with it the risk that when learners try to interpret these portrayals, they will make inappropriate inferences. Interpretative errors may arise when learners attempt to construct a dynamic mental model from an external representation that under-specifies the temporal changes involved (c.f. Schnotz, 2002). In contrast, animations present dynamic information in a form that is available to be read straight from the display itself. In principle, this direct reading of such information is much less likely to result in erroneous interpretations of temporal change. Further, to the extent that animations do not clutter their depiction of the subject matter with arrows or other added dynamic symbols required by a corresponding static depiction, they can provide the learner with a display that is perceptually less complex. Lower perceptual complexity can have benefits for processes that are fundamental to the extraction of information from displays, such as direction of attention and search (see Winn, 1993).

On the basis of the apparent processing advantages that animated graphics can offer over their static counterparts (particularly for dynamic subject matter), it is tempting to assume that learning from animations would be more effective. However, no general superiority for animations has yet been demonstrated (Tversky & Bétrancourt, 2002). Indeed, it seems likely that because of the particular way in which they present information, animations can sometimes even have negative effects on learning.

8.1.1 Negative Effects of Animation

One potentially problematic feature of animated depictions is the very aspect discussed above as likely to be beneficial - their capacity to present the referent situational dynamics in a fully explicit manner. At first glance, it may seem counterintuitive that explicit portrayal would be problematic rather than helpful to the learner. We have already noted that explicit portrayal of temporal change makes it unnecessary for the learner to perform the resource-intensive mental animations and inferences that are required with static depictions of dynamic content. However, it is possible that by alleviating learners of these demands, animations may have a negative effect on learning by engendering a passive approach to the presented information. In extreme cases, such passivity would be more akin to what happens in a 'mindless' TV-watching situation than to the active processing approach required for fostering effective learning. It could be argued that static graphics actually have advantages over animation as a means of learning about dynamic content precisely because they are likely to promote more active processing of presented information.

Another possibility is that animation can have negative effects on learning because of the distinctive types of processing demands that animations are considered to impose upon learners (Lowe, 1999, 2001). It has been suggested that such demands can be especially pronounced for 'fixed-play' (system controlled) animations in which the learner has no control over how the animated material is presented (see Narayanan & Hegarty 2002). Although system controlled animations are certainly capable of providing an explicit representation of the subject matter's situational dynamics, this does not necessarily mean that learners will be able to read relevant information from the display effectively. When animated content is presented via a fixed-play regime, opportunities for self regulation of learning are severely restricted. Learners cannot vary the speed, direction, or continuity of presentation in order to adapt the way information is offered to their specific needs or preferences. Given the capacity limits that constrain human information processing, fixed-play animations have the potential to result in considerable mismatches between the way they present their content and how well equipped the learner is to process that content effectively. For this reason, the provision of user control over animations has been advocated as a way of helping learners to match content presentation characteristics to their individual capacities. User-controllable animations would seem to be particularly appropriate for complex subject matter that is difficult for learners to comprehend. For example, learners could take advantage of this control to reduce the rate at which more demanding portions of the information are presented so that the complexity can be broken down. Present-day computer technology makes it comparatively easy to produce animations that provide a high degree of user control. Accordingly, multimedia learning resources increasingly incorporate user-controllable animations as a matter of course.

8.1.2 Searching Animation

User control has been characterised as a tool that provides learners with a potentially more effective means for extracting information from an animation. However, it does not follow from the mere *provision* of such a tool that learners will necessarily employ it to best effect. A fundamental pre-requisite for extracting task-relevant information from a user-controllable animation is that the learner carries out appropriate spatial and temporal search of the presentation. This necessity for well-targeted searching reflects the fact that not all aspects of the animation will be equally useful with respect to a specific learning task. For example, the information in some parts of the display *area* will be more useful than that in other parts. Similarly, some *periods* within the animation sequence will be more valuable than other periods. Spatial search explores aspects of the animation display area such as the constituents of the display, the characteristics of those constituents, and the various relationships that exist amongst them. In contrast, temporal search explores how these aspects change over the course of the presentation and so involves interrogation *across* a series of animation frames (rather than search *within* a particular frame). The provision of user control undoubtedly gives learners the freedom to interrogate a complex animation in ways that allow them to manage its complexity. They have the option of playing the animation slowly so that they are able to follow and analyse particular changes rather than being overwhelmed by the rapid flux of information. Further, they can choose to stop the animation on any specific frame, step through a series of frames, replay particular sections, and reverse the playing direction. Such possibilities offer learners ways of making dynamic representations more tractable than they would be if presented only in fixed-play mode (Schwan & Riempp, 2004). However, the effectiveness of user control as a tool for supporting learning ultimately depends on the capacity of learners to take advantage of these possibilities to obtain the type of information that is most relevant to the current learning task. Effective learner interrogation of an animation therefore requires exploration to be focused on the spatial and temporal regions in which this type of information is actually concentrated. Further, the learner's examination of these regions once they are located must be carried out in a manner that deals appropriately with the thematically relevant information they contain. This involves identifying the key entities depicted, determining which characteristics of those entities are relevant to the task at hand, and understanding how these various aspects are related.

8.2 Using User Control

Taking advantage of a computer's capacity to provide user control facilities for an educational animation greatly expands the range of possibilities for self regulated learning of dynamic content. However, although there is a trend towards increasing the degree of control learners have over such computer-based presentations, a meta-analysis by Niemiec, Sikorski, and Walberg (1996) failed to establish any clear evidence of benefit from user control. Indeed it has been argued that problems can actually arise as a consequence of giving learners this greater responsibility (Kay, 2001). Despite the existence of various theoretical justifications for user control in computer-based learning materials, we know comparatively little about the nature of the processing that learners engage in when confronted with such materials (Milheim & Martin, 1991). From a psychological perspective, the practical effectiveness of user control is likely to be heavily dependent on the capacities of learners to self regulate their approach so that the available control facilities are used in productive ways (see Schnackenberg & Sullivan, 2000). At a process level, Winne and Hadwin (1998) emphasise the importance of metacognitive aspects of self regulation in which students adapt their studying techniques as required to shape aspects such as their goal setting, planning, strategies and tactics to evolving requirements of the learning task. In the context of user controllable animations, the success with which learners interrogate the available information set will be heavily dependent on how appropriately they regulate their exploration strategies and tactics in response to both the moment-to-moment task demands and the central learning purpose.

8.2.1 Is User Control Effective?

Simply providing user control will not automatically result in the effective self regulation of learning by those who study an animation. If the facilities provided are used inappropriately and in an unprincipled way, it is unlikely that the intended learnings will occur. To be educationally effective, user control must be coupled with a learner who has the study skills and background knowledge necessary to properly exploit the opportunities that such control offers. Recent research confirms that in some situations the effectiveness of user control for aiding learning from animations may be limited. Such limitations appear to arise when the animation presents complex dynamic subject matter to learners who lack expertise in the depicted domain. Learners who were novices in the field of meteorology studied user-controllable animations of how meteorological markings on weather maps change over time (Lowe, 2003a, 2004). Participants were given a printed weather map (the 'Original') and asked to draw a prediction of the next day's meteorological markings on a blank outline map. This prediction was to be based upon their interrogation of an accompanying user-controllable weather map animation that showed the typical changes in markings occurring over a seven-day period. Data about the way participants built up markings on their prediction map were collected via a video camera positioned below the glass-topped table upon which they were drawing. It was found that participants tended to extract perceptually conspicuous aspects of the meteorological dynamics while neglecting those aspects that were thematically relevant but had lower perceptual salience. In addition, larger-scale spatial and temporal relations among the markings were far less likely to be incorporated into participants' drawn predictions than were those of a more local nature.

The learners who participated in this study lacked specialized background knowledge in the animation's content domain, while the animation itself depicted rich and complex dynamic information. It was inferred that the processing demands of this animation for these particular learners were such that participants were unable to take best advantage of the user control facility provided. The assumption was made that these learners were faced by a situation where far more information was being presented than they could deal with in an appropriate fashion. As a result, they adopted a 'survival strategy' which involved them being highly selective in how they searched the animation and thus very restricted in the information they extracted. Lacking the domain-specific knowledge required to carry out effective top-down processing of the animation, they processed its information in a largely bottom-up fashion that was strongly driven by the immediate perceptual characteristics of the display. As a result, much information of thematic relevance was either completely missed or interpreted inappropriately. It was hypothesized that in effect, the participants' self regulation of learning with respect to their employment of the user control facilities provided was poorly aligned to the requirements of the given learning task.

8.2.2 Methodological Challenges in Characterizing User Control

The research referred to above indicates that the exploratory flexibility available with user-controllable animations may not be uniformly positive in its effects on learning. If the educational potential of such animations is to be fulfilled, it is important to develop a detailed understanding of why learners may fail to exploit user control facilities effectively. Which specific aspects of the way learners extract information from the animation are ineffective and what opportunities exist for improving their performance? One way of developing an understanding of learners' deficiencies in this process is to collect fine-grained data about how they interrogate user-controllable animations. The utility of these data will depend to a large extent on how well they are able to capture details of both (a) the strategies and tactics that learners employ when interrogating the animation and (b) the reasoning processes behind these strategies and tactics, together with the influences of other aspects of self regulation such as goals, planning, monitoring, and adjustment. However, eliciting such data that is both valid and amenable to meaningful analysis in a practical sense poses considerable methodological challenges.

One of the more straightforward aspects of investigating learners' interrogation is the collection of data about which specific frame of the animation is displayed to the learner at any particular point in time. This is readily handled by well-established approaches such as the use of log files to directly capture the identity of these frames as they are visited by the learner and the length of time for which specific frames are viewed. However, merely being able to generate and record vast amounts of data via automatic capture is clearly of questionable value in itself (Maguire & Sweeney, 1989), particularly if the research focus is upon the subtleties of perceptual, cognitive, and metacognitive processing. For such data sets to be of value, they need to be interpretable with respect to the specific aims of the research. Multimedia data collection approaches offer a way to make the captured data more useful to the researcher by furnishing a basis for their interpretation. By tapping a varied range of behavioural indicators, these composite approaches can provide complementary perspectives on the phenomenon being investigated.

Although multimedia data collection approaches are useful in principle, collecting high quality data without disrupting learner processing can be challenging in practice. Further, challenges arise in analyzing these data to determine the underlying reasons that drive learner behaviour. Collection of concurrent think-aloud protocols is an option but the effectiveness of this approach is likely to be somewhat limited, particularly if the animation is already making considerable demands on learners' processing capacities (c.f. Rouet & Passerault, 1999). Because of these demands, insufficient processing resources may be available for the generation of useful verbalisations if performance of animation-based visual processing is to be sustained. Further, learners' thought processes may be disrupted if they are producing a think aloud protocol concurrently with performing the target task (Jourdenais, 2001). In addition, *verbal* data alone do not generally provide sufficiently specific identification and characterization of the *graphic* information being considered by learners during their reasoning processes. The requirement to convert visual thinking into a verbal utterance risks degradation or distortion of some aspects of that thinking, even assuming that words alone are actually capable of capturing the thought processes involved. Gestural data obtained by having learners point out, trace or otherwise physically indicate such information could help to provide more specificity as well as capture visual aspects that are not readily expressed in words (Trafton, Trickett, & Stilzlein, 2004; Hegarty, Mayer, & Kriz, 2004).

In the case of the weather map prediction investigations referred to above, an additional source of data was the video records of participants' drawing activity as they built up the set of predicted meteorological markings. It was clear from these investigations that a close coupling existed between interrogation activity and production of these markings. Understanding the learners' approaches to interrogation would therefore require analysis of synchronized records of these various aspects of their behaviour. Further, if participants' *concurrent* verbalizations about interrogation strategies are limited by the immediate demands of the learning task, having them give *retrospective* accounts of their approaches may provide valuable supplementary data. Van der Haak , De Jong, and Schellens (2003) suggest that these two approaches provide different but equally useful types of data, with retrospective accounts having their own distinctive advantages. The use of both concurrent and retrospective approaches allows participants to provide multiple explanatory perspectives on their approaches and this combination has the potential to provide richer data sets (Camps, 2003). Unfortunately, pilot studies showed that even if participants were debriefed straight after completing the task, they recalled relatively little detail about the strategies they used to interrogate the animation. This probably reflects the demanding nature of the task in which they were engaged. There was also a tendency for their recall to misrepresent what they had actually done while engaged in the task (c.f. Hoc & Leplat, 1983). It is possible that these deficiencies could be ameliorated by confronting participants with a record of their actual behaviour in order to stimulate more comprehensive and accurate recall (Camps, 2003). However, this would need to be done with a minimum of delay after completion of the task and in a way that allowed the participant to work with such a record in a flexible manner. This was the goal of the approach described below.

8.3 Investigating User Control

Consider a situation in which a learner is working with a particular user-controllable animation in order to carry out a specific learning task (as in the case described above of using a weather map animation to assist in the drawing of a future pattern of meteorological markings). Because some parts of the animation will be more valuable for this purpose than others, the learner's efforts should be concentrated on those aspects that are most relevant to the task at hand. For example, in the case of Australian summer weather maps, certain meteorological features (cold fronts, high pressure cells, etc.) are migratory and sweep across the animated display at reasonably regular intervals. In contrast, terrestrial heat lows tend to be stationary and persist for extended periods in much the same region. Further, various relationships exist between different types of meteorological features as exemplified by the way that the shape of terrestrial heat lows changes as cold fronts and high pressure systems wend their way across the map. An appreciation of the cyclic behaviour of key meteorological features and the transformations they undergo in association with other features is vital to being able to predict likely forthcoming meteorological patterns. The process of making a plausible prediction is assumed to involve the running of a high quality dynamic mental model from a given initial state to some nominated later state. In order to build a high quality mental model of meteorological dynamics from a weather map animation, the learner must first extract information of relevance to the prediction task. Such predictively crucial aspects will be distributed across space and time throughout the frames constituting the animation. Therefore in order to find information likely to be useful for the learning task, the learner must search across these two dimensions. A distinctive characteristic of user-controllable animation is that it allows learners to carry out temporal searches in a highly flexible manner. The aim of the approach described in the next section was to determine the way in which learners used this flexibility and how well their search strategies and tactics were suited to the task of extracting prediction-relevant information.

8.3.1 Integrating Multiple Data Sources

In order to collect richer and more illuminating data about how learners interrogated user-controllable animation of weather maps, the equipment used in previous studies was modified. Over the course of the procedure, three sets of video data were collected for each participant:

(i) a *composite* video of drawing activity embedded in animation interrogation
(ii) a *contextual* video showing the animation screen, original map, prediction map, and participant's gestures
(iii) a *stimulated recall* data obtained from the participant's explanation of the composite video.

In addition to collecting video records of the animation frames displayed and of the participants' drawing actions, a further video camera was used to collect gestural data. This video encompassed the computer display (showing the animation), the original map (from which the prediction was to be made) and the blank map (onto which the prediction was to be drawn). Further, video streams of the animation and the drawing activity were combined as shown in Fig. 8.1 to produce a composite video in which there was direct correspondence between animation interrogation and performance of the learning task so that their relation could later be analyzed in detail. This composite video also provided material for cueing of participants' retrospective accounts of their interrogation strategies.

In the composite recording, video of the participant's activity in drawing the meteorological markings is displayed as a 'picture-in-picture' inset within the main animation interrogation video (top left hand corner). The real-time

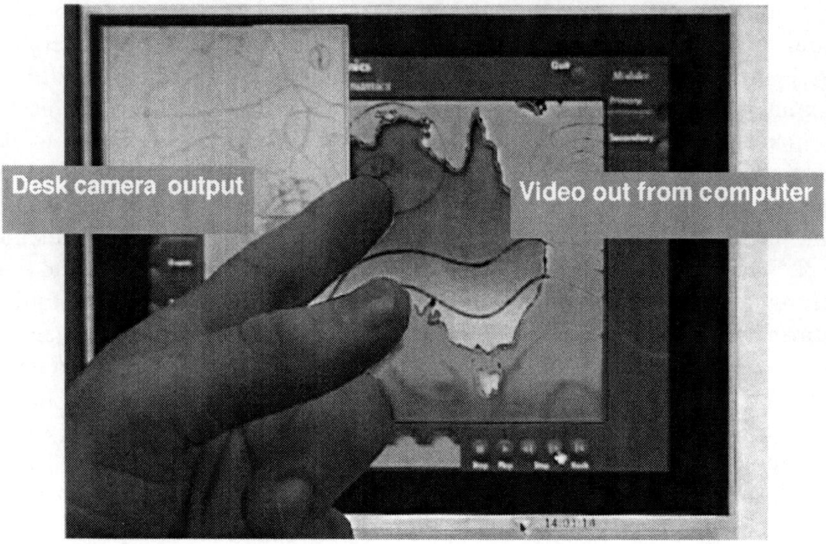

Fig. 8.1 Composite video being used to explain approaches used during animation interrogation and prediction

synchronized composite video was recorded straight to hard disk on a second computer. This made it available for immediate playback to the participant so that stimulated recall data could be collected as soon as the map prediction task had been completed. For this recall phase, the participant used the computer mouse to scan through the composite video (with its sound turned off) while explaining the approaches that were being used during the earlier interrogation and prediction drawing. Participants were also asked to use their other hand to point at the features being referred to on the screen. Each participant made a total of three sweeps through the composite video: (i) a *preview* sweep to familiarize themselves with the recording (ii) an *analysis* sweep to explain the approaches they used, and (iii) a *summary* sweep to identify the main stages in their performance of the task as a whole. The complete stimulated recall was videoed from the display screen so as to capture both the participant's sweeps through the composite video, and the associated explanatory gestures. For the purposes of analysis, the three sets of video recordings were transferred to DVD. This format provides powerful analytical advantages such as the capacity to bookmark material within the video, instant access to specific locations, and extensive options for precise control over playback.

8.3.2 Data and Analysis

Material from a participant's video records will be used to illustrate the types of data that can be collected from this approach and ways in which they can be

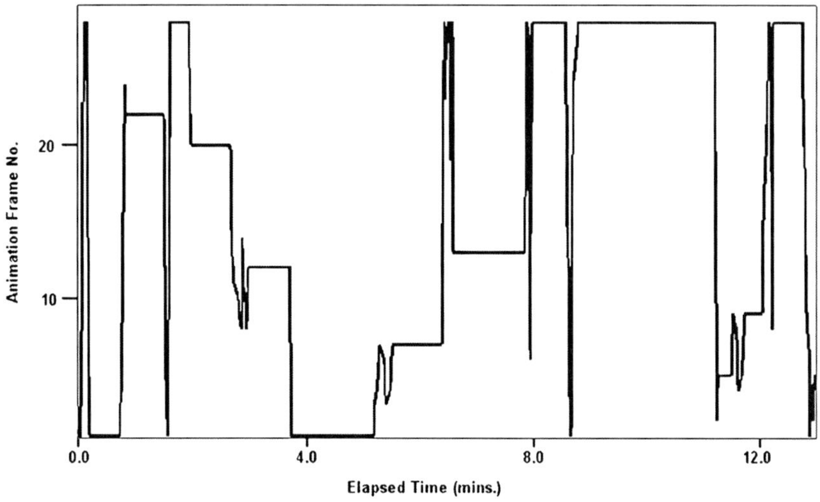

Fig. 8.2 Example interrogation graph showing search activity over time

analyzed. The video data provide the opportunity for fine-grained, coordinated quantitative and qualitative analysis of how user control is employed and the strategies underlying its employment.

Figure 8.2 is a graphical summary of the participant's interaction with the animation over the course of the task. The vertical axis indicates which frame (frames 1 to 28) of the animation was displayed on screen at any particular instant, while the horizontal axis indicates elapsed time. This graph shows that the overall interrogation pattern was made up of (i) periods where the animation was held static on a specific frame and (ii) various types of scans through a range of the animation's frames. To allow for the time lag involved in physically manipulating the computer mouse while changing animation play direction, the minimum threshold for a nominating an episode as 'static' was set at three seconds. Static episodes (represented by the horizontal portions of the graph) can be divided into *drawing* episodes during which the participant drew predicted markings, and *non-drawing* episodes. The scans are made up of individual sweeps (represented by the approximately vertical portions of the graph) that vary in both their scope and speed. Some sweeps cover most of the animation's 28 frames, while others are far more limited in scope. Scans also consisted of either single or multiple sweeps.

Figure 8.3 shows how key aspects of a participant's verbal and gestural activity are related to interpretation of the interrogation graph described above for Fig. 8.2. Only the initial part of that graph is shown here because the time scale has been expanded to reveal the fine structure of the interrogation (such as variations in the speed of sweeps which appear as differences in slope). This portion of the Fig. 8.2 graph has been rotated through ninety degrees in

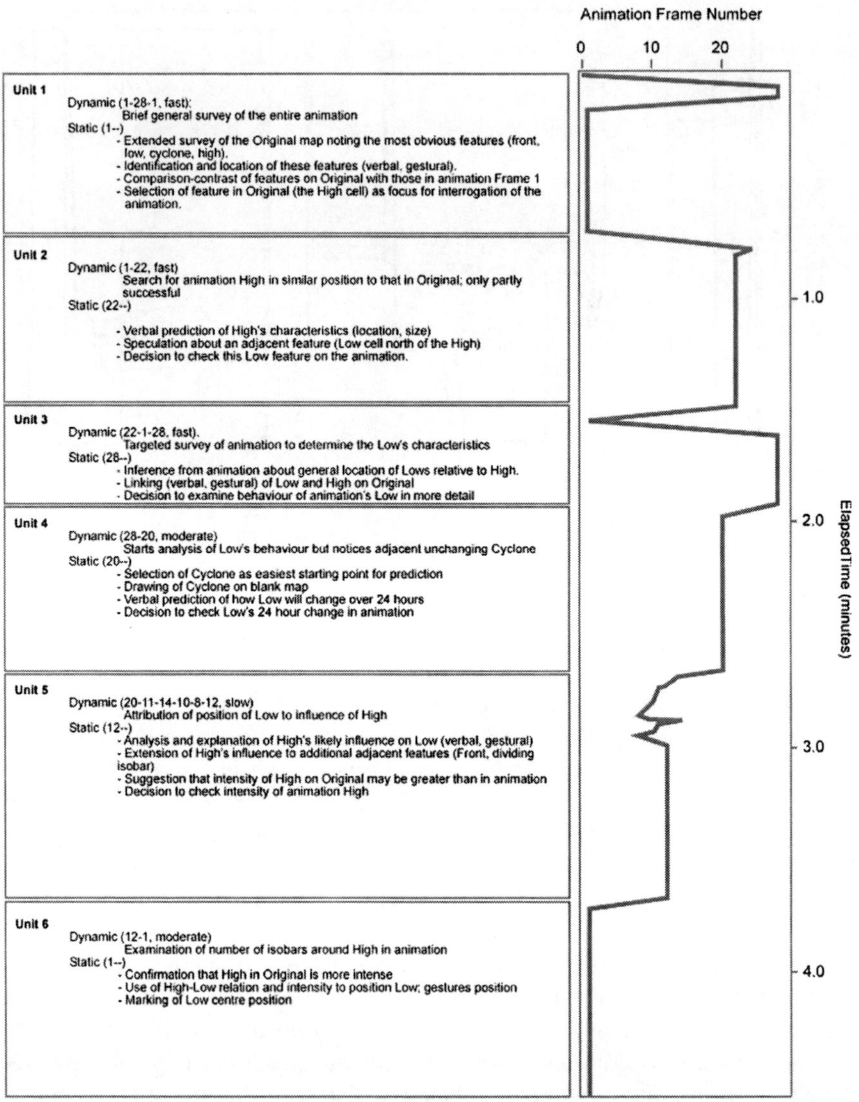

Fig. 8.3 *Right side* of figure is a portion of interrogation graph. *Left side* summarizes key aspects of verbal and gestural data generated by participant in each segment (unit) of interrogation

Fig. 8.3 to facilitate annotation with the associated verbal and gestural information. The example shown here is taken from the early part of the interrogation where the participant's particular focus is upon trying to predict what will happen to the low pressure areas over the north of the Australian continent in a 24 hour period. The original weather map pattern from which the prediction is to be made is shown in Fig. 8.4. In the annotations on the left hand side of

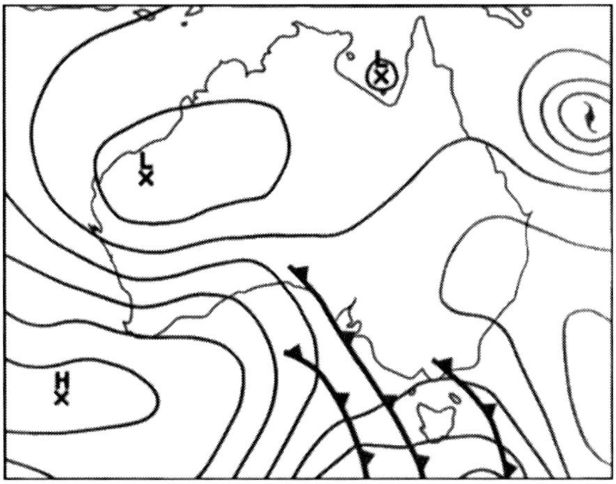

Fig. 8.4 'Original' map from which prediction was made

Fig. 8.3, details of the participant's activity are reported as a sequence of units, each of which consists of two main parts (i) a dynamic part (or scan) made up of one or more successive sweeps through the animation's frames, and (ii) a static part (or pause) that directly followed the dynamic part and during which the animation remained on a single frame for an extended period. These correspond to 'horizontal' and vertical regions of the Fig. 8.3 interrogation graph segment respectively. For example, the first unit's dynamic part, (1-28-1, fast), entailed a rapid sweep from Frame 1 of the animation to Frame 28 then back again to Frame 1, followed by its static part (1–) during which the animation was left paused on Frame 1. Typically, the dynamic part of each unit was of a shorter duration than its associated static part. Not surprisingly, most verbalizations and gestures occurred during these static parts, as did all of the drawing activity.

8.3.3 User Control Strategies and Tactics

In the example above, the participant employed the user control facility in a variety of ways that could have the effect of limiting the amount of information being processed at any time. The excerpt shows how the participant played animation segments of different lengths, depending on the exploratory goals at hand, so matching segment scope to the level of information sought. On some occasions, the entire sequence was swept in order to gain a general overview of how the marking patterns changed (e.g. Unit 1). This could be interpreted as 'skimming' across the surface of the available information without pursuing any particular aspect in any depth. For the case illustrated by Fig. 8.3, the following utterance made after the first sweep in Unit 1 suggests that the participant had skimmed through the frames to briefly characterise the features present in the animation:

> Front sweeping to the south and down, down like that. Only one low up top – there's only one low up the top there. There's one low there, quite large . . . more cold fronts, cyclones still there, highs still to that side . . .

This is essentially a basic roll-call of the components that occur during the course of the animation without any real attempt to deal with them in detail.

On other occasions, the interrogation was much more limited in scope with the stated goal being to obtain more specific information, such as how a particular component of the pattern changed over a 24 hour time period (e.g. Unit 2). This could be interpreted as 'burrowing' more deeply into a restricted subset of the available information. In Unit 2 of Fig. 8.3, the section of the participant's protocol associated with the more limited sweep to frame 22 suggests that the focus of attention has narrowed considerably.

> . . . so, if I wanted to position that high, I would drag that through but it doesn't quite do it. It's getting to a similar position there – we've got a low further down which is actually squeezing this up . . . so I am going to suggest that . . . the high is going to squeeze into the Bight, probably cover most of the Bight there . . . the low might stay where it is. I'm just going to check out what these lows are doing . . .

In this instance, the participant concentrates first on a detailed determination of the high pressure cell's path over time before noticing an apparent interaction between two features. Next, the extent of the high's coverage is dealt with together with the fate of the low. The excerpt ends with a decision to single out the lows for particular attention (followed by a further sweep in which the behavior of the lows is explored).

Despite their apparent differences, these two approaches could in fact impose much the same level of processing demands on the learner; they simply involve alternative ways of limiting those demands in order to achieve a workable match between information presentation and processing capacity. Further matching between the nature of the information sought and the manner in which the animation was interrogated occurred with the way the participant varied the playing speed. Compared with sweeps made when the goal was to survey the animation, relatively slow sweeps were made when the changes in a particular feature were being studied in detail. This latter more detailed study was particularly evident during the static segments.

As well as controlling the scope and speed of the animated segments examined, the participant appeared to constrain the processing burden further by mostly concentrating on only one meteorological feature at a time. In cases where more than one feature was being considered, the features were invariably adjacent to each other rather than widely separated on the map. The exploration sequence and focus of discussion were also dominated by the adjacency of features. The participant's interrogation of the animation progressed by chaining from feature to feature rather than by jumping between widely separated features. For example, the annotations in Fig. 8.3 show that the participant began with the high pressure cell, moved to the adjacent low pressure cell, then moved to cyclone next to that. This progression via adjacent features limited the spatial scope of exploration in a manner that is analogous to the way that the temporal scope of exploration was limited by the participant restricting the length of the animation sequence played.

Overall, this participant demonstrates a range of approaches consistent with employing user control to keep the processing demands within reasonable bounds. The constraints that the participant imposed on the scope of exploration were interpreted as a general strategy aimed at making this complex animation more tractable. However, not all aspects of the way the user manipulated the animation to limit the processing burden appear to be beneficial in terms of the learning task. One of these is the localization of exploratory activity to single or adjacent features. In order to draw a coherent weather map prediction, its component features need to be coordinated at a macro level (i.e. across the display area as a whole), not just in localised 'islands' of micro structure. The overarching macro level organisation is unlikely to be appreciated when interrogation is restricted to a mechanistic feature-by-feature search through the animation.

8.3.4 Example Results

The data collection approach reported above has been used to investigate how novices in the domain of meteorology interrogate user controllable animated weather maps (Lowe, 2003b). In that study, 10 Teacher Education students performed the task previously described, using the animation to help them predict the pattern of markings expected to appear on a forthcoming weather map. A particular focus of the investigation was the nature of the temporal exploration undertaken by the participants while constructing their weather map predictions. Participants varied greatly in (i) the total time they spent interrogating the animation, (ii) the intensity of that interrogation, and (iii) its distribution across the 28 frames comprising the animated sequence. However, despite the high degree of variation across participants, there appeared to be a general tendency to adopt exploration strategies that severely constrained the scope of temporal search. Interrogation was typically concentrated around those few frames of the animation bearing the closest superficial resemblance to the original weather map from which the prediction was to be made. These frames were more likely to be replayed several times by the participants than were the remaining frames. Further, much of the interrogation of these privileged frames was carried out in a slow stepwise manner rather than at sufficient speed to produce an illusion of continuous change. The frames examined were thus treated more as a series of static 'snapshots' than as a fluid dynamic system. In restricting their interrogation to this subset of frames, participants had much less exposure to the key information about temporal macro structures that is embodied in the intervening frames. Most of the interrogation consisted of short sweeps. Conversely, scans through large sections of the animation sequence were comparatively infrequent; they tended to be confined to preliminary surveys and were rarely used later in the interrogation. The temporally fragmented type of interrogation that comprised the bulk of the exploration activity is unlikely to provide opportunities for detecting the overarching patterns necessary for cohesion amongst the individual meteorological features comprising a weather map.

Data from the concurrent and retrospective protocols revealed why the learners limited their exploration in this manner. Participants' gestural data were particularly useful in disambiguating verbalizations, in providing direct spatial information, and in explicitly portraying dynamics. Together, verbalisations and gestures indicated that the user control was employed in a considered fashion with very particular goals in mind. Learners regulated their interrogation in a highly strategic manner and adapted exploration tactics on the fly to address emerging issues. However, their goals were typically ill-suited to the requirements of extracting the types of information required to build a high quality dynamic mental model of how Australian weather maps change over time. Rather, they tended to be concerned in the first instance with the immediate pragmatics of finding then characterizing material in the animation that matched individual features and local configurations exhibited on the original map. This matching process was restricted to a mechanical comparison of the most conspicuous perceptual properties of the material concerned. Once approximate matches were located, the typical strategy was to edge the animation forward by 24 hours to see what happened to a particular target feature or configuration over the period for which the participants were required to later make a prediction. This preoccupation with finding then progressing discrete fragments in the animation that superficially resembled those in the original map accounts for the frequent pauses and characteristic slow, deliberate, repeated approach to interrogation. It also explains why long sequences around the middle of the animation were neglected – the learners were concerned with comparing the superficial appearance of specific states rather than with making deeper connections throughout the animation to establish overall dynamic patterns. The protocols were generally lacking in references to the relationships between features that were separated in space or time. For example, in the retrospective data collection phase, participants often explained how they moved from one feature to the next on the basis of their proximity alone (i.e., noticing what was happening to a neighboring feature – perceptually based serendipity). However, they rarely compared spatially or temporally distant features that would have helped them detect macroscopic cyclic changes of key importance to meteorological prediction. Their verbalizations indicated little or no awareness of the predictive utility of super-ordinate spatial and temporal structures that are relatively low in natural perceptual salience. In sum, the concurrent and retrospective protocol data indicated that deficiencies in learners' interrogation approaches could be traced back to unproductive self regulation activities stemming from inappropriate task goals.

8.4 Conclusion

The approach reported in this chapter was designed to facilitate synchronized collection of fine-grained multi-perspective data about learner interaction with user controllable animations. A primary motivation for collecting such data was to help reveal why these animated learning resources can be less educationally effective than expected. A combination of quantitative and qualitative data sets that tightly integrated details of interrogation patterns with concurrent and retrospective verbalizations was used to link data about what learners were doing with data about why they were doing it.

Providing user control over educational animations has the potential to enhance their effectiveness as a resource for learning. However, fulfilling this potential in practice will depend on how successfully the learner interrogates the information that is presented in a particular animation. The uncritical faith too often placed in the efficacy of user control as a means of improving animation as a tool for learning may be misplaced because learners are not necessarily able to take best advantage of this facility. The available control needs to be exercised in a skilled and principled way so that all key task-relevant aspects of the presentation are located, examined, and appropriately interrelated. This requires well-targeted spatial and temporal search of the presented information set carried out in a comprehensive manner that provides the learner with all the raw material required for building a high quality dynamic mental model. For interrogation of animation to be effective, it must reveal to the learner the overarching relationships amongst the animation's various components that are the basis for forming an accurate, coherent, and task-appropriate knowledge structure.

A trial of the integrated data collection technique described above indicated that when left to their own devices, learners interrogated a user controllable weather map animation in a way that severely limited the number of animation frames examined in any depth. This restriction was interpreted as a learner response to the excessive demands faced when presented with complex animated content. As a consequence of learners adopting a superficial, pragmatic approach, key dynamic information concerning the generalizations required for making plausible coherent predictions was neglected. Likely underlying reasons for this neglect emerged from the complementary qualitative data obtained via concurrent and retrospective protocols. Verbal and gestural productions associated with the interrogation processes revealed that this neglect could be attributed to poor learner self regulation. Broad scale spatial and dynamic structures capable of supporting effective prediction tended not to be targeted in search. Instead, learners' perceptually-based strategies and tactics reflected their setting of task-inappropriate goals. Data about the deficiencies in self regulation that emerged from using this combination approach suggest that the learners were poorly equipped to handle user controllable animations of the complex dynamic subject matter on their own. For user control to be an effective addition to educational animations, it seems that learners may sometimes need guidance to help them perform their interrogation in a more appropriate way. In essence, such guidance could still help them make the animation more tractable by reducing the overall processing demands, but would do this by directing their processing towards those aspects having highest task relevance. This direction should help to re-orient learners' search goals towards finding more perceptually subtle high relevance aspects that lend coherence to the dynamic mental models constructed as a result of the interrogation process.

Investigating learners' interrogation of complex animated content requires the use of data collection approaches that both take account of the high demand situation involved and allow task-appropriate forms of data to be gathered in ways that capture their essential richness. The type of data collected using the approach described here can provide useful insights concerning how learners interact with animations. Because of its capacity to furnish rich explanatory data about why particular patterns of interrogation occur, this approach has potential for investigating the effectiveness of various intervention and support possibilities for guiding learners towards more effective employment of user control.

References

Camps, J. (2003). Concurrent and retrospective verbal reports as tools to better understand the role of attention in second language tasks. *International Journal of Applied Linguistics, 13*, 201–221.

Hegarty, M. (1992). Mental animation: Inferring motion from static diagrams of mechanical systems. *Journal of Experimental Psychology: Learning, Memory and Cognition, 1*, 1084–1102.

Hegarty, M., & Sims, V. K. (1994). Individual differences in mental animation during mechanical reasoning. *Memory & Cognition, 22*, 411–430.

Hegarty, M., Mayer, S., & Kriz, S. (2004, August). Gesture use while thinking about machines. In *Spatial cognition and gesture*, Symposium conducted at CogSci 2004, the 24th Annual Meeting of the Cognitive Science Society, Chicago.

Hoc, J. M., & Leplat, J. (1983). Evaluation of different modalities of verbalizations in a sorting task. *International Journal of Man-Machine Studies, 18*, 283–306.

Jourdenais, R. (2001). Cognition, instruction and protocol analysis. In P. Robinson (Ed.), *Cognition an second language instruction* (pp. 354–375). New York: Cambridge University Press.

Kay, J. (2001). Learner control. *User Modelling and User-Adapted Interaction, 11*, 111–127.

Lowe, R. K. (1999). Extracting information from an animation during complex visual learning. *European Journal of Psychology of Education, 14*, 225–244.

Lowe, R. K. (2001). Understanding information presented by complex animated diagrams. In J. -F. Rouet, J. J. Levonen, & A. Biardeau (Eds.), *Multimedia learning: Cognitive and instructional issues* (pp. 65–74). London: Pergamon.

Lowe, R. K. (2003a). Animation and learning: Selective processing of information in dynamic graphics. *Learning and Instruction, 13*, 157–176.

Lowe, R. K. (2003b, August). *Spatial and temporal search in learning from animation.* Paper presented at the 10th European Conference for Research on Learning and Instruction, Padua, Italy.

Lowe, R. K. (2004). Interrogation of a dynamic visualization during learning. *Learning and Instruction, 14*, 257–274.
Maguire, M., & Sweeney, M. (1989). System monitoring: Garbage generator or basis for comprehensive evaluation system? In A. SutcliffeSutcliffe & L. MacaulayMacaulay (Eds.), *Proceedings of CHI'89* (pp. 375–394). Cambridge, UK: Cambridge University press.
Mayer, R. E., & Anderson, R. B. (1992). The instructive animation: Helping students build connections between words and pictures in multimedia learning. *Journal of Educational Psychology, 84*, 444–452
Mayer, R. E., & Moreno, R. (2002). Animation as an aid to multimedia learning. *Educational Psychology Review, 14*, 87–99.
Milheim, W. D., & Martin, B. (1991). Theoretical bases for the use of learner control: Three different perspectives. *Journal of Computer-Based Instruction, 18*, 99–105.
Narayanan, N. H., & Hegarty, M. (2002). Multimedia design for communication of dynamic information. *International Journal of Human-Computer Studies, 57*, 279–315.
Niemiec, R. P., Sikorski, C., & Walberg, H. (1996). Learner-control effects: A review of reviews and a meta-analysis. *Journal of Educational Computing Research, 15*, 157–175.
Palmer, S., & Elkerton, J. (1993). Animated demonstrations for learning procedural computer-based tasks. *Human-Computer Interaction, 8*, 193–216.
Rouet, J. -F., & Passerault, J. -M. (1999). Analyzing learner-hypermedia interaction: An overview of online methods. *Instructional Science, 27*, 201–219.
Schnackenberg, H., & Sullivan, H. J. (2000). Learner control over full and lean computer-based instruction under differing ability levels. *Educational Technology Research and Development, 48*, 19–35.
Schnotz, W. (2002). Towards an integrated view of learning from text and visual displays. *Educational Psychology Review, 14*, 101–120.
Schwan, S., & Riempp, R. (2004). The cognitive benefits of interactive videos: Learning to tie nautical knots. *Learning and Instruction, 14*, 293–357.
Trafton, G., Trickett, S., & Stilzlein, C. (2004, August). Spatial transformations and gestures. In *Spatial cognition and gesture*, Symposium conducted at CogSci 2004, the 24th Annual Meeting of the Cognitive Science Society, Chicago.
Tversky, B., & Bétrancourt,Bétrancourt M. (2002). Animation: Can it facilitate? *International Journal of Human-Computer Studies, 57*, 247–262.
Van der Haak, M., De Jong, M., & Schellens, P. J. (2003). Retrospective vs. concurrent think-aloud protocols: Testing the useability of an online library catalogue. *Behaviour and Information Technology, 22*, 339–351.
Winne, P. H., & Hadwin, A. F. (1998). Studying as self-regulated learning. In D. J. Hacker & J. DunloskyDunlosky (Eds.), *Metacognition in educational theory and practice* (pp. 277–304). Mahway, NJ: Erlbaum.
Winn, W. D. (1993). An account of how readers search for information in diagrams. *Contemporary Educational Psychology, 18*, 162–185.

Chapter 9
Studying Eye Movements in Multimedia Learning

Huib K. Tabbers, Fred Paas, Chris Lankford, Rob L. Martens, and Jeroen J.G. van Merriënboer

Abstract This paper discusses the usefulness of tools that enable the analysis of eye movement data in dynamic interfaces for investigating theoretical issues in the area of multimedia learning. One of these tools, *GazeTracker*™, a program that links eye movement data to information about the internal computer processes and automatically combines the two for further analyses, is discussed. The functionality of the tool for studying the process of multimedia learning is illustrated with an experiment on the integration of text and pictures in a web-based lesson on instructional design. In the experiment, differences in fixation patterns between several presentation formats are investigated. It is concluded that tools like *GazeTracker*™ make it easier to study how people integrate text and pictures in dynamic interfaces like web browsers.

Keywords Eye movement · Integration · Picture · Text · Time constraints

9.1 Introduction

In educational psychology there is an on-going debate about how students learn with pictures and text, especially with the rise of multimedia learning environments where people have to integrate verbal and pictorial information. This has produced a large amount of empirical research on the effectiveness of different presentation formats (e.g., Mayer, 2001). However, as far as we know, hardly any research in this area has used eye-tracking methods to study looking behavior. Eye movement measures might be a very interesting addition to the research on multimedia learning, especially because the existing theories are partly based on assumptions about where people look when they are integrating text and pictures.

H.K. Tabbers
Institute of Psychology, Erasmus University Rotterdam, Woudestein, T12-39, P.O. Box 1738, 3000 DR Rotterdam, The Netherlands
e-mail: tabbers@fsw.eur.nl

J.-F. Rouet et al. (eds.), *Understanding Multimedia Documents*,
DOI: 10.1007/978-0-387-73337-1_9, © Springer Science+Business Media, LLC 2008

In the field of eye movement research, there are numerous studies on reading behavior and on scene perception (see Rayner, 1998, for an overview), but only a few studies on the integration of text and pictures (Duffy, 1992). These are notable exceptions like studies by Hegarty on mental animation (Hegarty, 1992a,b; Hegarty & Just, 1989, 1993), the work of d'Ydewalle and colleagues on television subtitles (for an overview, see d'Ydewalle & Gielen, 1992), some work on the perception of cartoons by Carroll, Young, and Guertin (1992), a study on how people look at advertisements by Rayner, Rotello, Stewart, Keir, and Duffy (2001) and a study of sentence-picture verification tasks by Underwood, Jebbett, & Roberts (2004). Most of these studies used static images so that the gaze position of the participants could easily be related to the different elements of the scene. Dynamic interfaces substantially increase the complexity of the data analysis because changes on the screen have to be directly related to the eye movement data (e.g., Goldberg & Kotval, 1999; Goldberg, Stimson, Lewenstein, Scott, & Wichansky, 2002). This makes eye tracking research in the area of multimedia learning not an easy task to do.

Fortunately, some interesting analysis tools have become available that integrate eye movement data with the dynamic processes that simultaneously take place on the computer screen (e.g., Crowe & Narayanan, 2000; Lankford, 2000b). In this article we will discuss the usefulness of these tools for examining theoretical issues related to the area of multimedia learning, and describe an experiment in which we applied one of these tools called *GazeTracker*™.

9.2 The Added Value of Studying Eye Movements in Multimedia Learning

Recent theories on multimedia learning like Mayer's generative theory (2001) and cognitive load theory (Sweller, 1999; Sweller, Van Merriënboer, & Paas, 1998) are based on a number of assumptions about the learner's cognitive architecture. Both Mayer's theory and Sweller's cognitive load theory stress the relevance of limitations in working memory capacity for processing multimedia instructions and the differences in processing verbal and pictorial materials. According to both theories, learners who are presented with a picture and an accompanying (visual) text have to split their attention between both information sources, resulting in a possible overload in (the visual part of) working memory. To prevent this overload and to enhance learning, several design guidelines have been proposed that have been tested in a number of empirical studies. For example, one design guideline is to replace visual (written or onscreen) text with spoken text in multimedia instructions (the so-called *modality* principle). Applying this guideline has resulted in superior learning in terms of faster problem solving (Jeung, Chandler, & Sweller, 1997); Mousavi, Low, & Sweller, 1995), higher scores on retention and transfer tests (Kalyuga, Chandler, & Sweller, 1999, 2000; Leahy, Chandler, & Sweller, 2003; Mayer &

Moreno, 1998; Moreno & Mayer, 1999) and less mental effort reported by the learners (Tabbers, Martens, & Van Merriënboer, 2001); Tindall-Ford, Chandler, & Sweller, 1997).

Although a great number of empirical studies support the design guidelines derived from the theories of Mayer and Sweller, none of these studies has actually taken a closer look at the process of multimedia learning. What are learners looking at when they are watching a multimedia instruction? And what exactly are people doing when they are trying to integrate text and picture? Eye tracking methods can give at least a partial answer to these questions, by providing information about the gaze position of the learner during the learning process. Moreover, an answer to these questions can help advance research on multimedia learning in at least two ways.

First of all, most researchers in the field of multimedia learning have developed their own multimedia materials for their experiments. They assume that both the textual and pictorial information in their materials are necessary for understanding (unless of course one is interested in the so-called *redundancy* effect). However, this assumption is not tested as measures like mental effort scales, time-on-task and learning results do not really tell if learners have actually looked at both pictures and text. After all, to mentally process an information source like a picture it will have to be perceived first. In order to know if learners treat the materials as real 'multimedia' instructions, measures of eye movements can provide the researcher with valuable information that can help in optimizing their multimedia materials for doing research.

The second advantage is that eye movement data can yield additional evidence for the theoretical rationale behind certain design guidelines. Different presentation formats of multimedia instructions do not only result in different cognitive processes (more or less cognitive load; more or less effective learning), but also lead to differences in looking behavior. For example, one of the guidelines deriving from cognitive load theory is that text should be physically integrated with a picture, in order to prevent unnecessary visual search (e.g., Chandler & Sweller, 1991, 1992). With eye-tracking research, the amount of visual search in the split-attention condition might be compared with the amount of visual search in the integrated condition. This way, the eye movement data can reveal if the underlying explanation of the guideline is supported or that alternative explanations are needed. For example in the case of split-attention, the crucial factor might be not the amount of visual search, but the fact that people in the split-format condition do not look at the right parts of the picture. So eye-tracking methods do not only test theoretical assumptions in multimedia learning, but can also provide alternative explanations for the effects that are found.

However, as far as we know, none of the studies inspired by Mayer's theory or by cognitive load theory has taken a closer look at the process of integrating text and picture by measuring the eye movements of the learners. One of the reasons is that the multimedia learning materials used in this research area are often presented as interactive web pages or animations. In these dynamic environments the analysis of eye movement data is a tough job, because the eye position is usually calibrated in relation to a static image. That is why tools are needed that integrate the eye movement data with the user's interactions with the computer and simplify the subsequent analyses.

9.3 The *GazeTracker*™ Software

GazeTracker™ is a tool for analyzing eye movement data in dynamic multimedia environments, and resulted from the work on the Eye-gaze Response Interface Computer Aid (*ERICA*) at the University of Virginia (Lankford, 2000a). The *ERICA* system helps individuals with disabilities communicate via the computer, and takes the eye movements of the user as input to operate mouse and keyboard functions in software applications. To facilitate the analysis of eye-movement data, the *GazeTracker*™ software was developed (Lankford, 2000b).

The program combines the input from eye-tracking systems like *ERICA*, *ASL* or *SMI* with information about the activities of the user of a computer application, like keystrokes and mouse clicks. It receives the eye-tracking data through a serial port and uses a global timer to synchronize the data it reads from the serial port with the mouse and keyboard data it intercepts from the operating system. *GazeTracker*™ accomplishes this by integrating itself into the low-level functions of the Windows operating system. The integration with Windows also allows the program to track the web pages that each test subject visits in the Internet Explorer, and to compensate the recorded eye-gaze and mouse data with the current scroll bar position. This ensures that all captured data is associated with the proper content shown on the screen during the experiment. Moreover, the program can parse the HTML-code of web pages and automatically create areas of interest (LookZones) for each hyperlink and image (based on information in tags like <a> and <img>). These LookZones can also be manually defined by the user and can take any size or shape. After recording, the data including the interactions of the user with the applications can be replayed, and can be displayed as a gaze trail, which depicts the scan path of a test subject superimposed on an application window (see Fig. 9.1).

So *GazeTracker*™ relates all activities on the screen to gaze position data, and has the opportunity to track eye movements in several applications simultaneously and even control for scrolling behavior. That way it becomes much easier to conduct eye movement research with dynamic interfaces like web browsers, and to study the way people integrate textual and pictorial information in these environments. Moreover, with LookZones information can be gathered on how long and how often a test subject observed different areas of interest like text boxes and pictures. For further analysis, the program provides several graphical methods, such as bar charts in Excel based on the LookZone data, or three-dimensional views of the application window with the time

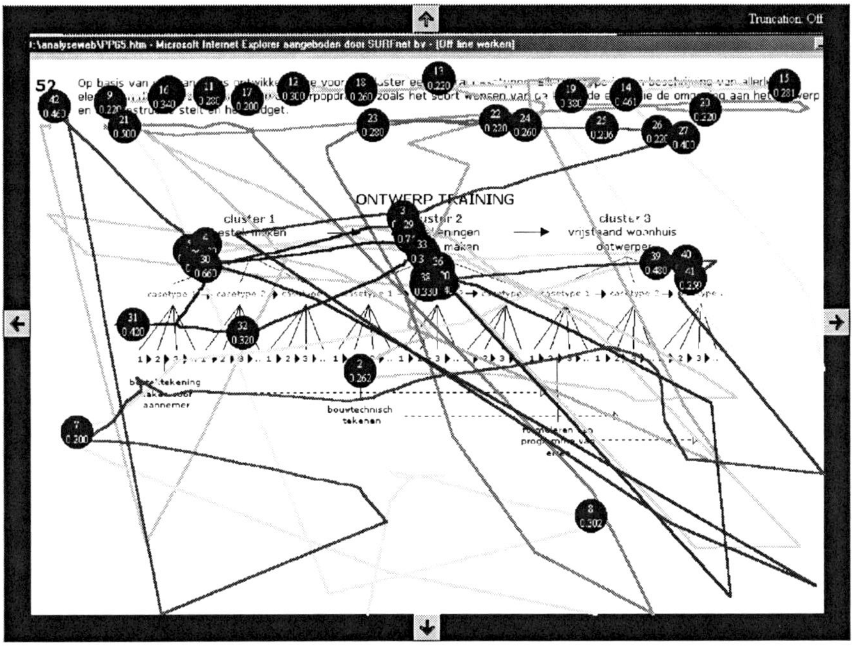

Fig. 9.1 Screen example of the gaze trail superimposed on a fragment of the multimedia materials used in the experiment described in this article. The gaze trail is depicted as a (*multicolored*) *line*, and the fixations are depicted as numbered *black circles* with the fixation duration printed inside

duration of the fixations in different regions depicted in the z-dimension. *GazeTracker*™ also allows experimenters to export the data to text files or Microsoft Excel for further statistical analysis in other statistical software packages.

9.4 Experiment

9.4.1 Objectives

To illustrate the usefulness of a tool like *GazeTracker*™ for research on multimedia learning, we set up a small experiment that builds on our previous work on the modality effect in multimedia learning (Tabbers, 2002; Tabbers, Martens, & Van Merriënboer, 2001, 2004). In these studies, we used a multimedia lesson that consisted of a series of diagrams accompanied with an explanatory narration. Not only did we vary the modality of the accompanying text (spoken text versus on-screen text), but we also varied the pacing of the instructions. Earlier research by Mayer and others had shown that giving learners control over the presentation rate might have a positive effect on multimedia learning in terms of higher transfer scores (Mayer & Chandler, 2001; see also Mayer, Dow, & Mayer, 2003). In Tabbers et al. (2001), we compared multimedia instructions with a pacing based on the speech rate of the narration with learner-controlled instructions. We found that with system-paced instructions, spoken text yielded superior learning results as would be predicted by the modality effect, whereas with learner-paced instructions, hardly any difference in effectiveness was found between spoken text and visual text. In Tabbers et al. (2004), we even found a reverse modality effect (superior learning with visual text) when the learners controlled the pace of the instruction. So based on these results we concluded that the modality effect does not apply when learners control the pace of the instructions.

However, the question is how to explain these findings. The general assumption behind the modality effect in multimedia learning is that the integration of spoken text and pictures is mentally less demanding than the integration of visual text and pictures. Sweller (1999) points out that the split format of visual text and picture requires holding components of the picture or the text in working memory while searching for the relevant referents in the text or picture. Furthermore, once the right section of the text or picture has been found, both information sources have to be mentally integrated. These processes of visual search and mental integration take up a good deal of working memory capacity, but are not essential to learning, according to Sweller. Preventing this unnecessary cognitive load, for example by physically integrating text and picture, will make extra working memory resources available for the learning process.

Another way of increasing the available working memory resources is by presenting text as spoken word. Both Mayer (2001) and Sweller (1999) base their explanation of this modality effect on the working memory model of Baddeley (1992). According to his model, working memory consists of separate processors for auditory and visual information. When text and picture are presented in visual form, they will both be processed in the visual channel (at least initially), so they have to compete for the same limited resources. Presenting the text in auditory form will take off the load of the visual subsystem. Moreover, the auditory subsystem will be used more optimally, so that the available working memory resources for learning will increase. Thus, the explanation of the modality effect is mainly in terms of cognitive processes (increasing working memory resources).

However, this cognitive explanation alone does not suffice to explain the disappearance or reversal of the modality effect with the introduction of learner control. Therefore, a closer look is warranted at what goes on when learners are watching a multimedia instruction. Apart from a cognitive advantage in terms of an increase in working memory resources, learners listening to a narration and watching a picture can immediately integrate text and picture, provided they are watching the right parts of the picture. Learners with visual-only instruction have to split their attention between visual text and picture and cannot process them simultaneously. That implies that if the pacing of the instruction is based on the narration, learners in the visual-only condition have less time available to study both text and picture. This might not be such a big problem. After all, as long as learners are reading faster than the pace of the narration, they will have enough time left to look at the picture as well. However, one could argue that giving the learners control over the pacing of the instructions will make it a lot easier for them to integrate visual text and picture, because more time can be spent on both text and picture. In fact, in one of our studies we did find that students in the visual-text condition spent 25% more time on the instructions when the instructions were learner-paced (Tabbers et al., 2001). That way, the cognitive load of the visual-only instructions may have been decreased, undoing the advantage of dual-mode instructions and making the modality effect disappear (or even reverse).

This hypothetical explanation for the disappearance of the modality effect with learner controlled multimedia instructions cannot be studied by looking at outcome measures alone. Process-based information is needed that reveals how much time is spent on either reading a text or looking at a picture. Measuring eye movements and looking at the different fixation patterns might provide exactly this.

Therefore we set up a small-scale experiment in which we studied eye movements using the same multimedia materials as in our previous studies (Tabbers et al., 2001, 2004). We compared three different presentation formats: system-paced instructions (in which the pacing was based on the narration) with either spoken text or visual text, and learner-paced instructions with visual text. Tabbers et al. (2001) showed that system-paced visual-text instructions resulted in the worst transfer performance, and explained this effect by stating that the students in this condition might lack the time to inspect the diagram after reading the text. Translated to eye movement data that results in the following hypothesis: Total time fixated in the diagrams will be shorter in the system-paced visual-text condition than in the audio and learner-paced visual-text condition.

Secondly, we wanted to check for the explanation of the modality effect in terms of differences in working memory load, and tried to see if eye movement data could provide additional support for this explanation. Therefore, we looked at some possible indicators of mental workload that are related to eye movements like fixation frequency (number of fixations per second) and average fixation duration (Van Orden, Limbert, Makeig, & Jung, 2001) and compared these to a more commonly used self-report measure of mental effort (Paas, Tuovinen, Tabbers, & Van Gerven, 2003). We expected memory load to be lowest in the audio condition, resulting in the lowest mental effort scores, the lowest fixation frequency and longest average fixation duration, and to be highest in the system-paced visual text condition, with the highest effort scores, highest fixation frequency and shortest average fixation duration.

9.4.2 Method

9.4.2.1 Participants and Design

The participants were 12 students from a Teacher Training College for Primary Education (age between 17 and 23; 1 male and 11 females). They had applied on a voluntary base and were paid 10 euros for their participation. Because of the large individual differences in looking patterns, we used a within-subjects design in this small-scale study. Each participant studied the multimedia instructions in three parts and each part was presented in a different presentation format (system-paced audio, system-paced visual text, learner-paced visual text). To prevent any sequencing effects, the order of presentation formats was counterbalanced between the participants.

9.4.2.2 Apparatus

The eye movements were recorded with a 50 Hz video-based remote eye-tracking device from SensoMotoric Instruments (*SMI*). The infrared camera was placed under the 21-inch display screen of the stimulus PC on which the multimedia instructions were presented. Special *SMI*-software to operate the camera and the calibration process ran on a separate PC that was connected to the stimulus PC. On the stimulus PC, the *GazeTracker*™ program combined the input of eye movement data from the SMI-PC with data of the user interactions with the web browser. A chin and forehead rest was placed in front of the screen in such a way that the subject's eye was 70 centimeters from the computer screen and level with its center. To calculate fixations (the relatively stable moments in the gaze trail during which information is most likely to be processed), *GazeTracker*™ uses a dispersion-threshold identification algorithm with a moving window (see Salvucci & Goldberg, 2000). The dispersion threshold was set at 25 pixels, which corresponds to approximately three or four letter spaces in the instructional material or 1 degree of visual angle, and the duration threshold was set at 100 milliseconds.

9.4.2.3 Materials

- Multimedia instructions.

The instructions used in the experiment discussed the four-component instructional design model (4C/ID model) of Van Merriënboer (1997) and were developed with Microsoft FrontPage as a linear sequence of web pages. Each page consisted of a diagram representing a skills hierarchy or an elaborated sequence of learning tasks and a textual explanation accompanying the diagram. The textual explanation that accompanied the eight diagrams was presented in smaller fragments of only one or two sentences long, that were presented one at a time. Together, the (eight) diagrams formed three worked-out examples showing how the 4C/ID model was applied in designing a blueprint for a training program.

Each of the three worked-out examples was presented in a different format: a system-paced audio format, a system-paced visual-text format or a learner-paced visual-text format (see Fig. 9.2 for screen examples of each presentation format). In the system-paced audio format, students could listen to the text fragments that accompanied a diagram, whereas in the system-paced visual-text format, students could read these text fragments from screen right above the

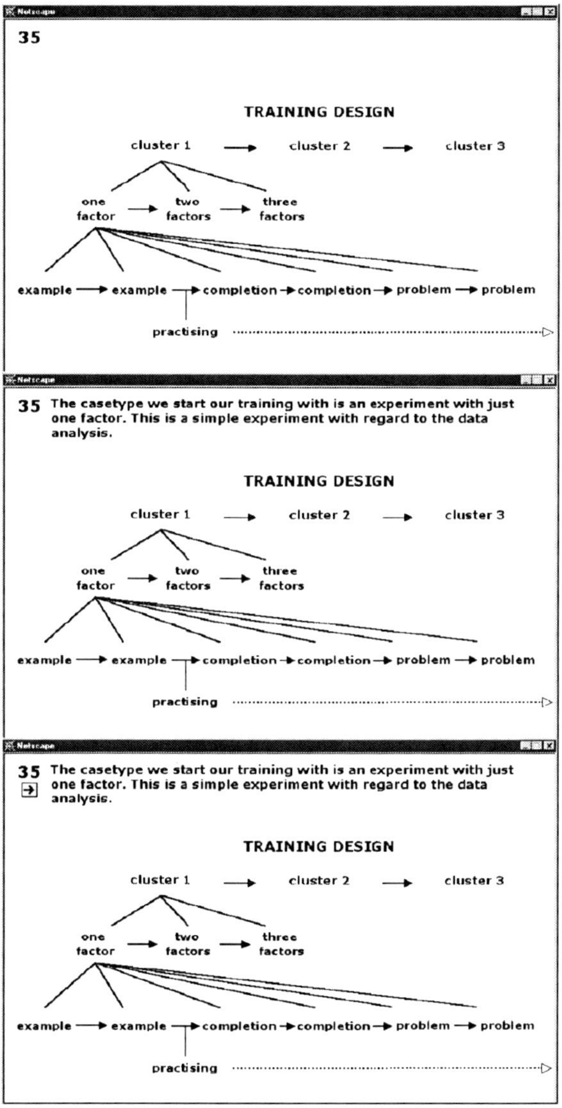

Fig. 9.2 Screen examples of the three different presentation formats (translated from Dutch). From top to bottom: the system-paced audio format, the system-paced visual-text format and the learner-paced visual-text format

diagram, with the same pacing as the audio fragments. With the learner-paced visual-text format students could reread each text fragment as many times as they wanted to before continuing with the next piece of text by clicking on a forward button. The presentation time of each worked example was about 6 minutes, except of course in the learner-paced visual-text format where the total time to study a worked-out example was variable.

- Mental effort scale

To measure mental effort a 9-point scale was used on which the students could rate the mental effort they had spent ranging from *very, very low mental effort* to *very, very high mental effort*. The scale was developed by Paas (1992), based on a measure of perceived task difficulty of Borg, Bratfisch, and Dornic (1971). The scale's reliability and sensitivity (Paas, Van Merriënboer, & Adam, 1994) and its non-intrusive nature make this scale a useful measure of perceived working memory load, and it has been used extensively in studies of multimedia learning (for an overview, see Paas et al., 2003).

- Evaluation questionnaire

The evaluation questionnaire contained 12 items about the instructional procedure, which were all accompanied with a 5-point scale on which students could indicate how much they agreed with the content of each item. We used this questionnaire to get an idea if the students had understood the instructions, if they had experienced any problems and if they had worked with sufficient concentration. It also contained the additional question which of the three presentation formats the student had liked best.

9.4.2.4 Procedure

The students were tested one at a time. They were seated in a solid chair that could not move and were told to put their heads in the chin rest that was positioned in front of the computer screen. First they read some general information about the experiment without anything being recorded. Subsequently, their eye movements were calibrated after which they could start studying the first worked example. After each diagram in the worked-out example, the students had to fill in the self-report mental effort scale that was presented on the screen. When a student clicked on one of the nine options, the program automatically continued with the next diagram. When the students had finished studying the first worked-out example, their eyes were once again calibrated and they started studying the second worked-out example (in a different presentation format) in the same way as the first. The same procedure was repeated for the third worked-out example. After they had studied the third example, students could remove their heads from the chin rest and the eye movement recording was stopped. Finally, the students completed the evaluation questionnaire that was presented on the computer screen. The whole procedure took about three-quarters of an hour.

9.4.3 Results and Discussion

The main dependent variables in the experiment were total time fixated and number of fixations (overall, in the text and in the diagrams), and average fixation duration, fixation frequency and perceived mental effort. We conducted a repeated measures MANOVA, with presentation format as the within-subjects factor. For any post-hoc analyses we used paired t-tests. For all statistical tests, a significance level of 0.05 was applied. Table 9.1 shows the means and standard deviations for all dependent measures.

For the overall eye movement results, we found a significant effect of presentation format on total time fixated and number of fixations (Wilks' lambda = 0.24, $F(4, 42) = 10.88$, $p < 0.01$), but no specific differences in the post-hoc tests. Looking at the division of attention over text and diagram, the results showed that students in the audio condition spent more than 98% of their total fixation time in the diagrams, versus 44% in the system-paced visual-text condition and 38% in the learner-paced visual-text condition. When analyzing the fixations in the diagrams separately, again a significant effect of presentation format was found on total time fixated and number of fixations (Wilks' lambda = 0.61, $F(4, 42) = 2.93$, $p < 0.05$). Post-hoc comparisons showed

Table 9. 1 Means and standard deviations of dependent measures

		Audio	System-Paced Visual Text	Learner-Paced Visual Text
	Number of Fixations	509 (302)	604 (340)	765 (420)
	Total Time Fixated (s)	158 (97)	139 (82)	174 (100)
Overall:	Average Fixation Duration (s)	0.31 (0.05)	0.22 (0.02)	0.22 (0.02)
	Fixation Frequency	2.26 (0.17)	2.79 (0.33)	2.89 (0.20)
	Mental effort score (1 – 9)	4.2 (1.0)	4.8 (1.4)	4.1 (1.0)
	Number of Fixations	497 (295)	243 (172)	250 (133)
Diagram:	Total Time Fixated (s)	156 (96)	66 (51)	69 (40)
	Average Fixation Duration (s)	0.31 (0.05)	0.25 (0.05)	0.26 (0.03)
	Number of Fixations		341 (226)	488 (305)
Text:	Total Time Fixated (s)		68 (44)	97 (63)
	Average Fixation Duration (s)		0.20 (0.03)	0.20 (0.03)

that in the audio condition, students' total fixation time was significantly longer and number of fixations was higher than in the system-paced visual-text condition ($t = 2.62$, $p < 0.05$ and $t = 2.46$, $p < 0.05$, respectively), and than in the learner-paced visual-text condition ($t = 2.71$, $p < 0.05$ and $t = 2.47$, $p < 0.05$, respectively). However, no significant differences were found between the visual-text conditions. When the visual-text conditions were compared on total time fixated and number of fixations in the text only, again no significant differences were found (Wilks' lambda = 0.87, $F(2, 10) = 0.77$, $p > 0.05$).

The effect of presentation format on the indicators of workload like average fixation duration, fixation frequency and mental effort was also significant, Wilks' lambda = 0.16, $F(6, 40) = 10{,}88$, $p < 0.01$. Post-hoc comparisons showed that the participants in the audio condition fixated less frequently than the participants in both the system-paced visual-text condition, $t = 4.85$, $p < 0.01$, and the learner-paced visual text condition, t 8.23, $p < 0.01$. Related to this finding, the average fixation duration was longer in the audio condition than in the system-paced visual-text condition, $t = 6.73$, $p < 0.01$, and the learner-paced visual-text condition, $t = 6.34$, $p < 0.01$. Although the participants reported a higher mental effort score in the system-paced visual-text condition than in the other two conditions, this difference did not reach statistical significance. Looking at the average fixation duration in the text, no significant difference was found between the learner-paced and system-paced visual-text condition.

Finally, the results of the evaluation questionnaire showed that two-thirds of the students had preferred the learner-paced visual-text version over the other two versions. Moreover, the students judged the part of the instructions presented in the learner-paced visual-text version as the easiest to comprehend.

So the results do show some clear differences in fixation patterns between the presentation formats, but not in the way that we hypothesized. Naturally, the looking pattern in the audio condition deviates from the patterns in the visual-text conditions, because there is no text to fixate on. However, the division of attention between diagram and text in both visual text conditions seems to be quite identical, contrary to what we expected. Moreover, no apparent differences in fixation data are found between system-paced and learner-paced instructions. A closer look at the different scan paths (how did the learner's gaze switch from text to diagram) might reveal other differences in switching behavior between the different visual-text formats, but such an analysis was beyond the scope of the current study. In their work on the integration of diagram and text, Carroll et al. (1992), Hegarty and Just (1993), Rayner et al. (2001) and Underwood et al. (2004) found that most subjects read the text first and then looked at the diagram, without much switching. As study time was not limited in these studies, the same fixation pattern could be expected in a learner-paced condition. It would be interesting to see if an identical pattern would be found in the system-paced condition, or that a different scan path would emerge.

Furthermore, looking at the possible workload indicators, it is interesting that the students fixate less frequently in the audio condition with a longer duration, just as we hypothesized. Primarily, this difference seems to reflect the 'calmness' of the looking pattern in the audio condition, where students do not have to switch between text and diagram. It is unclear, however, if this is also related to less cognitive load in the audio condition, because we do not find a similar difference between audio and both visual text conditions in the mental effort scores. The relationship between mental effort and fixation duration and fixation frequency might not be as direct as supposed, so further research in this area is needed.

In sum, we hypothesized that the students in the learner-paced condition would spend extra time in the diagrams, but we do not find it in the results. So the difference in effectiveness between system-paced and learner-paced multimedia instructions found in our earlier studies (using the same materials) does not seem to derive from an overall difference in fixation pattern, at least in terms of total time fixated or number of fixations. Nevertheless, students report a relatively high mental effort in the system-paced condition, and generally prefer the learner-paced visual-text version. It might be the case that the demonstrated superiority of learner-paced over system-paced visual-text is not the result of a general difference in fixation time, but because students can control the division of attention between diagrams and text more easily and adapt it to their individual needs. To fully test this hypothesis, an approach is needed that more directly links the eye movement data to a process model of how people integrate text and picture to construct meaning, like for example the model of Narayanan and Hegarty (1998, 2002).

9.5 General Discussion and Conclusions

Our study shows that the use of a tool for analyzing eye movements like *GazeTracker*™ can produce more specific insights on processes that take place during multimedia learning. By integrating eye movement data with computer processes, interesting information can be obtained on the way that people learn with text and pictures. Despite the dynamic nature of the presented material and the large number of different web pages in our experiment, the analysis could be done relatively easy, because *GazeTracker*™ automatically loaded the areas of interest in our study (i.e. the diagrams and the text boxes) as LookZones, and simplified the subsequent data analysis by offering the opportunity to indicate which data (of different participants, web pages and LookZones) should or should not be included in the analysis.

Of course, some elements of the analysis still can be improved upon. For example, the version of *GazeTracker*™ used in our experiment did not provide any summary data on the 'switches' from one LookZone to the other, like from text to diagram. However, newer versions of *GazeTracker*™ do provide the opportunity to create a LookZone Order Graph that displays the order and duration in which a subject observed different regions of interest, so that specific hypotheses on switching behavior can be studied more easily. Another drawback was that the program did not support some complex analyses, like aggregating data of multiple participants over multiple LookZones (for example all diagrams in one worked example), so we had to extract these data from the database file ourselves. Although that was not a real problem, it took us a lot more work to make these summary data available for further analyses.

These are of course only technical drawbacks of the program that can and hopefully will be solved in the near future. Nevertheless, some more general remarks can be made on doing eye tracking research in the area of multimedia learning. First of all, the quality of the analysis with *GazeTracker*™(or any other analysis tool) is very dependent on the quality of the eye tracking system used. For example, the system we used in our study had some drawbacks, like a relatively low resolution (50 Hz), and some difficulties in getting the participants' eyes calibrated. Care has to be taken to use optimal equipment for eye tracking research, especially when more fine-grained analyses of gaze positions are warranted. Furthermore, a more fundamental problem is that eye tracking methods produce huge amounts of process data. However, most of our current theories on multimedia learning do not provide hypotheses on the exact looking behavior of learners. This is of course complicated by the fact that large individual differences exist in the way that people process instructions. Therefore, researchers in the field of multimedia learning interested in eye tracking research should carefully consider if their hypotheses can be reformulated in such a way that they can be tested with eye movement data, and that they can indicate as precisely as possible which information they would like to extract from the data. Only then will tools like *GazeTracker*™ be of added value in simplifying the analysis of the eye movement data.

In conclusion, the use of tools like *GazeTracker*™ makes eye tracking methods available for the study of learning in dynamic multimedia environments, where different information elements are presented at different locations and at different times. With these tools, it is possible to identify where people look when they are studying multimedia materials, so that researchers can find out if learners treat their study materials as was intended in the design. Furthermore, with these tools the underlying explanations of theories of multimedia learning can be tested, at least those hypotheses that can be reformulated in terms of eye movement data. These advantages are not only interesting for the area of multimedia learning, but for any other study of human-computer interaction aimed at a further understanding of the cognitive processes that take place when people are working with a computer application.

Acknowledgments The experiment was part of a Ph.D. project that was co-funded by Aebly, a former multimedia company from 's Hertogenbosch, The Netherlands. We would like to thank Léon Sluijsmans from Hogeschool Zuyd in Heerlen for his helpful assistance in recruiting our participants.

References

Baddeley, A. D. (1992). Working memory. *Science, 255*, 556–559.

Borg, G., Bratfisch, O., & Dornic, S. (1971). On the problem of perceived difficulty. *Scandinavian Journal of Psychology, 12*, 249–260.

Carroll, P. J., Young, J. R., & Guertin, M. S. (1992). Visual analysis of cartoons: A view from the far side. In K. Rayner (Ed.), *Eye movements and visual cognition: Scene perception and reading* (pp. 444–461). New York: Springer-Verlag.

Chandler, P., & Sweller, J. (1991). Cognitive load theory and the format of instruction. *Cognition and Instruction, 8*, 293–332.

Chandler, P., & Sweller, J. (1992). The split-attention effect as a factor in the design of instruction. *British Journal of Educational Psychology, 62*, 233–246.

Crowe, E. C., & Narayanan, N. H. (2000). Comparing interfaces based on what users watch and do. In *Proceedings of the Eye Tracking Research and Applications Symposium* (pp. 29–36). New York: ACM Press.

d'Ydewalle, G., & Gielen, I. (1992). Attention allocation with overlapping sound, image, and text. In K. Rayner (Ed.), *Eye movements and visual cognition: Scene perception and reading* (pp. 415–427). New York: Springer-Verlag.

Duffy, S. A. (1992). Eye movements and complex comprehension processes. In K. Rayner (Ed.), *Eye movements and visual cognition: Scene perception and reading* (pp. 462–471). New York: Springer-Verlag.

Goldberg, J. H., & Kotval, X. P. (1999). Computer interface evaluation using eye movements: Methods and constructs. *International Journal of Industrial Ergonomics, 24*, 631–645.

Goldberg, J. H., Stimson, M. J., Lewenstein, M., Scott, N., & Wichansky, A. M. (2002). Eye tracking in web search tasks: Design implications. In *Proceedings of the Eye Tracking Research and Applications Symposium*. New York: ACM Press.

Hegarty, M. (1992a). Mental animation: Inferring motion from static displays of mechanical systems. *Journal of Experimental Psychology: Learning, Memory, & Cognition, 18*, 1084–1102.

Hegarty, M. (1992b). The mechanics of comprehension and comprehension of mechanics. In K. Rayner (Ed.), *Eye movements and visual cognition: Scene perception and reading* (pp. 428–443). New York: Springer-Verlag.

Hegarty, M., & Just, M. A. (1989). Understanding machines from text and diagrams. In H. Mandl & J. R. Levin (Eds.), *Knowledge acquisition from text and pictures* (pp. 171–194). Amsterdam: Elsevier.

Hegarty, M., & JustJust, M. A. (1993). Constructing mental models of machines from text and diagrams. *Journal of Memory and Language, 32*, 717–742.

Jeung, H., Chandler, P., & Sweller, J. (1997). The role of visual indicators in dual sensory mode instruction. *Educational Psychology, 17*, 329–343.

Kalyuga, S., Chandler, P., & Sweller, J. (1999). Managing split-attention and redundancy in multimedia instruction. *Applied Cognitive Psychology, 13*, 351–371.

Kalyuga, S., Chandler, P., & Sweller, J. (2000). Incorporating learner experience into the design of multimedia instruction. *Journal of Educational Psychology, 92*, 126–136.

Lankford, C. (2000a). Effective eye-gaze input into Windows™. In *Proceedings of the Eye Tracking Research and Applications Symposium*. New York: ACM Press.

Lankford, C. (2000b). GazeTracker™: Software designed to facilitate eye movement analysis. In *Proceedings of the Eye Tracking Research and Applications Symposium* (pp. 57–63). New York: ACM Press.

Leahy, W., Chandler, P., & Sweller, J. (2003). When auditory presentations should and should not be a component of multimedia instructions. *Applied Cognitive Psychology, 17*, 401–418.

Mayer, R. E. (2001). *Multimedia learning*. New York: Cambridge University Press.

Mayer, R. E., & Chandler, P. (2001). When learning is just a click away: Does simple user interaction foster deeper understanding of multimedia messages? *Journal of Educational Psychology, 93*, 390–397.

Mayer, R. E., Dow, G. T., & Mayer, S. (2003). Multimedia learning in an interactive self-explaining environment: What works in the design of agent-based microworlds? *Journal of Educational Psychology, 95*, 806–813.

Mayer, R. E., & Moreno, R. (1998). A split-attention effect in multimedia learning: Evidence for dual processing systems in working memory. *Journal of Educational Psychology, 90*, 312–320.

Moreno, R., & Mayer, R. E. (1999). Cognitive principles of multimedia learning: the role of modality and contiguity. *Journal of Educational Psychology, 91*, 358–368.

Mousavi, S. Y., Low, R., & Sweller, J. (1995). Reducing cognitive load by mixing auditory and visual presentation modes. *Journal of Educational Psychology, 87*, 319–334.

Narayanan, N. H., & Hegarty, M. (1998). On designing comprehensible interactive hypermedia manuals. *International Journal of Human-Computer Studies, 48*, 267–301.

Narayanan, N. H., & Hegarty, M. (2002). Multimedia design for communication of dynamic information. *International Journal of Human-Computer Studies, 57*, 279–315.

Paas, F. (1992). Training strategies for attaining transfer of problem-solving skill in statistics: a cognitive-load approach. *Journal of Educational Psychology, 84*, 429–434.

Paas, F., Tuovinen, J. E., Tabbers, H. K., & Van Gerven, P. W. M. (2003). Cognitive load measurement as a means to advance cognitive load theory. *Educational Psychologist, 38*, 63–71.

Paas, F., Van Merriënboer, J. J. G., & Adam, J. J. (1994). Measurement of cognitive load in instructional research. *Perceptual and Motor Skills, 79*, 419–430.

Rayner, K. (1998). Eye movements in reading and information processing: 20 years of research. *Psychological Bulletin, 124*, 372–422.

Rayner, K., Rotello, C. M., Stewart, A. J., Keir, J., & Duffy, S. A. (2001). Integrating text and pictorial information: Eye movements when looking at print advertisements. *Journal of Experimental Psychology: Applied, 7*, 219–226.

Salvucci, D. D., & Goldberg, J. H. (2000). Identifying fixations and saccades in eye-tracking protocols. In *Proceedings of the Eye Tracking Research and Applications Symposium* (pp. 71–78). New York: ACM Press.

Sweller, J. (1999). *Instructional design in technical areas.* Camberwell, Australia: ACER Press.

Sweller, J., Van Merriënboer, J. J. G., & Paas, F. (1998). Cognitive architecture and instructional design. *Educational Psychology Review, 10*, 251–296.

Tabbers, H. K. (2002). *The modality of text in multimedia instructions: Refining the design guidelines.* Unpublished doctoral dissertation, Open University of the Netherlands, Heerlen.

Tabbers, H. K., Martens, R. L., & Van Merriënboer, J. J. G. (2001). The modality effect in multimedia instructions. J. D. Moore & K. Stenning (Eds.), *Proceedings of the twenty-third annual conference of the Cognitive Science Society* (pp. 1024–1029). Mahwah, NJ: Erlbaum.

Tabbers, H. K., Martens, R. L., & Van Merriënboer, J. J. G. (2004). Multimedia instructions and cognitive load theory: Effects of modality and cueing. *British Journal of Educational Psychology, 74*, 71–81.

Tindall-Ford, S., Chandler, P., & Sweller, J. (1997). When two sensory modes are better than one. *Journal of Experimental Psychology: Applied, 3*, 257–287.

Underwood, G., Jebbett, L., & Roberts, K. (2004). Inspecting pictures for information to verify a sentence: Eye movements in general encoding and in focused search. *Quarterly Journal of Experimental Psychology, 57A*, 165–182.

Van Merriënboer, J. J. G. (1997). *Training complex cognitive skills: A four-component instructional design model for technical training.* Englewood Cliffs, NJ: Educational Technology Publications.

Van Orden, K. F., Limbert, W., Makeig, S., & Jung, T. P. (2001). Eye activity correlates of workload during a visuospatial memory task. *Human Factors, 43*, 111–121.

Chapter 10
The Interaction of Verbal and Pictorial Information in Comprehension and Memory

Mike Rinck

Abstract In two experiments, the author investigated how the correspondence between a verbal representation (a text describing data) and a simultaneously presented graphical representation (a graph showing data) affects comprehension of, and memory for, the results of empirical studies. Consistency of text and graph was varied by verbally describing observed differences between experimental conditions as small or large, and by using graphical depictions that made the effects appear to be small or large. In accord with the structure mapping hypothesis suggested by Schnotz and Bannert (2003), inconsistency of texts and graphs slowed down comprehension. Such inconsistency increased gaze durations on texts and graphs as well as the number of eye movements between text and graph. It also decreased confidence in a later memory task. Moreover, memory for the text was affected by the graph and memory for the graph was affected by the text, yielding distortions in cases of inconsistency.

Keywords Eye movement · Graph · Inconsistency · Integration · Memory · Text

10.1 Introduction

When empirical data are reported in scientific journals or other media, the authors have to decide how to describe the importance of the results. In specialized scientific publications, there are objective criteria for the importance, namely, significance levels, F-values, or effect sizes such as *f*, *d* or eta^2 (Cohen, 1988). In everyday media such as textbooks, journals, and newspapers, however, these objective criteria are usually missing, and effects of political interventions, medical treatments, or empirical research are often described as small or large at a subjective level. In general, there are two quite different means that authors may use to convince readers of the chosen subjective

M. Rinck
Behavioural Science Institute, Radboud University Nijmegen, PO Box 9104, 6500 HE Nijmegen, The Netherlands
e-mail: m.rinck@psych.ru.nl

J.-F. Rouet et al. (eds.), *Understanding Multimedia Documents*,
DOI: 10.1007/978-0-387-73337-1_10, © Springer Science+Business Media, LLC 2008

interpretation. First, the authors may use the text to verbally describe the effects (e.g., differences between experimental conditions) as either small or large. Second, they may use graphical depictions to make the effects look visually small or large. In fact, many reports contain verbal as well as graphical information in order to convey the intended message. From these two media, the reader has to create what has been termed a *Mental Model* or *Situation Model* (e.g., Glenberg & Langston, 1992; Rinck, 2000; Schnotz, 1993) of the data described.

There is a large body of research and suggestions on the optimal graphical presentation of data (e.g., Cleveland, 1993; Kosslyn, 1994; Tufte, 1983; Wainer, 1984), and also some illustrations of how graphical information may be used to cheat (e.g., Kosslyn, 1994). Moreover, many studies have investigated the comprehension of illustrated texts, for instance, expository texts describing the function of technical devices such as brakes or pumps (e.g., Mayer, 1989; Mayer & Gallini, 1990; for a review see Mayer, 1997). However, little is known about the interaction of information displayed concurrently in statistical graphs and texts, particularly if the sets of information conveyed by these different media do not match. In this case, it should be difficult, maybe even impossible, to create a coherent situation model of the situation described. Fortunately, Schnotz and Bannert (2003) recently presented a cognitive model of multimedia learning, which encompasses both the representation of textual information (termed the "descriptive" branch of representations) and pictorial information (the "depictive" branch of representations). According to the model, the textual information yields a propositional representation of the text and a mental model of the information conveyed by the text. The pictorial information yields a visual image, from which a mental model of the pictorial information is created. A crucial feature of the model suggested by Schnotz and Bannert (2003) is that the textual information and the pictorial information must be integrated into a coherent mental model in order to yield deep comprehension of the multimodal information. From their model, Schnotz and Bannert derive the *structure mapping hypothesis*, stating that in order for graphic representations to be beneficial for comprehension, their structural features should correspond to those of the textual representation. Moreover, the structure of the mental model derived from an illustration determines how easy it is to extract different types of information from the representation, therefore, illustrations vary in how efficient they are for different tasks. Empirical evidence for the hypothesis was provided by an experiment in which Schnotz and Bannert (2003) showed that two alternative graphical representations of the earth (called "carpet" diagram vs. "circle" diagram) were optimal for solving different tasks (time difference task vs. circumnavigation task). Thus, specific graphical representations did not yield superior or inferior performance in general. Rather, the interaction of tasks, graphics, and texts seems to be the key determinant of comprehension and performance in learning from illustrated text.

The research presented here follows the theoretical approach of Schnotz and Bannert (2003), and it takes the empirical test of the structure mapping hypothesis one step further. In the two experiments[1] reported below, the participants' task was held constant (comprehension of, and memory for, the results of psychological studies), and the correspondence between a graphical representation (statistical graph showing data) and a verbal representation (text describing data) was varied. Following the structure mapping hypothesis, it was predicted that performance should be better if the information conveyed by the two media is consistent. Consistency of text and graph was varied by verbally describing the effects observed in experimental studies (e.g., differences between experimental conditions) as either small or large, and by using graphical depictions of the results that made the effects appear either small or large. Moreover, the present experiments also assessed the relative impact of the *verbal message* communicated by the text and the *visual message* conveyed by the graph, by determining how memory for the verbal information was affected by the graph and how memory for the graphical information was affected by the text. Using graphs and texts to describe the size and importance of empirical results is particularly helpful in this context, because – as is often the case – objective information regarding effect sizes or statistical significance was not available to readers. Thus, the information described was open to subjective interpretation, and participants could not easily dismiss particular graphs or texts as "wrong".

10.2 Experiment 1

10.2.1 Objectives

Experiment 1 was designed to explore how the verbal message contained in a textual description of experimental results affects comprehension of, and memory for, the results, and how the visual message contained in a statistical graph showing the same results affects these processes. Participants in Experiment 1 read about experimental studies and their results, which were verbally described in a text and simultaneously depicted in a graph. Independently of each other, the text and the graph depicted the observed differences as either small or large. The experiment was designed to test the following hypotheses: (1) Comprehension of, and memory for, the experimental results will be diminished when text and graph convey inconsistent messages. (2) Memory for the verbal results description will be affected by the way the results are depicted in the graph. (3) Conversely, memory for the visual results depiction will be affected by the way the results are described in the text. (4) Participants will feel less confident in their memory for texts and graphs when these were inconsistent.

---

[1] To avoid confusion, the two experiments reported here are consistently referred to as "experiments", whereas the experiments described to the participants are called "studies" or "experimental studies".

10.2.2 Method

10.2.2.1 Participants

Sixty-two Psychology undergraduates of Dresden University of Technology participated, most of them in their first semester. Their participation fulfilled a curricular requirement, or they were compensated by a small monetary payment equivalent to 5 EUR. All participants were native speakers of German.

10.2.2.2 Materials and Procedure

The participants were asked to study descriptions of simple psychological studies in order to judge how interesting the studies were and whether they should be included in an introductory class. The studies (a practice study followed by eight experimental ones) were presented one after the other on the screen of a personal computer, controlled by the "*RSVP*" software (Williams & Tarr, no date). The software automatically recorded all responses of the participants and the corresponding latencies. All of the experimental studies employed here followed a 2×2 experimental design. They were modeled after existing studies, but adapted to the current purposes (e.g., the sample study shown below was similar to the study by Godden & Baddeley, 1975). For each study, the self-paced presentation followed the following pattern: First, an introductory description of the study including its purpose, methods, and hypotheses was presented (see Appendix for a sample). After pressing a key on the computer keyboard, the introduction was replaced by a description of the results, which included mean values but no information on standard deviations, significance levels, or objective effect size measures. The results sections contained verbal information (a text describing the results) accompanied by pictorial information (a bar graph or line graph depicting the results). The text and the graph were presented simultaneously, with the text always above the graph.

Independently of each other, the verbal message of the text and the visual message of the graph characterized the differences observed in the study as either very small or very large. In the text, this was achieved by using evaluative phrases such as "only a very small difference was observed" compared to "indeed a very large difference was observed". Appendix shows translations of the two different results descriptions used with the sample study. It should be noted that the two versions did not differ with regard to objective information: both contained identical numerical results. For the graph, manipulation of the depicted differences was achieved by varying the scale used on the ordinate of the graph. A large range of values shown on the ordinate was used to make the differences look very small, whereas a restricted range was used to make them look very large (see Kosslyn, 1994). Figure 10.1 shows this manipulation for the sample study: on top, values on the ordinate range from 26 to 34, making the differences look large, whereas the ranges chosen on the bottom (0–100) make

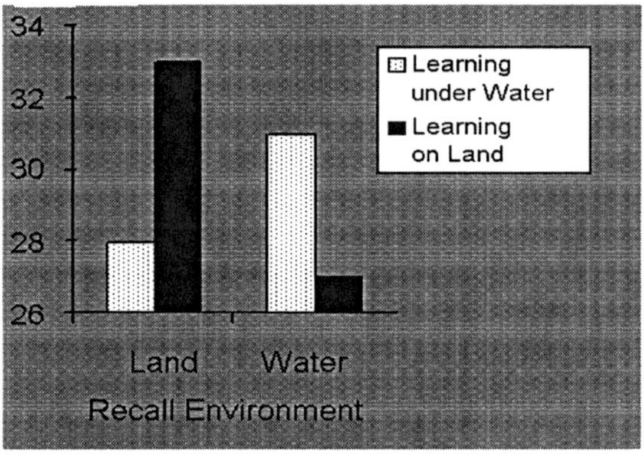

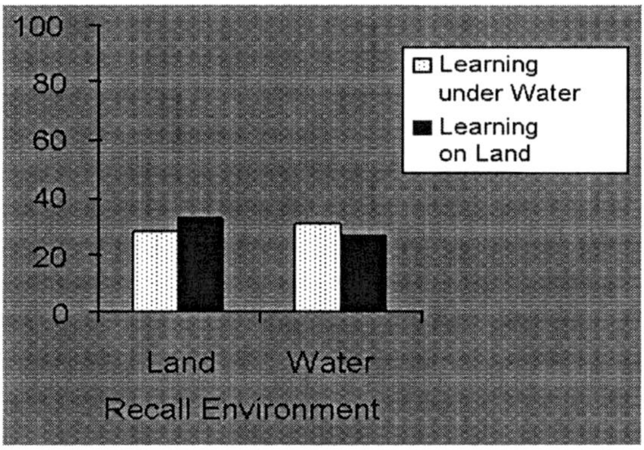

Fig. 10.1 Sample graphs presented in Experiment 1. *Top*: Graph depicting large effect. *Bottom*: Graph depicting small effect. Note: Original graphs were in color and text was in German

the same differences look small. Of course, both versions of the graph contained the same numerical data, which were also identical to the data contained in the text versions. After reading the results section, the participants indicated how interesting the study seemed to them and whether they had known about it before. Then, the next study was presented in the same way.

Effect size in the text and effect size in the graph were varied independently of each other as within-subjects factors, yielding a 2×2 experimental design. Each participant read two studies for which both the text and the graph consistently indicated that the observed differences were large. For two other studies, both the text and the graph indicated small differences. For the remaining four studies, the text and the graph contained inconsistent descriptions: for two studies, the text described small differences and the graph depicted large ones, whereas the reverse was true for two other studies. Across participants, each study occurred equally often in each of the 8 experimental conditions, to ensure full combination of conditions and materials.

After having read about all studies, participants were given a surprise memory test. For each of the described studies, this was a recognition test conducted in the following way: participants first read a short reminder text, describing the purpose and methods of the study. This reminder was identical to the introduction read earlier, except that the final sentence regarding the experimenters' hypothesis was deleted (see Appendix). Participants were then asked to identify the effect description used earlier in the text. For the sample study, they received the question *"How much better was the divers' recall of words if learning environment and recall environment were identical rather than different?"*, together with a five-point scale ranging from 0 (labeled "not better at all") to 4 ("very much better"). They responded by pressing one of the keys between 0 and 4. Next, the question *"How confident are you that your answer was correct?"* appeared on the screen. Participants indicated their confidence by pressing one of the keys between 0 (labeled "guessed") and 4 ("very confident"). After that, they were asked to identify the graph seen earlier: from five alternative graphs labeled A to E, they had to choose the original one. The five graphs were shown simultaneously, and they were identical except for the scaling of the ordinate. The graph labeled A was identical to the original one showing small differences (e.g., the one on the right of Fig. 10.1), and the graph labeled E was identical to the original one showing large differences (e.g., the one on the left of Fig. 10.1). The graphs labeled B, C, and D showed evenly spaced intermediate levels of differences. The five graphs were distributed randomly across five possible positions on the computer screen. After participants had responded by pressing one of the keys between A and E, they gave the same confidence rating as for text recognition. The order of the graph recognition test and the text recognition test was counterbalanced. For each participant, the eight experimental studies were tested in the same order they had been presented during the study phase. It took participants about 45 min. to finish the experiment.

10.2.3 Results and Discussion

The results of Experiment 1 are summarized in Table 10.1. All rating scales employed here (for text recognition, confidence ratings, and interest ratings) had five points, ranging from 0 to 4. The five possible graph choices A to E were converted to scores from 0 to 4, to achieve comparability of the dependent variables. All dependent variables were analyzed with a 2×2-ANOVA involving the within-participants factors *effect description in text* (small, large) and *effect depiction in graph* (small, large). All effect sizes reported below are f values according to Cohen (1988). Conventionally, f values of 0.10, 0.25, and 0.80 are considered to indicate small, medium, and large effects, respectively.

10.2.3.1 Comprehension Times of Results Sections

The 2×2 ANOVA of these comprehension times indicated that neither the effect description in the text ($F(1,61) = 2.76$, n.s., $f = .11$) nor the effect depiction in the graph ($F(1,61) = 1.99$, n.s., $f = 0.09$) yielded a significant main effect

Table 10.1 Mean values of dependent variables (with Standard Deviations) Observed in Experiment 1

Dependent Variable and Effect Size Depiction in Graph	Effect Size Description in Text	
	Small Effect	Large Effect
Comprehension Times of Results Sections (in sec)		
Small Effect in Graph	24.7 (8.2)	27.2 (11.1)
Large Effect in Graph	30.0 (10.2)	24.9 (10.1)
Interest Ratings (0–4)		
Small Effect in Graph	2.62 (0.74)	2.86 (0.83)
Large Effect in Graph	2.75 (0.74)	3.02 (0.69)
Recognition of Result Descriptions in Text (0–4)		
Small Effect in Graph	1.15 (0.43)	2.91 (0.53)
Large Effect in Graph	1.50 (0.56)	3.16 (0.67)
Confidence in Text Recognition (0–4)		
Small Effect in Graph	3.19 (0.43)	3.10 (0.62)
Large Effect in Graph	2.99 (0.57)	3.23 (0.48)
Recognition of Result Depictions in Graph (0 – 4)		
Small Effect in Graph	0.94 (0.67)	2.40 (1.08)
Large Effect in Graph	2.28 (0.94)	3.20 (0.85)
Confidence in Graph Recognition (0–4)		
Small Effect in Graph	2.12 (0.70)	1.85 (0.90)
Large Effect in Graph	2.01 (0.78)	2.52 (1.00)

on comprehension of the results. However, the interaction of text and graph was highly significant ($F(1,61)=17.64$, $p<0.001$, f$=0.24$), substantiating the expected pattern of comprehension times: It took participants longer to understand the experimental results, if the text and the graph were inconsistent (mean 28.6 sec) rather than consistent (mean 24.8 sec).

10.2.3.2 Interest Ratings

The interest ratings revealed that participants found studies with large effects more interesting: if the text indicated larger effects, interest ratings were significantly higher. In the 2×2 ANOVA, ratings were affected significantly by the effect description in the text ($F(1,61)=7.34$, $p<0.01$, f$=0.17$), in contrast to the effect depiction in the graph ($F(1,61)=2.56$, n.s., f$=0.10$). The text-graph interaction was not significant either ($F(1,61)<1$, n.s., f$=0.01$).

10.2.3.3 Recognition of Results Description in Text

As one would expect, participants' recognition of the results descriptions was strongly influenced by the real descriptions studied earlier. Thus, they chose larger effect descriptions if the text had indeed stated that the differences were large rather than small (mean 3.04 vs. 1.33, $F(1,61)=485.28$, $p<0.001$, f$=1.41$).

More importantly, however, their choices were also affected by the visual effect depictions ($F(1,61) = 21.56$, $p < 0.001$, f = 0.29): graphs showing large differences distorted memory towards recognition of larger verbal descriptions (mean 2.33), and graphs showing small differences yielded recognition of smaller effects in the verbal descriptions (mean 2.03). The interaction of text description and graph depiction was not significant ($F(1,61) < 1$, n.s., f = 0.04).

10.2.3.4 Recognition of Results Depiction in Graph

As would be expected, participants' recognition of the graphs was affected by the graphs they had seen earlier. Therefore, the effect depiction in the graph had a strong effect on the chosen graphs ($F(1,61) = 114.53$, $p < 0.001$, f = 0.59): if they had earlier seen a graph showing large differences, their recognition choices were larger (mean 2.74) than after seeing a graph showing small differences (mean 1.67). Of special interest, however, is the fact that their choices were also influenced by the verbal effect description ($F(1,61) = 86.76$, $p < 0.001$, f = 0.68). If the text had described a large effect, graph choices were larger (mean 2.80) than when the text had described a small effect (mean 1.61). Interestingly, the *f* values indicate that the text influenced graph recognition at least as strongly as the graph itself did. The text-graph interaction was significant as well, suggesting that the text's distorting effect was slightly more pronounced for graphs showing small rather than large effects ($F(1,61) = 5.57$, $p < 0.05$, f = 0.15).

10.2.3.5 Confidence in Text Recognition

As expected, the participants' confidence in their recognition of the verbal descriptions depended on the consistency of text and graph. If both media were consistent, confidence was higher (mean 3.21) than in cases of inconsistency (mean 3.04). Accordingly, the 2×2 ANOVA of the confidence ratings yielded a significant interaction of text and graph ($F(1,61) = 8.56$, $p < 0.01$, f = 0.19), whereas the main effects were not significant (text: $F(1,61) = 1.6$, n.s., f = 0.08; graph: $F(1,61) < 1$, n.s., f = 0.06).

10.2.3.6 Confidence in Graph Recognition

These confidence ratings mirrored the ones for text recognition: If both media were consistent, confidence in the graph choice was higher (mean 2.32) than when they were inconsistent (mean 1.93), yielding a significant text-graph interaction ($F(1,61) = 19.02$, $p < 0.001$, f = 0.27). In addition, confidence was also higher for recognition of large effect depictions studied earlier than for small effect depictions, yielding a main effect of effect depiction in the graph ($F(1,61) = 8.59$, $p < 0.01$, f = 0.19). The effect description in the text did not have a significant main effect ($F(1,61) = 1.56$, n.s., f = 0.08).

Taken together, the results observed in Experiment 1 demonstrate effects of both the verbal message contained in texts and the visual message conveyed by graphs. Regarding comprehension of the experimental results, consistency of text and graph was important: Conflicting messages caused longer comprehension times. Regarding memory, distorting effects of the text on memory for the accompanying graph were observed. Correspondingly, the graph also distorted memory for the accompanying text. Confidence in memory for texts and graphs was higher when text and graph had been consistent, reflecting the earlier ease of comprehending the results. Finally, large differences described in the text made the studies more interesting to the novice participants than small differences did.

10.3 Experiment 2

10.3.1 Objectives

Experiment 1 yielded clear effects of the visual message and the verbal message on students' comprehension of, and memory for, experimental studies. Therefore, Experiment 2 was designed to replicate the results of Experiment 1, and to extend them by investigating the process of text-graph comprehension in more detail. In particular, Experiment 2 served to find out how inconsistency of the verbal message and the visual message affects comprehension: Do comprehension times increase because participants spend more time reading the text, because they spend more time inspecting the graph, or because they look back and forth between the text and the graph more often? To answer these questions, participants' eye movements during the study phase of Experiment 2 were recorded. In most other respects, the second experiment was a replication of the first one, therefore, only the differences will be described below.

10.3.2 Method

10.3.2.1 Participants

Forty-nine students of Dresden University of Technology participated, most of them in their first semester. They participated to fulfill a curricular requirement, or they received a small monetary payment equivalent to 5 EUR. All participants were native speakers of German, and no one had participated in Experiment 1. Due to technical problems, the eye movement data of one participant were incomplete. Therefore, the analyses reported below are based on the data of the remaining 48 participants.

10.3.2.2 Materials, Procedure, Apparatus, and Design

The experimental studies presented to the participants were identical to those of Experiment 1. The procedure was also identical, except that eye movements were measured during the study phase. Eye movements were recorded by an

"*EyeLink*" eye tracking system, distributed by SensoMotoric Instruments GmbH, Germany. The eye tracker is an infrared video-based tracking system combined with hyperacuity image processing. Two cameras (one for each eye) are mounted on a headband, together with two infrared LEDs for illuminating each eye. The cameras sample pupil location and pupil size at the rate of 250 Hz. Registration was done binocularly, although monocular registration is possible as well. The resolution of eye position is 15 sec of arc and the spatial accuracy approximately 0.5 degrees. Head position with respect to the computer screen is measured with a head-tracking camera mounted on the center of the headband. Four LEDs attached to the corners of the computer screen are viewed by the head-tracking camera while the participant is facing the screen. Possible head motions are detected as movements of the four LEDs and are compensated for automatically. The compensation is better than 1 degree over the acceptable range of head motion. Thus, it is not necessary to use a head rest or other means to fixate the participant's head. Eye movements were not recorded during the surprise recognition test. The design of Experiment 2 differed from Experiment 1 only with regard to the additional dependent eye tracking variables, namely total gaze duration on text, total gaze duration on graph, and number of eye movements between text and graph.

10.3.3 Results and Discussion

The data of Experiment 2 were analyzed like the ones of Experiment 1, and the results are summarized in Table 10.2.

10.3.3.1 Comprehension Times of Results Sections

The 2×2 ANOVA of these self-paced comprehension times yielded results that replicated those of the first experiment: the interaction of text and graph was highly significant ($F(1,47)=28.99$, $p<0.001$, $f=0.39$), and it took participants longer to understand the experimental results, if the text and the graph were inconsistent (mean 26.2 sec) rather than consistent (mean 20.0 sec). As before, neither the effect size described in the text ($F(1,47)=2.51$, n.s., $f=0.11$) nor the effect size depicted in the graph ($F(1,47)<1$, $f=0.05$) yielded significant main effects.

10.3.3.2 Gaze Durations on Text

The analysis of these gaze durations mirrored that of the manual comprehension times just reported: participants spent more time fixating the text if it was inconsistent with the graph (mean 11.2 sec) rather than consistent (mean 9.8 sec). Consequently, the interaction of text and graph was highly significant ($F(1,47)=10.6$, $p<0.01$, $f=0.23$). Neither the effect size described in the text

Table 10.2 Mean values of dependent variables (with standard deviations) Observed in Experiment

Dependent Variable and Effect Size Depiction in Graph	Effect Size Description in Text	
	Small Effect	Large Effect
Comprehension Times of Results Sections (in sec)		
Small Effect in Graph	20.3 (6.5)	25.3 (8.0)
Large Effect in Graph	27.0 (8.3)	19.7 (6.2)
Gaze Durations on Text (in sec)		
Small Effect in Graph	10.4 (3.9)	11.2 (4.0)
Large Effect in Graph	11.2 (4.2)	9.2 (3.1)
Gaze Durations on Graph (in sec)		
Small Effect in Graph	1.6 (1.3)	3.8 (2.9)
Large Effect in Graph	4.9 (2.7)	2.0 (1.7)
Eye Movements between Text and Graph		
Small Effect in Graph	1.79 (0.73)	2.05 (1.24)
Large Effect in Graph	2.49 (1.35)	1.77 (0.96)
Interest Ratings (0–4)		
Small Effect in Graph	2.6 (0.59)	2.9 (0.68)
Large Effect in Graph	2.7 (0.66)	2.9 (6.0)
Recognition of Result Descriptions in Text (0–4)		
Small Effect in Graph	1.4 (0.48)	2.9 (0.52)
Large Effect in Graph	1.7 (0.62)	3.1 (0.55)
Confidence in Text Recognition (0-4)		
Small Effect in Graph	2.9 (0.73)	2.8 (0.56)
Large Effect in Graph	2.8 (0.63)	3.1 (0.66)
Recognition of Result Depictions in Graph (0–4)		
Small Effect in Graph	1.0 (9.1)	2.3 (0.82)
Large Effect in Graph	2.1 (1.1)	2.9 (0.77)
Confidence in Graph Recognition (0-4)		
Small Effect in Graph	2.5 (0.60)	2.1 (0.78)
Large Effect in Graph	2.2 (0.65)	2.4 (0.77)

($F(1,47) = 1.89$, n.s., $f = 0.10$) nor the effect size depicted in the graph ($F(1,47) = 2.6$, n.s., $f = 0.11$) yielded significant main effects.

10.3.3.3 Gaze Durations on Graphs

These gaze durations showed a pattern similar to the gaze durations on text: participants spent much more time fixating the graph if it was inconsistent with the text (mean 4.4 sec) rather than consistent (mean 1.8 sec). Consequently, the interaction of text and graph was highly significant ($F(1,47) = 46.7$, $p < 0.001$, $f = 0.50$). Effect size described in the text did not affect gaze durations on graphs ($F(1,47) = 1.87$, n.s., $f = 0.10$), whereas effect size depicted in the graph did ($F(1,47) = 7.74$, n.s., $f = 0.20$): graphs showing large effects were fixated for a longer time (mean 3.5 sec) than graphs showing small effects (mean 2.7 sec).

10.3.3.4 Eye Movements Between Text and Graph

Overall, participants did not look back and forth between the text and the graph very often (twice, on average). As expected, however, they did so more often if text and graph were inconsistent (mean 2.3) rather than consistent (mean 1.8). Consequently, the interaction of text and graph was significant ($F(1,47)=12.5$, $p<0.001$, $f=0.26$). In contrast, neither the effect size described in the text ($F(1,47)=3.01$, $p<0.10$, $f=0.13$) nor the effect size depicted in the graph ($F(1,47)=2.0$, n.s., $f=0.10$) yielded significant main effects.

10.3.3.5 Interest Ratings

Participants found studies more interesting if the effects were described verbally as being large (mean rating 2.9) rather than small (mean 2.6). In the 2×2 ANOVA, ratings were affected significantly by the effect description in the text ($F(1,47)=10.9$, $p<0.01$, $f=0.27$). In contrast, neither the effect depiction in the graph nor the text-graph interaction were significant (both $F(1,47)<1$, both $f<0.06$).

10.3.3.6 Recognition of Results Description in Text

As before, participants' recognition of the verbal results descriptions was of course strongly influenced by the real descriptions studied earlier. Thus, they chose larger effect descriptions if the text had indeed stated that the differences were large rather than small (mean 3.0 vs. 1.6, $F(1,47)=266.23$, $p<0.001$, $f=1.19$). More importantly, however, their choices were also affected by the visual effect depictions ($F(1,47)=14.76$, $p<0.001$, $f=0.28$): graphs showing large differences distorted text memory towards recognition of larger verbal descriptions (mean 2.4), and graphs showing small differences yielded recognition of smaller effects in the verbal descriptions (mean 2.1). The interaction of text description and graph depiction was not significant ($F(1,47)<1$, n.s., $f=0.03$).

10.3.3.7 Recognition of Results Depiction in Graph

As before, participants' recognition of the graphs was of course affected by the graphs they had seen earlier. Therefore, the effect depiction in the graph had a strong effect on the chosen graphs ($F(1,47)=39.57$, $p<0.001$, $f=0.46$): If participants had earlier seen a graph showing large differences, their recognition choices were larger (mean 2.5) than after seeing a graph showing small differences (mean 1.6). Of special interest, however, is the fact that their choices were also influenced by the verbal effect description ($F(1,47)=52.78$, $p<0.001$, $f=0.53$): if the text had described a large effect, graph choices were larger (mean 2.6) than when the text had described a small effect (mean 1.6), replicating the results of the first experiment. Again, the f values indicate that the text influenced graph recognition at least as strongly as the graph itself did. The text-graph interaction was marginally significant, suggesting that the text's distorting effect was again slightly more pronounced for graphs showing small rather than large effects ($F(1,47)=3.86$, $p<0.06$, $f=0.15$).

10.3.3.8 Confidence in Text Recognition

As before, the participants' confidence in their recognition of the verbal results descriptions depended on the consistency of text and graph. If the two media were consistent, confidence was higher (mean 3.0) than in cases of inconsistency (mean 2.8). Accordingly, the 2×2 ANOVA of the confidence ratings yielded a significant interaction of text and graph ($F(1,47)=4.72$, $p<0.05$, $f=0.16$), whereas the main effects were not significant (text: $F(1,47)=1.26$, n.s., $f=0.08$; graph: $F(1,47)=2.27$, n.s., $f=0.11$).

10.3.3.9 Confidence in Graph Recognition

These confidence ratings were also affected by the consistency of text and graph: participants' confidence in their graph choices was higher when text and graph were consistent (mean 2.5) rather than inconsistent (mean 2.1), yielding a significant text-graph interaction ($F(1,47)=19.1$, $p<0.001$, $f=0.32$). In contrast, neither the effect description in the text ($F(1,47)=1.19$, n.s., $f=0.08$) nor the effect depiction in the graph ($F(1,47)<1$, $f=0.01$) had a significant main effect on confidence.

In summary, the results of Experiment 2 clearly replicate the critical findings of Experiment 1: Inconsistency of text and graph slowed comprehension during reading of the results and lowered confidence in later recognition of them. Moreover, the verbal message contained in the text distorted memory for the accompanying graph, and the visual message conveyed by the graph distorted memory for the accompanying text. Experiment 2 also expanded the findings of the first experiment by eye tracking data. These data indicate that the increase in comprehension time observed for inconsistent text-graph combinations is due to longer fixations of the text as well as longer fixations of the graph. Moreover, inconsistency also caused participants to look back and forth between the text and the graph more often.

10.4 General Discussion and Conclusions

The two experiments reported here address two aspects of learning from verbal and pictorial information: (i) the consistency of the verbal message expressed by a text with the visual message depicted by a graph, and (ii) the relative impact of the two messages on each other. With regard to the consistency question, the experiments yielded clear answers. In accord with the structure mapping hypothesis introduced by Schnotz and Bannert (2003), the current findings indicate that the interplay of verbal and pictorial information contributes to the comprehension and retention of information about empirical studies. To arrive at a coherent mental representation of an empirical study and its results, readers need to process and integrate the verbal information given in the text and the pictorial information contained in the graph. If the verbal message and the visual message are consistent, creation of a coherent mental model is easier and faster than if they are inconsistent.

One may wonder what kind of representation readers build from inconsistent text-graph combinations. Although the current experiments were not designed to answer this question, they suggest that the representation is neither purely text-based (because the graph affected memory for the text) nor purely illustration-based (because the text affected memory for the graph). Moreover, the interactive effects of text and graph during the comprehension process imply that the comprehension process is not limited to creating separate representations of textual information and pictorial information, for instance, the propositional text base of the text and the mental model of the graph suggested by Schnotz and Bannert (2003). Instead, readers seem to make an effort to build the integrated "conceptual organization" suggested by Schnotz and Bannert (2003), even when integration of the verbal message and the visual message is difficult.

More research will be needed to determine the features of this attempted integration: does it fail because of the inconsistency, or is the contradiction solved by giving more credibility and weight to one type of information than to the other? If the latter is true, why is the resulting representation sometimes dominated by one type of information, sometimes by the other? A plausible answer would be that some participants favor verbal information, whereas others prefer pictorial information, depending on their individual abilities and experiences. However, the current experiments did not yield any evidence for this assumption: When analyzing the data individually, we did not find two separable groups of participants. Instead, most participants showed memory distortions for both types of information, such that graphs affected memory for texts and texts affected memory for graphs. This suggests that individual readers did not rely selectively on one or the other media during the creation of the mental model.

In general, however, the current results suggest that most participants put more emphasis on the information given in the text: gaze durations were much longer on the text than on the graph (on average, 10.5 sec vs. 3.1 sec), interest ratings were affected by the text more than by the graph, and the verbal message contained in the text affected memory for the graph more strongly than the visual message contained in the graph affected memory for the text. This might be due to two factors: First, the text was always displayed above the graph, therefore the text was usually fixated first. Second, the participants were novices who might find texts more credible and easier to process than graphs. It remains to be determined whether comparable results may be observed with other spatial arrangements of texts and graphs, and with more expert readers of empirical research. The latter may rely on graphical information more heavily, because of their experience in creating and reading graphs. Another open question concerns how the observed memory distortions develop over time: Future studies will have to examine whether the distortions increase with increasing retention intervals, and whether this is true for both verbal and pictorial information.

In the experiments reported here, the inconsistency was created with regard to the size and importance of the observed effects. An advantage of this variation is that it is possible to create inconsistencies regarding subjective aspects of the information without creating obvious contradictions of objective aspects. Thereby, even the inconsistent combinations of texts and graphs remained plausible. However, future research may use more obvious contradictions to assess the relative impact of verbal and graphical information on the processing of numerical data and other information. In that case, it should be impossible to create an integrated representation of verbal and pictorial information.

Acknowledgments Preparation of this paper was supported by grant Ri 600/3-3 from the German Research Foundation (DFG) to Mike Rinck. I would like to thank Ariane Bürkner, Constanze Hesse, Anja Pongracz, and Alexander Varchmin for their help in preparing and conducting the experiments. I am also grateful to two anonymous reviewers for helpful comments on an earlier version of this chapter.

Appendix

Sample Experimental Study Description, translated from German

1- Introduction:
This experiment investigated how memory depends on the context. A group of scuba divers learned lists of words. Half of them learned on land, and the other half learned under water. Afterwards, half of each group were asked to recall the words on land or under water. The experimenters counted how many words were recalled in each of the four possible combinations of learning environment (on land vs. under water) and recall environment (on land vs. under water). They expected that recall would be better when learning environment and recall environment are identical.

2a- Results Description Suggesting Large Effect:
Indeed, divers who both learned and recalled on land remembered a very high number of words (33 on average). Similarly, divers who learned and recalled under water, also recalled a very high number of words (31). However, if the environment changed, recall was much worse: Learning on land and recalling under water yielded a mean of only 27 words, and learning under water and recalling on land yielded only 28 words.

2b- Results Description Suggesting Small Effect:
However, divers who both learned and recalled on land remembered a medium number of words (33 on average). Similarly, divers who learned and recalled under water, also recalled a medium number of words (31). If the environment changed, recall was almost as good: Learning on land and recalling under water yielded a mean of 27 words, and learning under water and recalling on land even yielded 28 words.

References

Cleveland, W. S. (1993). *Visualizing data.* Summit, NJ: Hobart.

Cohen, J. (1988). *Statistical power analysis for the behavioral sciences.* Hillsdale, NJ: Erlbaum.

Glenberg, A. M., & Langston, W. E. (1992). Comprehension of illustrated text: Pictures help to build mental models. *Journal of Memory and Language, 31,* 129–151.

Godden, D. R., & Baddeley, A. D. (1975). Context-dependent memory in two natural environments: On land and under water. *British Journal of Psychology, 66,* 325–331.

Kosslyn, S. M. (1994). *Elements of graph design.* New York: Freeman.

Mayer, R. E. (1989). Systematic thinking fostered by illustrations in scientific text. *Journal of Educational Psychology, 81,* 240–246.

Mayer, R. E. (1997). Multimedia learning: Are we asking the right questions? *Educational Psychologist, 32,* 1–19.

Mayer, R. E., & Gallini, J. K. (1990). When is an illustration worth ten thousand words? *Journal of Educational Psychology, 82,* 715–726.

Rinck, M. (2000). Situationsmodelle und das Verstehen von Erzähltexten: Befunde und Probleme. (Situation models and the comprehension of narrative text: Findings and problems.) *Psychologische Rundschau, 51,* 115–122.

Schnotz, W. (1993). On the relation between dual coding and mental models in graphics comprehension. *Learning and Instruction, 3,* 247–249.

Schnotz, W., & Bannert, M. (2003). Construction and interference in learning from multiple representation. *Learning and Instruction, 13,* 141–156.

Tufte, E. R. (1983). *The visual display of quantitative information.* Cheshire, CT: Graphics Press.

Wainer, H. (1984). How to display data badly. *The American Statistician, 38,* 137–147.

Williams, P., & Tarr, M. J. (no date). *RSVP: Experimental control software for MacOS* [Online]. Available: http://psych.umb.edu/rsvp/ [1998, October 27].

Part III
Multimedia Research in Perspective

Chapter 11
Hypertext Was Born Around 1200

A Historical Perspective on Textual Navigation

Hervé Platteaux

Abstract This chapter considers non-linearity, a core feature of hypertext and multimedia systems, from a historical perspective. Based on a content analysis of ancient and contemporary historical sources, I review the evolution of text structuring devices (e.g., the table of contents) and their relationship with the social uses of text. I point out that the increasing sophistication of structuring devices over time was closely related to the shift from spoken, linear reading to silent, non-linear interactions with texts. Thus, non-linearity both characterizes modern texts and modern uses of text. I conclude that the navigational features of hypertext represent an evolution rather than a revolution in the history of text.

Keywords Codex · History · Hypertext · Non-linearity · Reading tools · Uses of text

11.1 Introduction

Non-linearity is often considered as a core difference between printed and hypermedia documents. Nelson (1967) created the word hypertext and defined it as: "a combination of natural language text with the computer's capacity for interactive branching, or dynamic display... of a non-linear text... which cannot be printed conveniently on a conventional page". This definition, which is still considered a reference by most authors, thus refers firstly to the technology of computers and networks, secondly to the linking process of information nodes in electronic documents and thirdly, to a particular information structure resulting from the network of linked nodes, i.e., non-linear text.

The present paper aims to reconsider the notion of non-linearity through a historical reanalysis of text structuring techniques. In the context of this

---

H. Platteaux
University of Fribourg, Centre NTE, Faucigny 2, CH – 1700 Fribourg, Switzerland
e-mail: herve.platteaux@unifr.ch

DOI: 10.1007/978-0-387-73337-1_11,

chapter, the word text means "All statement, whatever it is, spoken or writing, length or short, old or new" (Denhière & Baudet, 1992, 29). In the first part, I describe how the structure of the written text developed in the Middle Ages when the different book reading tools appeared. With the expression "reading tools", I mean both content representation devices (i.e., index, table of contents, bibliographical list, etc.) and orientation clues (page number, page of title, section titles, head of pages, etc.). By reconstructing the history of reading tools, I also describe how and why the reading activity evolved along with the introduction and development of reading tools in the codex. In the second part, I discuss the notions of linearity and non-linearity in documents and in reading activities. The present study thus tries to link historiography with a discussion of linearity and non-linearity in texts and in reading activities considered from a psychological standpoint.

A historical retrospective of book structuring devices may improve our understanding of non-linearity. Indeed, many text theorists have proposed that paper printed documents can also be non-linear. Foucault (1969) claimed that, from a discourse analysis perspective, the boundaries of scholarly books are not well defined because each book is linked to other books by a system of cross-references, namely the bibliography. Dillon (1991) pointed out that table of contents, index and page numbers are devices of printed text which facilitate direct access to relevant information. Mohageg (1992) emphasized that a table of contents gives a direct access to precise information nodes of texts and hypertexts. And Vandendorpe (1999) asserted that the organization of the printed books, starting with the design of the codex, transformed paper-based texts into non-linear systems.

Other authors have discussed the possibility of non-linear reading activities in printed texts. For example, Landow (1992) noted that readers can go from text to text by following footnotes and other referencing tools. Such non-linear, selective reading activities are driven by the reader's aim, which is to access directly to relevant information without reading each text completely (Rouet & Levonen, 1996). Espéret (1996) explained that the (non-)linearity of documents and that of reading activities are often confused. A linear document can be used into a non-linear way. For example, a student can look for the words that appear in a novel and that express a predefined idea.

Text structuring tools play a central role in the concept of non-linearity. On the one hand, they break the linearity of a text by proposing links to other text passages. On the other hand, they support the non-linear reading activity of the reader who can activate or not the proposed link, according to his navigation aims. They are fundamental to the navigation process that can be defined as: "To navigate in a hypertext firstly consists of setting up aims, maintaining them and finding orientation clues into the system so to make the appropriate selections" (Rouet & Tricot, 1995, 327). And this is why I proposed to take a look at the Middle Ages, period in which reading tools appeared in the written text.

11.2 Analyzing Reading Tools of Ancient Books: Methodological Aspects

11.2.1 Documentation Sources

In order to reconstruct a history of book reading tools and book structuring process, two main documentation sources were consulted. First, book historian publications were reviewed to assemble textual extracts dealing with reading tools, content structuring, book usages and their transformation through the ages. Second, old books, dated from 1482 to 1662, were consulted at the public and university library of Geneva.

Data collection was guided by several main objectives. First, a study of the evolution of book structure and usage has to look into the most important reading tools – table of contents and alphabetical index – without overlooking the evolution of page design and notion. Second, I also gathered, as much as possible, commentaries by middle ages scholars found as citations made by book historians. These materials provided first hand accounts of Middle Ages scholars' understanding and intentions about the structuring process. It was also foreseen that textual information would not be sufficient to support our study. In fact, a lot of reading tools have a graphical dimension that cannot be separated from their cognitive functions (Platteaux & Rickenmann, 1998). Different types of graphical examples were then assembled as another type of data. The reproductions of pages of old books were collected to visualise the graphical changes that took place in the appearance of the page. Illustrations representing people using books (reading, working with, etc.) completed the data.

All the textual data were then regrouped and globally structured into synoptic and chronological tables, which distinguish three main perods and present four information categories: reading tools, book types, book contents and usages of books. All the graphical examples and illustrations were structured into a database.

11.2.2 Study Limitations

Our work was based in part on publications by book historians that are centred on the evolution of reading tools and of reading activities. In the best cases, both the facts mentioned by these authors and their reconstructed historical context were relevant to our study. This is, for example, the case of Mary and Rouse's (1989) description of the birth of the index. However, in the majority of the consulted works, we could only extract a series of interesting but disconnected facts. We then had to reconstruct their importance with respect to their historical context, a process which faces a few obstacles that are worth mentioning here.

First, there is a large gap between contemporary thinking and the one of the Middle Ages. The historical novel Le nom de la rose (Eco, 1990) illustrates this gap very explicitly. Second, as Eisenstein (1991) highlighted, printing acts as a veil that hides the manuscript's context of production. The presentation and structure of written text evolved a lot before Gutenberg developed the technology of mobile letterpress, just before the middle of the 15th century. But, today, most of the old books that can be consulted were produced with printing techniques. Thus, are we able to see the transformations that happened before? Third, what can be said from one of the collected citations from Middle Ages' intellectuals? Is it reflecting a usage or a production way that was usual at the time, or exceptional, for the book readers and producers? Finally, it appeared through the collect of data that the book structuring process developed over fourteen centuries, from the 4th and until the 18th century. And this makes it impossible to reconstruct in detail a complete history. Platteaux (1999) presented an overview of the complete history which can be divided into three main periods: first, the birth of reading tools (4th–12th centuries); second, the development of reading tools (13th to 15th centuries) and, third, the generalisation of reading tools (16th–18th centuries). In this article, we summarize this history detailing all the elements which explain the big rupture that took place around year 1200 and introduced the efficient possibility of non-linear reading with written paper-based documents.

11.3 A Short History of Book Reading Tools

11.3.1 The Linear Codex: A Device to Memorize Orally Transmitted Knowledge

11.3.1.1 The Codex as a Major Shift in the Structuring of Textual Materials

The exact circumstances of the codex apparition are still not well known. But book historians agree that this page-bound document was a tremendous evolution, firstly adopted within Christian communities (Chartier, 1996). The codex replaced the Antiquity volumen, that consisted of a roll with one written side, during the 4th century (Johannot, 1994). Roberts (1954) showed that this transformation and its positive consequences for the scholars' work had already been noticed at that early time. The codex was considered the first major step in the text structuring process. In fact, because of its shape, the codex allowed the development of a large range of reading tools which required a material support made of sheets and pages.

11.3.1.2 Links Between Written Text and Orality

It is important to consider that for a long time (i.e., approximately from the Antiquity until the 4th century), written text was strongly linked to orality. Mesopotamian written text was the exception because its purpose was to store concrete facts (e.g., administrative lists, inventories, counts, etc.) and not to reproduce an oral speech (Martin, 1996). In general, throughout the Antiquity and early Christian era, written texts served as handbooks that merely helped people to memorize orally transmitted knowledge (Johannot, 1994). Written contracts, made by Greeks and Romans, always contained oral formulas that were spoken during the convention (Martin, 1996). Even in the Middle Ages, the primary purpose of a written text was to register and to visualize oral speech, because written text was always made to be read out loud in public (Zumthor, 1983). And this function of written text still exists in contemporary times: "Language and writing are two different systems of signs; (...) the second represents the first one" (De Saussure, 1972, 45).

In this way, the book remained just like a memorization tool and its contents, the written text, were organised according to the methods of mnemonic, the art of memory (Yates, 1975). Ong (1982) explained, for example, how the techniques of epic poems were based, in particular, on oral formats that were easier to remember. In these poems, everything was made to depict real and alive facts in the mind of listeners. The speech was narrated, accentuated and performed so that it was more easily transmitted and memorized. Nowadays, similar techniques are used in schools to memorize basic facts, such as multiplication tables (one surely remembers the music of "3 times 3... 9, 3 times 4... 12, etc.").

To summarize the social uses of text in the context of the early Middle Ages, books were made of purely linear text, and there was probably no need for visually structuring the written materials.

11.3.1.3 Oral Tradition vs. Written Memory

During this period, there appeared a conflict between written text and oral speech. This conflict was trying to solve the problem of the transmission of the Christian dogma. At first, people did not believe that they could extract useful information from text only. With time, however, the authority of text as a permanent, autonomous source of knowledge began to be better understood. Written documents allowed a text to be read again and again without having to memorize it, since the contents remained invariable (Johannot, 1994). As the importance of the form of poetic and narrative texts decreased, written prose gained momentum. In this way, the written text became a form to express the types and structures of different speeches. Books began to depart from strict linear texts. Johannot (1994) presented the Domesday Book, dated in 1066, that put together laws into a written form, as a piece of work that symbolizes the passage between oral tradition and written memory.

11.3.2 The Birth of Non-linearity in the Written Text

11.3.2.1 Reading Tools Needed Page as a Crucible to Develop

The generalization of the codex allowed the creation of reading tools, chiefly because of the specific characteristics of its primary constituent: the page. The word "page" acquired its present meaning during the 5th century (Hamman, 1985) and, since then, the art of designing pages evolved tremendously. In the beginning, there seemed to be little consideration for the concept of a page. Thus, the readability of codex pages remained quite poor. For several precursors, like Cassiodore in the 6th century, a clear presentation of text was very important (Johannot, 1994). But it is not until the 12th century that more codex designers became aware of it. In this time a uniform page presentation had been generally adopted: the text was divided in two columns so that the readers could see a complete line at once (Gilmont, 1993).

11.3.2.2 Divisions and Marks in Greater Variety

Scribes and scholars had already thought about the introduction of divisions and marks in the text to facilitate reading. Since the 3rd century, capitulations constituted a summary of the book and presented the structure of the contents. They were the first version of modern tables of contents (Mary & Rouse, 1989). As soon as codex replaced volumen (4th century), the words Explicit and Incipit were used to divide the contents of a book. But it is not clear if they delimited conceptual divisions like today's chapters or different volumen that were copied in a single codex (Hamman, 1985; Chartier, 1996).

In fact, as Vezin (1989) explained, the inventors of reading tools were very creative. Since the beginning of the 6th century, decorated initials were used to indicate separations in a text. Since the end of the 11th century, they were alternately presented red and blue. Since the 7th century, book producers started using numbers, called signatures, to identify the parts of the book and to bind them correctly. With the same purpose, a very ancient technique, called catchwords, placed the last words of one book piece on the next one and, in the 12th century, it was generalised in the Latin world. In the 8th century emerged another innovation: words began to be separated (Chartier, 1996). Word separation was very important, as it allowed the development of faster reading and of new reading tools. This technique generalized during the 11th century (Gilmont, 1993) but it remained in the monasteries before being introduced in the universities and schools in the 12th century (Chartier, 1996). Since the 12th century, many more tools appeared: systems to number sheets of paper, titles in red called rubrics, cross-references, names of cited authors, and so forth.

11.3.2.3 An "Embryo" of Non-linearity in Text and Reading

The invention of divisions and marks changed very much the appearance and the structure of the text. They introduced a fundamental mutation of reading. With time, they allowed to perform a visual and silent reading that was much faster. People had no longer to follow the order of the text, to read it aloud before catching its meaning and to memorize it (Cavallo & Chartier, 1997). Readers could have access to many and more complex texts (Chartier, 1996). And, from the 11th century on, all these changes created a completely new way to look at the text: "From now on, the reader does not listen to the text any more, but looks at the page, and his eyes move on the two dimensions of this one researching the marks or the letters of color which mark it out, or a given word" (Martin, 1996, 153).

Thus, all the inventions that took place between the 3rd and the 11th centuries were slowly transforming the linear, speech-like text into an autonomous, non-linear artifact. But this was only an embryo of non-linearity because there were no standards for the reading tools and their container: the books. Text and tools could have different presentation formats in different books because, for instance a copyist could add commentaries as in the case of gloss (Garin, 1968) or simply change the number of pages of the original text because of a larger handwriting. In this situation, a book could not play the role of a non-linear document. The innovation of non-linearity could in fact not diffuse easily because the world of written text was much partitioned in Europe and this was maintaining diversity of writing techniques until the 14th century (Martin, 1996).

Meanwhile, non-linear reading based on the use of reading tools was beginning to develop and, with it, "knowledge, even if it was fragmentary, became then first and got over everything else. Meditation gave way to utility and this was a deep modification that completely changed the impact of reading" (Hamesse, 1997, 133, my translation). This was true in learning and study activities but also in the domain of leisure where the book entered in the 13th century. Secular nobles and bourgeois began to read for their pleasure. They liked tales, fables and beautiful exotic novels like the story of the journeys of Marco Polo (Heers, 1983). And since the 14th century, these books were also made with tables of contents, alphabetical glossaries, indices, headings, etc. (Saenger, 1997). Other important domains of human activities, in particular commerce and law, knew a similar development, from the 4th century and until the 12th century, of their written documents (Martin, 1996). Documents were produced in order to weight off the memory, to be useful and they were based on a set of writing rules and reading tools.

Then during reading for study, work and leisure, memory could be used to retain the global meaning of a sentence and not the detail of the words and of their order (Saenger, 1997). This made possible the development of other cognitive skills (Eisenstein, 1991). It became possible to read more rapidly and that meant more texts and more complex texts (Chartier, 1996). Because the reading was no more made from the beginning and until the end of a text, everything changed in the relation between reading and time duration (Johannot, 1994). Also, when non-linear reading became totally efficient after the invention of printing, complete new ways of learning developed, in particular it became possible to learn alone (Eisenstein, 1991).

11.3.2.4 Written Text to Transmit the Fixed Word of God

The global objective of scholars who were developing reading tools also explains why the achieved form of the written document constituted an embryo of non-linearity. As soon as the written text was understood as being able to keep ideas without any alteration, it was used to transmit the Christian dogma that is the explanation of the world, created and organised by God in a way that cannot be changed. Then, scholars were not inventing a text but they wrote being directly inspired by God (Bréhier, 1971). Until the 15th century, illustrations in books showed Evangelists copying from a book kept by angels (Saenger, 1997).

Reading tools were developed with this objective. Capitulations that appeared in the 3rd century were summaries joined to biblical manuscripts. Tables of concordance, like those of Eusebe Cesaree of the 6th century, showed the existing correspondence between the four evangelists' books (Chartier & Martin, 1989). In the 3rd century took also place the birth of Index. It consisted in a list of texts considered as true by Church (Johannot, 1994). One of the most famous was the Décret Gélassien distributed since the beginning of the 6th century (Hamman, 1985). By extension, index would later mean forbidden books (index librorum prohibitorum). Hundreds of illustrations showed Christ pointing out a book with his index finger (Johannot, 1994) and everybody deduced that this meant: "This is the Bible and here is the truth".

11.3.3 How Written Text Became an Efficient Non-linear Artifact

11.3.3.1 Reading Tools Were Made for Readers

Since the invention of the codex, numerous reading tools were created. Nevertheless, it took a very long time before they became the reading tools that we know today. Their large diversity was an obstacle. They were also thought to help book producers. An example was the inclusion of page numbers, which were originally a technique to facilitate the copyists' work (Vezin, 1989). According to Mary and Rouse (1989), during the 13th century, a great advance was made as book producers used reading tools to facilitate readers' access to specific contents. Mary and Rouse added that it is very difficult to determine exactly when this happened for every existing technique. But they estimated that this new purpose was a norm in 1220, because a lot of scholars had this in mind. For instance, Guibert of Nogent divided very carefully his works in chapters to make private consultations easier (Saenger, 1997). Hughes of Saint-Victor advised his students to take care about the graphical presentation of information that he considered a pedagogical tool (Hamesse, 1997). Vincent of Beauvais paid special attention to his famous Speculum Majus (Big Mirror), an encyclopaedia edited for the first time in 1244, and to its first part he wrote as a very long table of contents. The author said about this reading tool: "This (...)

index of the whole work is the lantern lighting it up; it is the road through the contents of the books, it is used to show its order so that it appears more clearly to the reader in which chapter he will find what he is looking for with no lost effort" (Paulmier-Foucart, 1991, 222). He devoted his constant attention to utility for the readers of reading tools.

11.3.3.2 A New, "Radical" Reading Activity During the 13th Century

Why had reading tools not been directly applied to readers' usage during such a long time? Historians consider that, until the 13th century, the usual way of reading was the so-called divine reading (lectio divina). For instance, Benoît of Nursie explained during the 5th century that the aim of the reading activity was to go deep into the comments of the authorities (Bechtel, 1992). Scholars were certainly not reading only religious texts, but the reading of secular texts was strictly organised. For instance, during the 6th century, Cassiodore wanted his monks to read secular authors, but only so that they would be able to achieve a better understanding of the Holy Scriptures (Martin, 1996). And two centuries later, the school politic of the emperor Charlemagne was still dominated by this idea. There were courses of grammar, rhetoric and dialectic but these subjects were seen as allowing the understanding of religious texts. This importance of the religious texts remained for long time. Among the printed books of the period from 1450 to 1470, the proportion of religious books was 58% (Stillwell, 1972).

As mentioned above, the purpose of the typical reader was to memorize the Scriptures and not to understand them. The teaching principle of the great Bernard of Chartres according to the ideal monastic school in the 12th century was: reading and reading, tirelessly and day after day, the same famous texts that had to be learnt by heart in order to become the substance of the reader's soul (Garin, 1968). With this purpose, did scholars need reading tools to look for any information and to access easily to one part of the text? In fact, if they were reading a book, they memorized it from a to z. In this context, human memory was the most used tool for searching information.

However, the natural limitations of human memory were reached when scholastic medieval schools expanded and expected their students to really understand texts, to be able to compare across sources and to acquire knowledge (Hamesse, 1997). With this new purpose, reading tools and page design were used more systematically as memory and comprehension aids. On the contrary, the use of memory and mnemonic tools decreased because of their limits (Eisenstein, 1991). In the 12th century, there was a growing awareness of the complexity of reading. The first treatise on the art of reading was written by Hughes of Saint-Victor (Hamesse, 1997). A faster, selective scholastic reading replaced the slow and rigorous monastic reading method. This was a radical evolution in reading because a fragmentary, non-linear way of using texts was born (Hamesse, 1997). Non-linearity was enhanced in this new type of reading because it was including the consultation of reference books. For example, reading tools were used by scholars to organize their collections of citations from the authorities to support their argumentation. Some historians consider that this new approach of text revolutionized the methods of scholars (Martin, 1996).

11.3.3.3 Reading Tools to Support Non-linear Reading

The spread of the new reading process provided the ideal conditions to the development of efficient reading tools and they adopted their modern function: to support information search. From this moment, books became "communication tools" (Gilmont, 1993), that is, efficient non-linear documents.

Since the 13th century, scholars wanted to organize new ideas in systems presented in books as internal references. They were perceived as allowing the association of two passages that were separated in the book but logically linked together. The internal references permitted the reader to link two pages in order to find the logical origin of one argument and to compare the two text pieces (Saenger, 1997). This enhanced non-linear reading activities by providing a material support in the document.

With the considerable increase in literature production in the 12th century, it became impossible to read and remember everything and non-linear, selective reading became necessary. Scholars were facing two problems. The first one was how to access the essentials of a theme. The second one was how to be informed about new published books. The solution was the massive production of encyclopaedias, lexicons, glossaries, etc. (Cavallo & Chartier, 1997) that were made to give an easy access to their parts. This reinforced the development of reading tools.

During this period, the demand of the public to understand more difficult texts increased. Since the 14th century, scholars were convinced that reading tools were important for this comprehension process (Schmitt, 1987). Then the books which contained reading tools became reference works of the libraries and they had to be chained up in special consultation places to avoid the robbery (Saenger, 1997).

11.3.3.4 Two Important Tools: Index and Table of Contents

The alphabetical index appeared during the 13th century, but it is not possible to trace its exact chronological evolution because of a lack of precise dates (Chartier & Martin, 1989; Mary & Rouse, 1989). Precursors, like Papias, in his famous dictionary, had already used alphabetical order in the 11th century. The innovation of the 13th century was the systematization of its use into indices. The alphabetical order appeared as a method of classification that decreased the problem due to the use of memory as the main tool for information research. However, three obstacles remained before the alphabetical index could be efficient. First, in the Middle Ages, people did not like alphabetical order because they considered it was questioning the harmonious universe created by God (Chartier & Martin, 1989). Second, readers did not know the alphabetical order during the 13th century. Third, although page numbers were used since the 13th century (Cavallo & Chartier, 1997), they were only valid in the original book. However, readers saw more and more alphabetical indices and they got used to it. Individuals even wrote some for their own use (Eisenstein, 1991). The value of the index was then fully recognised at the end of the 13th century and it was mature in the 14th century after people specialised in its production.

A great effort was also done on the implementation of tables of contents. Scholars placed them into newly produced books. One significant work was the encyclopaedia of Vincent of Beauvais, dated around 1244 (Krynen, 1996). As mentioned above, his Speculum Majus (the big mirror) was organised so as to facilitate its use, proposing different paths through its contents (Paulmier-Foucart, 1991). The whole work was structured in about thirty books and every one was separated into 100 or 150 chapters. This structure was presented by tables of contents that introduced every book and one alphabetical table regrouped more than 12,000 entries. Also, from the 13th century and until the 15th century, scholars took ancient texts to subdivide them more precisely (Saenger, 1997). Some major works were renewed this way. For example, Hughes of Saint-Cher inserted new tables of concordance in the Bible in 1240, replacing the tables that Eusebe of Cesaree had written a thousand years before (Mary & Rouse, 1989). However, it was after long time that these examples became majority. For example, in the edition of 1467 of the widespread Saint-Augustin's Cité de Dieu, there was a table of contents but the book had no title, chapters, divisions or page numbers (Hamman, 1985). According to Boorstin (1986) the first table of contents in a printed book written in English was published in 1481.

11.3.4 The Generalisation of Non-linearity

11.3.4.1 Text Secularization Increased the Need for Reading Tools

Although for a long time the Bible remained the one reference book in the Christian world, books began to serve other, non religious functions. With time, writing and reading became increasingly important for a greater number of people. Literacy skills were valued since the end of the 12th century, even for a scholar who did not want to develop a religious carrier (Bechtel, 1992). Thus, secular books and uses of books increased, as illustrated by the aforementioned Domesday Book (1066) that assembled the English laws.

At the same time, reading entered the spheres of pleasure and of leisure in addition to those of learning, commerce and law (Gilmont, 1993). This did not mean, however, total freedom on the production and dissemination of knowledge. For example, Aristote's works, which had been rediscovered at the beginning of the 13th century, were censored because they contradicted Christian dogma, for example the Genesis story or the faith in the survival of soul (Orvas, 1998; De Boüard , 1991). The process of secularization tended to increase the number of books explaining the world, as it was understood by humans and not as described in the Bible. In order to present the new contents and to allow the new uses, more reading tools were needed and writing became a more creative art. Progressively, non-linear texts became prevalent in the middle of the 15th century, both in Church, University and the secular world (Bechtel, 1992).

11.3.4.2 New Systematic Reading Tools to Renew Knowledge

The traditional Christian dogma asserted that the world was finite and that it was possible to describe all the existing knowledge. That was precisely the purpose of Middle Ages encyclopaedias: to present the word organisation as it was revealed by God (Johannot, 1994). But the modern vision of the world as infinite opened the possibility for new knowledge to be elaborated. And a representation of knowledge to think about the world had to be built. In order to determine, organise and diffuse newly created knowledge, Lulle wrote in 1295 his Arbre de ciencia where he showed an organisational system that took the form of one information tree (Chatelain, 1996; Llinarès, 1991). This development was not part of the secularization tendency because Lulle had built this representation in order to present the divine creation. However it was remarkable because Lulle set up a dynamical approach that consisted in to apply a real process with the objective to renew knowledge. It made his work radically different from the earlier encyclopaedias (Llinarès, 1991). And Lulle's system has influenced much on encyclopaedias of the 16th century both on representations adopted as tables of contents and on division of contents. Pierre de la Ramée, called Ramus (Ong, 1958), took Lulle's idea during the 16th century and developed an objective, reasoned method to order and to present the knowledge systematically, without repetitions, without omissions and a perfect readability (Chatelain, 1996).

All the later encyclopaedias applied this method that constituted the basis of our hierarchical reading tools. One important example was the work of Francis Bacon, Proficience and advancement of learning divine and humane. It appeared in 1605 and it was based on a systematic tree organisation. With this work, he did not want to transmit knowledge and to favour readers learn it by hearth easily. He wanted to expose the knowledge to identify its limits and to make people aware of the topics where new knowledge should be produced (Le Doeuff, 1991). He summarized his idea of this process, in 1620, writing in head of his Novum Organum: "Many will pass and science will be augmented". This may have been the true origins of navigation as a knowledge reading metaphor.

11.3.4.3 Xylography and Gutenberg's Press Allowed the Generalisation of Non-linear Books

Since the 13th century, when readers began to favour non-linear reading activities, there was an effort to make the book and its reading tools much more uniform (Cavallo & Chartier, 1997). New techniques were developed to that aim, such as xylography. Since the 14th century and thanks to engraved pieces of wood, copyists could rapidly insert identical images into texts (Duby, 1976). Xylography allowed the multiplication of visual supports, which increased the importance given to visual communication, in particular in education (Eisenstein, 1991).

Gutenberg's typography also contributed to the "delinearization" of books, especially by allowing easier page numbering. Page numbering was originally devoted to the manual book production process (Vezin, 1989). I have mentioned the two techniques of signatures and catchwords into the different book parts called pieces (peciae). These marks were mostly used in manuscripts of the 13th and 14th centuries. Pages began to be individually numbered during the 15th century (Hamman, 1985) but numbering the pages remained a difficult and long task. On the contrary, with Gutenberg's discovery, uniformly paginated books could be made more easily and diffused in large numbers (Boorstin, 1986). Page numbering could really become a tool for readers even if the technique generalized very slowly. A single paginated book is known among all incunabula (i.e., printed books produced until 1501; Labarre, 1989). In contrast, pagination had become general about a hundred years after Gutenberg's discovery (Laufer, 1989; Hamman, 1985). Historians insist on the great influence that Gutenberg's technology had on reading tools (Eisenstein, 1989, 1991; Hindman, 1991; Hamman, 1985). First, by multiplying the number of books, it spread reading tools and their usage. Second, printing allowed the emergence of the concept of publishing. Book exemplars became identical, in particular for their pagination, and this permitted a true non-linear navigation based on cross-references.

11.4 Going Back to Non-linearity Principles

11.4.1 Standardized Reading Tools Made Non-linear Reading Efficient

The introduction of reading tools (index, table of contents, bibliographical list, etc.) in a paginated book radically transformed reading and made efficient a non-linear usage of paper based text between the 12th and the 13th centuries. Thus a new type of reading, very analogous to what is known as hypertext navigation, was born a long time before the birth of electronic documents. Before reading tools appeared, written documents could be read in a non-linear way. But written documents remained linear in the sense they were done and thought only for linear reading. On the contrary, texts became non-linear when they were associated to reading tools and also based on the idea that their contents could, or even should, be looked through different ways. They were conceived to reach the different purposes of different readers and to support different reading tasks and objectives.

The history of book design and production shows how parallel were the evolution of book reading tools and of non-linear reading. Relatively standard reading tools were needed to support efficient non-linear reading. Such standards concerned the presentation of contents, page numbers, header, page title, edition notion, etc. The diversity of early books was an obstacle to efficient non-linear reading. On the contrary, a "visual regularity" allowed its development (Vandendorpe, 1999, 29). Readers could easily access to the contents since the book – the container – has become predictable. Standards allowed readers to develop, enrich and use mental models applicable to all books and all book usages.

Nowadays, hypertext specialists also claim that a certain uniformity of the web should favour users' understanding of navigation principles (Foltz, 1996; Rouet, 2006; Weinreich, Obendorf, & Lamersdorf, 2001). In fact, it is true that "Hypertext permits and makes easy a non-linear reading of a set of documents" (Nanard, 1995, 31). But, associated with reading tools, paper-based text also allowed and made quite easy non-linear reading long time ago (Le Roy, 1995).

11.4.2 Linear vs. Non-linear Documents

In this section, I discuss the concepts of linearity and non-linearity in printed and electronic documents. In particular, I discuss the importance of reading tools in the operational process of non-linearity. Let me start with a specification of the concept of linear text. I have already mentioned that the origins of the written text are anchored in orality, where the audience "must follow the thread, irremediably linear because it is registered in time, of the recitation which is made by it" (Vandendorpe, 1999, 15). Thus the text was originally linear and dependent upon the temporal flow of speech. By extension, modern novels are considered linear because they are generally based on a chronological run and, in addition, because their development is reflected in the linear order of the pages. But linearity is not bound to written speeches and narratives. Indeed, texts that rest on a hierarchical organization, such as scientific accounts, are also considered linear because their organization corresponds to the course of the speech of a scientist who explains a set of themes. The concepts serving the explanation are articulated so as to show their logical links. And, generally, the same speech continues section after section because the new ideas that come with new sections still enrich the explanatory speech in accordance with what precedes. Thus, scientific discourse usually begins, in its first chapters, showing the basic concepts and then develops the set of themes in its more complex aspects. The linearity of the text comes from the uniqueness of the semantic link put forward between two concepts to express the continuation and the development of an idea. Indeed it "is not the loss but the repression of the thought multidimensional symbolic system" (Derrida, 1967, 128).

One can certainly also characterize linear texts through their global rhetorical structures. For example, a scientific article usually includes a sequence of standard sections, i.e. introduction, methods, results, discussion, bibliography. And experienced readers of such articles have a representation of this rhetoric structure that they can use to reorganize the isolated parts from the text in a logical whole (Dillon, 1991). The use of standard rhetorical structures facilitates the reader's comprehension of the text, and especially the construction of a macrostructure (Van Dijk, 1984; Van Dijk & Kintsch, 1983).

The linearity of a document then seems to rest basically on the concept of a semantic proposition which corresponds to "the smallest integrated semantic unit able to be processed and stored" (Le Ny, 1995, 386). Let us note however that the richness of the human thought creates a complex linearity because it can, for example, bring closer two ideas a priori very distant in an explanation. Similarly, the process of assembling ideas into a linear text is not trivial and it may even include some arbitrary decisions into the resulting conceptual thread, as Nodier (1985) noted: "Why first chapter? It would be as well everywhere else. Moreover, I must acknowledge that I wrote the eighth chapter before the fifth, which became the third here." But, once those decisions are made, the order of ideas is the same as the pages of its physical container. We find this parallelism in the table of contents of the linear document (Platteaux & Rickenmann, 1998).

Non-linearity in text may be defined as the existence of several linearities in a simultaneous way. These linearities and their tangles can be very varied since the interactive links which make operational non-linearity in a hypertext have a very wide spectrum of functions: they can take away the reader towards a glossary and bring back to a principal text or make the reader reach a completely different document.

To structure a document in a non-linear way means to offer readers various linear threads with the hope that those threads will allow them to achieve their reading goals. Thus, the author of a non-linear document needs to consider multiple readers and to favour the possibility of several readings. The document becomes thus non-linear because it assembles various linearities in a single artifact. Conklin (1987) showed that non-linear hypertexts were made of a hierarchical structure, combined with a transverse structure made up of associative links. Navigation in the hierarchical structure is implemented by a table of contents, whereas navigation in the transverse structure is made possible by a multitude of tools. Similarly, in the printed book, several reading tools serve various usages: footnotes to add details or specifications, bibliographical references to mention related texts, the alphabetical index to locate a concept or a quoted author, explanatory tables, illustrations or diagrams to complete or visualize some parts of the text. There are other tools and modes of text production that serve to orientate the reader: page numbers, headers, section and chapter titles, spaces between words and paragraphs and so forth (Rouet, 2006).

The global structure of the book can also be nonlinear. A usual example is the dictionary. The way terms are laid out in the book follows the alphabetic order. To read definitions successively does not produce any meaning because the text is globally non-linear. Another popular example is the edited book. Edited books gather contributions on a global theme, but subsequent chapters do not necessary follow up on each other. The table of contents of these works shows these differences and represents proposals for several simultaneous linearities.

11.4.3 Linear vs. Non-linear Uses of Text and Hypertext

Linearity may also be discussed in terms of the reading activity rather than the text. To read in a linear manner is to let one be guided by the thread recommended by the author. Examples include: following the logic of a sequence of arguments in a mathematical demonstration, the successive stages of a physical or biological phenomenon; or the charms of the music of the words of a poem.

Then as I have already mentioned in the introduction, to read in a non linear manner is to depart from the basic, default discourse thread. Such a departure can have multiple reasons. Among those is the reader who seeks specification information that is not readily offered in the thread of the book. The history of the book shows us in particular that the necessity for different readings was felt very early in the use of the book and that this necessity was that one of an intellectual life directed towards a production of knowledge. This is entirely the purpose of Francis Bacon's encyclopaedia in the 17th century. One cannot remain locked up indefinitely in an entirely preset and fixed linearity.

A good example of such a non-linear course is that one of a linguist seeking all the terms of a certain semantic field in a work of poetry. This example is a search for information, a task which very often is not following the principal structure of the consulted documents and rests on the use of tools like an alphabetical index (see also Cerdán et al., Chapter 7; Lowe, Chapter 8).

In front of a written text, the reader can set his or her reading rate, decide on a passage to read and the selection order of various segments. Many authors, like Martin (1996), noticed that non-linearity falls under the two dimension space of the page and is basically related to the presence of reading tools. In the same way, by distinguishing the linearity of the language from the non-linearity of the reading, linguists also remark that: "If the sequentiality remains constitutive of the language as a whole, (one cannot write 'cat milk drinks'), the bidimensionality of graphic space (of the writing) allows non-linear readings and a beaconing of the marks which creates legibility" (Anis, 1988, 146).

The history of the book shows that reading was freed from the constraints of orality only thanks to improvements in shape (from the roll to the codex), and by the invention of the "reference marks intended to facilitate the relationships between writing and reading" (Vandendorpe, 1999, 16). The bidimensionality of the text can be analyzed at various levels. At a local level, reading is mostly linear because it is constrained by the structure of sentences. But the text can also be seen as a whole which the reader must discover: at this level, reading tools allow the reader to know where he or she is and to make choices of sections of interest. This cognitive function comes from the correspondence that reading tools established between support and contents (Platteaux & Rickenmann, 1998). They make it always possible to answer the following two questions: "If I want to go to such contents, where should I go in the support?"; and "If I am in such place of the support, where am I in the contents?".

Can one carry out a linear reading in a hypertext, even though the ideas are connected in a non-linear network? Indeed, if there is no line of reference, as in a linear text, how can one distinguish between linear and nonlinear courses? Three types of criteria may be used to identify linear reading sequences in hypertext. First, the linearity of hypertext reading may be defined as the construction of a global meaning based on several passages and the reader of a hypertext must sometimes reconstruct global coherence, by making bridging inferences that connect different nodes (Foltz, 1996). Second, linearity may arise from the type of goal or objective that the reader pursues. Let us take the example of a search for information in the Web. Before a request has been formulated and sent by the user, there is no document to be read. Based on the user's request, the search engine proposes potentially relevant pages as a list of successive items that are presented in a specific order – a characteristic of linearity – according to their estimated relevance. And by looking up the different items, the reader performs a linear reading since he or she always pursues the same objective. In other words, search engine provide a new, on demand type of linearity. This is a major difference with the possibilities of a printed book. Third, there may exist local lines of references in a hypertext (e.g., series of coherent paragraphs on a page), and those will encourage linear reading episodes as in printed texts.

Thus, linearity is neither determined by the technological support nor by the arrangement of information and nor by the regular flow of time. It is rather a characteristic of the reading activity that rests on the objectives and the mental operations carried out by the reader. At this point, the question of linearity in reading meets a fundamental problem in pedagogy: Do the courses proposed to the user of a hypertext create meaning? Will the navigation tools of the hypertext facilitate a comprehension of the user and favour his tasks of reading and search for information?

11.5 Conclusions

The history of the book teaches us, on the one hand, that the paper-based text – handwritten or printed – is not essentially linear any more. Indeed, the term "text", which appeared in the 4th century, came from the Latin word "textus" meaning woven and fabric (Larousse, 1971). The text was construed, from a long time ago, not like a thread but rather like a weave. Indeed, since the revolution of the writing-reading which took place around 1200, the text was basically intended to offer several courses of reading. Nowadays, with hypertext, we are in a continuity of this development of the written text, rather than in an absolute rupture.

But then, where is the border between linear and non-linear documents located? The answer is certainly not so easy. Many texts are based on a linear structure, but they also feature tools which introduce non-linearity, such as the table of contents. By giving an overview of the contents and their hierarchical organization, the table of contents has the function of a summary. But, at the same time, the table of contents gives the reader a greater facility to reach a particular passage and to be extracted from the "principal" linearity of the text which he has created and recommends to follow.

Reading tools of texts and navigation tools of the hypertexts constitute a homogeneous set of meta-textual tools. They facilitate a type of reading-navigation, linear or not linear. They both belong to the writing and use of text and hypertext because they are exactly located at the intersection between writing and structuring of the document, intention and development of the course, comprehension of the contents and their supports. The history of the book clarifies this centrality and the necessity of standardized tools to make effective the reading-navigation.

References

Anis, J. (avec la collab. de Chiss, J.-L., & Puech, C.) (1988). *L'écriture : théories et descriptions*. Bruxelles : De Boeck, Collection Prisme Problématiques.

Bechtel, G. (1992). *Gutenberg*. Paris: Fayard.

Boorstin, D. (1986). *Les découvreurs*. Paris: Laffont.

Bréhier, E. (1971). *La philosophie du Moyen Age* . Paris: Albin Michel.

Cavallo, G., & Chartier, R. (1997). *Histoire de la lecture dans le monde occidental*. Paris: Seuil.

Chartier, R. (1996). *Culture écrite et société, l'ordre des livres (XIVème – XVIIème siècle)*. Paris: Albin Michel.

Chartier, R., & Martin, H. -J. (1989). L'objet livre. In R. Chartier & H.-J. Martin (Eds.), *Histoire de l'édition française: le livre conquérant, du moyen âge au milieu du XVIIème siècle* (pp. 567–568). Paris: Fayard.

Chatelain, J. -M. (1996). Du Parnasse à l'Amérique: l'imaginaire de l'encyclopédie à la Renaissance et à l'Age classique. In R. Schaer (Eds.), *Tous les savoirs du monde: encyclopédies et bibliothèques, de Sumer au XXIème siècle*. Paris: BNF et Flammarion.

Conklin, J. (1987). Hypertext: An introduction and survey. In *IEEE Computer* . september, 17–41.

De Boüard, M. (1991). Réflexions sur l'encyclopédisme médiéval. In A. Becq (Eds.), *L'encyclopédisme – Actes du colloque de Caen (12-16.01.1987)* (pp. 281–290). Paris: Aux Amateurs de Livres.

Denhière, G., & Baude, S. (1992). *Lecture, compréhension de texte et science cognitive*. Paris: PUF.

Derrida, J. (1967). *De la grammatologie* . Paris: Minuit.

De Saussure, F. (1972). *Cours de linguistique générale* . Payot.
Dillon, A. (1991). Reader's models of text structures: The case of academic articles. In *International Journal of Man-Machine Studie, 35* , 913–925.
Duby, G. (1976). *Le temps des cathédrales* . Paris: Gallimard.
Eco, U. (1990). *Le nom de la rose* . Paris: Grasset.
Eisenstein, E. (1989). Le livre et la culture savante. In R. Chartier & H. -J. Martin (Eds.), *Histoire de l'édition française: le livre conquérant, du moyen âge au milieu du XVIIème siècle* (pp. 671–697). Paris: Fayard.
Eisenstein, E. (1991). *La révolution de l'imprimé dans l'Europe des premiers temps modernes.* Paris: La Découverte.
Espéret, E. (1996). Notes on hypertext, cognition and language. In J. -F. Rouet, J. J. Levonen, A. Dillon, & R. J. Spiro (Eds.),*Hypertext and cognition* (pp. 149–155). New Jersey: Lawrence Erlbaum Associates Publishers.
Foltz, P. W. (1996). Comprehension, coherence and strategies in hypertext and linear text. In J. -F. Rouet, J. J. Levonen, A. Dillon, & R. J. Spiro (Eds.), *Hypertext and cognition* (pp. 109–136). New Jersey: Lawrence Erlbaum Associates Publishers.
Foucault, M. (1969). *Archéologie du savoir* . Paris: Gallimard.
Garin, E. (1968). *L'éducation de l'homme moderne (1400–1600)*. Paris: Fayard.
Gilmont, J. -F (1993).*Le livre, du manuscrit à l'ère électronique* . Liège: CEFAL.
Hamesse, J. (1997). Le modèle scolastique de la lecture. In G. Cavallo & R. Chartier (dir.). *Histoire de la lecture dans le monde occidental* (pp. 125–145). Paris: Seuil.
Hamman, A. -G. (1985). *L'épopée du livre, du scribe à l'imprimerie* . Paris: Perrin.
Heers, J. (1983). *Marco polo* . Paris: Editions Fayard.
Hindman, S. (Ed.) (1991). *Printing the written world: The social history of books circa 1450–1520.* Ithaca and London: Cornell University Press.
Johannot, Y. (1994). *Tourner la page: livre, rites et symboles.* Grenoble: J. Millon.
Krynen, J. (1996). Puissance et connaissance, royauté et aristocratie face aux savoirs du monde. In R. Schaer (Ed.), *Tous les savoirs du monde: encyclopédies et bibliothèques, de Sumer au XXIème siècle* (pp. 1107–1130). Paris: BNF et Flammarion.
Labarre, A. (1989). Les incunables: la présentation du livre. In R. Chartier & H. -J. Martin (Eds.),*Histoire de l'édition française: le livre conquérant, du moyen âge au milieu du XVIIème siècle* (pp. 228–255). Paris: Fayard.
Landow, G. P. (1992). *Hypertext: The convergence of contemporary critical theory and technology*. John Hopkins University Press.
Larousse (1971). *Dictionnaire étymologique* . Paris: Larousse.
Laufer, R. (1989). L'espace visuel du livre ancien. In R. Chartier & H. -J. Martin (Eds.), *Histoire de l'édition française: le livre conquérant, du moyen âge au milieu du XVIIème siècle* (pp. 579–601). Paris: Fayard.
Le Doeuff, M. (1991). Avant-propos. In F. Bacon (1605) *Du progrès et de la promotion des savoirs,* (texte original de 1605 traduit par M. Le Doeuff) (pp. VII–LXIV). Paris: Gallimard.
Le Ny, J. -F. (1995). L'analyse propositionnelle (prédicative). In Le Ny J. -F. & Gineste M. -D. (dir.). *La psychologie, textes fondamentaux* . Larousse.
Le Roy, H. (1995). Lettres, lignes, textes et hypertextes. Contre la linéarité de l'écriture. *Romaneske, 20*(1), 30–59.
Llinares, A. (1991). Esprit encyclopédique et volonté de système chez Raymond Lulle. In A. Becq (Eds.) *L'encyclopédisme – Actes du colloque de Caen (12-16.01.1987)* (pp. 449–458). Paris: Aux Amateurs de Livres.
Martin, H. -J. (1996). *Histoire et pouvoirs de l'écrit* . Paris: Albin Michel.
Mary, A. & Rouse, R. H. (1989). La naissance des index. In R. Chartier & H. -J. Martin (Eds.) *Histoire de l'édition française: le livre conquérant, du moyen âge au milieu du XVIIème siècle* (pp. 95–108). Paris: Fayard.

Mohageg, M. F. (1992). The influence of hypertext linking structures on the efficiency of information retrieval. *Human Factors, 34* (3), 351–367.
Nanard, M. (1995). Les hypertextes: au-delà des liens, la connaissance. *Sciences et Techniques Educatives, 2* (1), 31–59.
Nelson, T. H. (1967). Getting it out of our system. In G. Schechter (Eds.), *Information retrieval: A critical review* . Washington D. C: Thomson Books.
Nodier, C. (1985). *Moi-même* . (texte établi par D. Sangsue). Paris: José Corti.
Ong, W. J. (1958). *Ramus: method, and the decay of dialogue* . Cambridge MA: Harvard University Press.
Ong, W. J. (1982). *Orality and literacy: The technologizing of the word* . London: Methuen.
Orvas, G. (1998). Un nouveau type d'intellectuel. Les cahiers de Science et Vie, 43, Paris: Science et Vie.
Paulmier-Foucart, M. (1991). Ordre encyclopédique et organisation de la matière dans le Speculum maius de Vincent de Beauvais. In A. Becq (Eds.), *L'encyclopédisme – Actes du colloque de Caen (12-16.01.1987)* (pp. 201–226). Paris: Aux Amateurs de Livres.
Platteaux, H. (1999). *Quels outils de navigation pour les CD-ROMs de vulgarisation scientifique ?* Thèse de Doctorat, Université de Genève – FPSE, manuscrit non publié.
Platteaux, H., & Rickenmann, R. (1998). Dimension graphique et aspects cognitifs de la table des matières dans le livre imprimé et le livre électronique. *Sciences et Techniques Educatives, 5* (3), 221–243.
Roberts, C. H. (1954). The codex. *Proceedings of the British Academy, 40* , 169–204.
Rouet, J. -F. (2006). *The skills of document use: From text comprehension to Web-based learning*. Mahwah, NJ: Erlbaum.
Rouet, J. -F., & Levonen, J. J. (1996). Studying and learning with hypertext: empirical studies and their implications. In J. -F. Rouet, J. J. Levonen, A. Dillon, & R. J. Spiro (Eds.), *Hypertext and cognition* (pp. 9–23). New Jersey: Lawrence Erlbaum Associates Publishers.
Rouet, J. -F., & Tricot, A. (1995). Recherche d'informations dans les systèmes hypertextes: des représentations de la tâche à un modèle de l'activité cognitive. *Sciences et Techniques Educatives, 2* (3), 307–331.
Saenger, P. (1997). Lire aux derniers siècles du Moyen Age. In G. Cavallo & R. Chartier (dir.). *Histoire de la lecture dans le monde occidental* (pp. 147–174). Paris: Seuil.
Schmitt, C. (1987). Auctoritates, Repertorium, Dicta, Sententiae, Flores, Thesaurus and Axiomata: Latin Aristotelian Florilegia in the Renaissance. In J. Wiesner (Ed.), *Aristoteles, Werk und Wirkung* (pp. 515–537). Berlin.
Stillwell, M. (1972). *The beginning of the world of books: 1450–1470*. New York: The bibliographical society of America.
Vandendorpe, C. (1999). *Du papyrus à l'hypertexte, Essai sur les mutations du texte et de la lecture*. Paris: La Découverte.
Van Dijk, T. A. (1984). Macrostructures sémantiques et cadres de connaissances dans la compréhension du discours. In G. Denhière (Ed.), *Il était une fois....* (pp. 49–84). Presses Universitaires de Lille.
Van Dijk, T. A., & Kintsch, W. (1983). *Strategies of discourse comprehension* . San Diego CA: Academic Press.
Vezin, J. (1989). La fabrication du manuscrit. In R. Chartier & H. -J. Martin (Eds.), *Histoire de l'édition française: le livre conquérant, du moyen âge au milieu du XVIIème siècle* (pp. 21–51). Paris: Fayard.
Weinreich, H., Obendorf, H., & Lamersdorf, W. (2001). The look of the link – Concepts for the user interface of extended hyperlinks. In Proceedings of the twelfth *ACM Conference on Hypertext and Hypermedia ('Hypertext'01')–* - Aarhus, Denmark, August 2001.
Yates, F. A. (1975). *L'art de la mémoire* (trad. D. Arasse). Paris: Gallimard.
Zumthor, P. (1983). *Introduction à la poésie orale*. Paris: Seuil.

Chapter 12
From Film and Television to Multimedia Cognitive Effects

Lucia Lumbelli

Abstract Studies on the cognitive effects of film and TV medium-specific features are selectively reviewed. Particular attention is paid to the methodological problems involved in the comparisons between TV comprehension and reading comprehension. A solution is defined consisting of focusing the comparison on the level of those connective processes which are required for both kinds of comprehension inasmuch as they can be considered text comprehension, namely the bridging inferences to be drawn from prior knowledge and/or previous text information so as to preserve local text coherence. In this way, the same multiple-choice questions can be used to test both TV comprehension and reading comprehension. Two experimental investigations are reported which by using this methodology confirmed the hypothesis that less mental effort is invested by TV viewers, whose comprehension is hence lower than that of readers. A few suggestions are outlined for research into the comprehension of animation in multimedia inasmuch as it can be considered as a text.

Keywords Animation · Bridging inference · Mental effort · Reading comprehension · Situation model · TV comprehension

12.1 Introduction

Film and television can be considered as forms of multimedia inasmuch as they are forms of audio-visual communication. The visual component typically consists of dynamic images, while the verbal component typically consists of oral discourse. Furthermore, the primacy of the visual component and the overall difference from written communication are at the core of both popular, speculative characterisations and psychological theories, first about film and later about television. From both these perspectives, the effects upon the

L. Lumbelli
Universitá Degli Studi di Trieste, Dipartimento Di Psicologia, Via S. Anastasio 12, 34134 Trieste, Italy
e-mail: Lumbelli@univ.trieste.it

J.-F. Rouet et al. (eds.), *Understanding Multimedia Documents*,
DOI: 10.1007/978-0-387-73337-1_12,

viewer's mind specifically attributed to audio-visual communication are chiefly traced back to the visual component, and particularly to the dynamic images. Assumptions about these effects have been only partly subjected to empirical investigation, which has generally supported them by means of comparisons with written communication. Two experimental studies about the effects of audio-visual *versus* written communication will be presented here as contributions which also appear relevant to contemporary research about multimedia. Clearly, this possible relevance involves only those forms of multimedia in which the verbal component is oral and the visual component consists of moving images, whereas these contributions are obviously not relevant to those forms of multimedia which use static pictures and written text.

The presentation of these experimental studies will be the core of this chapter. It will be preceded by a selective review of the literature about theories of film communication and psychological research into the immediate mental effects of TV communication. In the third part of the chapter, the experimental results so far obtained about TV comprehension *versus* reading comprehension will be discussed in relationship to some questions of research on multimedia comprehension.

12.2 Medium Specificity and Television Comprehension

The selective review that follows covers just a small fraction of the copious literature on film analysis and on the various psycho-educational and psychosocial aspects of the rise of television in contemporary culture. The focus is on those definitions and analyses of the specific nature of film and television which emphasise the identifying feature of audio-visual communication, that is the characteristic of combining spoken discourse with moving images.

12.2.1 Early Studies of Film Viewers' Attitude

Early critics of the film experience characterised spectators as being imprisoned by the dynamism of moving images. They argued that films produce a more or less marked complacency which induces spectators to stop even trying to use their superior mental capacities. The suggestion is that 'thought remains powerless in a turmoil of shock-like emotions', because spectators are in the clutches of a kind of 'mental vertigo' and 'physiological tempests' (Cohen-Sèat, 1946, pp. 154–55).

However, this fundamental aspect was also stressed by theorists who are in favour of the new forms of consciousness introduced by cinema. Kracauer (1960) claimed that 'unlike the other types of pictures, film images affect primarily the spectator's senses, engaging him physiologically before he is in a position to respond intellectually' (p. 158). To explain this effect, Kracauer referred firstly to the strong and multiform presence of 'physical reality' which according to him distinguishes the film medium, and secondly to the fact that 'film renders the world in motion . . . movement is the alpha and omega of the medium'. Kracauer quoted the psychologist Wallon to illustrate the sort of fascination film exerts upon us: 'We cannot turn our eyes away from the film whose images supersede each other . . . because there is in the flow of the successive images a sort of attraction enjoining us, our attention, our senses, our vision, not to lose anything of that flow. The movement then is in itself something attractive and captivating' (p. 107).

These claims about the special fascination of film communication, and in particular the primacy of the moving images that characterise it, are rather fuzzy and difficult to translate into hypotheses which can be tested experimentally. But they do raise two interesting points: a shared introspective or phenomenological evidence and the tendency to posit, either explicitly or implicitly, a close connection between cognitive factors and emotional or motivational factors. This tendency is shared both by film theorists who are not psychologists, and by the first psychologists who reflected upon the specificity of this form of communication and its effects on the human mind (Balazs, 1952; Michotte, 1948).

From these theoretical claims was deducted an hypothesis which was experimentally checked (Lumbelli, 1974). If film viewers' mental control is weaker than the readers' one, then we can expect that film viewers are less likely to detect inconsistent verbal information than readers. In this experiment, the same inconsistency occurrence was inserted into two versions of the same text[1], i.e. into one version in which the verbal oral component was accompanied by dynamic images and into another in which only the verbal component was presented in a written form. In other words, a medium-specific effect was posited which consists of a lower ability to recognise an inconsistency, i.e. a lowering of the performance which is generally assumed as an indicator of metacognitive control of comprehension processes. More specifically, a piece of film (about ten minutes long) in which three characters were talking to each other in a very emotional exchange was re-dubbed so as to substitute one of the utterances of a girl who was expressing her intense feeling of love for her boyfriend with an utterance clearly inconsistent with all the others ('I want to give him a slap across the face right away!'). Two groups of highly educated participants were asked whether they noticed something wrong after having read the written and having viewed the piece of film, respectively. A significant difference in detection number was found in the two conditions ($\chi 2 = 20.778$; $p < 0.001$). The above mentioned claims about the medium-specificity of film processing can therefore be considered as confirmed, at least inasmuch as those claims are operationalised in terms of readiness to detect gaps in text coherence. A medium-specific effect was confirmed which consists of a tendency to decode only what is presented on the screen without further processing. This effect was also found with film of a documentary type (Lumbelli, 1974). In all types of film, the attractiveness of the moving images seems to give rise to a tendency to restore text coherence in a weakly controlled way.

12.2.2 Theories and Empirical Evidence About TV Viewers

Unlike the earlier analyses of film audience, reflections and studies about television viewing obviously had at their disposal more sophisticated understandings of the cognitive processes involved. I shall now examine the two main and contrasting theories of television comprehension: the *reactive theory* and *active theory*. Attempts to define the effects of television on the mind by taking into account both theories will also be discussed.

According to Anderson and Lorch (1983), the reactive theory 'has been popularly adopted, despite a paucity of evidence and a failure to consider alternatives' (p. 5). According to Singer (1980) the 'powerful appeal' of television can be explained as follows: 'the constant movement and pattern of change that characterise the screen produce a continuous series of orienting reflexes, and it is hard to habituate to the set' (p. 46). He tries to explain and support popular conceptions of television such as the advertiser Jerry Mander's (1978) assumptions about television's control over our attention: 'We become affixed to the changing images...we merely give ourselves over to them'. The consequence is that cognition is passive: 'no cognition, no discernment, no notations upon the experience one is having...the viewer is little more than a vessel of reception' (p. 204). The claims are apparently very similar to those quoted above about cinema, although no awareness of this similarity seem to emerge in the past and present (Sartori, 1997) literature.

Active theory. In contrast with the idea of spectator passivity, active theory is based on two lines of research: firstly, on the results of experiments on the relationship between comprehension and attention in children, and secondly on studies into the processes of comprehension of connected discourse or text, and in particular, into the fundamental notion that these processes are schema-driven. This idea is extended from the written text to the audio-visual one, since the processes in question pertain to *any form of elaboration of coherently organised information.*

This is the starting point for a re-evaluation of the active component of any kind of comprehension, regardless of the medium in which the information is presented. The resulting hypothesis is that of a spectator who is mentally active right from childhood, who decides if and when to pay attention to what happens on the screen. This hypothesis is tested using ingenious experimental procedures which demonstrate that attention (seen as visual orientation instead of visual fixation) depends on the comprehension or comprehensibility of what is happening on the screen (Lorch, Anderson, & Levin, 1979; Anderson, Lorch, Field, & Sanders, 1981). The conclusion is that since the spectator's attention is determined by comprehension, it is neither captured by the screen nor overpowered by 'electronic gimmicks' but is freely monitored by the spectator himself. These findings are chiefly used to make predictions about the effectiveness of the educational applications of the new medium.

The concept of *Amount of Mental Effort Invested* (AIME) upon which the definition of medium-specificity proposed by Salomon is based, encompasses the ideas of mindlessness (Langer, 1985) and 'the more veteran concept of shallow *versus* deep processing (Salomon, 1983, p. 186) into a theory which seems to insert into the active theory some aspects of the reactive theory. The basic assumption is that the amount of mental effort 'can be expected to increase when a unit of material cannot be easily fitted into existing schemata', whereas it is expected to decrease when 'the individual feels, rightly or wrongly, that there is little in the encountered material that warrants the investment of his or her mental efforts' (p. 187).

The experience of watching television engenders the general impression of something which is very easy to assimilate. In turn, this impression causes a decrease in the amount of mental effort invested in television processing. This argument has been used to explain the empirical finding that the comprehension of television texts is significantly lower than the comprehension of written texts (Salomon, 1981, 1984). However, some more experimental findings showed that both television comprehension and its relationship with the reading comprehension varied according to the cultural and educational background of the individual (Salomon, 1983) and according to the experimenter's instructions (Cohen & Salomon, 1983).

The theory of reduced mental effort seems to be the soundest definition of those effects of moving images which have been referred to using more colorful and fuzzy terms like *fascination* and *attractiveness*. The special form of attention triggered by moving images *per se* might affect the higher monitoring processes; the consequence might be a less accurate and exhaustive processing of all information items (both the visual items and the concurrent verbal ones), and therefore a less correct text comprehension. These higher processes can be considered common to both reading and TV comprehension, while the lower levels are different. In fact, Pezdek (1987) introduces his summary of empirical studies on television comprehension with the assumption that 'there are many similarities between comprehension of text and television' since 'both involve constructive processes such as integration and drawing of inferences' (Pezdek, 1987, p. 12). The medium-specificity of audio-visual communication might therefore be checked by examining that common level of processing which might be negatively affected by dynamic images.

12.2.3 Towards a Functional Definition of Mental Effort

The perspective argued for above is only partially adopted by Salomon. The operationalisation of the concept of AIME proposed by Salomon (1981, 1984, 1979–1994) and by Meringoff (1980) is based on the distinction between shallow and deep elaboration. According to Salomon and Meringoff, the amount of mental effort invested corresponds to the amount of inferences drawn in text processing. It is argued that readers comprehend better than TV viewers because they tend to draw more numerous inferences and so elaborate the text more deeply. In contrast, television viewers tend to make a more superficial elaboration, merely decoding the given verbal or visual information. Television viewers' comprehension is worse because they rely more exclusively on visually presented material, whereas readers tend to integrate verbal material by drawing inferences from their prior knowledge. On this analysis, the amount of mental effort invested is operationalised as the *amount of inferential activity in processing*.

The operationalisation suggested by Salomon is founded on the distinction between inferential and factual questions. Strictly speaking, only factual questions refer to the information to be gained directly from the text. They evoke explicitly expressed meanings which may have been stored in the memory either verbatim or in the form of paraphrases (see also Cerdán et al., Chapter 7). When factual questions are posed, there are no noticeable differences between comprehension of television texts and comprehension of written texts. By contrast, when answering inferential questions television viewers reveal a shallower comprehension than readers.

But are these inferential processes relevant to the *comprehension* of a given text? Are we not perhaps dealing with those inferences that must of necessity be drawn from within the text in order to integrate its components into a coherent meaning? Are these inferences indispensable in order to have a coherent and exhaustive comprehension of a text? The answer is uncertain because, in general, inferential questions seem to be aimed at assessing the *amount of inferential activity* overall and are chiefly targeted to information which *can* but *does not have to* be inferred from written and audio-visual text in order to understand it correctly. The distinction between *necessary bridging* inferences and merely *plausible* but not text-required inferences (Clark, 1977; Bransford, 1979; van Dijk & Kintsch, 1983; Mc Koon & Ratcliff, 1992; Trabasso & Suh, 1993; Kintsch, 1998) is rarely made in this research field. As a consequence, the measurement of medium-specific cognitive effects is made problematic.

In our opinion, the questions posed above should be answered through a more precise definition of those cognitive processes which appear to be affected by the decrease in mental effort provoked by television. We must clearly identify which aspects of text comprehension the comparison between audio-visual and written version should be based on. The *number* of inferences produced in the course of viewing or reading seems to be too fuzzy an operationalisation.

Kintsch (1998) states that 'long natural texts provide the subject with too many opportunities for misunderstandings, slips of attention, and a sheer unwillingness to co-operate, which makes illusory the predictions derived from the model of an ideal reader' (p. 205). In reality, many of his experimental and theoretical analyses seem to be a useful basis for predictions about possible misunderstandings and, consequently, for extension of experimental research to long natural texts. These predictions can be derived from both the bottom-up processes and some specific features of situation models. Kintsch (1998) deals with processes that may be subject to that kinds of failure which might become more likely in the audio-visual *versus* reading condition.

Misunderstanding may be caused by the fact that a mental representation is not held in working memory until 'its function of bridging previous and subsequent information item is satisfied'. As a consequence, integration processes are inadequate because they inevitably fail to link the items of explicit text information. The coherence finally attained is not the one required by the text (Kintsch, 1998, pp. 101–102).

Another significant source of miscomprehension is the use of situation models. According to Kintsch, the situation model is 'a construction that integrates the text-base and relevant aspects of the comprehender's knowledge; it depends not only on the text itself but also 'on the readers, their goals, motivation, and resources available' (Kintsch, 1998, p. 107). The knowledge used in the construction of situation models is also the reader's 'personal experience' (p. 103) and this type of knowledge, in particular, increases the risk of a *reader*-based integration instead of a *text*-based one. This risk is obviously greater when the inferences involved are not 'bridging inferences required for the maintenance of local coherence' but 'inferences that are necessary for global coherence' (p. 193). van Dijk and Kintsch (1983, p. 51) called the latter *elaborative inferences* and defined them as those inferences in which 'the reader uses his or her knowledge about the topic under discussion to fill in additional detail not mentioned in the text, or to establish connections between what is being read and related items of knowledge'.

The close connection between this kind of mental activity and the likelihood of distorted comprehension is made clearer in the following: *elaborative* inferences may be used 'to cover up an inability to recall details of the original text' and 'thus elaborations can also distort a text...if there is a misfit between the schema and the text, it is possible that the text will be adjusted to make it conform better to the schema' (van Dijk & Kintsch, 1983, p. 52). According to these authors, a situation model 'is different from a frame or script in that it is much more personal, based on one's own experiences, and therefore it will feature all kinds of details which, in learning, will be abstracted from' (p. 344) and will form 'a much-needed link between modalities' since it 'may be modified either through direct perception and action or through a discourse' (p. 341). *Cross-modality integration* is therefore a clue to the presence of a situation model in comprehension.

Kintsch (1998) claims that images intervene in verbal text processing too and that the interaction between propositional representation and images occurs also when only verbal information is processed. This interaction is considered as a provisional source of distorted outcome of processing. He optimistically assumes that if the text information read subsequently contradicts the inferences immediately drawn from the image of previous information, 'the network representation corrects errors easily' (p. 111). However, another equally plausible hypothesis is that the intervention of images in the processing of text introduces a source of possible comprehension error.

From this viewpoint, Kintsch (1998) seems to be close to Sadoski and Paivio's (2001) application of Dual Code Theory to text comprehension. According to them, 'mental models can take the form of mental language, mental images, or a combination of mental language and mental images together' (p. 79). By means of the universally assumed role of mental models in text comprehension, mental images become an important component of verbal text processing itself and the interaction between verbal and non-verbal elements becomes a matter of any kind of communication: 'the mental connections between language and the non-verbal experience serve to provide concrete referents for the language' (p. 70). In fact, the 'additional meaning' provided by referential imagery can be just as well obtained 'through images evoked by direct description, or inferentially. Mental imagery is central to *making sense* of text where that phrase is taken literally' (p. 74).

The assumption that Sadoski and Paivio Paivio (2001) seem to share with Kintsch (1998) is that the interaction between meanings drawn through a visual modality and meanings drawn from verbal text is essentially the same as the general interaction between imagery and meaning verbally expressed in the comprehender' s mind.[2] Regardless of the stance about the role of images in the representation of meanings verbally expressed, these authors share the assumption that situation models and their cross-modal nature affect comprehension processes.

This assumption helps us to identify another significant source of distortions in text processing and consequently hypothesise another possible effect of the decrease in mental effort triggered by dynamic images: the weakening of higher level mental activities might also entail a weakening of strategic control over the intrusion of personal knowledge and provisional images. It might render that intrusion a definite source of distorted internal representation of the text as a whole.

Lastly, there is another source of possible distortion in comprehension due to the weakening of higher level mental activities. It concerns the processes which organise information into microstructures (van Dijk & Kintsch, 1983; Kintsch, 1998) or substructures (Gernsbacher, 1985, 1988; Gernsbacher, Varner, & Faust, 1990). The theory of General Comprehension Skill by Gernsbacher (1985, 1989; Gernsbacher, Varner, & Faust, 1990) seems to be the most adequate to explain how the main points of a narrative structure common to both film and written text may be correctly or incorrectly selected. This theory refers to the comprehension processes common to both the linguistic and the visual information organised into a text. In the course of comprehension, substructures are built which are drawn from a sequence of sentences in which a comprehender recognises referential continuity and coherence. As soon as the reader encounters a sentence to which a new meaning is to be attributed, a *shift* occurs and the completed substructure is stored in the memory. The original superficial information (be it linguistic or iconic) from which the representation has been drawn becomes difficult to retrieve. After this shift, the construction of a new substructure begins. The adequacy and accuracy of the representation of the general meaning of a text depends on how well it reflects the hierarchical organisation of information in the text itself. Poor comprehension occurs when the reader shifts too hastily from one substructure to the next, because the excessive number of substructures is likely to negatively affect the identification of the right microstructures and macrostructures, i.e. the final selection of main points. This aspect of poor comprehension might be considered as another possible indicator of the effects of dynamic images on the viewers' state of mind, and consequently, of the lowering of mental effort invested as well.

12.2.4 A Comparability Problem

These specifications also serve to deal with another fundamental question which regards the conditions to be compared: how is it possible to guarantee that the comparison involves medium specificity alone (or primarily)? How can we be certain that all the other conditions are truly kept constant in order to exclude the influence of differences in content or structure of the information presented through the two different media?

This problem parallels the concerns raised by Clark and Salomon (1986) about comparisons between different communication media aimed at ascertaining their relative educational effectiveness. The often conflicting nature of experimental results may be explained by insufficient control over those aspects of educational strategy which are not necessarily connected to the medium. Similarly, when evaluating differences in comprehension attributable to medium-specific characteristics, it is difficult to keep control over possible differences in the cognitive processes required by the text presented through the different media being compared.

Inasmuch as the dependent variable is identified into the inferential activity needed for coherent representation of the information organised in the text, it is essential that the two versions being compared contain similar requirements for inferential integration by both readers and viewers.

Unlike the more recent studies on multimedia, in which the texts being compared are constructed intentionally, the bulk of research into film and television has dealt with pre-existing material. The complexity and variety of 'natural' text makes it extremely difficult to ensure that any possible comprehension difference found depends only (or mostly) on the nature of the media compared.

For example, in some studies with pre-scholars, Meringoff (1980) and Meringoff et al. (1983) compared the comprehension of an animated film for TV with the comprehension of a picture book about the same story. All they do is inform us that the two versions were comparable because the film version had been made as faithful as possible to the original book version. No further description of the material is provided.

In the study by Pezdek, Lehrer,Lehrer and Simon (1984) with children aged 9 and 12, the comparison consisted once again of a text version with pictures and a television version. Comparability was addressed by the experimenters editing both the narrative and the expository segments of text in order to guarantee two matched versions of each segment. The matching of experimental material is described in even more detail by Pezdek, Simon, Stoekert, and Kiely (1987) while presenting another comparison with adult subjects. The authors selected 12 segments of news presented on network television, which satisfied the following criteria: (1) four comprehension questions could be generated from each, (2) answers to those questions could not be easily inferred from general knowledge, (3) the visual portion of the segment included relevant filmed material that was 'a dynamic part of the information presented' and was relevant to the auditory presented material, 'providing a good fit', (4) the verbal text information was still comprehensible when presented alone in the text condition, in which the segments were presented as typed transcripts of articles from magazines. Pacing of the reading was adopted to assure the same exposure duration as in the television condition. In order to formulate the same open comprehension questions in both conditions, all questions were generated from information presented on the audio-track of each segment. The authors claim that 'each question probed information central to the theme of the segment'. The acceptable answers were specified in advance in order to make the scoring quite clear-cut.

It is worth mentioning that, despite the care taken both in the selection of the material (independent variable) and of the questions (dependent variable), these last two studies produced conflicting results. While in the first study, no correlation was found between the comprehension of the text with pictures and that of the televised version, in the second study this correlation was clearly significant (Pearson $r = 0.69$; $p < 0.001$) and the hypothesis of medium-specific effects was not confirmed. The important thing to point out here is that, even though the material was carefully selected and prepared, there is no guarantee that in the two cases the inferential processing required from the texts was similar; more precisely, there is not guarantee that in the alternative version to the audio-visual text adopted in the two studies, there were no important differences in the requirements of integration of the information expressed. These possible differences would also imply a risk that the lower comprehension scores obtained in the audio-visual condition might be traced back to the fact that the experimenter had unintentionally required easier, less demanding integration and connection processes from readers than from viewers.

To sum up, finding new ways of guaranteeing this comparability of the conditions compared entails guaranteeing more precise and definite confirmation or disconfirmation of the hypothesised medium-specific effect on text comprehension of the audio-visual *versus* reading (with or without pictures) condition.

12.3 Comparisons Focused on Similar Cognitive Text Requirements

In this section, two studies undertaken by the author and her colleagues will be discussed with the aim of introducing into the comparison between audio-visual and written communication some new methodological details in order to solve the problems raised above. These studies are based on the assumption that, in order to guarantee the comparability of written and audio-visual versions of the same text, it is necessary to adopt a measure of comprehension that refers to a well-defined cognitive performance. Such a performance must be capable of being described with sufficient precision so as to establish that it is kept unchanged across the different conditions. The following points have to be taken into account:

- The bottom-up decoding processes are by definition different in the two forms of communication since in one condition visual and (oral) verbal information have to be connected, while in the other one, all information is (written) verbal only;
- At this level, the internal representations are necessarily built through different types of processing depending on the medium involved, and thus, none of the decoding processes can be kept unvaried in the conditions compared;
- Comparable activity can be identified only at the higher levels of processing, in which the separate items of decoded information are connected up and integrated into a coherent representation; i.e. these processes consist either of recognising connections between explicit text information items or of drawing the inferences needed for text coherence (see also Rinck, Chapter 10).
- The comparison between viewing and reading condition has to therefore focus on those text sections which ask viewers and readers for a relatively complex performance at those higher levels, i.e. those text sections whose correct comprehension requires well-defined integration processes in *both* conditions; a preliminary text analysis is necessary to identify these sections and the points which the identical comprehension questions have to refer to.

12.3.1 Experiment 1: Restoring Coherence in Television Viewing and in Reading

In the first experiment (Lumbelli, 1999; Lumbelli & Zidari, 2001), the comparison between TV and reading comprehension was focused upon two TV news-reports, and precisely upon those sections whose correct comprehension appeared to require connection and integration processes which seemed to represent a sufficiently complex performance, i.e. a performance which could be made correctly only by investing a certain amount of mental effort into the higher level comprehension activities.

12.3.1.1 Hypotheses

It was predicted that in the audio-visual condition the connection and integration problems would be correctly solved less frequently than in the reading condition. This difference would be due to a diminution in the *quality* (instead of in the *amount*) of inferential activity. More precisely, in the audio-visual condition, the processes used to connect up and integrate the information items would be more likely to be incorrect. Previous qualitative observation of viewers' verbal protocols (Lumbelli & Cornoldi, 1994) about the same two news-reports used as experimental material had shown that even viewers with low comprehension ability exhibited a certain amount of inferential activity, although the inferences actually drawn were not the ones the text clearly needed, and could therefore be a clue to those comprehension distortions mentioned above. We used the evidence provided by think-aloud protocols in the manner suggested by Magliano and Graesser (1991), with the definition of their three-pronged method. According to this method it is possible to construct hypotheses not only through deduction from theories but also through induction from real-time observations about the processing of individual comprehenders. The experimental testing of hypotheses deduced from theories should be preceded by systematic observation of comprehenders' think-aloud protocols, which are a rigorous and reliable alternative to the classic introspective and/or retrospective reports (Ericsson & Simon, 1984; Olson, Duffy, & Mack, 1984; Pressley & Afflerbach, 1995).

The second hypothesis was that the negative effect of the dynamics images of a TV program on the quality of the viewers' integration processes would also be found in the condition in which the same program is presented on a computer; i.e. in a context which is different from the TV viewing condition as to other aspects. Two more conditions were therefore inserted into the design: audio-visual and written text presented on a computer.

12.3.1.2 Method

- Participants

465 high school students, aged either 14(225) or 18(240), participated to the experiment. Both the 4 main groups and the 8 subgroups were matched on a standardised reading comprehension test (Advanced MT Reading Comprehension test, 1991).

- Material and procedure

Two television texts were chosen containing critical passages which required fairly complex inferential integration in order to be understood. Their common characteristic was that in both the viewers had to notice a discontinuity or gap between successive information items. These items might be both expressed verbally or through a combination of linguistic and visual symbols. The comprehension problems varied with the specific critical passages, but a careful analysis of the text made it possible to identify:

- The critical text passages containing coherence problems which required some inferential integration, i.e. presented some coherence problem which could be solved by inferences from both prior knowledge and other textual information..
- The particular elements which those problems consist of, which had to be kept unchanged in the written text. In fact, the influence of the moving images on the quality of higher processing could only be ascertained by comparing participants' similarly difficult performances. In other terms, the two text versions had to be comparable in terms of the connection-integration processes on which the comparison was based.

In the written version, the audio information on the two television news-reports was kept completely unchanged, while the visual information was *translated* into sentences with a meaning which had to be connected and integrated through a kind of processing which was the same as in the audio-visual version. Depictions were translated into descriptions while the connection-integration problems to be solved for a correctly coherent text representation were carefully kept unchanged.

In the following paragraphs, we will refer in a more detailed way to: (a) the kind of critical passages which the comparison was focused upon, (b) the procedure adopted for constructing the written version, (c) the questions used to check whether the various sets of processes required by the text were performed or not.

The critical passages. Here is a short description of one critical passage. It belongs to a news-report about the high-speed TGV train in France. In presenting the item about the TGV, an off-screen speaker comments, ironically, that the interior was designed to encourage passengers to socialise. However, at the same time the images mostly show people reading, sleeping or eating on their own rather than socialising and only a few very short sequences show people chatting. The passage ends with the speaker's statement that 'the facts contradicted the intentions'. This statement is completely redundant for anyone who had noticed the contradiction between audio and video information and had therefore characterised the video data in such a way as to build internal representations of *people not communicating*. But the final audio information would be important for anyone who had previously paid too much attention to the very short (two seconds) sequences showing people chatting and thus failed to detect the inconsistency between the video data and the speaker's comments.

The construction of the written version. In writing the description which had to provide information essentially equivalent to that supplied by the original depiction, we were careful to avoid facilitating the construction of the representation described above (we carefully avoided inserting a sentence such as ‘Almost nobody is chatting in the train’) and alternated the pieces of faithfully transcribed verbal text with the description of passenger behaviour shown in the film.

The comprehension questions. In the questions about this text passage which were presented to both readers and to television viewers, only minor lexical adjustments in the stem of the questions were necessary for the different conditions. The total number of comprehension multiple-choice questions was 9 and therefore the score range was 0–9. The questions were asked immediately after each critical passage was either read or watched in order to make the response as concurrent as possible with local processing (Ericsson & Simon, 1984). In the two conditions in which the television news-reports and their written *translation* were presented on the computer, the procedure remained unchanged.

12.3.1.3 Results

Table 12.1 shows mean comprehension scores as a function of medium and presentation condition.

In both audio-visual conditions, viewers’ comprehension scores were significantly lower than readers’ comprehension scores in both reading conditions. This difference was found both in the comparison between reading *versus* television ($F(1, 271) = 28.378$; $p < 0.001$) and in the comparison between written *versus* audio-visual texts on the computer ($F(1, 194) = 12.844$; $p = 0.0004$). Since the comprehension questions were targeted at higher level processing, this difference may be traced back to the reduced mental effort invested in monitoring the connection and integration activities required by text.

Moreover, one particular finding should be underlined. In the comparison between the audio-visual and verbal condition on the computer, interaction between age and medium condition was significant ($F(1, 194) = 6.078$; $p = 0.0146$) whereas no significant interaction between age and condition was found in the comparison between audio-visual and reading condition without computer. This influence of age in the computer conditions was confirmed by

Table 12.1 Mean comprehension scores standard deviation of readers and viewers (with and without computer)

	Without computer		With computer	
	Reading	Video	Reading	Video
14-year-olds	4.6 (1.9)	3.4 (1.7)	3.7 (1.6)	3.4 (1.9)
18-year-olds	6.0 (1.7)	5.0 (1.9)	7.2 (1.5)	6.0 (2.0)
Overall	5.4 (1.9)	4.2 (1.9)	5.5 (2.3)	4.6 (2.2)

the results obtained when comparing the two reading conditions (*with* as opposed *without* computer) and the two video- conditions (*with* as opposed to *without* computer) While the overall data were confirmed for the subjects aged 14, the findings for the older subjects were different. There was a significant difference in favour of the computer condition *versus* the condition without computer, both in the case of written texts ($F(1,232) = 18.130, p < 0.0001$) and in the case of audio-visual texts ($F(1, 233) = 4.661; p = 0.0329$).

In conclusion, the depressive effect of moving images was shown to be present also in the computer-based presentation of audio-visual and written text. The difference between reading and viewing was significant at both ages. However, as far as the older participants are concerned, the difference between viewing on the computer and viewing on television shows that in the computer condition, factors may be at work which reduce that depressive effect. For instance, older participants might be more familiar with the computer and/or interested in its use. Obviously, the findings so far do not allow us to make any decision on this issue.

12.3.2 Experiment 2: Comparison Between a Literary and a Film Creative Text Comprehension

The second study was also aimed at checking the hypothesis that the presence of dynamic images triggers a special state of mind (decrease of mental effort invested) which can be observed through a lowering of the inferential activity in comprehension of the text as a whole, as to both visual and verbal information. This medium-specificity is once again ascertained by comparing an audio-visual text with a written text whose comparability is assured by keeping the higher level activity required unchanged. Whereas in the previous experiment, this condition was assured by 'translating' two TV programs into written accounts and therefore only the audio-visual condition was centered on a 'natural text', in this study (Lumbelli & Bechini, 2002) the original author's versions were used as materials for the two experimental conditions. The comprehension processes adopted as indicators of mental effort were once again above the decoding level, although they were selected using a partly different procedure. This study was carried out thanks to the Italian Ministry of University and Research fund n. MM11194814.

12.3.2.1 Hypotheses

The first main hypothesis was that the film condition would trigger a lower mental effort than the reading condition and that this lowering would be proved by significantly lower comprehension scores in the former condition than in the latter. The comprehension level would be measured by the same questions in both conditions.

A second hypothesis was connected to the time allowed for elaboration. In the previous study, the time available for reading the successive passages was uniformly predetermined and monitored by the experimenter (or by the program on the computer). There, we wanted to avoid the risk of differences in comprehension being attributable to the extra time available to the reader as compared to the viewer. The new hypothesis was that viewers' comprehension would be worse than that of readers, not only in the condition of externally-paced reading already tested, but also in the condition of self-paced reading. This hypothesis was deduced from the first one, that the medium-specific combination of moving images and oral language was a determinant factor in lowering comprehension rather than in reading condition.

12.3.2.2 Method

- Participants

All 146 participants were high-school students aged about 18. Sixty one participants watched the film, while 63 read the written text at a pace monitored by the experimenter, and 22 were allowed to choose their reading pace freely (the reduced number of the latter group was due to school schedule constraints). The three groups were matched on the same standardised reading comprehension test used in the previous investigation.

- Procedure and materials

The texts compared were the story 'Two Ladies of Berlevaag' by the writer Karen Blixen and the film 'Babette's Feast' made by the film director Gabriel Axel. The film text is so remarkably faithful to the original story (its audio-track repeats most parts of the written text verbatim) that it was possible to use the same procedural conditions as in the previous study. In fact, most of the video-track of the film can be considered as a depiction of the descriptions contained in the original story. It was enough to remove from the story the few text passages which had not been *translated* in the film.

The multiple-choice questions used to assess comprehension were once again the same for both versions and referred to text segments which had the following characteristics in common. As in the previous experiment, those segments required processes of connecting information and making inferential integration which text analysis had shown to be similar in both versions. A further criterion was added which concerned the nature of literary text, in which ambiguity is often intentional and is considered as an indicator of stylistic richness. Only those segments were chosen which conveyed clear information, whose decoding was not open to various interpretations. Lastly, the segments selected conveyed meanings which could be considered as main points. This criterion was made necessary by the fact that both texts (film and literary story) were much longer than the ones in the previous study. The selection processes were therefore more crucial here than in the previous case with short texts.

The procedure was the same as in the previous investigation. Both texts were divided into 4 sections which were obviously much longer than in the previous investigation. Immediately after having either read or watched each section, participants were presented with the same multiple-choice questions; the total number of questions was 10; the number of correct answers to these questions supplied the comprehension scores. Each experimental session, in which students (those in the self-paced condition too) participated in groups of around 12, was about 2 hours long.

12.3.2.3 Results and Discussion

Table 12.2 shows the mean scores obtained in the three conditions.

ANOVA analysis showed a significant difference between conditions ($F(2, 146) = 20.868$; $p < 0.0001$). Further analysis with Fischer's PLSD test showed that the only significant difference was between the film scores, on the one hand, and both reading conditions, on the other. The critical difference with the audio-visual group scores was 0.432 ($p<0.0001$) for the externally-paced reading group and 0.598 ($p = 0.0001$) for the self-paced reading group. No significant difference was found between the two reading conditions.

Both hypotheses were therefore supported. Overall, film comprehension was significantly lower than reading comprehension; the externally-paced versus self-paced condition did not affect reading comprehension scores. The difference in comprehension can therefore be attributed precisely to the influence of medium-specific characteristics on the quality of mental activity. In fact, it was found with different types of text, not only informative but also narrative.

On the basis of these studies, the explanations reported and discussed in the introduction seem to be supported. The higher level, strategic, processes of text comprehension seem to be negatively influenced by the specificity of the medium; i.e. by the dynamic images. A crucially important category of inferences is involved in the comprehension of a whole text – as opposed to single units of verbal or iconic meaning. This kind of comprehension is characterised, on the one hand, by its complexity and, on the other, by the absence of any voluntary, conscious control on the part of the subject. This very combination of complexity and unconsciousness may explain the hypothesised effect of moving images on the top-down processes by which the outcome of decoding is organised into a unified, coherent representation.

Table 12.2 Mean comprehension scores and standard deviation in film, monitored reading and self-paced reading conditions (Range: 0–10)

	Film	Monitored reading	Self-paced reading
Mean (SD)	7.2 (1.3)	8.5 (1.0)	8.4 (1.4)

12.4 Text Comprehension and Multimedia Comprehension

We shall begin by indicating some of the main aspects which distinguish multimedia investigations from studies on the medium specificity of TV and film.

One aspect is that in multimedia research, there is a clear prevalence of rigorous experimental design meeting the methodological requirements defined by Clark (1983), Clark and Salomon Salomon(1986) and Clark and Sugrue (1990): 'When examining the effects of different media, only the media being compared can be different. All other aspects of the mediated treatments, including the subject matter content and method of instruction, must be identical in two or more media being compared' (Clark & Sugrue, 1990, p. 509). The variables tend to be carefully defined and controlled by means of experimental manipulation.

In fact, the theories upon which investigations on multimedia comprehension are based either share Paivio's assumption of a different format for verbal and nonverbal internal representation (Mayer, 2001), or combine the propositional approach with the acknowledgement of an analogical component to internal representation (Schnotz, 2001). In any case, the basic problem of the quality of interaction between two kinds of external representation is posed as a question of interaction between two different formats of mental representation. Both Schnotz's definition of this critical multimedia question and the main points of his argumentation seem to imply the premises for dealing with the problems which have been posed here.

Schnotz's discussion also renders explicit the focus upon effective learning, and indeed, the crucial point is whether the activities which are supposed to be facilitated by multimedia 'support the cognitive processing required for effective learning' (Schnotz, 2001, p. 27). The key issue here is whether these activities actually do support the many instructional decisions that are required in self-directed acquisition of knowledge in an interactive learning environment. Factors which may prevent these decisions from being supportive include: a lack of a sufficiently specific goal of knowledge acquisition, by which information is to be searched for as a next step; a lack of knowledge about where the required information is to be found and how to locate it, and an inability to evaluate the information found 'according to its goal relevance, before a deeper semantic processing can take place' (ibidem). Cognitive load in working memory seems to depend solely or chiefly on these conditions; as a consequence, only the overload thereby brought about serves to explain the fact that learners pay insufficient 'attention to the characteristics of the respective sign system and the corresponding processing requirements' (ibid.).

Without calling these statements into question, we posit that insofar as multimedia can be considered as information coherently connected within a text, possible further causes of cognitive overload can be identified, which may not be connected to a shortage in the conditions required for effective learning processes.

A detailed analysis of multimedia texts in terms of the processes required for maintaining or correctly restoring local coherence should allow us to keep the text requirements under control and to make hypotheses about the conditions which improve educational effectiveness and those which can serve to predict difficulties and failures.

As for those studies aimed at comparing a particular kind of animation with other multimedia formats, one more indication can be derived from research into film/television comprehension *versus* comprehension of written text. If the effect of moving images is to reduce the mental effort invested in the activities of comprehension monitoring, those research findings which disconfirm the hypothesis of a greater educational effectiveness of animation can be traced back to the above posited effect of dynamic pictures on the comprehender's mind, that is to the fact that this effect has prevailed over the other factors. The effect of lowering the mental effort invested in text processing (measured in terms of the accuracy of comprehension strategic processes) can be studied in the first place independently of the other possible advantages and drawbacks of animation, and secondly, in interaction with them.

These assumptions can be further argued and illustrated by referring to a few chapters of the present book. Most references are aimed at showing the convenience of introducing a measure of comprehension as a dependent variable which be related to the processing level focused upon by the two experiments here reported.

The common feature of the mean measures adopted by Le Bohec and Jamet (Chapter 5), and Hidrio and Jamet (Chapter 6) is that they all refer to the extremes of a continuum of performance regarding, on the one hand, scores on the decoding and retention of single information items (*retention* questions and questions about *factual content*), and on the other hand, scores on *transfer questions* or *problem-solving tasks*. These measures tap either the lowest level of comprehension processes or something which can also be considered as being based on the outcome of higher level processes which are not, however, directly assessed. Those higher level processes consisting of connecting single information items to each other and integrating them into a coherent text representation are not taken into account in order to verify hypotheses about the educational effectiveness of certain formats *versus* other ones.

Moreover, from our standpoint about audio-visual communication, the ascertained feeling of 'attractiveness' experienced by the participants does not imply that animation improves the quality of students' mental activity. On the contrary, that feeling may actually be due to a decrease in the mental effort invested in the activities of connection, selection and integration. This specific effect, if any, cannot be verified by participants' answers either to factual questions or to the problem statements. Indeed, the feeling of something being more 'tiring' might be traced back to the fact that a great involvement in carrying out the higher level processes of text comprehension might interfere with the effect of lowering mental effort. This variable of students' involvement in a learning task might be controlled for, e.g. by gathering think-aloud protocols produced by participants in the course of text exploration/comprehension. It would thus be possible to make predictions regarding both the effect of dynamic pictures (decrease in mental effort) and the effect of a great involvement in a task (increase in mental effort associated with the feeling of tiredness).

12.5 Conclusion and Research Perspectives

In this chapter, some classic speculations, phenomenological reflections and empirical evidence about the medium-specificity of film and TV communication were selectively reviewed. From this review, a main hypothesis was derived regarding any kind of communication made up of texts with a verbal (oral) and a visual (dynamic) component. It was posited that any kind of audio-visual communication is characterised by a specific effect on the viewer's mind. On the one hand, this effect consists in viewers being attracted by the images on the screen and therefore likely to pay some kind of attention to them. At the same time, there is the effect of *reduction of the mental effort invested* (Salomon, 1979–1994) in the processing of audio-visual texts *versus* written texts. In fact, when the amount of connection and integration activity (and not retention of single superficial information) was measured, film and TV comprehension scores were lower than scores on verbal text comprehension. Since connection and integration processes were affected, rather than decoding ones, the conclusion drawn was that the medium-specificity of audio-visual communication is to lower the mental activity which consists of monitoring the comprehension processes of connecting and integrating the single text information items so as to build a coherent representation of the text as a whole.

In order to make this assumption clearer, some references were made to theory and research about those cognitive processes which seem (a) to be common to every kind of text comprehension, regardless of the nature of the information processed, and (b) to be direct indicators of the decrease of mental effort which might explain the lower text comprehension scores.

Our argument is that research on TV comprehension has failed to control for the textual dimension of the material used to compare the audio-visual condition with the reading condition , thereby neglecting the distinction between *plausible* and *necessary* inferences, i.e. between those inferences with which comprehenders draw more information from a single information item, and those inferences which must necessarily be drawn from text information in order to provide local coherence between adjacent information items.

Interestingly, this focusing upon connective inferences in text comprehension seems to find some grounds in neuropsychological research, and precisely in the identification of a brain region in which the function of a supervisory system is localised (anterior cingulate cortex). This region was shown to be more activated when cognitive tasks are difficult and demanding and when a top-down supervisory modulation of several processing systems is required by a performance (Posner & Di Girolamo, 1998; Jack & Shallice, 2001). Our stance is that isolating the higher level comprehension processes also means focusing comprehension comparisons upon a dependent variable (the amount of activation of the anterior cingulate) which can also be used as a clue to the effect of text with dynamic images. The amount of that activation might be a clue to the lower mental effort invested while viewing a given passage than while reading it.

Conclusions were drawn which are relevant to every kind of audio-visual text and therefore to educational multimedia as well. Obviously, these can only be relevant to those kinds of multimedia which consist, on the one hand, of a spoken component and a dynamic visual one, and on the other, can be defined as a text; insofar as the comprehension of the information items presented necessarily requires those reasoning processes which serve to connect and integrate those items into a coherent representation of them. Research perspectives are referred especially to experimental designs aimed at checking the influence of presentation medium on the educational effectiveness of the learning material presented.

These designs should comprise a measure of dependent variable directly related to those comprehension processes which do not coincide either with the decoding and memorising of single content units, or with those learning processes (such as transfer) which cannot be considered as comprehension processes but are necessarily founded upon them. At this level of comprehension, errors (omissions and distortions) are very likely to make learning processes more problematic. This is the reason why focusing the assessment of multimedia comprehension upon these processes also means measuring an important factor in the educational effectiveness of multimedia.

Obviously, this methodological proposal may be only applied to those multimedia which are endowed with a text structure. This is a necessary condition for identifying those text passages upon which the comparison between different multimedia conditions (narration only, narration with static illustration and with animation, etc.) should be made and the effect of dynamic pictures in terms of text comprehension should be checked.

The assumption drawn from our research on TV and film comprehension is that an error in connecting and integrating text information pieces in the course of the first exploration of text, i.e. text comprehension, can interfere significantly with the recall of text as a whole, and therefore with learning processes. In fact, that kind of error might affect comprehension outcome in such a way as to represent an instance of *extraneous cognitive load* (Sweller, 1988; Sweller, van Merrienboer,van Merrienboer & Paas, 1998) in learning from a given multimedia material. This application of cognitive load theory can fit both when students manage to detect and fix those errors, and when, on the contrary, they failed to notice them, thus making adequate learning difficult and even unlikely.

Another contribution from the study of educational multimedia can help us to clarify the influence of comprehension outcome on learning problems. This regards the distinction between *underwhelming* and *overwhelming* situation

(Lowe, Chapter 8). It may be posited that precisely the dynamic nature of the pictures might render the situation less cognitively demanding and therefore *underwhelming* The very nature of the dynamic images makes the students invest less effort into processing the text, thereby taking into account only superficial information.

This special kind of *underwhelming* situation might be concurrent with an *overwhelming* one as a direct consequence of the inadequate comprehension outcome. In fact, because of that inadequacy, students have to tackle an additional, highly demanding task, i.e. revising and fixing the comprehension outcome so as to use it as a foundation for the learning processes.

Thus, a risk can be predicted of a lower educational effectiveness for animation which seems to be similar to the risk defined by Lowe through his analysis of demands in terms of learning processes. The tendency to circumvent the cognitive overload by casually selecting only a few information items, and thus processing those items only partially and incorrectly, seems to apply to that higher level of comprehension processes which our approach is focused upon. According to this approach, students might find themselves in an *overwhelming* situation precisely as a consequence of the insufficient amount of mental effort invested in text processing; i.e. precisely because they have also been faced with an *underwhelming* situation.

Lastly, our approach also provides a further reason why interaction opportunities should be appreciated in educational animation. Insofar as animated material, like any kind of dynamic pictures, leads to rather superficial and inaccurate processing of text, any opportunity in support of student interaction with animated text has the additional function of counteracting this negative effect, i.e. serves to counteract the lowering of mental effort invested in processing, thus making correct connection and integration processes more likely. The interaction opportunities in the case of animation might work in a similar way to the special curricula of television literacy which were shown to counteract the reduction of mental effort in the case of TV comprehension (Cohen & Salomon, 1979; Salomon, 1983). In the case of both multimedia and TV we can predict, a reduction in the effect of lower mental effort invested in the strategic comprehension activities thanks to the presence of conditions which enhance student involvement into these activities.

Notes

1. The meaning assigned to the word *text*, as unusual in psychology as in everyday language, calls for an explanation. Textual linguistics is based on the distinction between a mere collection of sentences and a set of sentences coherently and hierarchically organised; the cognitive psychology of processes of textual comprehension looks at how the processes of connection and integration of the information organised into texts ensure the construction of a coherent mental representation of it. The definition of *text* can include audio-visual communication since those processes of connection and integration are just as necessary when the *coherent set* of information is partly visual and partly verbal.

2. There is obviously one fundamental difference between the two theories of comprehension. Kintsch (1998) not only maintains the propositional character of mental representations for reading comprehension, but also extends it to imagery and non-verbal representation. Although he recognises the risk of this extension and admits that it 'does not necessarily highlight relations that are significant in the realm of action and perception in a direct, analogous manner' (p. 47); although he recognises that 'it is not clear how to interface linear and spatial analogue representations with such units' (p. 45), he decided to translate both imagery and linear strings into predicate-argument format 'only because of practical considerations', that is because he knows 'how to work with predicate-argument units' (p. 45).

   Apart from this preference for the propositional format, Kintsch (1998) emphasises the neuropsychological evidence in support of the distinction between the two types of representation and the importance of perception and mental images in his own theory of comprehension. He argues for 'the need to interpret the propositional units in terms of perceptual and spatial-functional considerations, not purely in terms of a linguistic and abstract level' (p. 44). He not only agrees that 'language developed to reflect the constraints of human action and human perception, probably as well as they can be reflected in any medium' (ibid.), but also suggests that , since 'we talk successfully all the time about what we do and perceive, we ought be able to do science in a similar way' (ibid.).

   The last point seems to suggest that the propositional format is not inevitable and to leave open the question of whether interaction between different external representations should also involve the distinction between propositional as opposed to analogical internal representation.

References

Anderson, D. R., Lorch, E. P., Field, D. E., & Sanders, J. (1981). The effects of TV program comprehensibility on pre-school children's visual attention to television. *Child* development, 52, 151–157.

Anderson, R. D., & Lorch, E. P. (1983). Looking at television: Action or Reaction? In J. Bryant & D. R. Anderson (Eds.), *Children's Understanding of Television* (pp. 1–33). New York: Academic Press.

Balazs, B. (1952). *Theory of the film*. London: Dennis Dobson.

Bransford, J. D. (1979). *Human cognition, learning, understanding and remembering*. Belmont: Wadsworth.

Clark, H. H. (1977). Bridging. In P. N. Johnson-Laird & P. C. Watson (Eds.), *Thinking: Readings in cognitive science* (pp. 243–263). Cambridge, England: Cambridge University Press.

Clark, R. E. (1983). Reconsidering research on learning from media. *Review of Educational Research, 54,* 445–460.

Clark, R. E., & Salomon, G. (1986). Media in teaching. In M. Wittrock (Ed.), *Handbook of research on teaching* (pp. 464–478). New York: Mac Millan.

Clark, R. E., & Sugrue, B. M. (1990). North American disputes about research on learning from media. *International Journal of Educational Research, 14,* 507–520.

Cohen, A., & Salomon, G. (1979). Children's literate television viewing: Surprises and possible explanations. *Journal of Communication, 29,* 156–163.

Cohen-Séat, G. (1946). *Essai sur les principes d'une philosophie du cinéma*. Paris: Denoel.

Ericsson, K. A., & Simon, H. A. (1984). *Protocol analysis: Verbal reports as data*. Cambridge, Ma.: MIT Press.

Gernsbacher, M. A. (1985). Surface information loss in comprehension. *Cognitive Psychology, 17,* 324–363.

Gernsbacher, M. A. (1989). Mechanisms that improve referential access. *Cognition, 32,* 99–156.
Gernsbacher, M. A., Varner, K. R., & Faust, M. E. (1990). Investigating differences in general comprehension skill. *Journal of Experimental Psychology*, 3, 430–445.
Jack, A. I., & Shallice, T. (2001). Introspective physicalism as an approach to the science of consciousness. *Cognition, 79,* 161–196.
Kintsch, W. (1998). *Comprehension: A paradigm for cognition.* Cambridge: Cambridge University Press.
Kracauer, S. (1960). *Theory of film.* Princeton, N.J.: Princeton University Press.
Langer, E. J. (1985). Playing the middle against both ends: The usefulness of adult cognitive activity as a model for cognitive activity in childhood and olden age. In S. R. Yussen (Ed.), *The growth of reflection in children* (pp. 267–285). New York: Academic Press.
Lorch, E. P., Anderson, D. R., & Levin, S. R. (1979). The relationship of visual attention to children's comprehension of television. *Child Development, 50,* 722–727.
Lumbelli, L. (1974). *Comunicazione filmica* (Film Communication). Firenze: La Nuova Italia.
Lumbelli, L. (1999). Learners as TV audience and as readers: What is similar and what is different? Keynote Address at the *Eighth European Conference of EARLI.* Goeteborg, August 24–28.
Lumbelli L., & Bechini, B. (2002). Audio-visual versus written text comprehension: What about creative work? Paper presented at the meeting on *Multimedia Comprehension*, Poitiers, August 29–30.
Lumbelli, L., & Cornoldi, C. (1994). Interaction between verbal and visual information in audio-visual text comprehension. In F. P. C. M. De Jong & B. van Hout-Wolters (Eds.), *Process-oriented instruction and learning from text* (pp. 183–193). Amsterdam: VU University Press.
Lumbelli, L., & Zidari, C. (2001). Comprehension processes compared: Reading, TV and computer. Paper presented at *the Ninth European Conference of EARLI.* Fribourg, August 28 – September 1.
Magliano, J. P., & Graesser, A. C. (1991). A three-pronged method for studying inference generation in literary text. *Poetics, 20*, 193–232.
Mc Koon, G., & Ratcliff, R. (1992). Inference during reading. *Psychological Review, 99,* 440–466.
Mander, J. (1978). *Four arguments for the elimination of television.* New York: Morrow.
Mayer, R. E. (2001). *Multimedia learning.* Cambridge: Cambridge University Press.
Meringoff, L. (1980). Influence of the medium on children's story apprehension. *Journal of Educational Psychology, 72,* 240–249.
Meringoff, L., Vibbert, M., Char, C., Fernie, D., Banker, G., & Gardner, H. (1983), How is children's learning from television distinctive? In J. Bryant & D. R. Anderson (Eds.), *Children' understanding of television* (pp. 151–179). New York: Academic Press.
Michotte, A. (1948). Le caractère de 'réalité' des projections cinèmatographiques. *IKON. Révue Internationale de Filmologie, 3–4,* 298–322.
Olson, G. M., Duffy, S. A., & Mack, R. L. (1984). Thinking-out-loud as a method for studying real-time comprehension processes. In D. E. Kieras & M. A. Just (Eds.), *New methods in reading comprehension research* (pp. 253–286). Hillsdale, NJ : Erlbaum.
Pezdek, K. (1987). Television comprehension as an example of applied research in cognitive psychology. In D. Berger, K. Pezdek, & W. P. Banks (Eds.). *Applications of cognitive psychology: Problem solving, education and computing* (pp. 3–15). Hillsdale: Erlbaum.
Pezdek, K., Lehrer, A., & Simon, S. (1984). The relationship between reading and cognitive processing of television and radio. *Child Development, 55,* 2072–2082.
Pezdek, K., Simon, S., Stoeckert, J., & Kiely, J. (1987). Individual differences in television comprehension. *Memory and Cognition, 15,* 428–435.
Pressley, M., & Afflerbach, P. (1995). *Verbal protocols of reading.* Hillsdale: Erlbaum.

Sadoski, M., & Paivio, A. (2001). *Imagery and text: A dual coding theory of reading and writing*. Mahwah, N.J.: Erlbaum.

Salomon, G. (1979–1994). *Interaction of media, cognition and learning*. San Francisco: Jossey-Bass.

Salomon, G. (1981). Introducing AIME. The assessment of children's mental involvement with television. In H. Gardner & H. Kelly (Eds.), *Children and the world of* television (pp. 89–102). San Francisco: Jossey-Bass.

Salomon, G. (1983). Television watching and mental effort: A social psychological view. In J. Bryant & D. R. Anderson (Eds.), *Children's Understanding of Television* (pp. 181–198). New York: Academic Press.

Salomon, G. (1984). Television is easy and print is "tough": The differential investment of mental effort in learning as a function of perceptions and attributions. *Journal of Educational Psychology, 76*, 647–658.

Sartori, G. (1997). *Homo videns*. Bari: Laterza

Schnotz, W. (2001). Sign systems, technologies, and the acquisition of knowledge. In J. F. Rouet, J. J. Levonen, & A. Biardeau (Eds.), *Multimedia learning: Cognitive and instructional issues* (pp. 9–29). Amsterdam: Pergamon.

Singer, G. L. (1980). The power and limitations of television: A cognitive-affective Analysis. In P. H. Tannenbaum & R. Abeles (Eds.), *The entertainment functions of television*. Hilldale, N.J.: Erlabaum.

Sweller, G., van Merrienboer, J. J. G., & Paas, F. G. W. C. (1998). Cognitive architecture and instructional design. *Educational Psychology Review, 10*, 251–296.

Sweller, J. (1988). Cognitive load during problem-solving: Effects on learning. *Cognitive science, 12*, 257–285.

Trabasso, T., & Suh S. (1993). Understanding text: Achieving explanatory coherence through on-line inferences and mental operations in working memory. *Discourse Processes, 16*, 3–34.

Van Dijk, T. A., & Kintsch, W. (1983). *Strategies of discourse comprehension*. Orlando, Fl.: Academic Press.

Chapter 13
How Should We Evaluate Multimedia Learning Environments?

Shaaron Ainsworth

Abstract Early research with multimedia environments questioned whether these environments are effective in supporting learning. More recently it has been acknowledged that this question should really be about the specific conditions and reasons why multimedia is effective. However, while the argument has become more sophisticated, the techniques for evaluating learning with multimedia environments have not always followed suit. The dominant approach at present involves factorial designs with novices as participants, learning something for a short period of time with outcomes tested by an immediate pen and paper post-test. In this chapter, the positive aspects of this approach are reviewed, but it will be argued that such an approach limits the questions that can be answered. Four important such questions about learning with multimedia are proposed and then the chapter describes a range of methodologies that can be used to answer them.

Keywords Experimental methods · Flexible designs · Evaluation · Microgenetic

13.1 Introduction

In common with the introduction of other forms of learning technologies when multimedia learning environments were first becoming available, they seemed to promise a solution for the problem of how to teach in complex domains. Learners would be motivated to learn by novel forms of representations such as animations, videos, dyna-linked pictures and text. Moreover, their understanding of the domain would be enhanced by the opportunity to interact with many forms of representations. Learners would identify which representations best revealed the particular aspect of the domain they were currently studying and

S. Ainsworth
University of Nottingham, School of Psychology and Learning Sciences Research Institute, University Park, Nottingham, NG7 2RD, UK
e-mail: shaaron.ainsworth@nottingham.ac.uk

J.-F. Rouet et al. (eds.), *Understanding Multimedia Documents*,
DOI: 10.1007/978-0-387-73337-1_13,

by making connections across these forms of representation, they would come to understand the domain in a less superficial, more expert way.

Research on learning with multimedia and multi-representational software has shown that this rosy promise can be achieved (e.g. for reviews see Ainsworth, 2006; Najjar, 1998) but that it is not an invariant feature of learning with multimedia. For every study published showing that such environments facilitate learning, it seems that an equal number show that learners find such environments overwhelming and that in the worse cases, such environments are not just neutral but can even harm learning (e.g. Ainsworth, Bibby, & Wood, 2002; de Jong et al., 1998; Moreno & Mayer, 2000). Consequently, the research question has changed from the overly simple one of whether multimedia is an effective form of learning environment to questioning why specific examples of multimedia can help particular learners in some contexts.

The purpose of this chapter is to argue that now we have acknowledged the complexity of the question, we need to adjust our research methodologies to this new complexity. In this chapter, I am not going to discuss the range of philosophical positions that underlie these methodologies in order to argue whether positivist, interpretive and critical approaches are most appropriate. I am also going to assume the overall agenda is one of evaluation research – i.e. the goal is to perform a rigorous study to assess the effects and effectiveness of a multimedia learning environment. To this end, I will start by describing a typical approach to understanding multimedia learning. However, whist such an approach does have many positive factors, I will argue that alternative approaches are also needed. Four 'second generation' questions that concern whether learning with multimedia will be effective are proposed and the remainder of the chapter reviews alternatives way of researching multimedia that can help answer those questions. The point ultimately is to argue that there is no single "right" method with which to evaluate multimedia, only right methodologies for specific questions.

13.2 First Generation Experiments

This approach has been probably been the commonly applied method for evaluating multimedia – it might be considered the prototype for what Goldman (2003) calls 'first-generation' multimedia learning research. A typical scenario could be considered to have the following characteristics.

> Participants for an experiment are recruited in return for credit on the psychology or education courses they are studying or are paid a small amount in reward for their time. They have no prior knowledge of the science topic and what they are about to learn will not benefit them in their future studies. They may be given a short pen and paper multi-choice pre-test to check that they have little prior knowledge of the concepts of the domain and then are randomly assigned to two groups. The first group receives the special multimedia condition that has been previously designed to be "good" according to the predictions of a current fashionable theory. The second group receives the same

material but in a text-only control. A short orientation phase is provided to ensure that students know how to use the interface. They learn with this material for 30 minutes and are then immediately given a pen and paper multi-choice post-test of the domain concepts, which typically will include some harder elements than the pre-test. They are debriefed, thanked for their participation and told not to sign up for further experiments, as they are not naïve to the material. The whole experience takes about an hour. The multimedia group do statistically better on the post-test than the control group and the results are interpreted to support the predictions of the current theory.

We should acknowledge a couple of things about this scenario. Firstly, a single experiment rarely has all of these characteristics, but many do include a substantial proportion. I do not think I'm attacking a 'straw man' here but a fairly common paradigm. Secondly, I have conducted a number of these sorts of experiments myself (and still do); so lest anyone think I am pointing the finger of blame, imagine it pointing squarely at myself. I often use this methodology because it has a number of desirable characteristics.

13.2.1 Positive Features

- Use of theory to guide experimentation

One of the strengths of recent research in multimedia learning is the emergence of theoretical frameworks, which integrate what might appear to be unrelated findings into a consistent whole. The two most commonly applied theories (which are strongly related) are the Cognitive Theory of Multimedia Learning (e.g. Mayer, 2001) and Cognitive Load theory (e.g. Sweller, van Merrienboer, & Paas, 1998). They focus on the nature of working memory (and its relation to long term memory) with its multiple, modality-specific limited capacity subsystems and identify the benefits that can accrue by presenting information that uses multiple modalities so that learners who actively process such information can learn effectively.

- Robust and replicable results

The wide spread acceptance of these theories means that a substantial number of researchers are contributing to the development of the theories and showing the robustness of their results across multiple laboratories. For example, research concerning the "split attention effect" – that separating pictures and text results in worse learning than integrating them into a single representation has been confirmed in many experiments (e.g. Chandler & Sweller, 1992; Kalyuga, Chandler, & Sweller, 1999; Mayer & Moreno, 1998). This can be enhanced when materials are shared across laboratories, (e.g. Bétrancourt, Dillenbourg, & Clavien Chapter 4).

- Reasonable statistical rigour

As opposed to relying on intuition about the benefits of multimedia learning environment, these experiments use statistical methodologies to show when these intuitions are justified and when they are not. Furthermore, effect size analysis (Gain in Experimental Group's Scores – Gain in Control Group's Score)/St Dev in Control Group's Gain Scores) can be used to allow at least some comparison about the relative effects of different treatments. This was not widely seen in the reports of early experimental research but is becoming more commonplace (e.g. Mayer, 2003).

- Publishing "negative" data

Generally, negative data or results are those that confirm the null hypothesis – in the imaginary experiment above the null hypothesis is that there is no difference in learning outcomes between those students who learnt with multimedia and those who learnt with text. For example, the animation literature is contains a number of experiments showing no difference between those students who learnt with dynamic representations and those who learnt with static materials (e.g. Pane, Corbett, & John, 1996; Price, 2002); Rieber, 1990). Similarly, a significant amount of published research on learning with multiple representations has found no benefits for this approach (e.g. Guercin, 2001; Van Someren & Tabbers, 1998; Yerushalmy, 1991). By publishing negative as well as positives results, we are in a stronger position to weight up the costs as well as benefits of the impact of new technologies on learning.

- Use of within system control

Typically, these experiments use within system controls, *i.e.* both groups of learners interact with the same technology, which only differs in the specific aspect of the interface that is under investigation. General explanations about the effects of computers of learning are therefore ruled out (increased motivation, immediate feedback, etc.) and so we can be certain that the results are due to the specific features under investigation.

13.2.2 Negative Features

However, although these first-generation experiments have all these positive features, I believe that on balance this approach has more flaws than benefits.

- Use of artificial populations

One concern with this approach is that it is common for people with no background knowledge to participate in return for payment or course credit. One could argue that many multimedia environments are designed for people who are in the early stages of learning a topic and hence experimental participants provide a good analogue of this population. However, it is commonly the case that multimedia environments are used by students after initial exposure to the topic in other forms, (e.g. lectures, readings) and often as part of a more extensive curriculum. Furthermore, people learning with multimedia outside experimental settings are presumably doing so because they want to know something about the topic, perhaps because they are fulfilling some personal learning objective or because they are required to learn to pass examinations. It may not be wise to generalise about the suitability of different approaches to multimedia from this experimental population to the actual intended users of the learning environments.

A second worry with using artificial populations is that many explanations of the effects of multimedia are based on limited capacity working memory. People differ in their working memory capacity (Daily, Lovett, & Reder, 2001) and so what may overload some learners will not overload others. What is often overlooked in the applications of such theories by multimedia designers (although not in the original conceptualisation of the theory) is the interaction between the limited capacity working memory and constructivist nature of human cognition. Working memory capacity refers to chunks not items and so it is as much about long-term memory as short-term. Thus, the string 441159515314 will be difficult for you to remember but as I know that is the UK international dialling code followed by the Nottingham dialling code, followed by my office phone number it is easy for me (3 chunks of information rather than 13). Thus, everyone's different long-term memory (schemata) will influence how they can interact with different representations. Broad assumptions about certain representations overloading working memory may not always be justified. But, in particular, complete novices when acting as participants in these experiments are likely to be the ones without relevant schemata and who are most likely to suffer most from representations that are working memory intensive.

- Description of representations

One current problem when trying to generalize across multiple studies is that an insufficient level of detail is presented about the design of multimedia environment and the representations that are used. In much multimedia research, representations are described simply in terms of modality – pictorial/graphical or textual. Pictorial representations are depictive in that they explicitly preserve geometric and topological information whereas textual representations are descriptive as they have an arbitrary relationship to the object that they represent (e.g. Schnotz, 2001). The other common classifying dimension in multimedia research is sensory channel (*i.e.* auditory, visual, and less often haptic). The current theoretical focus on dual coding and cognitive load theories has tended to lead to a situation where these dimensions of modality and sensory channel are seen as the only ones important for representational analysis. Yet, there are many of ways that representations can differ from one another. For example, other dimensions that have been used to classify representations include precision (the level of accuracy of information e.g. qualitative to quantitative), specificity (the extent to which a representation permits expression of abstraction), perspective (what is represented such as functional or structural relationships) and complexity (the amount of information) (see de Jong et al., 1998). We need to widen our theoretical stance to understand how representations influence learning (see also Klein, 2003; Reimann, 2003) and to do that we need to describe the representations used in multimedia environments in much greater detail.

- Lack of domain variability

One problem with generalizing from this type of research to widespread applications of principles is that the majority of research has been conducted in the pure sciences, with much less research addressing social sciences, humanities or arts. These subjects typically don't have a single correct answer and may need different forms of representations to help convey the shades of grey involved in understanding these topics.

- Timescale of the study:

Another concern with the nature of the tasks used in most experiments is the timescale of the learning experience. In the vast majority of experiments, participants only interact with the learning environment once and that for a short amount of time (normally for less than one hour). This leads to a number of questionable practices. Firstly, it tends to confound the time learners must spend in coming to understand new interfaces and representations with the time spent learning the domain though these representations. New forms of representations must be learnt and in many cases this will be a complex task. Learners must come to understand the syntax and semantics of representations, may need to learn how to select and construct representations, and in multi-representational cases may need to translate between representations. It is unlikely that the short training sessions that most experiments employ will allow learners to have completed all these tasks. Secondly, the interesting questions of how learners change and adapt as their expertise grows is not addressed in this sort of methodology. Finally, it is questionable whether the results would apply to situations where learners are interacting with environments over more extended periods of time.

- Assessment of Learning Outcomes

Positively, many experiments distinguish between different types of learning outcome – for example, Mayer, (2003) uses both retention and transfer tests; Ainsworth and Loizou (2003) examined explicit, implicit and knowledge inference questions. However, there remains a reliance on multi-choice and true-false questions which is understandable as they are quick to administer and mark. However, this has a tendency to bias outcomes towards declarative knowledge. Secondly, the majority of experiments rely on an immediate post-test to assess learning outcomes. Yet, different styles of intervention can differentially impact on the outcomes of learning at different rates. For example, research comparing collaborative to individual learning has shown that benefits of collaboration become more apparent on a delayed rather than immediate post-test (Howe, Tolmie, Anderson, & Mackenzie, 1992). Thirdly, limited emphasis is placed on the modality of the test items. Typically, irrespective of the modality of the learning material, post-test items have a tendency to be textual. We may be underestimating the benefits of different forms of representation this way. If dynamic representations lead to dynamic mental models, should we give learners tools to create dynamic representations at post-test?

Furthermore, the representational aspect of what is learnt is often not assessed separately from the conceptual. Given that much multimedia research involves novel representations formalisms it would be nice to routinely differentiate between learners'' understanding of representations and the way they encode domain. For example, Cheng (2002) showed that learners could solve complex electrical circuit problems more easily when using a novel form of diagram – a law-encoding diagram. To truly understand the contribution that this diagram made to facilitate problem-solving, it would be beneficial to see if learners could apply this form of representation to domains with similar deep structures and whether they could solve problems in this electrical circuit domain more easily with other forms of representation.

13.3 The Need for Alternative Approaches to Evaluating Multimedia Learning

These criticisms of 'first generation' experiments have identified common features of this format of experiment that we might want to improve, but intrinsically there is no reason why experiments of this form could not recruit participants from 'real' populations, explore different types of representation and in a wider variety of domains as well as assessing learning outcomes in multiple ways and at a delay. In fact, many experimental evaluations do include some of these characteristics, even if a very few have all of them. However, I want to argue that there are four important questions that experiments such as these have difficultly in answering, namely:

1. Who benefits from learning with (specific forms of) multimedia?
2. How do people learn with multimedia?
3. How does learning with multimedia change over time?
4. How does the wider context influence learning with multimedia?

In this section, I will try to justify why I consider these questions as fundamental to understanding the effectiveness of multimedia and will show how a range of methods including second generation experiments, computer modelling, case studies of representation use in 'real world' contexts and microgenetic accounts of learning with multimedia can be used to answer these questions.

13.3.1 *Who Benefits from Learning with (Specific Forms of) Multimedia?*

One of the key benefits that is commonly used to justify multimedia learning environments is that different types of learners may differentially benefit from alternative forms of representation. Multimedia can present the same information in many different ways so that learners can chose to focus on the representations that they find most useful. This intuition is not always backed up by research as it ignores the fact that learners may find representations difficult to integrate or that learning to select appropriate representations is a significant task in itself and learners may not always make sensible decisions. However, it does acknowledge one key aspect of multimedia learning – that people differ in what and how they learn with multimedia.

One way that this has been addressed experimentally is by the exploring aptitude by treatment interactions i.e. that some forms of representations (treatments) are more or less effective for particular individuals depending upon their specific abilities For example, research on learning with pictures has often explored aptitude by treatment interactions. Winn (1987) proposed that factors such as IQ, spatial reasoning, locus of control, field dependence, verbal ability, vocabulary, gender and age will mean that learners with different characteristics will differentially benefit from different forms of representation. It is commonly suggested that both lower achieving learners or learners with high spatial or visual preferences will benefit most from pictures (e.g. Snow & Yalow, 1982; Mayer & Sims, 1994). However, there is not necessarily a simple or face-valid relation between representational preference and task performance. For example, Roberts, Gilmore, and Wood (1997) showed that high visual problem-solvers understood when to abandon visual strategies better than low visual problem-solvers.

Recent experimental approaches to multimedia learning are revisiting aptitude treatment interaction research to ask what sort of learner most benefits from dynamic or multi-representational learning environments. Increasingly common practice is to include pre-tests that examine learners' prior knowledge to ask whether learners with different expertise will benefit from the approach. For example, Mayer and Gallini (1990) showed that learners with less domain-specific knowledge benefit more from multimedia material (text and pictures) than from text alone. Seufert (2003) placed learners into one of three categories based on their prior domain-specific knowledge of chemistry before they learnt complex chemical concepts with multimedia software. They also received one of three types of help for supporting their understanding of the relation between representations – directive, non-directive or no help. Seufert found that learners with medium levels of prior knowledge increased their comprehension of the material most when given help – learners with too much or too little knowledge did not benefit to the same degree and in some cases, help was even harmful. An important addition to understanding the relation between learners' prior knowledge and learning with multimedia is to disentangle learners' familiarity with domain concepts from their familiarity with the representations employed. This is exemplified by Stern, Aprea, and Ebner (2003) who examined both prior knowledge of the domain under investigation (economics) as well as understanding of linear graphs.

However, an approach that relies on classifying learners into categories is still limited in the questions it can answer, as it does not tell us much about **why** certain learners benefit whilst others do not. Furthermore, in most experiments even if there are significant differences between conditions, there is also significant overlap between subjects' learning outcomes in all conditions. Yet, this is simply ignored as the error term in an ANOVA rather that considered an interesting focus for exploration. Why are some learners in the "bad" condition able to surpass the performance on those in the "good" condition? Does it simply relate to their prior knowledge or ability to learn new material or perhaps they have better strategies and approaches for learning with the multimedia.

One of the key advantages of experimental approaches to multimedia learning is the opportunity to collect easily and automatically a wealth of data about how learners interact with the representations without changing the learning experience. Examples of learner-system interaction traces that can be used include time on task data, progression through curriculum, use of various systems features (e.g. learner control of dynamic representation, selection of different representations, etc.), amount of help sought or provided, performance on questions (see Rouet & Passerault, 1999). This data is often (though not necessarily) more difficult to collect in more naturalistic situations – for example, time on task data collected in real contexts is normally too noisy to provide reliable information. Such interaction traces can be used to explain why some learners are more successful than others in different experimental conditions. For example, Zahn, Barquero and Schwan (2004) compared subjects learning with different hypervideo designs and with the text and video materials presented without hyperlinks. Irrespective of the specific condition it was those students who activated more links and spent longer reading the content who scored better on the multi-choice pen and paper post-test. Lowe (2003) shows how subtle perceptual features can strongly influence what novices comprehend and remember from animated weather maps. Participants attended to features that dynamically contrasted with their surroundings. However, these features were not necessarily the ones of most conceptual interest (see also Lowe, Chapter 8).

A second type of measure that can be used to understand why some individuals benefit more than others does involve changing the nature of the learning experience. Examples of these process measures include eye-movement data (see Tabbers, Paas, Lankford, Martens, & Merriënboer, Chapter 9), poor men's eye trackers (e.g. Romero, du Boulay, Lutz, & Cox, 2003) which only uncover parts of a screen when a cursor is moved over them, videoing learners to capture gesture and other forms of non-verbal behaviour, and various forms of protocol data. For example, Lewalter (2003) collected verbal protocols from students as they learned with text, which in two cases was supplemented with either graphical dynamic or static representations. She found no difference between the two illustrated conditions, but both were better than text only. However, she found that learners provided with static representations in addition to text produced more rehearsal strategies. A similar analysis was conducted by Ainsworth and Loizou (2003) who asked students to self-explain when learning about the cardio-vascular system with either text or pictures. They completed multi-choice questions (half pictorial, half text) and completed a blood-path diagram at pre and post-test and also answered extended textual questions at post-test which tested their mental model construction. Those students presented with pictures scored higher at post-test (particularly on mental model questions) produced significantly more self-explanations, were more likely to produce explanations that included goals or principles and self-explaining was more strongly related to learning outcomes in the pictures rather than the text conditions.

I would argue that a key feature of 'second generation' research is the routine collection and analysis of learner system interactions. This information could tell us much about how learners actually use such systems and help us answer the question of which learners benefit most from learning with multimedia. Collecting process data is obviously much more difficult and may not always be possible to use within experiments as it can significantly change the nature of the learning experience. However, collecting process data is almost always necessary if we turn from asking which learners benefit from multimedia to asking how do people learn with multimedia.

13.3.2 How do People Learn with Multimedia?

Experiments are sometimes referred to as black box evaluations – they focus on the inputs (prior knowledge and ability) and outputs (learning outcomes) of an experience but pay less attention to the describing the process of an experience. Interaction measures within experiments obviously go someway to addressing the 'black box' criticism but still have limitations. For example, Ainsworth, Bibby,Bibby and Wood (2002) conducted an experiment to see whether it more effective to present children with feedback about the accuracy of their mathematical problem-solving (estimation) in either pictures, mathematical representations or a combination of pictures and mathematics. Learning outcome measures showed that whilst pictorial and mathematical representations helped learning of the estimation task, the combination of pictorial with mathematical representations inhibited learning to estimate. Interaction data goes someway to explaining why this occurred as it was possible to isolate the problem as resulting from relating representations. Each representation in the mixed system was present in either mathematical or pictorial systems where it was used successfully, so it is known that learners could understand the representations. Analysis of the similarity of behaviour over the representations suggested that in the mixed case, learners did not relate the representations. However, what this interaction data does not tell us if whether learners were trying and failing to relate the mixed representations or whether they did not even try to relate them.

Consequently, to explore how people learn with multi-media may require different forms of evaluation design – often referred to as flexible rather than fixed design (e.g. Robson, 2002) of which typical examples include ethnography, case studies and grounded theory. A number of researchers have used case studies to explore how people learn in multi-media and multi-representational situations. Typically case studies involve an in-depth analysis of a small number of cases and use multiple data sources (such an interviews, observation and video, analysis of physical and virtual artefacts. For example, Kozma, Chin, Russell and Marx (2000) followed up an experimental study of expert-novice differences in using chemical representations by analysing the behaviour of professional chemists engaging in professional practice in laboratories. The researchers observed and interviewed the chemists as well as recording interactions and analysing representations. They confirmed the experimental finding that chemists did use multiple representations to help them understand complex phenomena, however they also revealed in more detail how this understanding occurred. For example, they showed how specific forms of representation were useful for different aspects of chemistry and they showed how chemists working together would slowly converge upon joint understanding through a combination of dialogue and representation construction, interpretation and coordination. Tsui and Treagust (2003) analysed students' learning of genetics with a multi-representational tool by observing classrooms, interviewing students and analysing interaction data. One of the results of their study was identification of processes that successful students engaged in when coming to understand the topic of genetics through multiple representations. They summarise these processes as 'mindful'; i.e. ones that involve effortful learning guided by students reflection into their own current state of knowledge. Similarly, Buckley (2000) explored how students developed a model of the structure and function of the cardio-vascular system by interacting with multimedia. By performing very detailed analysis of a student's use of software, her notes and performance on off-lines tests, Buckley was able to describe how learner's interactions with particular representations contributed in both positive and negative ways to the development of specific parts of a learner's mental model.

Computational modelling is a very different approach to exploring the processes involved in learning with multimedia and multiple representations. Whilst it is obviously not an evaluation research methodology itself, it can be used to explain the behaviour of learners interacting with multimedia and ultimately can help it predicting the likely effectiveness of particular forms of learning environment (Card, Moran & Newell, 1983).

Tabachneck-Schijf, Leonardo,Leonardo and Simon (1997) describe CaMeRa – which consists of a production system and parallel network. CaMeRa is based on a number of assumption (drawn from a variety of empirical sources), for example, that mental images closely resemble visual stimuli and that different modalities have different (internal) representations. Consequently, it consists of a pictorial external display, pictorial and verbal short-term memories and pictorial and verbal long-term memories. Knowledge is organized into small chunks, which can be connected by associations within or between modalities, but modified only from short-term memory structures of their own modality. It also has semantic knowledge of a particular domain (in this case, economics). The performance of the model and the processes that the model uses as it makes inferences about economics principles (e.g. supply and demand) and its use of multiple representations (e.g. graphs and verbal explanations) can be compared to the behaviour and protocols of human reasoning. Then the way, for example, that the model uses it semantic knowledge to guide its interpretation of a visual display can help explain why the processes and outcomes of learning with multimedia can depend upon a learners' prior knowledge.

Lane, Cheng, and Gobet (2000) developed a computational model of how learners solved electrical circuit problems when presented both with the conventional diagram and a diagrammatic representation which encodes the main laws of electricity, including Ohm's Law. The model consists of a simulated eye and pen, a pictorial short term memory which has both an iconic representation of what the eye is looking at as well as pointers to information held in long term memory (modelled as a discrimination network). Lane et al.'s model was compared to human learners and was found to have drawn diagrams in similar ways. This model is interesting as it complements work with eye-trackers in exploring exactly how what people look at informs what and how they learn.

13.3.3 How does Learning with Multimedia Change Over Time?

Many experiments of learning with multimedia have used only one intervention session and so have little to say about how learning may change as learners become increasingly experienced with the environment, domain and representations. Furthermore, it could be argued that this can confound learning a new representation with learning through a representation. One way to address this would be to use experimental designs such as interrupted time series but another technique that has been specifically developed to addresses the problem of analyzing changing behaviour are the microgenetic methods. Siegler (1995) characterises microgenetic methods as involving a high density of observations relative to the rate of change, a large number of observation in the time in which change is taking place and intensive trial-by-trial analysis using both quantitative and qualitative methods with the goal of inferring the processes that give rise to change. Although originally applied with developmental psychology, it has been applied to multi-representational learning.

Schoenfeld, Smith, and Arcavi (1993) examined one student's understanding of function using a multi-representational graphing environment. Using microgenetic analysis, they describe in detail the mappings between the algebraic and graphical representation in this domain. Working with one student over a number of sessions, they showed how a student could appear to have mastered fundamental components of a domain both in terms of algebra and in terms of graphs. However, because some of the connections between these modes of representation were missing, her behaviour with the representations was often misguided.

Van Labeke and Ainsworth (2003) explored three learners using a very complex multi-representational simulation of population biology (up to 16 representations are available simultaneously including simple animations, tables, equations, graphs and phaseplots). Each learner had a different background (e.g. computer science, undergraduate biology) and they worked with an experimenter for eight hours to explore models of increasingly complexity. This study revealed a number of fine-grained details about how prior knowledge influenced the way that learners used the software and what they could learn from it. It addition, it showed how learners changed over time. At the beginning, learners began by opening all representations, rejecting some very swiftly (and not necessarily rejecting those which were least informative). Learners tended to select representations by working down the menu of choices, they then selected a number for more intensive study, but typically selected too many to focus upon all of them. Learners interacted with the representations by running the simulations over and over again. However, by the end of the eight hours, their behaviour changed substantially. Now, typically they would only run the simulation once or twice, selected far fewer representations and used them more deliberately.

Studies such as these reveal how multimedia learning may change as learners come to understand how they should learn with these types of environments. They also show how complex learning with multiple representations can be – both studies showed that learning was brittle and that students needed considerable time to practice with the environments before they really developed a deep understanding of the concepts under investigation.

13.3.4 How does the Wider Context Influence Learning with Multimedia?

Researchers from a situated perspective have reminded us that people's understanding and interactions with multimedia will be influenced by their cultural background, the activities they are engaged in and the current context in which the multimedia is found. They emphasize that learning is socially constructed.

Ethnography provides a very useful tool for exploring these issues. Ethnographers spend considerable time in the field, observing and interviewing people as they go about their everyday practice. Whilst ethnographic studies have rarely been used to study multi-media learning precisely, they have been used to explore the learning and use of representations. For example, Roth and Bowen (2001) explored how a water technician uses graphs of the water level of a creek in her local environment. This is an aspect of a job she has being doing for many years and she is extremely familiar with both the representation and the environment which it is depicting. In contrast to research in laboratory which often focuses on incompetency (see diSessa 2004), this research provides a striking account of the competency. The experience of the professional with these forms of graphs and her knowledge of the geography they were representing shows how 'transparent' the process of reading graphs can be. A peak on a graph is not seen as a representational feature which must be interpreted with effort but immediately evokes a causal explanation at the phenomena level (a non-natural event caused by clogged pipe). Such accounts imply that multimedia learning environments must help students not just come to understand a representational system and the object is represents but must focus on providing the opportunities for deep understanding which comes from translating between the two levels.

Given that multimedia learning often takes place in the classroom, one very important context to explore is how teachers can scaffold learners' interaction with multimedia to enhance its effectiveness. For example, Waldrip and Prain (2004) observed classroom practice and interviewed students and teachers to capture crucial incidents in students learning. One successful teacher used questioning to help students to see relationships between different modes of representation. By beginning with a particular mode, and then introducing other modes of representation, he eventually provided students with the cognitive tools to utilise multi-modal representations and to explain the concepts they were studying.

13.4 Conclusion

This chapter has considered how we should evaluate multimedia learning environments. It has argued that as the field has matured we have moved from just assuming that multimedia would be better to assessing the effectiveness of multimedia – initially with fairly simple experiments and now with a wide variety of methods including second generation experiments, computer modelling, case studies, ethnography and microgenetic methods. Each method obviously needs to be performed to high standards which are appropriate for each method. For example, experiments should have clear hypotheses, random allocation of subjects to groups, should manipulate independent variables and use systematic procedures to test the hypothesised causal relationships and case studies should use rigorous data collection in multiple forms with appropriate analysis and generalisation (see Robson 2002 for an excellent introduction to the practice of 'real world' research). Rather than becoming entrenched in methodological warfare, with everyone fighting for their favourite method, the answer to the question of "how we should evaluate multimedia learning environments" is to recognise that the general question can never be answered at this level of abstraction, but must be answered by matching methodologies to a specific questions under investigation.

References

Ainsworth, S. (2006). DeFT: A conceptual framework for considering learning with multiple representations. *Learning and Instruction, 16*(3), 183–198.

Ainsworth, S. E., Bibby, P., & Wood, D. (2002). Examining the effects of different multiple representational systems in learning primary mathematics. *Journal of the Learning Sciences, 11*(1), 25–61.

Ainsworth, S. E., & Loizou, A. T. (2003). The effects of self-explaining when learning with text or diagrams. *Cognitive Science, 27*(4), 669–681.

Buckley, B. C. (2000). Interactive multimedia and model-based learning in biology. *International Journal of Science Education, 22*(9), 895–935.

Chandler, P., & Sweller, J. (1992). The split-attention effect as a factor in the design of instruction. *British Journal of Educational Psychology, 62*, 233–246.

Card, S., Moran, T., & Newell, A. (1983). *The psychology of human-computer interaction.* Hillsdale, NJ: Erlbaum.

Cheng, P. C. H. (2002). Electrifying diagrams for learning: principles for complex representational systems. *Cognitive Science, 26*(6), 685–736.

Daily, L. Z., Lovett, M. C., & Reder, L. M. (2001). Modelling individual differences in working memory performance: a source activation account. *Cognitive Science, 25*(3), 315–353.

de Jong, T., Ainsworth, S. E., Dobson, M., van der Hulst, A., Levonen, J., Reimann, P., et al. (1998). Acquiring knowledge in science and math: The use of multiple representations in technology based learning environments. In M. W. Van Someren, P. Reimann, H. P. A. Boshuizen, & T. de Jong (Eds.), *Learning with multiple representations* (pp. 9–40). Amsterdam: Elsevier Science.

diSessa, A. A. (2004). Metarepresentation: Native competence and targets for instruction. *Cognition and Instruction, 22*(3), 293–331.

Goldman, S. R. (2003). Learning in complex domains: When and why do multiple representations help? *Learning and Instruction, 13*(2), 239–244.

Guercin, F. (2001). Can children process complex information from different media? In J.-F. Rouet, J. L. Levonen, & A. Biardeau (Eds.), *Multimedia learning* (pp. 59–64). Amsterdam: Pergamon.

Howe, C., Tolmie, A., Anderson, A., & Mackenzie, M. (1992). Conceptual knowledge in physics: The role of group interaction in computer-supported teaching. *Learning and Instruction, 2*, 161–183.

Kalyuga, S., Chandler, P., & Sweller, J. (1999). Managing split-attention and redundancy in multimedia instruction. *Applied Cognitive Psychology, 13*(4), 351–371.

Klein, P. D. (2003). Rethinking the multiplicity of cognitive resources and curricular representations: alternatives to 'learning styles' and 'multiple intelligences'. *Journal of Curriculum Studies, 35*(1), 45–81.

Kozma, R., Chin, E., Russell, J., & Marx, N. (2000). The roles of representations and tools in the chemistry laboratory and their implications for chemistry learning. *Journal of the Learning Sciences, 9*(2), 105–143.

Lane, P. C. R., Cheng, P. C. -H., & Gobet, F. (2000). CHREST+: A simulation of how humans learn to solve problems using diagrams. *AISB Quarterly, 103*, 24–30.

Lewalter, D. (2003). Cognitive strategies for learning from static and dynamic visuals. *Learning and Instruction, 13*(2), 177–189.

Lowe, R. K. (2003). Animation and learning: selective processing of information in dynamic graphics. *Learning and Instruction, 13*(2), 157–176.

Mayer, R. E. (2001). *Multimedia Learning*. Cambridge: Cambridge University Press.

Mayer, R. E. (2003). The promise of multimedia learning: Using the same instructional design methods across different media. *Learning and Instruction, 13*(2), 125–139.

Mayer, R. E., & Gallini, J. K. (1990). When is an illustration worth ten thousand words? *Journal of Educational Psychology, 82*(4), 715–726.

Mayer, R. E., & Moreno, R. (1998). Split-attention effect in multimedia learning: Evidence for dual processing systems in working memory. *Journal of Educational Psychology, 90*(2), 312–320.

Mayer, R. E., & Sims, V. K. (1994). For whom is a picture worth 1000 Words – extensions of a dual-coding theory of multimedia learning. *Journal of Educational Psychology, 86*(3), 389–401.

Moreno, R., & Mayer, R. E. (2000). A coherence effect in multimedia learning: The case for minimizing irrelevant sounds in the design of multimedia instructional messages. *Journal of Educational Psychology, 92*(1), 117–125.

Najjar, L. (1998). Principles of educational multi-media user interface design. *Human Factors, 40*(2), 311–323.

Pane, J. F., Corbett, A. T., & John, B. E. (1996). Assessing dynamics in computer-based instruction., *Proceedings of ACM CHI'96 Conference on Human Factors in Computing Systems*. Vancouver.

Price, S. J. (2002). *Diagram representation: The cognitive basis for understanding animation in education* (Technical Report CSRP 553): School of Computing and Cognitive Sciences, University of Sussex.

Reimann, P. (2003). Multimedia learning: beyond modality. *Learning and Instruction, 13*(2), 245–252.

Rieber, L. P. (1990). Animation in Computer-Based Instruction. *Educational Technology Research and Development, 38*(1), 77–86.

Roberts, M. J., Gilmore, D. J., & Wood, D. J. (1997). Individual differences and strategy selection in reasoning. *British Journal of Psychology, 88*, 473–492.

Robson, C.(2002) *Real world research*. Oxford: Blackwell Publishing.

Romero, P., du Boulay, B., Lutz, R., & Cox, R. (2003). The effects of graphical and textual visualisations in multi-representational debugging environments., *Proceedings of 2003 IEEE Symposia on Human Centric Computing Languages and Environments*.

Roth, W.-M., & Bowen, G. M. (2001). Professionals read graphs: A semiotic analysis. *Journal for Research in Mathematics Education, 32*, 159–194.

Rouet, J.-F. & Passerault, J.-M. (1999). Analyzing learner-hypermedia interaction: An overview of online methods. *Instructional Science, 27*(3/4), 201–219.

Schnotz, W. (2001). Sign systems, technologies and the acquisition of knowledge. In J.-F. Rouet, J. J. Levonen & A. Biardeau (Eds.), *Multimedia learning: Cognitive and instructional Issues* (pp. 9–30). Amsterdam: Pergamon.

Schoenfeld, A. H., Smith, J. P., & Arcavi, A. (1993). Learning: The microgenetic analysis of one student's evolving understanding of a complex subject matter domain. In R. Glaser (Ed.), *Advances in instructional psychology* (Vol. volume 4). Hillsdale, NJ: LEA.

Seufert, T. (2003). Supporting coherence formation in learning from multiple representations. *Learning and Instruction, 13*(2), 227–237.

Snow, R. E., & Yalow, E. (1982). Education and intelligence. In R. J. Stenberg (Ed.), *A handbook of human intelligence* (pp. 493–585). Cambridge: Cambridge University Press.
Siegler, R. S. (1995). How does change occur: A microgenetic study of number conservation. *Cognitive Psychology, 25*, 225–273.
Stern, E., Aprea, C., & Ebner, H. G. (2003). Improving cross-content transfer in text processing by means of active graphical representation. *Learning and Instruction, 13*(2), 191–203.
Sweller, J., van Merrienboer, J. J. G., & Paas, F. (1998). Cognitive architecture and instructional design. *Educational Psychology Review, 10*(3), 251–296...
Tabachneck-Schijf, H. J. M., Leonardo, A. M., & Simon, H. A. (1997). CaMeRa: A computational model of multiple representations. *Cognitive Science, 21*(3), 305–350.
Tabbers, H. K., Martens, R. L., & Van Merriënboer, J. J. G. (2001). The modality effect in multimedia instructions. In J. D. Moore & K. Stenning (Eds.), *Proceedings of the 23rd annual conference of the Cognitive Science Society* (pp. 1024–1029). Mahwah, NJ: Lawrence Erlbaum Associates.
Tsui, C. -Y. & Treagust, D. F. (2003). Genetics reasoning with multiple external representations. *Research in Science Education, 33*, 111–135.
Van Someren, M. W., & Tabbers, H. (1998). The role of prior knowledge qualitative knowledge in inductive learning. In M. W. Van Someren, P. Reimann, H. P. A. Boshuizen, & T. de Jong (Eds.), *Learning with multiple representations* (pp. 102–119). Amsterdam: Pergamon.
Waldrip, B. G., & Prain, V. (2004, April). *Enhancing learning through using multi-modal representations of concepts.* A paper presented at the Annual Meeting of the American Educational Research Association, San Diego.
Winn, B. (1987). Charts, graphs and diagrams in educational materials. In D. M. Willows & H. A. Houghton (Eds.), *The psychology of illustration: I. Basic research* (pp. 152–198). New York: Springer.
Yerushalmy, M. (1991). Student perceptions of aspects of algebraic function using multiple representation software. *Journal of Computer Assisted Learning, 7*, 42–57.
Zahn, C., Barquero, B., &, S. (2004). Learning with hyperlinked videos – design criteria and efficient strategies for using audiovisual hypermedia. *Learning and Instruction, 14*(3), 275–291.

Chapter 14
Memory Processes in Text and Multimedia Comprehension: Some Reflections and Perspectives

Michel Fayol and Jean-François Rouet

Abstract We reflect on the cognitive skills involved in comprehending text and multimedia documents. Multimedia comprehension involves a multiplicity of processes and places heavy demands on the individual's working memory. We propose that two key factors determine learners' ability to construct knowledge from multimedia documents: first, the automaticity of some processing components, such as word decoding, reference assignment or inference generation; second, the mastery of effective processing strategies, allowing the learner to take into account the constraints and affordances of specific task contexts and combination of media. We conclude that the development of comprehensive theories of comprehension may improve the practice of designing and using multimedia resources in educational contexts.

Keywords Applications · Language · Learning skills · Strategies · Working memory

14.1 Introduction

Multimedia comprehension is a relatively recent topic within the broader domain of cognitive psychology. It rests, however, on theories of attention, language and memory that are common with other areas of investigation, in particular the study of language and comprehension processes. Of particular interest is a reflection on how individuals come to be experts at processing, comprehending and using multimedia materials. In the present discussion note, we reflect on the notion of skilled multimedia comprehension, based on a review of cognitive theories and on a synthesis of the contributions presented in this book.

M. Fayol
Université Blaise Pascal, Laboratoire de Psychologie Sociale de la Cognition, Centre National de la Recherche Scientifique, 34 avenue Carnot, 63 037 Clermont-Ferrand Cedex, France
e-mail: michel.fayol@univ-bpclermont.fr

J.-F. Rouet et al. (eds.), *Understanding Multimedia Documents*,
DOI: 10.1007/978-0-387-73337-1_14,

A clear lesson emerging from the studies presented in this book is that multimedia comprehension is a complex cognitive activity, which may raise as many difficulties as it provides potential benefits for learning. Any reflection on the potential of multimedia as an instructional medium has to be firmly grounded into a comprehensive theory of the complex mental processes involved in processing multimedia materials.

The main challenge children and adults are faced with when comprehending text or multimedia documents is most likely the on-line management of several cognitive processes, which have to be coordinated in order to achieve a coherent mental representation, i.e. a mental model or a situation model, adapted to the task at hand. Two general features of comprehension are worth mentioning at this point:

- First, *comprehension involves various cognitive subcomponents (or subprocesses)*. Most if not all of these subcomponents make some demands on a shared, limited pool of cognitive resources.
- Second, managing the competing demands of the different subcomponents requires readers/understanders to make *skilled use of their working memory* (WM). Managing working memory does not just consist in maintaining as much information as possible; it also involves continuously selecting, updating, and integrating the incoming information.

In this discussion note, we reflect on those two important aspects of comprehension and synthesize the contribution of some of the chapters on those issues, in light of research studies conducted in the area of reading.

14.2 Comprehension as a Complex Task Involving Costly Components

14.2.1 Comprehension is Goal-Directed

As a cognitive activity, comprehension is goal-directed. Readers engage in comprehension relative to a text or a multimedia document as a function of explicit or implicit objectives (e.g. entertainment, acquisition of new information, or concrete performance such as assembling a model, cooking a recipe, solving a word problem, preparing for a talk and so forth). The constraints bearing on the elaboration of the mental model vary depending on the type of text on the one hand and the reader's objective on the other (see also Rouet, Lowe, & Schnotz, Chapter 1). Thus, the reading of reports, of assembly instructions (often including text and pictures), or problem statements require the detailed assimilation of the information and the construction of a rather constrained mental representation (Hegarty & Just, 1993). In contrast, the reading of a crime novel for entertainment can lead to the elaboration of a relatively more condensed mental model whose internal coherence may be more or less tenuous. We therefore have to think of *comprehension as an interpretive activity which offers a greater or lesser level of flexibility* as a function of the text, the standards which readers set for themselves or which are imposed on them, and the prior knowledge which they possess. Even though the importance of contextual constraints is acknowledged in various chapters within this volume (see e.g. Cerdán et al., Chapter 7), this dimension of comprehension is still to be fully understood.

In particular, the contextual flexibility of comprehension raises the problem of designing or selecting appropriate methods to assess *readers' level of performance*. A number of tasks are typically used in comprehension research: statement recognition, text recall, summaries, comprehension questions (literal or inferential), transfer tasks, problem solving and so forth. How these techniques map onto comprehension purposes, processes and products has so far been overlooked by researchers (but see Ainsworth, Chapter 13). Of particular interest are the differences in cognitive costs associated with different assessment procedures. These differences are problematic because people involved in multimedia experiments tend to adjust to the perceived demands of the situation: they do what is expected from them. For instance, if the expected test requires literal information, participants will concentrate on literal information and not care so much about inferencing or transfering to new tasks or situations. As a consequence, researchers need *to carefully match the goal and the instructions given to readers/understanders and the methods used to assess their comprehension*.

14.2.2 Comprehension is a Real-Time Activity

The comprehension activity takes place in real time. Current cognitive theories assume that human beings have *a limited pool of general cognitive resources* (including attention and working memory) that can be *flexibly allocated to accommodate the real-time needs of the processing system*(Baddeley, 1986; see also Schnotz, Chapter 2; Hidrio & Jamet, Chapter 6). In other words, people have limited information processing capacities in order to select and utilize the relevant information at the right moment.

A large body of literature (see e.g. Daneman & Merikle, 1996 for a meta-analysis) has shown that WM is strongly involved in reading and text comprehension. However, conflicting findings exist as to *whether the correlations between WM tasks and reading measures are primarily mediated by modality-specific processes* (e.g. the phonological vs. visuo-spatial WM subsystems; Baddeley, 1986; Daneman & Tardiff, 1987) *or a general system* (Engle, 1996; Shah & Miyake, 1996, for a review). Such a question is especially important for multimedia comprehension because documents very often include both text and images, and/or a combination of auditory and visual information. Verbal (phonological) information and visuo-spatial information may thus function independently and complement each other, making the use of two modalities more efficient than just one (Pazzaglia,

Chapter 3). However, a number of studies show that the joint use of the two modalities may sometimes increase cognitive load, and thus decrease comprehension performances. For instance, full redundancy between written and spoken messages generally hinders comprehension (Le Bohec & Jamet, Chapter 5); and the visual presentation of text and pictures may result in a split attention effect (see Tabbers, Paas, Lankford, Martens, & Merriënboer, Chapter 9).

Research into the attentional mechanisms that underlie information processing helps interpret those phenomena. At any given point in time, cognitive resources are normally focused on a single information source and on processes relevant for the source and the task at hand. The processing of complex information requires *quick shifts between modality-specific or detail-specific processes*, these shifts being controlled by a central component (e.g., Baddeley's 1986 central executive). The online recording of attentional shifts requires sophisticated techniques, for instance eye movement technology. Eye movement studies help understanding when and why using two modalities or sources is detrimental or useful for understanding and/or memorizing information (see e.g. Tabbers et al., Chapter 9; Rinck, Chapter 10).

As understanding is a goal-directed activity, most resources are devoted to *the global control of comprehension processes.* Controlled processing requires focused attention and conscious mental effort. Control is generally slow, and deals with serially organized information because it is either impossible or very difficult to execute different complex operations simultaneously (Brown & Carr, 1989). However, in order to achieve their goal, readers/comprehenders have to exert different component sub-skills such as decoding, exploring pictures, segmenting and grouping informations, and drawing inferences in order to make sense of successive pieces of information. Under certain task conditions, *an inefficient subcomponent (e.g., inferencing) can disrupt performance because it draws resources away from focused activities.* Such disruptions can affect either higher-order components (e.g. the formation of a macrostructure) or lower-level processes (e.g., the speed of word decoding or feature extraction in a picture).

Several chapters in this volume have demonstrated the role and place of cognitive control in multimedia comprehension. Control is important, for instance, when locating objects or parts mentioned in an audio commentary within a picture (see e.g. Hidrio & Jamet, Chapter 6), or when resolving discrepancies between a text and an embedded illustration (Rinck, Chapter 10). Control is also important (and problematic) when making decisions as to what sections of a complex document must be read carefully, just skimmed, or skipped when search answer to complex questions (see Cerdán et al., Chapter 7). In the case of animated visuals, control is essential for the learner to cope with time limitations (see Lowe, Chapter 8; Tabbers et al., Chapter 9). Throughout the theoretical discussions and empirical findings, effective control appears to be dependent upon general cognitive abilities (e.g. memory span), but also one's experience in studying complex documents. In fact, most studies report large inter-individual variations in both online indicators (e.g. allocation of study time or gaze) and post-measurements of memory and learning, regardless of the task, context and display at hand. Whether skilled multimedia comprehension strategies can be trained in a general, domain-independent way, as well as the conditions for effective training remain to be found.

14.2.3 Comprehension as a Strategic Activity

Depending on the characteristics of the text (such as e.g. sentence complexity, vocabulary difficulty), their prior domain knowledge and the objectives they have set for themselves, *readers must allocate their attention in the most suitable and effective way possible*. Resource allocation must make it possible to elaborate a mental model which is suited to the constraints of the task at hand (e.g. to solve a problem, answer questions, search for information) as well as to the authors' (and/or, sometimes, teachers') intentions. Thus *readers must possess resources to assess their own level of comprehension in real time*, to detect possible inconsistencies and to deal with them. Readers may then initiate corrective procedures (or actions) which are specific to reading or to multimedia processing, such as modulating the speed of information intake, rereading re-exploring texts or pictures, taking notes, etc (Fayol, 1992).

Comprehension strategies appear to be specific to the printed medium. Take as an example Bell and Perfetti's (1994) work. These authors have reported that college students with good or poorer reading skills obtained equivalent results in the comprehension of short texts (200 words) for both oral and written presentation. In contrast, in the case of long texts (2000 words), performances were better in reading. This result suggests that when reading under habitual conditions, experienced readers use specific procedures which are capable of improving comprehension especially in the most difficult situations (e.g., reading long texts about scientific topics). This applies, in particular, to two types of procedures: first, *going back and re-reading the text already read* in greater or lesser detail (or going back to the previous picture in order to explore it more extensively); secondly, the modulation of the speed with which the segments are read during processing (pausing between information intakes, slowing down reading or visual exploration; see also Walczyk, Marsiglia, Bryan, & Naquin, 2001). It is worth noting that all these control procedures rely on the permanence of the written trace.

In summary, comprehension is a context-dependent activity that requires the coordination of a number of component processes. Executive control processes thus play an important role, especially for the reader to be able to adjust strategically to specific contextual demands or specific textual difficulties.

14.3 On the Coordination of Components Skills in Comprehension

14.3.1 Two Different Coordination Mechanisms

The coordination of the different subcomponents can proceed in a number of different ways. At least two different mechanisms can be involved in the reduction of costs necessary to make comprehension tasks manageable.

- Automaticity

The first mechanism is automaticity, which exploits the constancy of either task information or task operations, for example by strengthening the internode associations between components of a skill such as producing sequences of search or using particular devices (Anderson, 1995; Brown & Carr, 1989; Logan, 1988; Logan & Klapp, 1991; MacKay, 1982). As everywhere, practice makes perfect, and novelty may be a problem. For instance, using a new keyboard or a new piece of software increases the mental load, and thus very often entails a decrease in performance. This is why, among other reasons, people are generally reluctant to change. This is also why even experts' performance suffers when they modify the tools they work with. However, practice improves quickly the use of the keyboard or the software (or hardware), and performance improves too. Those changes may be explained by the automaticity (or lack thereof) of the procedures involved in accomplishing the task.

Consider now the reading activity. Most theoretical conceptions of the reading-understanding activity may be described as involving various, interrelated components. Some components are thought to process a precise type of information (e.g., identification of letters, identification of words, syntactic analysis). Others are thought to have a more general function and manage the interactions between components. The processing operations mobilized by these components should each be associated with a certain cognitive cost. This cost would vary as a function of the level of automation: the more automated a processing operation is, the lower its cost should be. In contrast, the more attentional control a processing operation requires, the higher its cost should be. As text comprehension demands the "simultaneous" application of a variety of processing components, the cognitive cost of the processing operations being performed at a given point in time should be approximately equal to the sum of the costs of each of the components involved added to the possible cost of their co-ordination. If this total is lower than the total capacity which the reader is able to mobilize, the activity continues without a problem. In contrast, if the total exceeds this capacity, certain processing operations will be negatively affected unless they can be deferred (Carpenter, Miyake, & Just, 1994; see also, Schnotz, Chapter 2).

The relationship between automation and cognitive cost outlined above predicts that readers who have only partially automated the so-called low-level processing operations (e.g., word identification) should have to allocate attentional resources to them and should, therefore, possess fewer resources to devote to so-called high-level activities (e.g., calculation of the pronoun references, elaboration of inferences). Empirical data have convincingly supported this theoretical view in the area of reading (Perfetti, 1985). The studies presented in this volume suggest that it may be fruitfully extended to the area of multimedia learning. At the moment a huge number of people are only beginning to use keyboards, operating systems, and Web browsers. The many low-level procedures involved in «running» electronic multimedia documents most likely need to be automated to allow readers to become skilled multimedia comprehenders. Again, the instructional conditions for such an automation need to be further explored.

- Task combination strategies

The second coordination mechanism has to do with the combination of component tasks within a complex activity (Brown & Carr, 1989). It involves changes over time in the relations between the components of the tasks which are combined. For example, attention switching between pictures, graphs, and written comments require flexible allocation of cognitive resources as a function of the task demands. Task combination strategies enable finely adapted moves from parallel to serial organization, for instance between visual and auditory information processing or between written text and pictures (see e.g., chapters by Pazzaglia; Le Bohec & Jamet, Bétrancourt, Dillenbourg, & Clavien et al.). It must be pointed out, however, that a task combination strategy both *decreases the cognitive load* by distributing it over time, and *adds some extra-load* for the fine-grain management of the different processes and their coordination. This is why beginning using strategies very often impairs understanding and performances. And this may be why the inclusion of extra cues or redundant information within a multimedia environment does not always results in the expected outcomes (see e.g. chapters by Bétrancourt et al.; Le Bohec & Jamet, Hidrio & Jamet).

An example of highly demanding component of comprehension is the production of inferences. Inferential processes relate to the information needed for comprehension but which is not readily available from the data explicitly present in the text (Zwaan & Singer, 2003). Three broad categories of inferences may be defined: Inferences concerning the anaphoric relations which are established by means of pronouns or articles; inferences concerning causal relations; and inferences which establish temporal and spatial coherence (see also Kintsch, 1998). Yuill and Oakhill (1991) have shown that the resolution and interpretation of anaphora represents a problem. Readers, especially younger ones, experience difficulties when processing anaphora and do not seem to use their knowledge of the world spontaneously in order to make relevant inferences. Causal inferences relate to the elaboration of composite chains of actions, events and statuses in which these components are associated by links of antecedence to consequence (Van den Broekvan den Broek , 1994). Their elaboration depends on domain prior knowledge. Their identification is all the more infrequent and difficult, the greater the distance between the clauses containing the facts to be related. The cognitive cost of causal inferences should be relatively high and should vary as a function of the reader's/listener's prior knowledge.

Empirical research into adult performances suggests that most inferences are not made automatically (see e.g. the minimalist hypothesis; McKoon & Ratcliff, 1992). Instead, complex inferences are only made under textual or contextual conditions that permit the activation of causally related concepts (see e.g. the constructionist hypothesis; Graesser, Singer & Trabasso, 1994). When the constraints are weak, readers/listeners are thought to implement a voluntary, controlled activity for the elaboration of causal relations. That is, they have to shift from word decoding or surface picture exploring to deeper situation model construction processes. As a consequence, *drawing inferences depends both on the effective use of prior knowledge and on working memory resources* (Singer & Ritchot, 1996).

The application of strategies is dependent on contextual conditions, and especially on time pressure. When people have to read a text or to process a multimedia document in a limited time, their performance decreases and becomes highly dependent on their basic reading capacities (reading span, word naming, etc). However, when reading does not occur under time pressure, less verbally efficient readers use more compensatory strategies and achieve comparable levels of literal understanding as more efficient readers. Walczyk et al. (2001) have shown that these readers pause and reread more often as they access words and resolve anaphors. Those who experienced difficulties during anaphor resolution looked back more frequently. Similarly, when combining text and graphics into a single mental representation, readers need time in order to combine the sources of information (see Tabbers et al., Chapter 9).

14.3.2 Automaticity and its Limits

When a subcomponent skill is automated, it becomes faster, effortless and non-interfering. As a consequence, the reader can deal with relatively large amounts of information and perform various processes in parallel. Automated processing skills do not overload the limited capacity of the working memory system. However, *automaticity is not an all-or-none phenomenon* (Logan & Klapp, 1991): Practice effects can be observed even after automaticity is achieved. Overtraining beyond automaticity leads to limited but significantly reliable gains in speed and, more importantly, to a dramatic reduction in interference from concurrent tasks (Klapp, Boches, Trabert,Trabert & Logan, 1991). Consequently, the more a skill is over-trained, the more it can be used in parallel with another activity. For example, automatic decoding enables to devote more and more resources to searching for concepts and to inferencing. However, even when activities are (relatively) automated, people can simultaneously carry out only a limited number of them. When two activities can occur simultaneously within the "band-width" of the limited capacity, it is difficult to determine their respective cognitive cost. Secondary tasks, reaction times and other online techniques are then quite useful.

14.3.3 Adapting the Processing/Comprehension Rhythm

When readers/understanders face difficulties in integrating subcomponent skills in real time, they must adjust their information intake speed by decreasing reading or exploring rates and/or by increasing pause duration. They thus use compensatory strategies (Walczyk, 2000). For instance, Walczyk and Taylor (1996) have shown that among adults who were able to read and comprehend a passage of text (as assessed by comprehension questions), those with the lower performance on a working memory measure were more likely to look back in text as they were reading. That is, *readers compensated for their lowest instantaneous processing capacity by distributing processing over time.*

Sometimes it is impossible to conduct several activities in parallel. Readers may then delay one of them and focus on the other(s), strategically allocating more or less time and effort to managing his own comprehension (Walczyk, 2000). The more efficient the time and effort sharing, the better the comprehension outcomes. However, even if the sequencing of activities (or sub-processes) over time is generally not a problem, *even experts are sometimes unable to deal with specific problems, due to a temporary overload.* For example, even expert adults may be disrupted in a language comprehension activity when they have to deal with an unusual task component, for instance when they have to use a brand new display or a different keyboard. The unusual task component acts as a concurrent task that forces the reader/learner to divide his or her attention. Comparing recall performance under normal *vs.* divided attention conditions, Jou and Harris (1992) reported that, under the divided attention condition, less information was recalled, whereas speech defects and pause durations increased.

Very few studies have examined the global processing strategies used by children or adult readers in multimedia comprehension. As a consequence, it is difficult both to describe these strategies, to study their relationships to some low-level processing components, and to teach and learn them. Hyönä, Lorch, and Kaakinen (2002) have used eye movements to describe what global strategies adults use to read expository texts (and more specifically to process sentences related to the topic structure of those texts) to summarize them. They have found *several very different strategies with complex relationships to the quality of summaries. Interestingly, huge inter-individual differences were found,* far more than was expected. It could be that processing multimedia documents is associated with still more and still more varied strategies, and a first step would be to describe them (see e.g. Hegarty & Steinhoff, 1997). As the chapter by Tabbers et al. illustrates, however, the relationship of time constraints, cognitive load and eye movements is far from a simple one.

14.4 Challenges and Perspectives for Multimedia Research

The ultimate purpose of scientific research is to help people. Theoretical and empirical studies have to produce new data in order to increase both our understanding of the world and our efficiency in dealing with it. As regards multimedia comprehension, the studies gathered in the present volume have explored at least two promising avenues: One consists in improving the design of multimedia documents; the other consists in empowering multimedia comprehenders with strategies that increase their efficiency and their autonomy.

14.4.1 Interventions in Textual Formulations and Document Design

Texts and documents can be modified so as to accommodate readers' specific needs (Mayer, 1984). For instance, one can reduce the length of the segments to be processed. Breaking down the text into simpler sentences improves poor comprehenders' performance, because it reduces the load on their processing capacity (Cromer, 1971; Mason & Kendall, 1979). One can also reduce the amount of inferencing needed for the reader to comprehend. To do this, authors can make explicit the relations between subsequent clauses and improve co-reference across clauses. Texts which are rewritten using these principles are generally easier to read, to understand and to memorize (Britton & Gülgöz, 1991; Garnham, Oakhill, & Johnson-Laird, 1982; Gilabert, Martinez, & Vidal-Abarca, 2005). Those and other textual improvements reduce the processing load and indirectly facilitate the elaboration of a mental model, at least in readers with low prior knowledge (McNamara, Kintsch, Songer, & Kintsch, 1996). Overviews and other organizers are also efficient techniques to facilitate the integration of the information from complex documents (Goldman & Rakestraw, 2000; Mannes, 1994; Reder, 1985; Rouet, 2006).

Nevertheless, the potential of a design quality approach is necessarily limited. On the one hand, the level of explicitness, referential clarity, or causal coherence depends on the person whom the text is intended for. If made too explicit, a document may be boring to the reader and does not induce learning (Kintsch, 1994; McNamara et al., 1996). On the other hand, it is practically impossible to adapt each text/document to each reader/understander. Thus, any document must be designed as a function of predefined objectives and with a specific readership in mind.

As pointed out by Platteaux (Chapter 11), the history of printed communication techniques is that of a constant evolution toward greater sophistication, based in part on text designers' recognition of the (changing) readers' needs.

Thus, the continuum of design problems and solutions transcends the sometimes overstated distinction between the realms of printed and electronic information. As regards multimedia learning, various contributors to this volume have proposed original approaches to improving document design. To start with, pictorial information do add some value to textual documents when the information to be conveyed is highly spatial in nature (Pazzaglia, Chapter 3), even though there seems to be a dominance of verbal over pictorial information (Rinck, Chapter 10). When dealing with dynamic phenomena, computer animations may prove more efficient than series of static slides (Bétrancourt et al., Chapter 4; Hidrio & Jamet, Chapter 6). The inclusion of cues, however, does not necessarily facilitate comprehension, probably due to the fact that, as the saying goes, « too much information kills information ». For instance, the repetition of information across modalities (i.e., print and speech) can hinder rather than support comprehension (Le Bohec & Jamet, Chapter 5).

14.4.2 Improving Readers' Processing of Texts and Documents?

Is comprehension specific to the medium or is it a general, independent skill? The latter view is supported by the generally high correlations between oral and written comprehension reported in the literature (e.g. Bell & Perfetti, 1994; Gernsbacher, 1989). But at the same time, the specific conditions that surround listening, text and multimedia processing allow specific comprehension procedures to be implemented. An issue of importance is to identify those medium-specific procedures and to teach them to students.

At any moment during multimedia comprehension, people have to deal with the management of several subcomponent processes. More efficient management can be obtained by automating some skills (e.g., decoding; Perfetti, 1985; but also, maybe, picture exploration and other components of multimedia comprehension), by teaching stereotypical discourse structures (e.g., story schemata, standard expository patterns, basic multimedia designs) and, obviously, by increasing the student's knowledge base. However, as illustrated in several chapters of the present volume, even experts readers may be subjected to cognitive overload during multimedia comprehension, because of the high cost of coordinating task constraints, information intake, integration and coordination of processes (Cerdán et al. Chapter 7). To cope with the complexity of multimedia comprehension, learners have to develop adaptive strategy choices (Siegler & Shipley, 1995).

Specifically, learners have to select different procedures in response to problem difficulties (are they highly knowledgeable about the topic?), changes in their own competences (how costly are information search and question answering?), task instructions (is it important to focus on literal or inference information?), and so on. That is, they have to become experts in controlling and regulating their own capacities, so to say to become metacogntive understanders (see e.g. chapters by Cerdán et al.; Lowe, & Lumbelli).

In the future, researchers will have to further examine the conditions for children and/or novice multimedia users to become efficient enough in adjusting their study rate, focusing their attention, and planning ahead what they have to do next in rich and complex multimedia environments. Researchers will then have to study how experience shapes students' strategy choices as a function of the contextual constraints. These advances in multimedia research are a precondition for the design of effective training procedures and tools. They are also necessary steps in order to bridge the gap between the cognitive, the social, and the instructional approaches of multimedia comprehension.

References

Anderson, J. R. (1995). *Learning and Memory*. New York: Wiley.

Baddeley, A. (1986). *Working Memory*. New York: Oxford University Press.

Bell, L. C., & Perfetti, C. A. (1994). Reading Skill: Some Adult Comparisons. *Journal of Educational Psychology, 86*, 244–255.

Britton, B. K., & GülgözGülgöz, S. (1991). Using Kintsch's computational model to improve instructional text: Effects of repairing inference calls on recall and cognitive structures. *Journal of Educational Psychology, 83*, 329–345.

Brown, T., & Carr, T. (1989). Automaticity in skill acquisition: Mechanisms for reducing interference in congruent performance. *Journal of Experimental Psychology: Human Perception and Performance, 15*, 686–700.

Carpenter, P. A., Miyake, A., & Just, M. A. (1994). Working memory constraints in comprehension. In M. A. Gernsbacher (Ed.), *Handbook of psycholinguistics* (pp. 1075–1122). New-York : Academic Press.

Cromer, W. (1971). The difference model : A new explanation for some reading difficulties. *Journal of Educational Psychology, 61*, 471–483.

Daneman, M., & Merikle, P. M. (1996). Working memory and language comprehension: A meta-analysis. *Psychonomic Bulletin & Review, 3*, 422–433.

Daneman, M., & Tardiff, T. (1987). Working memory and reading skill reexamined. In M. Coltheart (Eds.), *Attention and Performance XII: The psychology of reading*. (pp. 491–508). Hillsdale, NJ: Erlbaum.

Engle, R. W. (1996). Working memory and retrieval: An inhibition-resource approach. In J. T. E. Richardson (Ed.), *Working memory and human cognition* (pp. 89–119). Oxford: Oxford University Press.

Fayol, M. (1992). Comprendre ce qu'on lit: De l'automatisme au contrôle [Understanding what one reads: from automatism to control]. In M. Fayol, J. E. Gombert, P. Lecocq, L. Sprenger-Charolles & D. Zagar (Eds.), *Psychologie cognitive de la lecture* [*cognitive psychology of reading*]. Paris: Presses Universitaires de France.

Garnham, A., Oakhill, J. V., & Johnson-Laird, P. N. (1982). Referential continuity and the coherence of discourse. *Cognition, 11*, 29–46.

Gernsbacher, M. A. (1989). *Language comprehension as structure building*. Hillsdale, NJ : Erlbaum.

Gilabert, R., Martinez, G., & Vidal-Abarca, E. (2005). Some good texts are always better: Text revision to foster inferences of readers with high and low prior background knowledge. *Learning and Instruction, 15*, 45–68.

Goldman, S. R., & Rakestraw Jr., J. A. (2000). Structural aspects of constructing meaning from text. In M. L. Kamil, P. B. Mosenthal, P. D. Pearson, & R. Barr (Eds.). *Handbook of reading research, volume III* (pp. 311–335). Mahwah, NJ, Erlbaum.
Graesser, A. C., Singer, M., & Trabasso, T. (1994). Constructing inferences during narrative text comprehension. *Psychological Review, 101*, 371–395.
Hegarty, M. & Just, M. A. (1993). Constructing mental models of machines from text and diagrams. *Journal of Memory and Language, 32*, 717–742.
Hegarty, M., & Steinhoff, K. (1997). Individual differences in use of diagrams as external memory in mechanical reasoning. *Learning and Individual Differences, 9*, 19–42.
Hyönä, J., Lorch, R. F., Jr., & Kaakinen, J. K. (2002). Individual differences in reading to summarize expository text: Evidence from eye fixation patterns. *Journal of Educational Psychology, 94*, 44–55.
Jou, J., & Harris, R. J. (1992). The effect of divided attention on speech production. *Bulletin of the Psychonomic Society, 30*, 301–304.
Kintsch, W. (1994). Text comprehension, memory, and learning. *American Psychologist, 49*, 294–303.
Kintsch, W. (1998). *Comprehension: A paradigm for cognition*. Cambridge, MA: Cambridge University Press.
Klapp, S. T., Boches, C. A., Trabert, M. L., & Logan, G. D. (1991). Automatizing alphabet arithmetic: II. Are there practice effects after automaticity is achieved? *Journal of Experimental Psychology: Learning, Memory, and Cognition, 17*, 196–209.
Logan, G. D. (1988). Toward an instance theory of automatization. *Psychological Review, 95*, 492–527.
Logan, G. D., & Klapp, S. T. (1991). Automatizing alphabet arithmetic: I. Is extended practice necessary to produce automaticity? *Journal of Experimental Psychology: Learning, Memory, and Cognition, 17*, 179–195.
MacKay, D. G. (1982) The problems of flexibility, fluency, and speed-accuracy trade-off in skilled behavior. *Psychological Review, 89*, 483–506.
Mannes, S. (1994). Strategic processing of text. *Journal of Educational Psychology, 88*, 577–588.
Mason, J. M., & Kendall, J. R. (1979). Facilitating reading comprehension through text structure manipulation. *The Alberta Journal of Educational Research, 25*, 68–76.
Mayer, R. E. (1984). Aids to text comprehension. *Educational Psychologist, 19*, 30–42.
McKoon, G., & Ratcliff, R. (1992). Inference during reading. *Psychological Review, 99*, 440–466.
McNamara, D. S., Kintsch, E., Songer, N. S., & Kintsch, W. (1996). Are good texts always better? Interactions of text coherence, background knowledge, and levels of understanding in learning from text. *Cognition and Instruction, 14*(1), 1–43.
Perfetti, C. A. (1985). *Reading Ability*. New York: Oxford University Press.
Reder, L. M. (1985). Techniques available to author, teacher, and reader to improve retention of main ideas of a chapter. In S. F. Chapman, J. W. Segal, & R.Gloser (Ed.), *Thinking and learning skills, Vol. 2: Research and open questions* (pp. 37–64). Hillsdale, NJ: Erlbaum.
Rouet, J. -F. (2006). *The skills of document use: from text comprehension to Web-based learning*. Mahwah, NJ: Erlbaum.
Shah, P., & Miyake, A. (1996). The separability of working memory resources for spatial thinking and language processing: An individual difference approach. *Journal of Experimental Psychology: General, 125*, 4–27.
Siegler, R. S., & Shipley, C. (1995). Variation, selection, and cognitive change. In T. J. Simon & G. S. Halford (Eds.), *Developing cognitive competence: New approaches to process modeling* (pp. 31–76). Hillsdale, NJ: Erlbaum.
Singer, M., & Ritchot, K. F. M. (1996). The role of working memory capacity and knowledge access in text inference processing. *Memory and Cognition, 24*, 733–743.

Van den Broek, P. (1994). Comprehension and memory of narrative texts. In M. A. Gernsbacher (Ed.). *Handbook of psycholinguistics* (pp. 539–588). New-York: Academic Press.

Walczyk, J. J. (2000). The interplay between automatic and control processes in reading. *Reading Research Quarterly, 35*, 554–566.

Walczyk, J. J., Marsiglia, C. S., Bryan, K. S., & Naquin, P. J. (2001). Overcoming inefficient reading skills. *Journal of Educational Psychology, 93*, 750–757.

Walczyk, J. J., & Taylor, R. W. (1996). How do the efficiencies of reading subcomponents relate to looking back in text? *Journal of Educational Psychology, 88*, 537–545.

Yuill, N., & Oakhill, J. (1991). *Children's problems in text comprehension. An experimental investigation.*Cambridge University Press.

Zwaan, R. A., & Singer, M. (2003). Text comprehension. In A. C. Graesser, M. A. Gernsbacher, & S. R. Goldman (Eds.), *Handbook of Discourse Processes* (pp. 83–122). Mahwah, NJ: Erlbaum.

Author Index

Subject Index

Printed in the United States
119097LV00001B/5/P

9 780387 733364